ONTARIO'S EDUCATIVE SOCIETY / I

The expansion of the
educational system

ONTARIO'S EDUCATIVE SOCIETY / I

The expansion of the educational system

W.G. FLEMING

UNIVERSITY OF TORONTO PRESS

© University of Toronto Press 1971
Toronto and Buffalo

Printed in Canada

Volume I
ISBN 0-8020-3267-2

Volumes I–V
ISBN 0-8020-3258-3
Microfiche ISBN 0-8020-0079-7
LC 77-166928

Preface

The series entitled ONTARIO'S EDUCATIVE SOCIETY, of which this volume is the first, deals with many formal and informal aspects of education as they have developed in Ontario in recent years. The province of Ontario is particularly suitable for a study of this kind. Its population of approximately 7.5 million, the largest of any Canadian province, demonstrates a rich and varied mosaic of cultures and traditions. Its extended territory includes a wide range of topographical and climatic features shaping the lives of its people in many different ways. During the post-war period it has surged with unprecedented life and vitality, striding ahead in population, in resource development, in technology, and in culture. As both a highly developed and a rapidly developing society, it offers examples of many of the problems and difficulties involved in meeting the challenges of the modern world.

Recent educational progress in Ontario has been impressive in both quantity and quality. Such a judgment has been made by numerous observers from other provinces and from abroad. This does not mean, of course, that the province has become the universal model; in some respects it is in the process of catching up with developments already completed elsewhere. It is perhaps not unreasonable to suggest, however, that many of its achievements are at least worthy of attention, if not of emulation, in other parts of the world.

Education is defined in a broad sense to include training activities of many kinds, even those with very limited goals. Such treatment does not imply that there is no value in distinguishing between education and training as concepts. The danger in dwelling excessively on such distinctions is that it becomes difficult to discern the larger pattern in which both types of activity have a part. They are often in practice so inextricably intertwined that any effort at separate treatment becomes highly artificial.

The reader will be conscious of two somewhat different approaches, one for the great majority of events and developments, where I have been largely or exclusively a bystander, and the other for situations where I have had some significant personal involvement. Examples of the latter are the operation of the departmental grade 13 examination system and the origin and early expansion of the Ontario Institute for Studies in Education. No matter what the topic, I have attempted to present an objective factual account. However, where direct experience has seemed to justify it, I have been much freer about offering opinions and assessments than where my material has been obtained at second hand. I trust that I have been successful in keeping fact separated from opinion. A second feature distinguishing the two types of material is that I have presented a relatively large amount of information about the developments in which I have had a substantial role. As a result, my attempt to present a fairly complete overview of education in Ontario has perhaps been somewhat distorted. I can only hope that there is value in the more thorough treatment which I have felt particularly qualified to provide.

For the whole series I have used the title ONTARIO'S EDUCATIVE SOCIETY. In doing so, I have deliberately obscured a valid distinction between the ideal and the actual. Imperfect human society will not soon be truly educative in the sense that education in all its manifestations is universally accepted as the central activity to which all others are subordinated. Yet if modern civilization, and even humanity itself, is to survive, I firmly believe that there will have to be a strong and consistent move in that direction. Future generations, if any, will have to ask themselves first of any activity: "Is it educative?" Only when they have answered affirmatively will they then be justified in asking: "Is it productive of material goods?" "Is it entertaining?"

If Ontario does not yet, strictly speaking, have an educative society, a study of the record of recent years suggests that remarkable strides have been made toward that objective. The extension of formal opportunities for learning has been impressive enough in itself. When one also considers the multiplicity of informal influences that are actually or potentially educative, the over-all effect is awesome. It is possible to feel in moments of optimism that the ultimate ideal is not completely unattainable.

Volume I, *The expansion of the educational system*, provides an introduction to the whole series, in which some of the major contemporary issues and problems in education are discussed briefly, followed by seven chapters containing most of the quantitative information in compact form. For many readers it may serve chiefly for reference purposes. Volume II, *The administrative structure*, deals with the development and functions of the Department of Education and of local school systems, the financing of education, and the educational activities of the provincial and federal governments. Volume III, *Schools, pupils, and teachers*, covers the evolution of the school structure and curriculum, and attempts to show how the process of education has operated up to the end of secondary school. Volume IV, *Post-secondary and adult education*, deals with the development and activities of universities, colleges of applied arts and technology, and other institutions of post-secondary education, as well as with public and private training activities in business and industry. Volume V, *Supporting institutions and services*, relates to a variety of institutions and activities such as teacher preparation, research and development, educational television services, and externally administered examinations. Volume VI, *Significant developments in local school systems*, indicates some of the educational contributions arising chiefly from local initiative. Volume VII, *Educational contributions of associations*, attempts to demonstrate the extent to which educative activities in Ontario are initiated and conducted through voluntary effort as a supplement to formal and official services. A companion volume to the series, *Education: Ontario's preoccupation*, contains a review of the main highlights of educational development in Ontario, with less emphasis on fact and more on interpretation.

The main focus of the series is on the recent period. An attempt was made to record developments of major importance up to early 1970, just before the first five volumes were delivered to the publisher. Volumes VI and VII, which were written during the latter part of the same year, contain a certain amount of more recent material. Very few additions or changes were made during the editorial stage. The result is that a number of the speculations about future developments have already lost some of the value they might have had earlier.

The treatment of the topic is essentially descriptive. As a means of conveying a reasonable understanding of recent developments, it was thought desirable to trace the origins of many current institutions and practices back into the nineteenth century. For the relevant material in the earlier period, I have relied almost exclusively on secondary sources. Treatment of the last four decades, particularly the period since the Second World War, involved increasing use of primary data.

Acknowledgments

I am deeply indebted to the Honourable William G. Davis, Minister of Education and of University Affairs at the time of writing, for providing me the full co-operation of his departments in the production of the series of volumes constituting ONTARIO'S EDUCATIVE SOCIETY. In this task I was given access to all pertinent material in the two departments under his direction. His officials at the time of writing, headed by Dr J.R. McCarthy, Deputy Minister of Education, and Dr E.E. Stewart, Deputy Minister of University Affairs, were also extraordinarily co-operative and helpful. I am particularly grateful to these officials for enabling me to pursue the work in a way that most appeals to a member of the university community: that is, I was completely free to choose, present, and interpret the facts according to my own best judgment. I did not feel the slightest pressure to adapt or modify the material in any way so as to present an "official" version of educational developments in Ontario. As a consequence, I am completely responsible for any opinions or interpretations of the facts that the work contains. The generous assistance for the project provided by the Ontario government, without which publication would have been impossible, does not involve any responsibility for the contents.

I would like to express my particular gratitude to those who assisted me so devotedly in the project: Miss L. McGuire, my loyal secretary, who served from the time the work began in the spring of 1968, Mrs E. West, who also served with extraordinary devotion and competence during most of the same period, and Mrs S. Constable, Miss D. McDowell, and Mrs G.J. Moore, each of whom participated during an extended period. Mr C. Westcott, who served as Executive Assistant to the Minister of Education and University Affairs, gave me continuous encouragement and helped to deal with practical problems relating to production and publication. Particularly helpful advice and information were given by Dr C.A. Brown, Professor E.B. Rideout, and Dr J.A. Keddy. Arrangements by Dr G.E. Flower to relieve me of the majority of my other professional obligations during most of a three-year period are also greatly appreciated. In addition, I would like to acknowledge my general indebtedness to the hundreds of people who supplied information so willingly in a variety of forms. That I am unable to name them all individually does not mean that I am any the less grateful for their contributions.

W.G. FLEMING
May 1971

Contents

PREFACE / v

ACKNOWLEDGMENTS / ix

TABLES / xiii

CHARTS / xxiii

Introduction
Current issues in education / 1

1
Characteristics of the Ontario population / 42

2
Enrolment in schools and in courses sponsored by the Department of Education / 93

3
Educational institutions / 143

4
University enrolment and degrees awarded / 174

5
Enrolment and certificates awarded in other post-secondary educational institutions / 224

6
Status and characteristics of teachers / 259

7
The financing of education / 305

Notes / 360

Contents of volumes in ONTARIO'S EDUCATIVE SOCIETY / 365

Tables

1-1 / Total population of Ontario and Canada as a whole, 1945–70   43
1-2 / Natural increase in Ontario's population, 1937–68   44
1-3 / Number of births in Canada per 1,000 population, 1945–69   44
1-4 / Population of Ontario by age, 1941–66   47
1-5 / Ontario population percentages by age and sex, 1941–66   49
1-6 / Successive population projections for Ontario   51
1-7 / Estimated population growth in selected countries, 1965–80   52
1-8 / Projected population of Ontario by age, 1971–91   53
1-9 / Projected Ontario population percentage by age and sex, 1971–96   55
1-10 / Immigration to Canada and Ontario, 1946–69   56
1-11 / Immigration to the United States, 1941–67   58
1-12 / Population of Ontario by place of birth, 1941–61   59
1-13 / Percentages of immigrants to Ontario from various sources, 1959–68   60
1-14 / Percentages of immigrants from outside Canada to Ontario by age, 1958–68   62
1-15 / Ontario labour force in relation to total population by sex, 1946–68   65
1-16 / Percentages of population of Ontario 14 years of age and over by labour force status, 1946–68   66
1-17 / Percentages of labour force employed in Canada and Ontario, 1946–69   68
1-18 / Percentages of employment in selected countries, 1953, 1958–66   68
1-19 / Percentages of Ontario labour force by occupational groups, 1951 and 1961   69
1-20 / Percentages of immigrants entering the labour force in Ontario, 1956–68   70
1-21 / Percentages of immigrants to Ontario by intended occupational groups, 1946–68   71
1-22 / Percentages of population of Ontario by mother tongue and age, 1941–61   73
1-23 / Population of Ontario 14 years of age and over by age and level of education, 1960 and 1965   75

1-24 / Population of Ontario 14 years of age and over by sex and level of education, 1960 and 1965   77
1-25 / Comparison of certain age groups in Canada and the United States by percentage at each level of education, 1965   78
1-26 / Population density in selected countries, 1966   80
1-27 / Population of Ontario by county or census division, 1941–66   82
1-28 / Rural and urban population trends in Ontario, 1941–66   85
1-29 / Population in largest urban units in Ontario, 1941–66   87
1-30 / Income level in Ontario, 1945–69   88
1-31 / Average constant dollar income in Ontario, 1950–69   88
1-32 / Consumption expenditure per capita by economic region of Ontario, 1967   89
1-33 / Average income per person in Canadian provinces and territories, 1960–7   91
1-34 / Per capita income in certain states of the United States, 1950–67   92

2-1 / Enrolment in elementary and secondary schools of Ontario, 1945–70   95
2-2 / School enrolment in Ontario as percentages of certain age groups, 1950–69   98
2-3 / Grade distribution in public elementary schools, 1945–70   100
2-4 / Grade distribution in Roman Catholic separate schools, 1945–70   102
2-5 / Age-grade distribution of enrolment, 1949–50   103
2-6 / Age-grade distribution of enrolment, 1955–6   104
2-7 / Age-grade distribution of enrolment, 1960–1   105
2-8 / Age-grade distribution of enrolment, 1966–7   106
2-9 / Enrolment in publicly supported bilingual elementary schools, 1945–70   108
2-10 / Enrolment in public elementary and Protestant separate schools operated by each type of school board, 1955–68   109
2-11 / Enrolment in elementary schools in each type of municipality, 1960–70   111
2-12 / Enrolment in secondary schools by grade, 1950–70   112
2-13 / Percentage of total enrolment in each secondary school grade, 1950–70   112
2-14 / Enrolment in secondary schools by course, 1955–63   113
2-15 / Enrolment in secondary schools by branch and program, 1963–70   115
2-16 / Enrolment in five-year programs in Ontario secondary schools by branch and grade, 1963–9   119
2-17 / Enrolment in four-year programs in Ontario secondary schools by branch and grade, 1963–9   121
2-18 / Enrolment in Ontario secondary schools in special or ungraded

courses, 1963–70   122
2-19 / Estimated progress of students through Ontario secondary schools, 1951–69, by percentage of grade 9 enrolment in each subsequent year   123
2-20 / Percentages of retirements from Ontario schools according to grade level, 1955–69   124
2-21 / Percentages of pupils leaving Ontario elementary and secondary schools for various reasons, 1959–68   125
2-22 / Enrolment in secondary schools operated by each type of school board, 1966–8   126
2-23 / Enrolment in secondary schools in each type of municipality, 1960–70   127
2-24 / Number of Ontario Secondary School Honour Graduation Diplomas issued by pattern of school attendance, 1950–69   128
2-25 / Number of papers written and number and percentage passed in the grade 13 examinations, 1950–69   130
2-26 / Percentages of certain Ontario grade 13 examination papers passed, 1964–9   132
2-27 / Number of Ontario Secondary School Graduation Diplomas issued, 1960–5   132
2-28 / Number of Ontario Secondary School Graduation Diplomas issued to graduates of the Reorganized Program, 1966–9   133
2-29 / Number of Certificates of Standing issued to students successfully completing grades 9 and 10 of the two-year program in Ontario secondary schools, 1964–9   134
2-30 / Enrolment in private schools in Ontario by level of instruction, 1963–70   135
2-31 / Enrolment in private schools in Ontario by type of school, 1963–70   136
2-32 / Enrolment in private schools in Ontario by grade, 1963–70   137
2-33 / Enrolment in schools for the blind and deaf operated by the Department of Education, 1950–70   138
2-34 / Enrolment in schools operated by the Retarded Children's Authorities, 1965–8   138
2-35 / Active enrolment in Department of Education correspondence courses, 1950–69   140

3-1 / Number of publicly supported elementary schools, 1945–70   144
3-2 / Number of publicly supported elementary schools operating kindergartens, 1955–70   144
3-3 / Number of public elementary schools by enrolment, 1960–70   145
3-4 / Number of Roman Catholic separate schools by enrolment, 1960–70   146
3-5 / Number of publicly supported elementary schools using French as a language of instruction, 1955–70   147

3-6 / Number of teaching areas in publicly supported elementary schools using French as a language of instruction, 1955–69   147
3-7 / Number of public elementary and Protestant separate schools operated by each type of school board, 1955–68   149
3-8 / Number of school boards of each type operating public elementary and Protestant separate schools, 1960–8   150
3-9 / Number of elementary schools by type of municipality, 1960–70   152
3-10 / Number of publicly supported secondary schools in Ontario by type of school, 1955–69   152
3-11 / Number of publicly supported secondary schools in Ontario by enrolment, 1960–70   154
3-12 / Number of publicly supported secondary schools offering Français and number of students enrolled, 1950–70   155
3-13 / Number of publicly supported secondary schools in Ontario by type of municipality, 1965–70   155
3-14 / Number of school boards of each type operating secondary schools, 1960–8   156
3-15 / New schools and additions built in Ontario, 1945–69   158
3-16 / Number of private schools in Ontario by level of instruction, 1963–70   161
3-17 / Number of private schools in Ontario by type, 1963–70   162
3-18 / Number of private schools in Ontario by size, 1963–70   163
3-19 / Number of private vocational schools, 1960–8   163
3-20 / Number of schools of nursing in Ontario and enrolment, 1945–70   163
3-21 / Founding dates of the provincially assisted universities   165
3-22 / Dates of establishment and changes in status of institutions for technological and trades training supported by the Department of Education   167
3-23 / General information about Ontario libraries, 1960–8   169
3-24 / Stock and services of municipal and county public libraries in Ontario in centres with population 10,000 and over, 1960–8   170
3-25 / Stock and services of municipal public libraries in Ontario in centres with population under 10,000, 1960–8   170
3-26 / Regional library systems, 1966–8   172
3-27 / Number of county library co-operatives in Ontario, 1945–69   172
3-28 / Stock and services of association libraries in Ontario, 1945–65   172

4-1 / University and college enrolment in Ontario, 1951–69   177
4-2 / Full-time undergraduate enrolment in Ontario universities in relation to 18–21 age group and grade 13 enrolment, 1950–68   179
4-3 / Total full-time enrolment in provincially assisted universities in Ontario, 1955–70   181

4-4 / Total full-time undergraduate enrolment at provincially assisted universities in Ontario, 1955–70   186
4-5 / Total full-time graduate enrolment at provincially assisted universities in Ontario, 1955–70   187
4-6 / Part-time enrolment in regular and summer sessions at provincially assisted universities in Ontario, 1966–70   189
4-7 / Full-time enrolment by program of study at provincially assisted universities, 1964–70   192–3
4-8 / Full-time enrolment by program of study at Brock University, 1964–70   195
4-9 / Full-time enrolment by program of study at Carleton University, 1964–70   196
4-10 / Full-time enrolment by program of study at the University of Guelph, 1964–70   198
4-11 / Full-time enrolment by program of study at Lakehead University, 1964–70   199
4-12 / Full-time enrolment by program of study at Laurentian University, including Algoma and Nipissing Colleges, 1964–70   200
4-13 / Full-time enrolment by program of study at McMaster University, 1964–70   201
4-14 / Full-time enrolment by program of study at the University of Ottawa, 1964–70   202
4-15 / Full-time enrolment by program of study at Queen's University, 1964–70   204
4-16 / Full-time enrolment by program of study at the University of Toronto, including Erindale and Scarborough Colleges, 1964–70   206–7
4-17 / Full-time enrolment by program of study at Trent University, 1964–70   208
4-18 / Full-time enrolment by program of study at the University of Waterloo, 1964–70   209
4-19 / Full-time enrolment by program of study at the University of Western Ontario, 1964–70   211
4-20 / Full-time enrolment by program of study at the University of Windsor, 1964–70   212
4-21 / Full-time enrolment by program of study at York University, 1964–70   213
4-22 / Number of degrees and diplomas of each type awarded by Ontario universities, 1955–69   214–15
4-23 / Number of bachelors' or first professional degrees conferred by individual colleges and universities in Ontario, 1959–69   219
4-24 / Number of masters' degrees conferred by individual colleges and universities in Ontario, 1959–69   219
4-25 / Number of earned academic doctorates conferred by individual universities in Ontario, 1959–69   220
4-26 / Projected enrolment in Ontario universities, 1970–82   220

4-27 / Projected full-time enrolment in each provincially assisted university in Ontario, 1970–5   222
4-28 / Projected graduate enrolment in each provincially assisted university in Ontario, 1970–5   222

5-1 / Enrolment in Ontario teachers' colleges, 1945–70   225
5-2 / Enrolment in Ontario colleges of education by course and program, 1945–70   228
5-3 / Number of first certificates of each type awarded intramurally in the colleges of education, 1955–69   234
5-4 / Number of additional certificates of each type awarded intramurally in the colleges of education, 1955–69   235
5-5 / Number of first certificates of each type awarded extramurally in the colleges of education, 1955–69   237
5-6 / Number of additional certificates of each type awarded extramurally in the colleges of education, 1955–69   237
5-7 / Enrolment in Department of Education summer courses, 1945–69   238–9
5-8 / Full-time enrolment in institutions for technological and trades training supported by the Department of Education, 1962–7   241
5-9 / Evening class enrolment in institutions for technological and trades training supported by the Department of Education, 1962–7   242
5-10 / Number of certificates of each type issued in provincial institutes of technology, 1960–7   242
5-11 / Full-time and part-time enrolment in the colleges of applied arts and technology, 1967–70   243
5-12 / Projected enrolment of full-time fee-paying students in the colleges of applied arts and technology, 1970–7   244
5-13-1 / Enrolment in colleges of applied arts and technology in full-time business and applied arts programs, 1967–8   246
5-13-2 / Enrolment in colleges of applied arts and technology in full-time technological, technical, apprenticeship, short, and Ontario Manpower Retraining programs, 1967–8   247
5-14-1 / Enrolment in colleges of applied arts and technology in full-time business and applied arts programs, 1968–9   248
5-14-2 / Enrolment in colleges of applied arts and technology in full-time technological, technical, apprenticeship, short, and Ontario Manpower Retraining programs, 1968–9   249
5-15-1 / Enrolment in colleges of applied arts and technology in full-time business and applied arts programs, 1969–70   250
5-15-2 / Enrolment in colleges of applied arts and technology in full-time technological, technical, apprenticeship, and Ontario Manpower Retraining programs, 1969–70   251
5-16 / Enrolment in adult leadership courses offered by the Community Programs (Youth and Recreation) Branch, 1960–8   253

5-17 / Enrolment in courses for leaders of special groups offered by the Community Programs (Youth and Recreation) Branch, 1962–9   255
5-18 / Enrolment in training courses for municipal recreation directors offered by the Community Programs (Youth and Recreation) Branch, and number completing, 1955–69   256
5-19 / Enrolment in newcomer classes offered by the Community Programs Branch, 1947–61   256
5-20 / Number of trainees in business and industry in programs sponsored by the Applied Arts and Technology Branch of the Ontario Department of Education, 1963–8   256
5-21 / Number of trainees in Ontario under the *Technical and Vocational Training Assistance Act*, by program, 1961–7   257
5-22 / Number of trainees in Canada under the *Technical and Vocational Training Assistance Act*, by program, 1961–7   257

6-1 / Numbers of acquisitions and withdrawals of teachers from elementary and secondary schools in Ontario, 1945–70   260
6-2 / Ratio of pupils to teachers in Ontario schools, 1945–70   263
6-3-1 / Number of full-time teachers in elementary schools in Ontario by sex, 1945–70   264
6-3-2 / Number of full-time teachers in Ontario schools by sex, 1945–70   265
6-4 / Teacher acquisitions in Ontario elementary schools from various sources, 1957–69   267
6-5 / Teacher acquisitions in Ontario secondary schools from various sources, 1957–69   269
6-6 / Number of withdrawals from elementary school teaching force for various reasons, 1957–69   271
6-7 / Percentages of withdrawals from elementary school teaching force for various reasons, 1957–69   272
6-8 / Number of withdrawals from secondary school teaching force for various reasons, 1957–69   273
6-9 / Percentages of withdrawals from secondary school teaching force for various reasons, 1957–69   274
6-10 / Salary frequency distribution for full-time teachers in Ontario schools as of September 1950   276
6-11 / Salary frequency distribution for full-time teachers in Ontario schools as of September 1955   277
6-12 / Salary frequency distribution for full-time teachers in Ontario schools as of September 1960   278
6-13 / Salary frequency distribution for full-time teachers in Ontario schools as of December 1966   279
6-14 / Salary frequency distribution for full-time teachers in Ontario schools as of April 1968   280
6-15 / Median salaries of teachers and principals in Ontario schools

by sex, 1950–69 281
6-16 / Salaries of elementary and secondary school teachers in the United States, 1955–69 282
6-17 / Percentage distribution of public elementary and secondary school classroom teachers in the United States by degrees held, 1964 and 1967 283
6-18 / Percentage distribution of public elementary and secondary school classroom teachers in the United States by age, 1964 and 1967 285
6-19 / Percentage distribution of public elementary and secondary school classroom teachers in the United States by teaching experience, 1964 and 1967 286
6-20 / Number of full-time teaching staff in the provincially assisted universities of Ontario, 1964–9 289
6-21 / Ratio of students to instructors in each provincially assisted university in Ontario, 1960–9 291
6-22 / Mean salaries by rank and yearly percentage increases in Ontario universities, 1966–9 294
6-23 / Mean salaries and annual percentage increases for all ranks in each Ontario university, 1966–70 295
6-24 / Mean salaries by rank in each Ontario university, 1968–9 296
6-25 / Number of instructors in Ontario teachers' colleges, 1951–70 298
6-26 / Ratio of students to instructors in Ontario teachers' colleges, 1951–70 299
6-27 / Salary scales for teachers' college masters, 1947–69 300
6-28 / Number of full-time faculty in institutions for technological and trades training supported by the Department of Education, 1960–7 301
6-29 / Number of part-time faculty in institutions for technological and trades training supported by the Department of Education, 1960–7 302
6-30 / Number of faculty in colleges of applied arts and technology, 1967–70 303

7-1 / Ontario gross provincial product, 1945–69 306
7-2 / Canadian gross national product, 1945–68 307
7-3 / Net general revenue of government of Ontario, 1945–71 309
7-4 / Ontario government net general revenue by major sources, 1962–71 310
7-5 / Major sources of Ontario government net general revenue as percentages of total, 1962–71 311
7-6 / Payments made by the federal government to Ontario for education, 1960–6 312
7-7 / Federal financial contributions to training in Ontario under the *Technical and Vocational Training Assistance Act*, by program, 1961–7 313
7-8 / Federal financial contributions to training in Canada under the

Technical and Vocational Training Assistance Act, by program, 1961–7   314
7-9 / Total and per capita net provincial debt, 1944–70   315
7-10 / Net public debt of the government of Canada, 1946–69   316
7-11 / Net general expenditure by ministerial responsibility in Ontario government, 1964–71   317
7-12 / Percentage of total net general expenditure spent by the Departments of Education and University Affairs, 1964–71   319
7-13 / Net general expenditure by the Ontario Department of Education on various items, 1965–71   320
7-14 / Expenditure by the Department of Education on summer courses for teachers, 1950–69   321
7-15 / Net general expenditure by the Ontario Department of University Affairs on various items, 1965–71   321
7-16 / Miscellaneous grants by the Department of Education for 1969–70   322
7-17 / General legislative grants to school boards, 1945–69   323
7-18 / Percentage increase of provincial grants to school boards, 1945–69   327
7-19 / Revenues of Ontario school boards from major sources, 1945–68   328
7-20 / Receipts from the provincial government and local taxation as percentages of the sum of receipts from both sources, 1945–68   330
7-21 / Revenues of Ontario school boards from various sources, 1950–68   331
7-22 / Revenues of Ontario elementary school boards from various sources, 1950–68   333
7-23 / Revenues of Ontario public elementary school boards from various sources, 1950–68   334
7-24 / Revenues of Ontario Roman Catholic separate school boards from various sources, 1950–68   335
7-25 / Revenues of Ontario secondary school boards from various sources, 1950–68   337
7-26 / Education levies as a percentage of total municipal taxation in Ontario, 1945–68   338
7-27 / Expenditure by Ontario school boards on various items, 1950–68   339
7-28 / Expenditure by Ontario elementary school boards on various items, 1950–68   341
7-29 / Expenditure by Ontario public elementary school boards on various items, 1950–68   342
7-30 / Expenditure by Ontario Roman Catholic separate school boards on various items, 1950–68   343
7-31 / Expenditure by Ontario secondary school boards on various items, 1950–68   344

7-32 / Expenditure by Ontario secondary school boards on various items, academic schools, 1950–67   345
7-33 / Expenditure by Ontario secondary school boards on various items, vocational schools, 1950–67   346
7-34 / Expenditure on instruction as a percentage of total Ontario school board expenditure, 1950–68   347
7-35 / Annual per pupil cost of average daily attendance for day school education in Ontario, 1945–69   348
7-36 / Municipal and school board debt, 1945–67   349
7-37 / Percentages of total income of provincially assisted universities of Ontario by source, 1965–9   351
7-38 / Student fees and grants from provincial and federal governments as percentages of total income of provincially assisted universities of Ontario, 1965–9   351
7-39 / Provincial operating grants to provincially assisted universities of Ontario, 1957–70   352
7-40 / Federal operating grants to provincially assisted universities of Ontario, 1957–67   354
7-41 / Combined provincial and federal operating grants to provincially assisted universities of Ontario, 1957–67   355
7-42 / Regular provincial capital grants to provincially assisted universities of Ontario, 1957–70   356
7-43 / Operating and capital funds provided to colleges of applied arts and technology by Ontario government, 1966–70   357
7-44 / Expenditure for public libraries in Ontario, 1960–8   359

Charts

1-1 / Number of births in Ontario per thousand of population, 1945–68   45
1-2 / Number of births in Ontario, 1945–68   45
1-3 / Number of births in selected countries per thousand of the population, 1960–6   46
1-4 / Number of immigrants to Ontario, 1946–69   57
1-5 / Percentages of men and women aged fourteen and over in the labour force, 1946–68   67
1-6 / Ontario population by mother tongue, 1941–61   74
1-7 / Population density in Ontario, 1966   79
1-8 / Population growth patterns in Ontario, 1941–66   83
1-9 / Per capita income in Ontario, 1945–69   89
1-10 / The economic regions of Ontario   90

2-1 / Enrolment in Ontario elementary and secondary schools, 1945–70   96
2-2 / Enrolment in public elementary and Roman Catholic separate schools in Ontario, 1945–70   97
2-3 / Percentage of secondary school enrolment in Ontario in each branch, 1963–70   116
2-4 / Percentage of secondary school enrolment in Ontario in each program, 1963–9   117
2-5 / Percentage of secondary school enrolment in Ontario in each branch and program, 1963–9   118
2-6 / Enrolment in adult elementary school level correspondence courses provided by the Ontario Department of Education, 1960–9   141
2-7 / Enrolment in academic secondary school correspondence courses provided by the Ontario Department of Education, 1960–9   142

3-1 / Estimated cost of school building projects in Ontario, 1945–69   160

3-2 / Location of the universities of Ontario   164
3-3 / Location of the colleges of applied arts and technology of Ontario   168
3-4 / Regional library systems in Ontario   171

4-1 / Percentage increase in full-time undergraduate and graduate enrolment in the universities of Ontario, 1955–69   178
4-2 / Full-time undergraduate enrolment in Ontario universities as a percentage of the 18–21 age group, 1950–68   179
4-3 / Enrolment in five senior provincially assisted universities in Ontario, 1960–70   182
4-4 / Enrolment in nine provincially assisted Ontario universities chartered in the twentieth century, 1960–70   183
4-5 / Full-time enrolment at the University of Toronto as a percentage of full-time enrolment at all provincially assisted universities in Ontario, 1960–70   184
4-6 / Percentage of undergraduate degrees awarded in each of five leading faculties in all Ontario universities, 1960–9   216
4-7 / Percentage increase in undergraduate and graduate degrees awarded by all Ontario universities, 1960–8   217

5-1 / Total enrolment in Ontario teachers' colleges, 1960–70   226
5-2 / Enrolment in regular winter and special summer courses at the Ontario colleges of education, 1960–70   229
5-3 / Enrolment in the regular session in the academic departments of the Ontario colleges of education, 1945–70   231
5-4 / Enrolment in the regular session in the academic and vocational departments of the Ontario colleges of education, 1950–70   233
5-5 / Total enrolment in Ontario Department of Education summer courses, 1960–9   240
5-6 / Percentage of total enrolment in colleges of applied arts and technology in each program, 1967–70   252

6-1 / Numbers in the Ontario teaching force, 1945–70   261
6-2 / Pupil-teacher ratios in public elementary, Roman Catholic separate, and secondary schools, 1945–70   263
6-3 / Percentages of teacher acquisitions in Ontario elementary schools from major sources, 1957–69   268
6-4 / Percentages of teacher acquisitions in Ontario secondary schools from major sources, 1957–69   268
6-5 / Numbers of full-time instructors in institutions for technological and trades training and Ryerson Polytechnical Institute, 1960–7   300

7-1 / Gross provincial product in Ontario and gross national product in Canada in current and constant dollars, 1945–69   308

7-2 / Net general expenditure by ministerial responsibility in selected departments of the Ontario government, 1964–71   318

7-3 / Provincial grants for elementary and secondary schools in Ontario, 1945–69   324

7-4 / Provincial grants for public elementary and Roman Catholic separate schools in Ontario, 1945–69   325

7-5 / Provincial grants for academic and vocational programs in Ontario secondary schools, 1945–68   326

7-6 / Total school board revenues and receipts from local taxation, 1945–68   329

7-7 / Local taxes, receipts from the provincial government, and other revenues as percentages of the total revenue for public elementary and Roman Catholic separate school boards, 1950–68   336

ONTARIO'S EDUCATIVE SOCIETY / I

The expansion of the educational system

INTRODUCTION

Current issues in education

This first section of volume I is intended as an introduction to the whole series on *Ontario's Educative Society* rather than as an integral part of the volume. Its purpose is to identify briefly some of the issues and problems of greatest concern to those involved in Ontario education in recent years. These are not, for the most part, matters of purely provincial interest but tend to have international dimensions. Some are of worldwide application, and others are typical of technically advanced countries alone. In certain cases Ontarians have contributed some element of originality in dealing with them. In others, perhaps, they have faced these problems with the same bewilderment as have their neighbours in other Canadian provinces and abroad.

THE ECONOMIC VALUE OF EDUCATION

Importance of the belief in economic benefits
It would be inspiring to think that Ontario was prepared to pour enormous sums of money into an enterprise designed primarily to upgrade the quality of its intellectual and cultural life. In fact, the phenomenal increase in educational expenditure in the post-war period has had popular support mainly because of the anticipated economic returns. Parents of earlier generations did their best to discharge their obligations to their children by leaving them a financial nest egg. Their modern counterparts try to give their offspring the means to security and social prestige by providing them with the best possible education. Even those with no children have been persuaded that the benefits of education permeate the whole economy and contribute to the welfare of all. The government has felt able to count sufficiently on public foresight and sophistication to resist pressure for more tangible goods and services in favour of an approach that promises to provide amenities ultimately in greater abundance.

There are some important questions about education as investment. For example, to what extent does it benefit the individual? the economy as a whole? What are the returns from different types and levels of education? Is it possible that some forms work to the advantage of the individual but not to that of the economy? Reliable answers to these questions become more urgent as the size of the investment increases.

The case for individual benefit
A case for individual benefit has often been made on the basis of the high positive correlation between levels of education and earnings. The Dominion Bureau of Statistics performed such an exercise on data from the 1961 census. The results showed the average salary in the male non-farm labour force in the fifteen- to twenty-four-year age group as $1,928 for those who had only an elementary education as compared with $3,408 for those who had a university degree. The discrepancy increased progressively with age to the point where the comparable figures were $3,480 and $10,609 for the fifty-five- to sixty-four-year age group.[1] This means that those with only an elementary school education earned about 57 per cent as much as the university graduates in the youngest age category and only 33 per cent as much in the oldest.

The case for benefit to the economy as a whole
The process of identifying the general economic benefits of education is more complicated. Some American investigators have undertaken to analyse the factors contributing to the growth of the economy over a period of several decades and to assess the relative importance of each factor in quantitative terms. A common approach is to allocate as much as possible of the economic growth to factors such as the increase in the labour force and in physical capital, and to attribute the remainder, or some arbitrary percentage of it, to educational investment. Denison, following such a procedure,[2] attributed over 20 per cent of the 2.9 per cent annual growth rate of the gross national product in the United States between 1929 and 1957 to expenditure on formal education at all levels. He allocated to education three-fifths of the differences in earnings corresponding to differences in schooling. On the basis of his own calculations, with reinforcement from those of Denison, Schultz[3] concluded that between 1909 and 1929 material capital contributed almost twice as much as schooling to economic growth, but between 1929 and 1957 the contribution of schooling exceeded that of material capital.

The report *Financing Higher Education in Canada*, published by the Association of Universities and Colleges of Canada in 1965, traced some of the implications for higher education of the concept of education as investment as opposed to education as consumption. It noted first that, even if we were justified in adopting the education as consumption view, we might well choose to increase our consumption of the educational commodity as we add to our wealth. We would, under such circumstances, be forced to choose between education and some alternative goods and services, or content ourselves with a lesser investment in physical capital and a consequent slower rate in growth. But it is quite probable that education would still fare reasonably well. Taking the other view, however, that the growth in the gross national product is dependent in part on an increase in investment in higher education, the consequence of choosing to make such an investment will be that we have not only more education, but also more to spend on other things. Some rather persuasive arithmetic was used to illustrate the point. In 1963-4 university expenditures were about $429 million, or approximately 1 per cent of a gross national product of about $43 billion. Projected university expenditures for 1974 were $2 billion, which would constitute close to 2.5 per cent of an estimated gross national product of $83 billion. From the point of view of education as consumption, Canadians would have to decide whether to spend on higher education the $1.2 billion over the $800 million that a maintenance of the existing rate of support would provide, or whether to spend the same amount on some alternative benefits. Viewed as investment, the extra $1.2 billion would not need to account for a very large proportion of the $83 billion figure to justify its use in that way.

The *Second Annual Review* of the Economic Council of Canada made a strong case for both individual and social returns from educational investment. According to what it called a cautious estimate, the real income per person in the male labour force was roughly one-quarter higher in 1961 than it would have been if the average educational attainment had remained at the 1911 level.[4] Comparable calculations for the United States had suggested a gain of no less than 40 per cent attributable to education in the same period. The report concluded that a surprisingly large part of the discrepancy between American and Canadian average income levels could be explained by differences in educational level.

The Economic Council pointed out that it takes an extremely powerful combination of factors to bring about any substantial short-term or medium-term change in a country's educational stock. Basic factors may have prolonged and cumulative effects stretching over many decades. The Council suggested that the notable vigour and dynamism that characterized Canadian education in the early part of the twentieth century, which was not maintained after the early 1920s, had important effects lasting at least until the Second World War. Conversely, the lagging educational efforts after the early 1920s had adverse effects through the 1940s and 1950s. The rate of improvement was also restricted by the relatively small number of new entrants to the labour force emerging from the domestic educational system. The higher school retention rates and the increased enrolment ratios in the 1950s had little effect in that decade, but would show up in the 1960s, the 1970s, and beyond.[5]

The process by which general economic benefit occurs
If general economic benefits are to accrue from an improvement in the educational level of the population, it must be because greater technologi-

cal and organizational skills lead to a shift in the balance of different occupations. Means are devised to eliminate jobs requiring lesser skills, while opportunities are multiplied for the exercise of competencies at a higher level.

Confidence that this process would actually occur was being severely shaken by the beginning of the 1970s. The recession that occurred at that time left many young people without much immediate prospect of finding the interesting and challenging work they had been led to expect. The economy did not seem to be evolving quickly enough to provide a need for their educated talents. Those menial tasks such as farm labour which did remain had so little appeal that workers from the Caribbean were admitted to perform them at a time when unemployment among Canadians reached a level that had not existed for years. There was a prospect of social disruption caused by the boredom and dissatisfaction felt by over-educated people for whom the economy had no use.

The optimists hoped that an upswing in the economy would correct the difficulty by producing an employment structure that would absorb most of the young people emerging from the educational system. It seemed difficult to imagine, however, that full employment would return in the near future. Until nearly the end of the 1960s, Canada had had no surplus of people equipped for professional, managerial, and other occupations requiring a high level of education, skill, and flexibility. J.R. Nicholson, then Minister of Citizenship and Immigration in the federal government, said in 1965: "Everyone knows full well that new techniques and methods are creating demands for higher levels of skills and knowledge, and that our rapid expansion is creating jobs in the skilled and professional categories faster than we can produce qualified workers through Canadian sources."[6]

Doubts about the extent of individual benefit

While the statisticians who have compiled various figures have concluded that education appears to be the most important explanation of inter-occupation and inter-age earning differences, the basis for this reasoning is open to some question, since causation is attributed to one of two factors that have merely been shown to be related. There is room for the argument that the difference in earnings can be accounted for more by the qualities such as intelligence and persistence that lead to the achievement of a high level of education than to anything the education itself contributes. Account must also be taken of the effect of prevailing attitudes toward the value of education, whether or not they are soundly based. For example, if a certain certificate or diploma is required for a particular job, an under-qualified aspirant never gets an opportunity to demonstrate whether he could perform as well as one with the prescribed educational background. The salary that accompanies the job is also out of his reach. A further factor has to do with socially based inequalities in educational opportunity. Those who have advanced furthest up the educational ladder have tended to come from families with connections that have opened up for them some of the most advantageous occupational opportunities.

There is no very satisfactory way to determine the relative importance of all these factors. To the extent that education makes a real addition to the occupational value of an individual, actual financial benefits will accrue to him and to the society of which he is a part. But to the extent that education is simply one of those factors that distinguish individuals in terms of social and occupational privilege, increasing everyone's educational level by an increment of a given size merely moves the whole structure up a peg without otherwise changing anything.

Paul Goodman has expressed many of these doubts. After noting a set of figures showing the relationship between the number of years of schooling and unemployment rates, he commented as follows.

But these figures are unimpressive ... the *prima facie* explanation of the correlation is the parents' income: By connections, manners and aspirations, middle-class children get middle-class jobs; schooling is an incidental part of it. Lower-class children used to get lower-class jobs, but just these jobs have petered out; in the present *structure* of the economy, the money and jobs do not filter down. Similarly, the docility, neatness of appearance, etc. that are useful for getting petty jobs, are not created by years of schooling but they are accurately measured by them. In my opinion, the same line of criticism strongly applies to the spectacular correlations between life-time income and years of schooling. Looking for his first job, a middle class youth decides he wants $80 to start, and he can afford to shop around till he gets it; a poor boy must take anything and starts at $35. For obvious reasons, this initial difference will usually predetermine the whole career. Conversely a sharp poor boy, seeing that this is the score, might choose not to bestir himself and prefer to look for a racket.[7]

Questions about the economic contribution of university education
There is little evidence of any serious decline in confidence in the general economic value of most forms and levels of education. A rising degree of scepticism has, however, begun to develop over university education, particularly the type offered in faculties of arts and sciences. There is real evidence that a public antipathy has appeared over the extent of financial support provided in this particular area.

A paper entitled "Education: Cause or Effect of Economic Growth?" delivered by Professor David A. Dodge during the Secondary School Principals' course at Queen's University on July 21, 1969, attracted a good deal of attention. Press reports unfortunately created the impression that Dodge had discovered some major factors not previously taken into account in attempts to determine the economic proceeds from educational investment. The real significance of the paper was that he had interpreted the facts in such a way as to arrive at conclusions other than those that were generally accepted. Two of his four concluding statements were as follows.

3. The payoff to this investment in education is quite high for the individual but, contrary to popular opinion, quite low for society as a whole.
4. If the Province of Ontario wished to achieve maximum economic growth through investment in education, increased expenditure on university education does not appear to be the best way to achieve its objective. If economic considerations are paramount, the Province should cease to increase public expenditure on university education for the return on this investment appears to have become too low. The economy is not fully utilizing the training of the quantity of university and high school graduates being produced in Ontario today.[8]

Dodge compared average lifetime earnings for those who attained different educational levels, taking into account the costs of obtaining an education, including earnings foregone. He pointed out along the way that financial returns varied greatly according to the student's selection of courses and careers. While the rate of return for dentistry was over 20 per cent, that for social work was zero, and that for theology, −15 per cent. It was highest of all, an astonishing 75 per cent, for those obtaining a teaching certificate at a teachers' college. These figures, however, had to be modified by taking into account the fact that those who pursued higher education were brighter on the average than those who did not, and would presumably have earned better than average incomes even if educational achievement had been equalized.

In considering the question of the economic value of educational investment to society, Dodge asserted that the figure of 9–10 per cent accepted by the Economic Council of Canada was in error. His reasoning was as follows.

First, the estimated 9 or 10% should be reduced to take into account differential ability of students. Doing this reduces the estimated return to about 7%. But then one must ask the question, does extra education make one more "productive" or does it merely serve as a "barrier to entry" into a profession or trade in which wages are high? Some research that I have been doing indicates that as much as half of the differential between earnings of graduates and high school graduates may occur because of the "barrier to entry" effect. That is, the real social return to investment in post secondary education may only be a scant 3½%.[9]

Explaining the point further, Dodge gave examples of occupational and professional groups that kept their numbers small, and their wages consequently high, by demanding a level of general education that he thought had little, if any, relationship to the work itself. The social returns from such education were nil.

Even among those who remain favourably disposed toward the concept of education as investment, reactions to a high level of government spending do not necessarily produce a favourable reaction at the polls. Wage-earners have been persuaded during the post-war period of general prosperity and rising income that they are entitled to a continuous increase in the amount of funds at their private disposal. There is a widespread impression that the average citizen is entitled, despite losses attributable to inflation, to be a little better off each year. If the tax collector prevents him from realizing this expectation, he often reacts negatively, regardless of how worthy the cause for which the money is spent.

The Deputy Minister of Education, J.R. McCarthy, gave expression to the problem.

... because the return on the capital investment is not clearly identifiable on a balance sheet at the end of each fiscal year, there is a strong tendency, when the bills are rendered, to forget the necessity for capital investment in human resources as the essential ingredient for a healthy economy in the future.[10]

The increasing scepticism about the costs of education, which became pronounced at the beginning of the 1970s, was reflected in debates in the Legislature. On December 2, 1969, Walter Pitman said:

In a strange "gut" way, the people of Ontario are questioning the explosion in expenditures and activity all in the name of education. Unless we do something in this jurisdiction, I am afraid the worship will turn to disdain and cynicism. During this period of expansion, we have acted as though any expenditure in the name of education was good and worthwhile. Citizens are wondering to what extent the rising cost of education can be tolerated, as long as it appears that decisions are made which are completely uncritical. The argument that money spent on education will be repaid with interest, that, indeed, all educational spending is an investment, will simply no longer hold water. We are realizing slowly that all spending on education is not necessarily going to produce growth of any kind.[11]

Effect of the utilitarian emphasis on the content of education
It is reasonable to deduce that the prevalence of the concept of education as investment has generated pressure in favour of utilitarian courses and programs with a clearly demonstrable relationship to production. The federal government, for example, has intervened to swing the balance toward vocational programs in the high schools. Its activities in the field of manpower training and retraining have also been frankly designed to develop job skills. The support provided by the Ontario government for institutions of technology and trades training and the enormous effort

devoted to the creation of a system of colleges of applied arts and technology reflect some of the same attitudes.

The humane and liberal interests have fared reasonably well under the circumstances. To some extent they have prospered by virtue of the unproved and perhaps unprovable claim that the best provision for long-term occupational success, in an economy where the average person must expect to have his job rendered obsolete x number of times during his career, is to educate for flexibility, for the understanding of general principles, for the ability to think creatively and critically, and for other such objectives of a general education. Since these views are held firmly by many educators and the man who is interested largely in practical results has no grounds for disproving them, they have helped to maintain the traditional orientation of the educational system.

Attitudes of young people
There is a very pronounced tendency among some young people to denigrate the highly organized industrial and commercial society in which they live. They reject the idea of an education to prepare them to fit into some prescribed niche. Such a process seems to them to be antithetical to the concept of education for individual self-realization. At the most extreme, they appear to believe that the whole system is some kind of malign plot to rob idealistic youth of its soul. They show no interest in relating the creation of wealth by the industrious people of the past to the kind of educational opportunities they are able to enjoy. Since these young people tend to be highly voluble, they are serving increasingly as a focus for complaints on the part of those who object to the high level of financial support that education has recently received. Prime Minister Robarts sometimes expressed an apprehension lest the apparent lack of value placed on education for employment, and the lack of appreciation of educational opportunities for any other purpose, might lead to an undue demotion of education on the priority list, to the province's ultimate serious disadvantage.

THE GENERATION GAP
Whether Ontario or any other province or country will in the long run succeed in maintaining a close relationship between education and economic growth hinges on the attitudes of the mass of young people and the effect education will have on them. There are some extremely vital questions that must be asked. For example: 1 / Are the present differences between the established and the younger generation simply a normal expectation or are they so deep and fundamental as to constitute something unique in human history? 2 / If the latter, what are the implications for existing society of the values held by the younger generation? 3 / If these values are incompatible with present-day social forms and structures, or with anything into which these might evolve through normal

growth process, are they likely to be modified as young people grow older, or are we facing a social revolution that will invalidate many of the old assumptions?

The most complacent view is that current differences between the generations are no more than a normal phenomenon. The fact that they are wider than in any preceding era is simply an inevitable consequence of the speed of social change. They are thought, however, to arise from the same basic cause: the adolescent search for independence. Departures from conventional adult behaviour are seen as a phase that will pass as young people gain maturity. The after-dinner speaker who proclaims that any student who is not a radical is abnormal may utter under his breath that the middle-aged radical is probably equally abnormal.

An example of the view that there is no problem was offered in a Toronto newspaper in 1968. Entitled "Where is the generation gap?" it described the young people who were temporarily employed in the editorial department for the summer. According to expectation, they conformed to certain fashions typical of their age group: for example, there were plenty of miniskirts and the occasional psychedelic sport shirt, and the parking lot contained a collection of motorcycles. But there was no evidence of the reputed problem of communication, and no sign that the young people mistrusted their elders. In fact, discussion revealed that a large proportion of the opinions of both groups were held in common. The students did not believe that young people should be compelled to give up years of their lives for military service in peacetime, and they did not agree that every war that a democracy gets into is just or necessary. They believed that the educational systems should respect the student as an individual and that it should serve his needs rather than those of the professional hierarchy. They were concerned about fair treatment for minorities. They wanted to eliminate unjust poverty from Canadian society and to ensure a decent start for every Canadian child. Most important, perhaps, these clear-eyed young idealists saw a productive role for themselves in existing society, much as it might have needed reforming in certain aspects. They were taking advantage of their opportunities to prepare themselves for satisfying and rewarding careers.

A search for the generation gap was recently conducted by Mildred Henry and Paul Heist of the Center for Research and Development in Higher Education at the University of California, Berkeley.[12] The participants were students from three colleges with respective enrolments primarily from upper, middle, and lower socio-economic levels. They were asked for their opinions, and those of their parents, on a variety of current socio-political issues and on personal behaviour and interests. Their responses gave no evidence of a true generation gap. Students at all colleges disagreed overwhelmingly with the statement that it is difficult for the person over thirty to understand the young person today. An interesting result of the study was that the respondents from the different colleges differed rather sharply in their views. It was thus concluded that the "social strata gap" was much wider than the generation gap.

Edgar Z. Friedenberg analyzed the issue on a more abstract level some years ago.[13] He expressed surprise that adults everywhere should be bewildered at the current behaviour of young people, since they were acting according to a standard pattern in technically developed countries throughout the world. He felt, however, that there was cause for concern in that many of them were in serious trouble. Adolescence should be a natural and normal stage in the unfolding of human life rather than a crisis-ridden period of transition.

Friedenberg saw no sign of an original, stable, coherent set of values among young people that had any chance of standing up against those of the older generation. He described the situation as follows.

"Youth cultures" vary from the more flamboyant forms of delinquency to the conservative eroticism of the college fraternity. But all of them have been altered by continuous interaction with the adult world; the youngsters, unlike natives of a primitive tribe, have never known anything else and have no traditions wholly their own. The idols of the "teen-age" culture are the entertainers who use their "teen-age" clientele to make it as disk jockeys, on TV, or within the residually "teen-age" enclave of the B-movie. The explicit values of the juvenile gang are taken from the adult world; they, too, covet status and success and do not imagine that these could be conceived in terms more compelling than those they find familiar.[14]

Much of the problem of youth appeared to Friedenberg to be attributable to the widespread feeling that it cannot be allowed to proceed without massive intervention. He called young people the last social group in the world to be given the full nineteenth-century colonial treatment.

Our colonial administrators, at least at the higher policy-making levels, are usually of the enlightened sort who decry the punitive expedition except as an instrument of last resort, though they are inclined to tolerate a shade more brutality in the actual school or police station than the law allows. They prefer, however, to study the young with a view to understanding them, not for their own sake but in order to learn how to induce them to abandon their barbarism and assimilate the folkways of normal adult life. The model emissary to the world of youth is no longer the tough disciplinarian but the trained youth worker, who works like a psychoanalytically oriented anthropologist. Like the best of missionaries, he is sympathetic and understanding toward the people he is sent to work with, and aware and critical of the larger society he represents. But fundamentally he accepts it, and often does not really question its basic values or its right to send him to wean the young from savagery.[15]

This interpretation suggests the existence of a problem with no easy remedy, but it leaves no room for the idea that young people are formulating a set of values that pose a revolutionary threat to the adult order.

During the same period, Paul Goodman expressed views much like those of Friedenberg.[16] He saw the youth subculture as very similar in motivation and style to that of adults, and called it "only an absurd imitation of an absurd adult culture." He felt that there was nothing authentic in it except "its youthful vitality, its disappointment in being cut off from the adult world, and its spite against the adults' demands." In the background was the organized system, to which most of the young people would eventually conform. His verdict was expressed thus.

Writers about the youth culture tend to overrate its contents and underrate its importance. It has no cultural value; it is base rather than juvenile. The valuable juvenile is the adolescent-romantic, the crush, the stupid-stubborn honest, the daydream, the religious conversion, the frantic daring, the unbelievable loyalty, etc.; and these probably exist as much as ever and the same as ever. The way to tap these values is to let them grow up further. But the attempt to manipulate "adolescent society" as such for adult purposes ... can lead only to trivial and base results. But the importance of youth-culture is its protest, that the adults are alien and that they are not worth growing up to. The problem it raises in education is a simple but hard one, how to make the adult culture more available, more useful, and more noble.[17]

Seymour L. Halleck recently presented a rather different view of the situation.[18] His observations of youth's value system suggest something much more significant than a distorted reflection of values held by the adult society. He found that the most striking aspect of students' orientation is the importance they place on immediate gratification. They seem to have little reverence for the past and little hope for the future. They have become so aware of the rapidity of change that they believe it futile to make long-term plans. They see little point in competitive striving for success. They are hesitant to spend many years in preparation for professional careers like medicine because they are uncertain of the form such careers will assume by the time they are through. Uncertainty about the future also leads to a downgrading of the value of property. Few young people are attracted by a life dedicated to trade and the acquisition of wealth. A lack of respect for property is manifested in shoplifting and minor pilfering.

Halleck was impressed by the value present-day youth place on human relationships. While he thought it debatable whether they are any more capable than their parents of finding rewarding relationships, he considered their commitment to the search indisputable. Their ideal appears to be, not the person who is physically attractive or the possessor of qualities that guarantee success, but the one who can relate openly and warmly to others.

If Halleck's assessment of young people's attitudes toward the objectives of education is accurate, there may well be cause for concern as to whether education will produce in the future the economic dividends that have characterized past decades.

Not only creative activities but also intellectual pursuits are increasingly valued as ends rather than means. This change has important ramifications for our educational system. Adults are accustomed to thinking of education as a means to success and progress. Since these values do not have the same meaning to youth, they are skeptical of the practical benefits of learning. They tend to see education as an end in itself, something to be enjoyed, even worshiped as a noble activity of man. There is much emphasis on doing away with the competitive aspects of education, with the regimentation and emphasis on grading that has served to produce citizens who would easily fit into an industrial society. Nothing enrages students more than the feeling that they are being processed to take their place in a competitive society rather than being educated to become better people.[19]

THE CHALLENGE OF THE AUTOMATED SOCIETY

Warnings have been uttered for years that the advent of the automated society will make many of the existing forms of work obsolete. A large proportion of the population will either have to go through meaningless motions or else find new and creative uses for their time. The fact that there is not yet a disastrous shortage of work does not mean that the crisis will not come. It may be that young people perceive more accurately than their parents what is in store for them, and are responding by developing attitudes and life styles to harmonize with the conditions under which they will live. A reduced respect for the value of property and a decreased interest in striving to accumulate it are consistent with the prospect of great material abundance. A desperate search for productive human relationships can be seen as a healthy reaction against the overpowering machine and the impersonal organization. Some see a danger that these attitudes will take hold to such an extent that even that nucleus of highly skilled individuals which is required to operate the mechanisms of the automated society will not be available. It seems unlikely, however, that the human drive for achievement is in that much danger of disappearing.

Some people see a great danger for the future in the work ethic that is so deeply ingrained in the Canadian character. People's existence has been closely attuned to work. They can feel secure, respected, and self-confident only if they have a job, and consider themselves disgraced if they are unemployed. They count on maintaining their morale by draining away most of their energies in their jobs. The remainder of the time can then be disposed of in rest or in passive activities that need no justification. The assertion that they are too tired is accepted as an adequate excuse for their failure to add creative dimensions to their lives. They ostensibly, and in a sense genuinely, look forward to a vacation, but after a couple of weeks they are completely bored and relieved to resume normal activities. Work is glorified to such an extent that the "work addict" expects sympathy, and gets it, because he never takes a vacation and spends his evenings and weekends dealing with mountains of homework. If he had a similar compulsion to eat or drink, he would be despised as a glutton or a drunkard, even though such vices might do him no more harm than an addiction to work.

The schools have been held partly responsible for inculcating this attitude, not so much because they have over-emphasized vocational preparation as because they have downgraded recreation and leisure. No school planners have ever considered giving priority to anything but classrooms or, to use a more modern expression, "teaching areas." In most of the 1950s the Ontario government did not pay grants for the construction of school auditoriums, and the Minister of Education was generally reputed to regard them as frills. The official attitude is more enlightened today, but the change in educational priorities is not very pronounced. For the school, life is a serious business. One makes his contribution in the world of work and gets his reward.

Arnold Toynbee says of leisure:

... the creative use of leisure by a minority of the leisured minority in societies in process of civilization has been the mainspring of all human progress beyond the primitive level .... The Greeks had a truer vision in seeing in leisure the greatest of all human goods; and they did indeed use leisure for worthy ends – as is witnessed by the fact that the Greek word for leisure has provided most of the modern Western languages with their word for "school."[20]

The philosopher Eric Hoffer, who has made no mean contribution to the view that manual work can be a productive and rewarding experience, maintains that play is the primary human and humanizing activity. He regards it as the natural function of man through which he can liberate all kinds of constructive and creative impulses. If he succeeds in ridding himself of guilt feelings over his indulgence in it, he will rise to new heights of satisfaction and self-realization.

The "if" is extremely important. Hoffer gives grounds for a conviction that there is a real solution to the problem of enforced leisure, but he does not offer much hope that it will be grasped. Evidence up to this point does not seem very promising, to judge by the actions of those who are forced into unemployment. The listlessness, the time-killing, the waiting for something to happen that characterize this group are anything but hopeful portents of the days to come. Some grounds for optimism can be found in the theory that these undesirable manifestations are mainly attributable to the anxiety and insecurity resulting from the lack of confidence that a minimum income will be available, rather than to the actual absence of work. Also, it is felt that the attitude will improve when leisure becomes the common lot of most citizens rather than evidence of inadequacy and failure. Nevertheless, it would be foolish to suppose that, even if the serious organizational problem of ensuring an equitable distribution of income is solved, the majority of people will easily take the transition in their stride.

If the problems are accurately identified, it appears that education must provide the answer. The cultural subjects such as art, drama, and music must be given new emphasis and greater prestige. Young people must be taught the satisfaction of developing skills that can be exercised in hobbies. There must be greater attention to individual and group sports and to various kinds of games. Students must learn to regard subjects judged "serious" according to traditional values as worthy of study as ends in themselves rather than as means to an occupational end. (As has been noted, they may be teaching themselves this lesson so quickly that their elders cannot understand what is going on.) Adults must be persuaded of the appropriateness of the role of the perpetual student. Perhaps most important of all, young and old must learn that they do not need to justify themselves through constant overt activity. The virtues of contemplation perhaps have some prospect of being rediscovered.

If education does not accommodate itself to these needs, and do it very quickly, the prophets warn that the consequences are likely to be extremely unfortunate. Human energy will be released in some form or other. If it is not directed toward constructive uses, it will rend the social fabric and perhaps even destroy the technical apparatus that should have been the source of its joyous liberation.

It is remarkable how different a picture some of the most expert economists have presented. They propose to ward off unemployment not by cultivating leisure, but by providing new opportunities for work in a more productive economy. Their concerns are with producing trained manpower and deploying it in such a way that the need for employment can continue to be met and that production can be maintained at the highest possible level. Such an attitude was expressed by J.J. Deutsch, Principal of Queen's University, in an address to the Annual Meeting of the Association of Professional Engineers of the Province of Ontario on March 2, 1968.[21]

Deutsch pointed out that, since the Second World War, Canada had never come close to educating enough young people to fill its own needs for professional, technical, and other highly skilled manpower, but had had to depend on a large infusion from other countries. Even allowing for a substantial drainage to the United States, the net gain was large. Despite such gains, Canada had 40 per cent fewer scientists and engineers employed outside educational institutions than had the United States, in relation to population, in 1961. Over the previous three years, American universities had graduated proportionately one and a half times as many engineers as had those in Canada. Thus there was a great deal of catching up to do, and a great many opportunities available for those who were willing and able to acquire the necessary skills. But there were more important reasons why this type of need should be adequately filled. A high level of scientific and engineering skill was required if the Canadian economy was to take the fullest advantage of the fastest growing industries which were science-based and technically sophisticated. These industries would offer the kind of employment that would provide for the growing number of young people who were coming on the labour market. Deutsch recognized quite clearly the potential problem of unemployment and its dangers. He noted projections indicating that Canada's labour force would increase by one-half between 1965 and 1980, while its population would increase by only one-fourth.

It may be that the weakness in the proposal that much of the work force be diverted to leisure and recreation lies in the factor of international competition. If some countries insisted on employing every marginal increment that human efforts could add to those of the machines, they might undermine the economies of those that decided to accept limits on production on the grounds that enough was enough. The latter would thus be forced back into competition lest their whole structure collapse. The possibility that any international agreement could be reached so that all would play the game in the same way may be regarded as non-existent.

THE ROLE OF THE SCHOOL

It is difficult to open up a discussion of the role of the school without being lured into a full-blown exploration of the aims of education. Such treatment as that topic receives, however, is reserved as much as possible for volume III. The intention at this point is merely to suggest what aspects of the educative process the schools of Ontario have been permitted or required to deal with, and how this responsibility compares with that of other agencies that also assume an educational role.

Since schools, colleges, and universities are identified in the public mind as primarily or exclusively educational agencies, it has been easy enough to act as if they had the sole responsibility for education. This kind of assumption necessarily implies that education is what the schools do, or at least what they are supposed to do – a very narrow and limited concept indeed. There is of course nothing new in the definition of education as a broad, comprehensive, lifelong process, almost paralleling existence itself. But the genuine acceptance of this view on the part of the public has only recently begun to be in evidence. Such a development has focused a lively interest on the question of what should and what should not be expected of the school.

Responsibility for development of the intellect
The responsibility of the school and university for the training of the intellect has appeared to be beyond dispute. That does not mean, of course, that society at large has understood just what it was consigning to these institutions, nor that the school and the university themselves necessarily had any consistent or coherent ideas about the matter either. Innumerable students have, for example, spent countless hours acquiring an extremely superficial and defective knowledge of the classical languages, which were originally introduced into the curriculum as essential keys to the storehouses that contained most of the learning available to western society. This process has been considered to constitute training of the intelligence, although the idea that it can confer skill in performing other intellectually demanding tasks was long ago thrown into complete discredit. The acquisition of great quantities of facts, related or unrelated, important or unimportant, has also been equated with intellectual training, although it has become very much the fashion in recent years to deride such a concept. The standard cliché of the present era is that the student should primarily be taught to "think," to "think creatively," or to "think for himself." Many of those who advocate this objective envision such a skill operating within very definite limitations. The prospective employer who wants his employees to "think" usually means that he wants them to devise superior ways to do their work and make money for the company. He probably does not want them to go so far as to think about the validity of the company's role in the social structure, or about the ethics of some of the less admirable business practices. The last person he would care to hire would be an "intellectual" in the usual sense of the term. Even the university, which is reasonably tolerant of thinking about almost anything else, finds its patience strained when it has to deal with those who challenge the fundamental assumptions underlying its own existence. So the educational institution has its problems even with the function that it is willing to claim as a central responsibility.

Responsibility for cultural and physical development
Ontario's educational institutions, like their counterparts elsewhere in the western world, have given a place to education for physical and for aesthetic ends. Plato is usually held responsible for the fact that these have traditionally been assigned a distinctly inferior place, although some of the other influences shaping the Hebrew-Christian outlook ought to share the responsibility. In any case, the low status of physical and aesthetic studies has been indisputable. Even the physical education teachers do not often propound the idea that achievement in their field should be averaged with that in academic subjects in order to determine a student's over-all standing. The student who is endowed with superior strength or reflexes must not be given any advantage on that account over his weaker or clumsier colleague, although it is not regarded as equally unfair if the

latter happens to excel in academic work. For their part, the subjects of primarily aesthetic interest have had a long history of treatment as frills. They have been added to the "basic" subjects only if the school could afford to provide something extra; they have been permitted as options only after a core of obligatory "hard" subjects has been provided for; a student has been limited in the number he could take (e.g., art or music, but not both, has been a specification of many courses of study). It was only in the dying years of the departmental grade 13 examinations that provision was made for an examination in art. One of the most marked changes in the Ontario educational system in recent years has been the great increase in provision for cultural subjects in the average school. They are not, however, likely to reach the status of the academic subjects in the near future.

Responsibility for vocational training

The school's role in occupational training is a complex issue. Those who feel that the position of some professional school in a university is under attack are fond of pointing out that the earliest universities were established to provide professional training, and that the idea of liberal education came later. For the most part, the university is quite prepared to offer occupational preparation 1 / provided that, if it is almost entirely technical, like medicine, it caters to a select clientele, it is highly prestigious, and it is associated with that type of institution by long-standing tradition, or 2 / provided that it involves a large enough component of general theory, and particularly if it includes a reasonable proportion of liberal studies.

Ontario secondary schools, which evolved from grammar schools, have through most of their history reflected highly academic attitudes. Their most valued and respected function was, and still is, to prepare students for the university. When responsibility for vocational education was foisted on them, they had to sugar the pill by claiming that they could not provide only straightforward preparation for a job, but must include a reasonable proportion of academic studies in order to turn out graduates with some claim to education as well as skill. Arguing validly that it was impossible for them to keep up to date with changing equipment and techniques, they proposed to teach even the technical skills for their general educational value and for a broad job orientation rather than as a preparation for immediate employment. Many schools and teachers failed to grasp the difference and handled the courses just as trade schools might have done, but the intention is what is important here rather than the practice. The displeasure of the secondary schools over their obligation to provide vocational education was long demonstrated by the inferior status, or even contempt, shown toward everyone who was involved with vocational education. Vocational inspectors in the department were paid less than academic inspectors, and their operations were kept separate. A teacher who began his professional career in the vocational branch of a composite school about 1950 tells of women teachers in the academic wing who refused to speak to him in the corridors, even though his honours degree was of a higher level than their own qualifications.

Academic snobbery is not by any means exclusively an Ontario problem. Climbing the academic ladder has been almost universally regarded as a way of rising from menial, usually manual, work to the more desirable white-collar clerical and professional occupations. The underdeveloped countries have been plagued with the difficulty of avoiding the production of literate unemployables as opposed to the much-needed artisans, technicians, and technologists. Technical progress has been very closely related to a nation's success in ridding itself of undesirable attitudes. In this respect Ontario entered the post-war period without very much to its credit, but during recent years has made remarkable progress in developing a different point of view. The federal government made a very substantial contribution by pouring in large sums of money for vocational education, while the provincial government, with its encouragement for the building of vocational schools and its Reorganized Program, took full advantage of its opportunities. At the tertiary level the rapid development of colleges of applied arts and technology has been another major step in the process.

Responsibility for social and emotional development
Recent years have seen more dispute about the educational institution's responsibility for the social and emotional development of its charges than about any of the other functions already mentioned. The elementary schools have shown a moderate affinity for the slogan that "the whole child" should be educated. They have been prevented from putting it into practice with complete effectiveness less because of the influence of the arguments of its opponents, such as Hilda Neatby in *So Little for the Mind*, than by ill-trained and inexperienced teachers, over-sized classes, and a shortage of specially qualified consultants.

During the 1950s, spokesmen for Ontario secondary schools were often emphatic in their assertion that they had quite enough to do to develop their students' minds without having to socialize them, let alone treat their emotional aberrations. In some cases it was hard to tell whether this attitude was based on the heavy burden the average teacher bore in keeping up with and teaching his own subject or subjects, or whether it represented a fundamental conviction. The same view is expressed less often nowadays. It may be that there is an increasing realization, resulting in part from the gradual seepage of psychological findings into educational practice, that the different aspects of the human personality cannot be dealt with in isolation. Certainly the interrelationships between emotional health and positive social attitudes on the one hand and the motivation to learn on the other are increasingly understood. Larger school boards have done a great deal to provide specialized services for those with conspicuous problems. It has often been claimed, however, that too little has yet been done to modify the authoritarian atmosphere of the schools in order to provide a more realistic environment for the development and exercise of social skills.

Whether the universities' hasty attempts to give students a voice in various committees and councils, and their somewhat more reluctant concession of places on their governing bodies, represent a recognition of their responsibility to contribute to the students' social development would be debatable. Apart from that, there have been substantial efforts, particularly in the newer institutions, to provide counselling services and facilities for the treatment of the more moderate emotional problems. These developments are partly attributable to the accumulating evidence of difficulties contributed to, if not caused by, the impersonality of the institution, the pressure of the program of studies, and the threat of examinations. While the university may be said to be showing an increasing awareness of the scope and variety of the student's needs, it is moving further away from the idea of moulding or shaping him as a person.

Limits of the school's role
It has been customary for spokesmen for the school, when under attack, to repeat the familiar litany about education being a shared responsibility of the home, the school, the church, and various other agencies. Numerous calculations have been made to show how many more hours the child spends in the extra-school environment than he does in the institution itself. The amount of time he spends in front of the television set alone not infrequently exceeds the amount he spends in school. If he has poor motivation or negative attitudes toward learning, it is legitimate to ask how much the school can be expected to do to counteract the influences that produce them. Even if it is possible, as some have claimed, for the most sympathetic teacher working under the most ideal conditions to overcome almost any attitudinal handicap, realistic expectations must be based on the capacities of the average teacher in the average school.

The school and the family
In Ontario, as in other democratic societies, the family has hitherto been regarded as relatively sacrosanct. It takes fairly substantial evidence of serious abuse or neglect before a child can be removed, and such action is taken with relative infrequency. Yet sociological studies show that a large proportion of parents exert an undesirable or downright destructive influence on their children. Such an influence in many cases predisposes the latter, when they reach adulthood, to chronic unemployment, delinquency, and crime. Much more often, there is a failure through ignorance or indifference to develop latent curiosity and learning capacity. By the

time the child reaches the age when he is delivered by compulsion into the hands of the teachers, the best opportunities for constructive action have gone.

Margaret Mead has noted the breakdown of parents' ability to give their children clear ethical direction. She observes that moral counsel has become either out of date or vacillating. Despairing of the capacity of the family to regain the functions it once performed, she indicates the necessity for alternatives.

Today selective devices by which communities can take over what the individual parent seems no longer able to do – give ethical direction to children's lives – are urgently needed. This will mean the articulate delegation by the individual family of a moral role which it has long since lost, and the development of new ways for parents, teachers, and citizens to take responsibility for protecting *all* of the children of the community, the State, the Nation, and ultimately of the world.[22]

The prospect is clearly that the chief remedial agency under public control, the school, must expect continuous pressure to take an increasing amount of responsibility in this area.

How successful the school will be in assuming a larger share of responsibilities once considered in the province of the family will depend to a considerable extent on the family's attitude toward the school. As might be expected, research has shown that children do better in school, and stay there longer, if they have parental approval for doing so. The results they achieve also depend to a high degree on the feelings of acceptance or rejection within the family. Covert feelings of hostility toward their parents are vented against the school. Thus those to whom the school should offer the most help are the ones who are most likely to reject it.

Among the many criticisms of the family as a responsible social agency, it has long been assumed that some of the most serious ills can be traced to the working mother. To hear certain opinions, one might suppose that the remedy for most of the trouble would be to put the mother back in her traditional place in the kitchen, from which she could prepare the children's lunches, send them off to school, and greet their arrival home. This kind of reasoning fails to give her credit for being able to manage her affairs so that the children are adequately looked after in some alternative fashion. In fact, there is nothing disadvantageous in her being out of the home *per se*. An outside occupation may well provide the interest and stimulation that more than compensate for her absence at certain times. Research studies have usually failed to uncover any definite relationship between the mother's occupational status and children's achievement, the school's appraisal of their behaviour, the length of time they remain in school after the end of the period of compulsory education, and other factors.

Encouragement for the school to reach into earlier age groups than formerly is being provided in rather impressive fashion by certain studies of infant and early childhood behaviour. It is being shown that very young children not only can learn much more than was once supposed, but, to all appearances, benefit from doing so. The old apprehensions about undesirable side-effects or after-effects are being dispelled. One of the experiments in this area, conducted by the National Institute of Mental Health in co-operation with Catholic University in Washington, involved sixty-four fifteen-month-old boys from a Negro section of the city. Half of these boys were tutored for an hour each weekday by women college graduates, while the others were not. The tutoring involved reading to the children and walking, talking, and playing with them in an effort to stimulate their mental and verbal capacities. After twenty-one months, the average measured IQ of the tutored group was 106, while that of the others was 89. When the tutoring was discontinued, the boys' IQs began to drop, but their language skills did not.[23] No matter how firmly such findings are established, it is unlikely that even the families that exert the healthiest and most beneficial effects on their children will be able to take full advantage of them. Thus the general effect will be to encourage the intervention of the school. Such a tendency is shown in the establishment of junior kindergartens in Ontario school systems, particularly in areas in larger cities where the children are considered to be culturally deprived.

The role of the church
It is quite unrealistic to expect the church as an institution to play any substantial part in the educative process. Even if a major proportion of children and young people belonged to a church, the amount of their time it had at its disposal would be insufficient to yield major results. In pioneer days, when the church was the centre of social, and to some extent recreational, as well as religious life, the situation was different. But it has fared so ill in the competition with other centres of attraction that to leave it with any important educational obligation is tantamount to a complete abandonment of responsibility.

The school and the mass media
Apart from informal social contacts, the most important remaining influence is that exerted by the mass media. By all estimates this influence is very great, although there is considerable question just how great, and in what direction it operates. As long as our society retains any claim to be regarded as free, the media are not likely to be controlled in the interests of someone's concept of education. Censorship is falling increasingly into disrepute, and it is doubtful that parents who fear the effect of disapproved books, films, or television on their children's manners or morals will be able to reverse the trend. Thus again the school must expect to be called upon to counteract the undesirable effects of other agencies.

The school versus the alternatives
The expectation that the school will make up for the deficiencies of other agencies rests both on an underlying belief on the part of parents that it has the potential capacity for the task and on parental hopes for the improvement of their children. On this latter point, Paul Goodman says: "The private home will not completely give up its claim to the children – including usually the claim to be as stupid as the day is long. But also, the parents dumbly want for their children a 'better' future than the dominant present, including courses in Art and Music Appreciation."[24] Such a general feeling is a tremendous asset to the school, but it also presents a danger, specifically that the latter may assume that anything it does for or to the children is better than turning them loose on the streets. At the height of the teacher shortage in the 1950s, there were many derisive things said about official determination to get some kind of body in each classroom as long as it was warm. Thus some of the least capable of grade 12 students were dignified with the name of teacher after a six-week introduction to the profession. While it would be quite unfair to condemn the efforts of this whole group as worthless or harmful, some of the inspectors who appraised their work are prepared to attest that such a description would, in certain specific cases, have been entirely appropriate. Had it been possible to take a logical approach, instead of acting on the basis of a public myth, the proper course of action would have been to close the school until a teacher capable of exerting a positive influence had been found.

The school is often justified as if its existence were all that prevented the child from growing up as an ignorant savage. This assumption involves an absurd failure to assess the educative capacities of the other agencies. Despite their many deficiencies, a bad school is not a preferable alternative. And for some individuals even a good school may not be a preferable alternative. Whatever influences are to blame, there are children and young people who have built up such a negative attitude toward the school and all its works that it would be common sense to recognize that it would be better to give "the street" a chance. This proposition is not offered as support for those teachers who would welcome the opportunity to unload their more difficult pupils so that they could concentrate on the most intelligent, the most docile, and the most attractive. It is rather a suggestion that the school's superior educative virtues not be taken as proved, but rather that the best of the available opportunities from the whole spectrum of educative influences be selected to meet each individual's special needs. In Paul Goodman's view,

Education is a natural community function and occurs inevitably, since the young grow up on the old, toward their activities, and into (or against) their institutions; and the old foster, teach, train, exploit, and abuse the young. Even neglect of the young, except physical neglect, has an educational effect – not the worst possible.

Formal schooling is a reasonable auxiliary of the inevitable process, whenever an activity is best learned by singling it out for special attention with a special person to teach it. Yet it by no means follows that the complicated artifact of a school system has much to do with education, and certainly not with good education.[25]

In view of the assumed necessity of avoiding unmanageable precedents, there is likely to be strong resistance to any relaxation of the rule of compulsory attendance to age sixteen. Yet, in the light of an increasing realization of the incompatibility of true education and compulsion, there has been a sharply rising demand that the question be subjected to a searching examination. Just as the student is being given unprecedented opportunities to decide what he will learn, so also thought is being given to the idea that he should have the option of rejecting the school itself, provided always that he is given full information about the implications of his decision.

The school as an agent of change
Despite the hopes of some philosophers that the school might move to the forefront of agencies producing social change, it is not usually thought to have fulfilled such a role very effectively. It is more often considered a preserver of established community values. Generalizations in this area, as in so many others, are likely to be meaningless without a careful definition of terms.

If it deliberately undertook to introduce concepts differing from those idealized by the community in areas of ethics and morality as applied to the conduct of business, political behaviour, family and neighbourhood relationships, and other aspects of public and private life, the school would very soon find itself brought up short. This kind of initiative is simply not tolerated. The fact is so well accepted that there is no need to organize angry demonstrations or to threaten to dismiss teachers in order to ensure that no one will forget it. Most teachers below the university level hardly even aspire to the privilege of trying to devise and propound more adequate adaptations to the changing conditions of life and work in the modern age.

Many of them would, in fact, be satisfied with a much more modest role, that of dealing with society on the basis of reality rather than in terms of myth. Throughout the whole pre-adolescent stage, at least, the school's picture of the family, at its most extreme, is always one of harmony and good will; the children are never dominated by sibling rivalries; father never dozes in front of the television set in a semi-drunken stupor; mother never goes around looking like a slattern with a pile of dirty dishes in the sink and the beds unmade; father and mother never stay together merely because they lack the initiative to separate. The world outside the home consists of happy and contented firemen, policemen, milkmen, postmen, storekeepers, and doctors, each making his contribution to a smoothly functioning community where life is sheer pleasure. The school cannot even admit the language of the street exists. It cannot acknowledge the base and selfish motives that interweave business and social relationships. Even in dealing with adolescents whose contact with real life has made some of the most blatant fantasies impossible to maintain, the school can offer only a very restrained acknowledgment of the less pleasant aspects of existence. Its idealized version persists long after it has lost all credibility.

Two defences of this approach have been offered, both with an air of plausibility. First, it is said that the child must be shielded from the harsher features of life until he has developed the strength and maturity to cope with them. Second, it is maintained that the school has an obligation to provide a model for human betterment. The trouble with the first of these propositions is that, even if the approach were desirable, comparable efforts are not made to insulate the child from unpleasantness in other spheres. He is quite aware that real families are seldom like the one in the primer. He knows that other children and adults steal and bully and cheat and manipulate one another to their own advantage. Thus he perceives the school as a highly artificial environment without much relevance to things as they are. It accordingly loses its chance of operating as a really effective model. The teacher who is restrained from doing or saying things that are permitted of others is not seen as an example to be followed but as a kind of curiosity separated from the mainstream of humanity. In discussions with the writer in 1969, an instructor in one of the colleges of applied arts and technology identified institutional artificiality and the tendency to present a false view of reality as a basic defect even at that level.

The amorphous public is usually blamed for these conditions. Every once in a while something happens that seems to demonstrate that the schools are kept on a very tight rein. In 1968–9, for example, the Toronto Board of Education, which ought in theory to consist of the most enlightened citizens in view of the wide range of potential candidates from whom a choice could be made, showed itself determined to fire a teacher who, while running for a position on the board, had dared to criticize its previous performance. No one seemed to be able to accuse Mrs Fiona Nelson of anything worse than injudicious behaviour. Reliable reports indicated that she was a teacher of superior quality. The threat of a review of the case by a board of reference forced the Toronto board to retract its action, but Mrs Nelson resigned with the claim that the incident had made it impossible for her to carry on effectively. It would be an obtuse member of the profession indeed who would fail to learn from such an incident that it is risky to depart from conventional modes of behaviour. Not many have an opportunity comparable to that of Mrs Nelson in winning a place at the next election on the very board that made things so difficult for her.

Despite this kind of example, it is by no means certain that the community at large is entirely responsible for the school's failure to lead in the process of social innovation. Undoubtedly many educators feel comfortable and secure in their artificial world. They find no particular attraction in the role of innovator. They share the approval of the general public for the idea of change in general, but tend also to be opposed to any specific change beyond superficial tinkering with existing customs and practice. If they were really determined to lead, they could find the strength through professional cohesiveness to have their way.

Although the school is denied, or denies itself, any major role in initiating direct social change, it does nevertheless contribute to the transformation of the community in somewhat indirect ways. By helping to supply students with intellectual and vocational tools, it provides the means for a shift in the prevalent occupational patterns. The preparation of future scientists and technologists ensures an alteration of the physical environment that ultimately generates pressures forcing social and cultural adaptations. As a feeder of the universities, the school provides a necessary foundation for the preparation of scholars on whose ideas social change must ultimately be based.

THE INDIVIDUAL AND SOCIETY

At one extreme of the issue of the individual's relation to society, we have the position that the most vigorous effort must be made, through education and other means, to preserve and strengthen individual integrity against the threat of the collectivity. At the other extreme, we have the assertion that there is no issue at all — that the interests of the individual and society are identical.

One of the strongest philosophical positions denying the existence of an individual-social conflict has been taken by Teilhard de Chardin. His view has been expressed in these terms.

... we must rid ourselves of a prejudice which is deeply embedded in our thought, namely the habit of mind which causes us to contrast unity with plurality, the element with the whole and the individual with the collective, as though these were diametrically opposed ideas. We constantly argue as though in each case the terms varied inversely, a gain on the one side being *ipso facto* the other side's loss; and this in turn leads to the widespread idea that *any* destiny on "monist" lines would exact the sacrifice and bring about the destruction of all personal values in the Universe.[26]

According to a widely held view, the individual may be regarded both as a product of the group and as a potential sufferer from its too close embrace. He becomes human by virtue of his group memberships. It is in the group that he satisfies his thirst for recognition as well as his need for security. He develops the distinctiveness of his personality by the clash of his ideas and opinions against those of his fellows. If he chooses to be eccentric, his eccentricity has meaning only in terms of norms of group behaviour.

The school places considerable emphasis on the proposition that it is necessary for the individual to recognize his dependence on the group, and desirable for him to learn to avoid undesirable conflict with those with whom he must associate in order to fulfill his own needs. To put it more positively, he will benefit by learning to co-operate with his fellows for the achievement of common purposes. To the extent that he does so, he will have maximum scope for the expression of his individuality. Difficulties arise when education seems to encourage undue conformity, involving the abandonment of independent tastes, attitudes, interests, and preferences in the face of group pressures. The term "adjustment" developed a bad name when it had become associated with the definition of narrow group norms and with the school's assumption of the responsibility for shaping the child's development so as to reduce variation from these norms. Dewey has received a good deal of blame for inspiring such practices in the past. It is thus interesting that the Provincial Committee on Aims and Objectives of Education in the Schools of Ontario has produced a report that owes so much to Dewey's influence, and yet stands as an eloquent exponent of the concept of the primacy of individual development.

It is difficult to reach the happy position where the individual can express his personality with maximum effectiveness in a group setting. Elizabeth L. Simpson expresses the problem in this way.

The more thoroughly the child is socialized – that is, the more thoroughly the child accepts the standards and norms of the group – the more he also accepts its perceptions and abandons his own. He is freed from the fears of isolation and loses in the process the tension and awareness which force him to utilize his own senses and mind. In the integrative process, the group makes man less himself and more everyone. His discreteness is questioned. He loses his right to be idiosyncratic and original at the same time that he gains reinforcement through commonality.[27]

This writer goes on to ask whether education should encourage individuation and separation at the cost of cohesion. She points out that no society whose members reject their membership can survive. Obviously education cannot be allowed to become an instrument for the destruction of the society that provides it. The ideal, delicate balance is described thus.

The group for which we are educating the child must not ask too much of the individual – if by *too much* we mean the loss of selfhood – nor the individual too much of the group – if by *too much* we mean its disintegration as an entity. If either side joggles the scales, the balance is destroyed. No man can live well, fully human, fully social, fully himself, without it achieved.[28]

The individual versus society issue is often seen as one of deciding whether the best interests of the individual will be served by catering to him directly or by concentrating on building and maintaining the economic structure that will alone ensure the satisfaction of material and cultural needs. Despite the similarity of their ultimate objectives, these two approaches involve the adoption of quite sharply contrasting ways and means. The first approach is exemplified by the Provincial Committee on Aims and Objectives of Education in the Schools of Ontario, which calls for encouragement of the individual to reach the highest levels of self-realization. The assumption appears to be that if this goal is given primacy, adequate material prosperity will follow. The alternative orientation may be described as the trained manpower approach. It tends to concentrate on vocational preparation leading to the existence of a highly skilled population whose efforts will produce the environment in which creative leisure and cultural pursuits can flourish.

Those with the trained manpower orientation face a serious dilemma in a democratic society. They carry out studies to determine existing and future needs for particular kinds of technical and professional skills. Elaborate techniques are being developed for the conduct of this kind of planning activity, even though the complexity of the task ensures that many sources of uncertainty will long remain. The problem is, however, that people cannot be arbitrarily assigned to training for particular jobs or to the jobs themselves. They are inclined to follow their own individual preferences. The standard solution, where compulsion is ruled out, is to provide extra incentives, such as special bursaries and scholarships for the preparatory course. If such incentives are not provided artificially to avert future dislocation, the labour market will itself provide them when the dislocation becomes serious. The question is whether intervention to divert students from their first occupational preference represents a conflict between the demands of society and the interests of the individual. The answer is perhaps that in the long run the interests of the individual are best served if he is dissuaded from preparing for an occupation that is likely to be glutted. Economic planners, however, do not usually go out of their way to express concern for the welfare of the individual. They seem to treat the growth and health of the economy as the beginning and end of their concern. To what extent this impression is conveyed merely because they neglect to identify humanitarian assumptions underlying their activities would be difficult to say.

It was those who saw things primarily from the trained manpower viewpoint who showed the greatest concern during the 1950s for Canada's position in a competitive world. Expressions of this concern reached a high point at the National Conference on Engineering, Scientific, and Technical Manpower at St Andrews-By-The-Sea in New Brunswick in 1956. A brief to this Conference attempted "to measure the growth that will be required in both the number and type of engineering, scientific and technical manpower in Canada to ensure that we, as a nation, will remain competitive and progressive as an industrial power and will maintain our position as a front-rank defender of the free world."[29] The brief was said to be based on two prime considerations.

1. We cannot grow, or even survive, as an industrial power if we are content to use second-hand technology.
2. Our democratic way of life, in a world riven with ideologies opposed to it, is in serious jeopardy unless we educate our scientific and technical manpower in a more effective manner.

The success of the Soviet Union the following year in launching the first earth satellite did not take those who expressed these sentiments by surprise. The event was more in the nature of a confirmation that the western world was indeed falling behind in the competition; it was taken as additional evidence that all educational resources must be mobilized for survival.

Some of the same attitudes were revealed in a report on the development of student potential prepared for the second Canadian Conference on Education, held in 1962.

A democratic society cannot function successfully unless a large majority of its citizens have received education and training which makes them competent and co-operative workers, as well as informed and intelligent voters. To the extent that he is less than he could be, each individual lessens his potential contribution to society, and one of the weaknesses of present-day democracies lies in the effect produced by the total of these individual deficiencies. In a totalitarian country, where the interests of the state take priority over those of the individual, direct control is exercised over the development of human resources. The apparent efficiency of this authoritarian control in converting student potential into productive manpower is causing much concern to many people in the Western world. They fear that an educated and trained communist world will become such a threat to the free world that similar controls may replace our freedom.[30]

Canadian education has never shown any real sign of being converted into a mechanism for the exclusive production of the human and technological tools required for a smoothly running economic machine. But it is nevertheless remarkable how definitely the voluble exponents of educational objectives have shifted their emphasis from social to individual goals, and from narrow occupational preparation to the pursuit of knowledge for its own sake or for the liberation of the human spirit. The fact that young people are accepting this trend so avidly does not mean that they have independently generated a new set of values in competition with those prevailing among their elders. They are deriving much of their inspiration from adults who are expressing current trends of thought.

IMPLICATIONS OF THE KNOWLEDGE EXPLOSION

Perhaps no cliché has endeared itself more to speakers on issues and problems of education than that knowledge is increasing at an accelerating rate. The amount of information available to the human race is said to have doubled between 1900 and 1950, to have doubled again between 1950 and 1960, and to have done the same during the decade just completed. Equally impressive developments are anticipated in the foreseeable future.

One might be tempted to quibble with the significance of these estimates – to wonder just what it means to have twice as much knowledge as we had a decade earlier. To say that it takes twice as much paper, or twice as many feet of tape, or twice as much microfilm, or twice as many written characters, to record everything written does not seem to amount to quite the same thing. An estimate based on this kind of quantitative measure makes no allowance for repetition and duplication. It also treats knowledge as if it consisted of comparable units that can be cumulated to form a meaningful total. Few would claim that any single decade has doubled our resources of significant philosophical theories or of the fundamental scientific principles. There is also some fault to be found with the practice of equating knowledge with information. If knowledge exists only as a meaningful organization of information in human minds, it clearly cannot be said with any assurance to accumulate at the same rate as information. Apart from these considerations, however, there is no denying that the situation confronts education with a serious challenge.

One type of visceral response to the educational implications of the growth of knowledge is to act as if the student must try to keep up with it. Psychological research has given a kind of spurious support to such an approach by showing that human beings are capable of learning and retaining a great deal more under ideal conditions than they have traditionally done. We have been told that the student of the future will have to learn two or three times as much as his parents did at the same stage in their careers. Subliminal devices will presumably maintain continuous pressure on the mind during both waking and sleeping hours in order to supplement learning programs which are organized to perfection in the schools.

It may indeed be necessary in certain circumstances to stretch minds to the limit in this way. It has long been perfectly obvious, however, that the accumulation of knowledge has far outstripped the storage capacity of the mind, and that the fundamental solution must lie elsewhere than in a futile effort to try to keep up. The educator's efforts must be directed toward two goals: 1 / to determine what factual foundation must be established in the mind so that the individual has a reasonable concept of the nature of knowledge, an understanding of what further information he needs under particular circumstances, and a framework into which he can fit such accretions of information; and 2 / to ensure that the learner knows where and how the information he needs is stored, and how he should go about retrieving it. It requires continuous study and modifications in approach to attain these goals. As far as the first is concerned, in many fields the accumulation of new knowledge requires a continuous modification in the essential core of interrelated facts that should be stored in the mind and accessible for use in thought processes. Means of attaining the second goal must be adapted as new and improved methods of storage and retrieval are developed.

The knowledge explosion is really only forcing educators to take more serious account of principles that have long been recognized. There has always been a strong justification for education to concern itself with the ability to make generalizations and to learn how to seek and find information from external sources at the time it is needed. We are not moving from an era when rote learning by itself was sufficient to an era when it is no longer adequate. Learning not associated with purpose or meaning has always been dysfunctional except where the real role of the school has been to keep the population mentally dormant and docile so as not to disturb the prerogatives of the group in power. Modern conditions are demanding an end to wasteful and useless educational practices.

GENERAL VERSUS SPECIALIZED EDUCATION

The knowledge explosion, or, perhaps more accurately, the information explosion is making it harder for education to deal with the dilemma of generalization versus specialization. The essence of the problem is that the individual who wishes to become genuinely competent in a given area of human knowledge, or contribute to its extension, must burrow further and further into the tunnel excavated by those who preceded him. If he devotes intensive efforts to doing so, he becomes less and less capable of achieving a balanced understanding of the basic structures of civilization and of seeing the significance of life and society. The more specialized he becomes, the less his chance of becoming truly wise. If he decides to try to balance his grasp of his specialty with brief forays into broader areas, he finds that casual efforts give him little but shaky knowledge and superficial understanding. To increase his efforts undermines his claim to specialized expertise. On the other hand, the individual who seeks generalized competence and concentrates on gaining a broad comprehension of human affairs runs the risk of failing to understand the very nature of present-day knowledge. In seeing only the surface of many areas, he gains no concept of what the depths may hold.

A position not infrequently taken by scholars is to deny the existence of any real dilemma of specialization. According to this view, concentrated intellectual effort in a restricted area is the route that leads to an understanding of the universe and of man's place in it. By seeing one element clearly, one observes the world in microcosm. When the area of specialization is in the humanities, this view can be presented with an air of plausibility. As far as the sciences and mathematics are concerned, it is completely unconvincing. Education is left with the problem of combining sufficient specialization to meet the modern world's need for further knowledge with enough forays into more general fields to maintain the specialist's humanity in the face of dehumanizing forces, and to ensure that he has minimum competence to contribute to the management of human affairs.

EDUCATION AND SOCIAL CLASS

It is a firmly established and well-known fact that the length of time young people continue their formal education and the success they achieve are closely related to the social class to which their families belong. Frank E. Jones has reviewed a number of the research studies which confirm the facts.[31] A rather plausible effort can be made to reconcile the situation with the proposition that Canadian society offers equality of educational opportunity. One need only attribute the superior scores obtained on tests of scholastic aptitude by children from higher social classes to the superior ability of their ancestors, the factor which has enabled them to rise on the social scale and maintain their position there. With their inherited ability, the children naturally get better test scores, stay in school longer, and achieve more. While this explanation has serious inadequacies, there is no point in rejecting it outright in an excess of egalitarian sentiment. People of higher ability *do* tend to rise in society and mental abilities *are* to some extent hereditary, just like other human traits. But there is a great deal more to the story.

Some of the major reasons for searching for other dimensions of the phenomenon are as follows. 1 / It is a well known fact that measures of academic aptitude are highly dependent on social environment. Abundant and varied experiences, the opportunity for mental stimulation, the availability of books, and the emphasis on verbal expression all make an important contribution, and all of them are more characteristic of higher- than lower-class groups. Aptitude as a cause of class status declines in credibility to the extent that it can be shown also to be an effect of such status rather than of heredity. 2 / Differences in aptitude do not account for nearly all the differences in persistence and achievement. Students from upper-class families are more likely to continue and succeed in their education with a given level of measured aptitude than are those from lower-class families.

During the 1950s a great deal of attention in Ontario and other provinces was focused on the financial explanation for the failure of many young people to reach the limit of their potential for education. Some people seemed to assume that, if enough money were supplied, class-based inequalities would simply disappear. It was recognized not only that fees and living expenses involved in university attendance had to be kept low, but that the major factor, lost earnings, had to be taken into account. But surveys of opinion did not put a lack of funds at the top of the list of reasons for failure to attend university. There were obviously deeper and more fundamental reasons.

Accumulating evidence from sociological research has placed increasing emphasis on class influence on life styles and on the varying degrees of importance placed on education. Despite the occupational mobility characterizing current society, many parents, even while hoping for something better for their children, cannot shake off the general expectation that they will find employment among opportunities at their own level. Lower-class families assume that their children will get lower-class jobs, and encourage them, often in a negative way, to choose the appropriate preparation. Also, certain qualities are much more stressed in middle-class value systems, particularly initiative, independence, competitiveness, and willingness to defer gratification. These qualities are all valuable in the pursuit of formal education.

Perhaps the most promising approach to the maximum development of human potential lies in accepting in full the implications of the research on early childhood. One such study has already been referred to. The whole area has become one of overwhelming fascination to a group of psychologists. Using the latest of equipment, including computers, and very detailed and careful observation, they have completely exploded the older idea that, for the newborn infant, the world is a "big buzzing confusion." Quite to the contrary, he is capable of an intelligent visual response to his environment almost from the moment of birth. And apparently the business of ensuring that, many years later, he will derive the most complete satisfaction from learning depends on what kind of stimulation he gets from that time on. The warmth and security that a loving mother and family can provide are needed to give him mental health. But if he is not at the same time granted the wherewithal to develop his intelligence, he can become merely a secure and mentally healthy dullard. While his family's attitude and the values it places on various life goals are undoubtedly of great importance, perhaps of equal or greater importance is the kind of start he has in using his capacities.

Tim Reid, member of the Ontario Legislature for Scarborough East, has taken up the cause of providing something closer to real equality of educational opportunity by assigning a higher priority to early childhood education. He describes the effects of a poor start on later educational progress.

One essential aspect of the "poverty syndrome" is that poverty homes produce too many children without adequate words at the age of 4 and 5. Such children have not had the opportunity or the encouragement to pick up the basic skills of communication and understanding of language that are largely a prerequisite for success in senior kindergarten and Grade 1.

All later learning will be influenced by this lack of basic learning – having names for things is essential in the learning process. The average child from such a background will have difficulty and constant frustration from the demand of a typical primary school programme. He cannot cope with the change and with expectations about what he should achieve, and he is baffled and feels inadequate. No wonder the desire grows to escape from the virtual imprisonment which school comes to represent as he experiences failure year after year.[32]

Solutions in the form of pre-kindergartens would help matters at the four-year and five-year age levels, and are easily within reach of an affluent society. But it is not so easy to see how stimulating influences can be provided for younger children who most need them. The prospects of influencing and educating lower-class parents to take the necessary measures do not appear good. The traditional sanctity of the family seems to put direct public intervention out of reach. To achieve the desired ends will pose one of the most difficult problems faced by educators in the future.

Canadians would generally agree that class differences in educational achievement are undesirable, both from the point of view of social efficiency and that of equity. On the first point it seems plausible that there should be no obstacles to prevent the most able from rising to the highest positions of power and influence. Only if every career is fully and exclusively open to talent can society function to the optimum benefit of all. But of course if Canadians really wanted this kind of society, they would have to do more than wish for it. There would have to be some means of combating the inevitable tendency on the part of those who reach the top to try to ensure that they and their progeny stay there by fair means or foul.

On the point of equity, it is a source of embarrassment to citizens of British descent and to those of Jewish faith to be told by John Porter that the proportion of them increases from the lowest to the highest class.[33] There should be no surprise at a show of resentment, on the other hand, from all the other groups to be told that they show the opposite tendency. Porter has presented overwhelming evidence that the dominant groups maintain their position not by demonstrating superiority in a continuous battle of wits with potential challengers, but by a network of influence that excludes whole groups on the basis of a combination of background factors adding up to the verdict that they are simply not the "right" people.

CANADIAN UNITY

It would be out of place here to undertake a detailed review of the causes of disunity within Canada, or to predict how they will be resolved. The issue has, however, been recognized as one of the greatest importance in Ontario education. Hodgetts assigns some of the blame for the problem to the past failings of education.

[Y]oung English- and French-speaking Canadians are being raised on sharply opposed views of our history, which create entirely different value systems for each group. Thus, the lack of understanding between our two linguistic communities is in part the direct result of what these young people have been taught in school.

Here, then, in a particular Canadian problem area, our educational systems have failed in their responsibilities to the nation ... we have not given our students a meaningful sense of Canadian identity.[34]

He identifies the failure in more general terms.

By neglecting the slow process of formal education, a society can fail to provide the public support, the basic consensus, needed to ensure its stability. In other words, it can fail, as we seem to have in the relations between our two major linguistic communities, to encourage the skilled and contemporary public opinion needed to resolve deep-seated differences before the tension levels become dangerously high. It is indeed strange, in a democracy professing to believe in the value of education, that we should be making this mistake.[35]

The change in approach called for to remedy this situation is a very deep and fundamental one. It requires not only a modification in the content of social science courses in the direction of better balance and greater honesty of treatment, but the acceptance of a different purpose in the teaching as well. Only a large measure of good will and the strongest sense of urgency could produce any substantial improvement over the short run. The good will may perhaps exist in Ontario, but whether there is sufficient sense of urgency is another question. In any case, for the moment, the maintenance of the tenuous links between the two main segments of the country must rest on political habits and on whatever economic advantages seem to accrue from operating within the same framework. At best, education can only gradually build up a more positive underpinning.

During an earlier period, Ontario contributed substantially to the lack of cordiality between itself and Quebec by the kind of educational provision it made for its French-speaking minority. Although the use of French was tolerated in some schools during the nineteenth century, the language was placed in much the same category as German. From the end of the century on, the policy alternated between neglect and half-hearted efforts at suppression. Ontarians took a long time to recognize that French culture deserved more consideration than that of other language groups. The fact that the English-speaking minority in Quebec received more favourable treatment did not carry much weight. These privileges were apparently considered the natural right of members of the group in a position of dominance in the country as a whole.

Things might, of course, have been worse. Members of cultural groups in a dominant political position in many countries have embarked on a deliberate policy of eradicating minority cultures. That they have failed more often than not is less because the task was impossible to accomplish than because the repressive policy was not enforced firmly enough or over a long enough period of time. French culture has never faced the remotest possibility that this kind of policy would be adopted against it in Ontario. But many must have wondered whether slow starvation was really any more desirable.

It would be hard to say to what extent motives other than the threat of Quebec's secession have played a part in the official change of heart during the last few years. Although the necessity for decisive action has no doubt been brought home by the prospect of the break-up of the country, positive action must obviously depend also on a desire for fairness and justice. Prime Minister Robarts emphasized that Ontario's steps to provide more adequately for the needs of its French-speaking population did not depend either on what Quebec did with respect to Confederation or how it treated its English-speaking minority. Whether or not these issues can actually be kept separate is another question.

Efforts in Ontario to recognize the status of the French language and culture and to promote understanding and harmony between the two official groups have taken the following forms. 1 / Provision is being made for students to follow an uninterrupted program of studies in the French language through school and university. 2 / Cultural activities among the French-speaking group are receiving increased encouragement. 3 / The study of French is being extended down through the elementary school about as fast as teachers can be provided. 4 / French is being studied as the language of French Canada, and illustrations and literature are being provided accordingly. One need only examine earlier textbooks to deduce that France was the almost exclusive focus of attention in former years. 5 / Contacts between Ontario English-speaking and Quebec French-speaking students are being actively encouraged.

These gestures will not hold Quebec in Canada if the current runs strongly in the other direction. Many Quebeckers regard such measures as insignificant tokens. If they mean by that charge that English-speaking children in Ontario will never learn to speak French in three or four half-hour classes a week, they are of course right. But it would be only fair to acknowledge that there is, despite the deficiencies in their educational background, a desire among Ontarians to have Quebec remain in the union, not merely for economic reasons, but because they value the association with a linguistic and cultural group that is lively, creative, and different from the majority.

The problem of national unity cannot of course be seen as one involving only relations between Quebec and the other provinces. There has been a general growth of regionalism affecting various parts of the country. The Prairie provinces blame the east because their wheat is not sold. British Columbia openly speculates on whether it could not do better by going it alone. The Maritime provinces wonder if they would not fare better economically as part of the United States. The failure of the educational agencies pointed out by Hodgetts is indeed a pervasive one, and no superficial tinkering will be enough to reverse the process.

EDUCATION AND POVERTY

There are appeals to education, of varying degrees of practicality and realism, to alleviate or solve practically all social problems. While it is impossible in the present context to identify and analyse these problems one by one, some comments on poverty seem appropriate, especially since it is often seen as the breeding ground for many other social ills.

The existence of poverty in the midst of increasing affluence seems to be one of the strangest anomalies of developed countries in the modern world. It implies both a lack of humanitarian concern for those not physically or mentally equipped to deal with the complexities of society and an inability to organize the social structures needed to produce a fair distribution of material benefits.

Many of those in comfortable circumstances do not really believe that genuine poverty exists in present-day Canada. With memories of the 1930s still vivid, they feel that the poverty line, as defined in terms of annual income, is unrealistically high. Even allowing for inflationary reductions in the value of the dollar, they see no reason why there should be hunger or malnutrition. Few families appear to be unable to afford a television set. Welfare services stand ready to prevent or relieve actual suffering.

Among those who acknowledge the reality of poverty, recognition does not necessarily evoke sympathy. Paralleling "middle America," there is a middle Canada that has not divested itself of the subconscious feeling that poverty is essentially the fault of its victims. Leaving aside those who cannot fend for themselves because they are too old, too young, or too infirm, there are seen to be unprecedented opportunities for occupational and educational advancement. Those who fail to take advantage of such opportunities are not really forgiven for lacking the necessary intelligence or drive. The punitive attitude is reinforced when they produce more children than they can support, or when they opt for liquor instead of proper nutrition.

Poverty in a wealthy nation must be seen in relative rather than in absolute terms. It is of no help to a person who is deprived of the amenities which the great majority of his fellows enjoy that the average income in some backward country is $75 a year. He does not make a quick calculation and congratulate himself on being much more fortunate. He looks instead at the material possessions and the social and recreational opportunities of his more prosperous neighbours and, bombarded by appeals to buy houses, automobiles, furniture, clothing, vacations in the sun, and other things that he cannot afford, he feels deprived. And this feeling of deprivation is being recognized increasingly as a destructive social force.

The poor, as defined in Canadian terms, feel trapped by imponderable forces which they have no power to control. Generally speaking, they accept with relative passivity the failure of landlords to keep their residences in good repair, the appropriation of the buildings they occupy by public agencies or private developers, the discriminatory treatment they receive at the hands of the law courts and the police, the patronizing attitude of a certain proportion of social workers with whom they deal. Direct individual protest is avoided lest it bring on still greater misfortune. Some attempt to escape through the use of liquor or drugs. Resort to crime sometimes completes the process of alienation from the rest of society.

There is increasing interest in providing some form of guaranteed annual income. For many of those who are unavoidably poor, this measure might essentially solve their problem. There are others, however, for whom it would be only a beginning. A guaranteed income would not in itself ensure that wise spending priorities would be followed, that children would be properly clothed and nourished, that constructive recreational activities would be selected, or that minds would be open to challenging and rewarding cultural experiences. Education is thus called upon to complement measures to ensure the more even distribution of wealth.

To a large extent, education's contribution to the problem of poverty must be the very difficult one of shaping attitudes. For their part, those in a favoured economic position must want to cure poverty and its attendant ills, even at some considerable expense and inconvenience to themselves. The appeal to them may be based on a combination of humanitarian concern and enlightened self-interest. Complementing an effort in this direction, the mentality of poverty must be successfully combated among those for whom it is a destructive legacy. One might say that the solution lies in promoting middle-class values in the poor, and especially among their children. It is hardly the fashion in the present era to exalt middle-class attitudes and virtues. In a sense, however, poverty in an affluent country is a meaningful concept only from a middle-class point of view. The poor man is pitied or despised, and pities or despises himself, because he accepts the middle-class definition of failure. Whether philosophically or morally justified from the ultimate perspective, the obvious solution is to encourage him to develop those middle-class characteristics that will enable him to succeed – ambition, drive, perseverance, willingness to defer gratification, and confidence in his own ability to overcome environmental or personal handicaps. Only if he has a fair measure of these will he be willing to undergo the long periods of education and training which have become the essential prerequisites for reasonably remunerative jobs.

As a commonly identified bastion of middle-class values, the school is already acquainted with the complexities of trying to change the attitudes of children who do not arrive with a middle-class orientation. They may greet the unfamiliar environment with incomprehension, indifference, or hostility. If, on the other hand, through the efforts of especially sympathetic and perceptive teachers, they accept a new set of values, they are pulled in opposite directions by the school and the home. Given that the school's values are the right ones, the solution would seem to lie in educating the parents along with the children. Unfortunately, however, although the capacity of adults to learn and to change has been effectively demonstrated, there has been little progress in developing methods of teaching those who do not wish to learn.

It would indeed be ironical if a supreme educational effort produced an entire population imbued with traditional middle-class virtues just when the prophecies of an automated age of leisure were being realized. What were once considered constructive and desirable attributes would become stumbling blocks to creative living. The *desiderata* of the age would include the ability to accept play and idleness without guilt. Whether such an eventuality should be considered in efforts to solve the immediate problem of poverty is an open question.

THE USE OF HALLUCINATORY DRUGS AND NARCOTICS

The rapid increase in the use of hallucinogens and narcotics, despite the existence of repressive legal sanctions, has puzzled and frightened many adults in Canada as in other countries. Again the cry goes up, whether reasoned or instinctive, that the answer to the problem must be found in education. The difficulty is that the problem has not been defined clearly enough to provide the basis for a solution through education or any other means.

It might appear that the crucial question is whether or not a particular drug is mentally or physically harmful. Once sufficient research has been carried out and objective evidence secured, a rational decision could be made and enforced. There are, however, a number of difficulties associated with this approach. 1 / The criterion "harmful" is exceedingly imprecise. While there is not much question that addiction to heroin produces mental and physical deterioration, a great many users and non-users of marijuana are prepared to assert that there is no conclusive evidence that the same is true of the latter. The least partial view might be one of tentative agreement, with the warning that adequate investigation might very well reverse such a claim. But even if clinical evidence did not produce an adverse judgment, a great many people would remain opposed to the use of any substance that cushions the healthy individual against reality. Their philosophical position is that man's purpose should be to come to terms with the world rather than to escape from it. 2 / When a particular drug is on the borderline between being generally harmful and harmless, the verdict is likely to be that it produces ill effects on people with certain physical or psychological characteristics, but not on others. Making differential judgments among individuals is a difficult matter, and securing their implementation is even more difficult, especially if it is considered desirable or necessary to employ legal means. 3 / The knowledge that a drug may produce moderately undesirable consequences does not necessarily deter some people from using it. Even a general acceptance of the slogan "speed kills" may not prevent them from deliberately trying out the substance known colloquially as "speed." They may have the impression that they can control their own degree of indulgence, even if others cannot. Some may even be prepared to trade a few years of what appears to be a very vague future for the thrills that seem to be available in the present. 4 / Even when research has greatly extended the factual basis for decisions, the emotional concomitants of the issue make it unlikely that such decisions will be made on an objective basis.

Since there is no uniformity in attitude on the place of drugs in society, there are no clearcut goals for the school to follow. One possible course of action would be to try to present the known facts to young people in as objective a manner as possible, without any philosophical speculation or moral conclusions. However, even while asserting their right to reject adult advice, especially when backed by irrational authority, young people still generally look to adults to provide them with guidance in their search for answers. A bloodless "on the one hand but on the other hand" approach may be anything but satisfactory. As an alternative, the school may accept the "safe" traditional view that the use of any kind of drug is undesirable and morally wrong. Young people compare this attitude with their own observations, and reject the strictures of their uncomprehending elders. Their temptation to try drugs is likely to be reinforced when it becomes associated with the normal adolescent drive for independence. The familiar rejoinder to an adult who takes a position against drugs is that they are no more injurious than liquor or tobacco, and perhaps in some cases considerably less so. The response is likely to be feeble: either that the longer established vices ought to be repressed as well, or that they have become so firmly rooted that it would be a practical impossibility to eradicate them.

Apart from the question of whether or not specific drugs are harmful, and according to what definition, there are great differences of opinion over society's regulatory role. The present approach in Canada, as in many other countries where the situation has rapidly developed new dimensions, is of course one of continuing legal repression. No serious effort has been made to distinguish formally between hallucinogens and narcotic drugs. The familiar criticism of this approach is that widespread disagreement with the law has eliminated any serious effort to enforce it, and that law enforcement agencies make only sporadic efforts to do their theoretical duty. When an example is made of some offender, the penalty seems unduly harsh, especially when it leaves him with a criminal record. Public sympathy is aroused, and the result can only be to add to the general lack of respect for legislation that seems not to be meant to be taken seriously. Educators are in a very awkward position if they must say in effect: "There is no obvious harm in this practice but there is a law against it, and that settles the matter." Young people are not impressed by this kind of reasoning.

Some people, including many who look with disfavour on the use of drugs, feel that the solution lies in the complete abolition of all efforts at legal repression. Regulation would involve only measures to ensure that the purchaser was getting an unadulterated product. The individual would be entirely free to decide whether indulgence served his interests or not. The state would provide for facilities for treatment and rehabilitation for those who wanted and needed it, just as it does for those whose shortsightedness, bad judgment, or stupidity produces ill health or accidents. To those who envision a massive, wholesale corruption of the population under such conditions, they respond with the theory that normal people have a predominant drive toward health and productivity which would place strict limits on the spread of any practice that had obviously deleterious effects. The abolition of restrictions would have the advantage that profits from "pushing" the drugs would be slashed if they were sold near actual cost. Also, their use would no longer serve as a vehicle of protest against aspects of society with which an individual disagreed.

These views would no doubt have greater currency if society were entirely made up of adults who could be held responsible for their own decisions. But, although there is a great deal of disagreement on where the line should be drawn between immature dependence and adult responsibility, no one really rejects the proposition that children should be protected against the consequences of decisions they would be unlikely to make on reaching maturity. It might seem reasonable to prohibit the sale of drugs only to minors, as it the present practice with respect to liquor and tobacco. This solution loses appeal in view of the ineffective enforcement of restrictions on the latter. People shudder at the idea of making heroin, or even LSD, as accessible as are liquor and tobacco.

It would appear that the legal framework must be considerably revised before education's role is clear with respect to the drug issue. Reforms must be based on at least two basic principles: 1 / that whatever restrictions are necessary must, despite the problem of definition already noted, distinguish among drugs in terms of their capacity to do harm; and 2 / that the approach must, again despite serious difficulties, differentiate between those who need protection because of their immaturity and those who should be allowed to make their own choices. The difficulty of devising an appropriate legal framework was brought out clearly when a leading government official declared that, if too many people disagreed with the existing laws, they would have to be changed. He was accused widely of being prepared to abandon principle in favour of expediency. His critics did not appear to see that he was proposing the only course of action consistent with democratic government. Elected officials have no mandate to impose principles which are not supported by the voting public.

Education's ultimate contribution must be one that does not involve any necessary reference to drugs at all, but rather one of encouraging positive attitudes to life and experience. For those who see the world as a place full of exciting challenges, there is little attraction in escape mechanisms. If the child must find his way to the world through the school, he must first meet such challenges there. On the other hand, if he learns to be cynical, blasé, or bored, all the laws in the books will not keep him from experimenting with substitutes for real living.

THE OVERRIDING ISSUE

There is one question that transcends all others at this crucial stage in history. It is not whether the pollution of the environment can be brought under control, whether the population explosion can be contained, whether the vicious limited wars that have succeeded conflict on a global scale can be stopped, whether poverty throughout the world can be banished, whether racial antagonisms and other forms of hostility can be overcome. It is not any specific economic or social problem, formidable as some of these undoubtedly are, whether considered individually or in combination. It is rather whether or not man can summon and sustain the will to use the means at his disposal to save himself from the dangers that surround him. When viewed with a cold, unemotional eye, the portents do not look promising. On every hand there are signs that people have resigned themselves to despair and impotence. They have no hope that their own efforts can make any difference or that the collectivity can be organized for effective action. Can education help humanity to rescue itself from its perilous state? We can only hope.

ONE

Characteristics of the Ontario population

The number, rate of growth, age pattern, origin, and rural-urban distribution of Ontario's population have combined to place their own particular stamp on the province's educational development. Education has both responded to certain demographic factors and exerted a major influence on the evolution of these factors.

GROSS POPULATION GROWTH

During the years since the end of the Second World War, Ontario has been conspicuous among comparable political units for the pace of its growth. The fundamental aspect of this phenomenon is the rapid increase in population. The figures to the nearest thousand are shown for Ontario and Canada as a whole in Table 1-1 for five-year intervals from 1945 to 1960, and for single years thereafter to 1970; actual figures are given for census years and estimates for the others. The population of Ontario thus grew from four million to nearly 7.5 million, that is, by 84.8 per cent between 1945 and 1969 or, using the estimated figure, by 86.0 per cent between 1945 and 1970. The comparable figures for Canada as a whole are 12.1 million and 21.3 million in 1945 and 1970 respectively, representing an increase of 76.2 per cent. For Canada, and particularly for Ontario, the challenge of population growth has been almost unique among developed countries, and has demanded an educational response without parallel anywhere else. When to this growth is added the unprecedented rise in the level of education needed to contribute to a continuously expanding economy and to cope with the changes resulting from the technological revolution, it is hardly surprising that education has become Ontario's preoccupation.

The percentage increases in Ontario for the successive five-year intervals between 1945 and 1970 were as follows: 1945–50, 11.8; 1950–5, 17.8; 1955–60, 16.0; 1960–5, 11.1; and 1965–70, 9.6. Thus it is evident that, despite the rise in the birth rate and the rate of immigration immediately after the war, the rate of increase did not reach its peak until the 1950s. That was the decade when the crisis of numbers had its greatest impact in the elementary schools. The declining rate of population increase in the 1960s corresponded to an easing of educational difficulties at that level.

Characteristics of the Ontario population 43

TABLE 1-1

Total population of Ontario and Canada as a whole, 1945-70 (numbers in thousands)

YEAR	POPULATION		YEAR	POPULATION	
	Ontario	Canada		Ontario	Canada
1945	4,000	12,072	1964	6,631	19,290
1950	4,471	13,712	1965	6,788	19,644
1955	5,266	15,698	1966	6,961	20,015
1960	6,111	17,870	1967	7,149	20,405
1961	6,236	18,238	1968	7,306	20,744
1962	6,351	18,583	1969[a]	7,392	20,940
1963	6,481	18,931	1970[a]	7,438	21,269

SOURCES: Ontario, Department of Treasury and Economics, *Ontario Statistical Review 1968*, June 1969, p. 31; Dominion Bureau of Statistics (DBS), *Canadian Statistical Review*, publication no. 11-003, XLIV: 4, 1969, p. 1; Metropolitan Toronto Planning Board, Research Division, *Metropolitan Plan Review*, Report No. 2, Appendix, Population Projections 1966-2001, Metropolitan Toronto Planning Area, Ontario and Canada, September 1968. Mimeographed.

[a]Metropolitan Toronto Planning Board: projection estimates based on assumption of net migration of 60,000 to Ontario and 100,000 to all Canada.

The changes in numbers of births,* birth rate, natural increase, and rate of natural increase for the period between the lowest ebb of the depression of the 1930s and 1968 are given in Table 1-2. A slight rise in the birth rate during the Second World War brought the rate from seventeen or eighteen per thousand up to about twenty. Immediately after the war, it began a steady climb until it reached almost twenty-seven in 1957. The rate for Ontario was always somewhat below that for Canada as a whole, as indicated in Table 1-3, no doubt reflecting the fact that the population was more urbanized. In both the provinces and the country the figure at its peak was considered very high for a developed industrialized economy.

The rate of natural increase also reached its peak in 1957, although the absolute number of births and the absolute natural increase continued to rise until 1960. After reaching 159,000 and 108,000 respectively, these figures began a steady decline, reaching 127,000 and 71,000 in 1968.

The decline in the birth rate during the 1960s has left sociologists and demographers somewhat at a loss for an adequate explanation. A rising rate of marriage and a decline in the average age at which it occurred should, according to traditional theory, have had the opposite effect. Lack of prosperity does not provide a satisfactory answer, as it did for a similar phenomenon in the 1930s. While the widespread use of oral contraceptives no doubt had a depressant effect, the trend toward a lower birth rate was well established several years before such techniques became generally available. Other suggested answers are the high rate of female

*Where births are referred to in the present volume, they may be assumed to be live births.

TABLE 1-2
Natural increase in Ontario's population, 1937–68 (numbers in thousands)

YEAR	BIRTHS No.	Rate per 1,000 population	NATURAL INCREASE No.	Rate per 1,000 population	YEAR	BIRTHS No.	Rate per 1,000 population	NATURAL INCREASE No.	Rate per 1,000 population
1937	62	16.9[a]	23	6.4	1953	130	26.3	85	17.1
1938	66	17.9	29	7.8	1954	136	26.6	92	17.9
1939	64	17.3	27	7.2	1955	140	26.5	94	17.9
1940	69	18.3	30	8.0	1956	144	26.6	96	17.9
1941	72	19.1	33	8.7	1957	151	26.8[b]	102	18.1
1942	78	20.1	39	10.0	1958	153	26.2	104	17.8
1943	81	20.7	40	10.2	1959	157	26.3	107	17.8
1944	78	19.7	38	9.7	1960	159	26.1	108	17.7
1945	79	19.7	39	9.8	1961	158	25.3	107	17.1
1946	97	23.8	58	14.1	1962	156	24.6	104	16.4
1947	109	26.1	67	16.1	1963	155	23.9	101	15.6
1948	104	24.4	62	14.5	1964	153	23.0	101	15.2
1949	107	24.3	63	14.4	1965	142	20.9	87	12.9
1950	109	24.3	65	14.5	1966	132	19.0	78	11.2
1951	115	25.0	71	15.4	1967	129[c]	18.0	74	10.4
1952	124	25.9	79	16.6	1968	127[c]	17.4	71	9.7

SOURCE: Ontario, Department of Treasury and Economics, *Ontario Statistical Review 1968*, June 1969.

[a] The lowest figure on record for Ontario.
[b] The highest figure on record for Ontario.
[c] Data from DBS, *Vital Statistics*, monthly, December 1967, 1968. These cumulative monthly figures are not strictly comparable with the annual data of previous years. Monthly statistics represent the number of registrations filed in Ontario Vital Statistics offices during the period in question, while annual data are compiled according to the actual month of occurrence and province of residence.

TABLE 1-3
Number of births in Canada per 1,000 population, 1945–69

YEAR	NO.	YEAR	NO.
1945	24.3	1964	23.5
1950	27.1	1965	21.3
1955	28.2	1966	19.4
1960	26.8	1967	18.2
1961	26.1	1968	17.6
1962	25.3	1969	17.1[a]
1963	24.6		

SOURCE: DBS, *Vital Statistics 1968*, publication no. 84-201, 1970.

[a] Estimate.

CHART 1-1
Number of births in Ontario per thousand of population, 1945–68

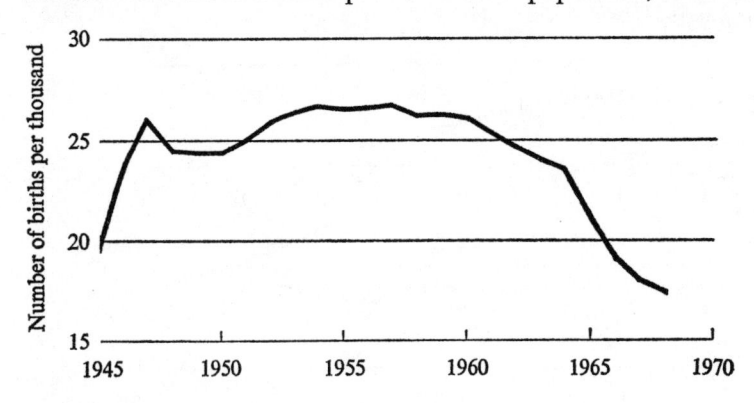

CHART 1-2
Number of births in Ontario, 1945–68

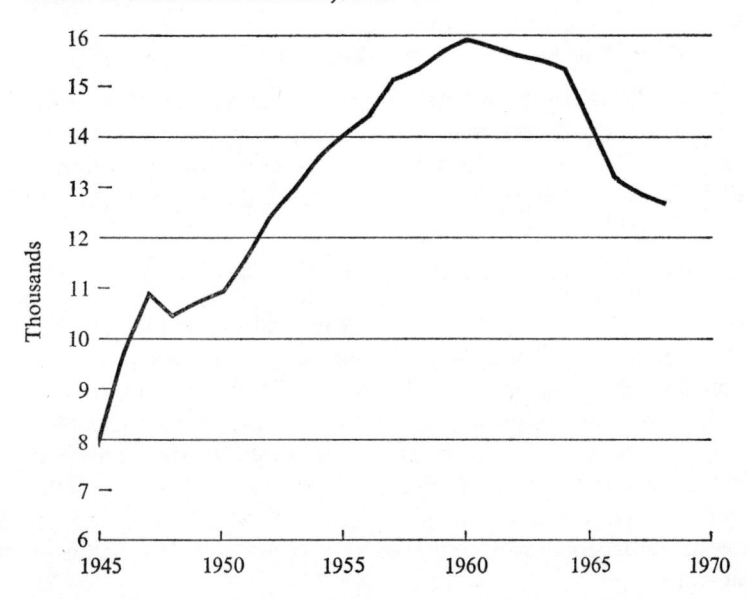

employment and the changing role of women, the high level of consumption expectations in today's society, and the trend to longer formal education. The lack of certainty about the explanation gives educational planners considerable difficulty, since they are left with so little basis for anticipating a possible reversal of the trend.

Whatever the reasons, the trend is consistent with that in certain other countries with comparable economic development. Between 1960 and 1966 birth rates fell steadily in Australia and the United States, in the former reaching the same rate as that in Canada, and in the latter remaining consistently somewhat lower. The rate in France presented a contrast,

CHART 1-3
Number of births in selected countries per thousand of the population, 1960–6

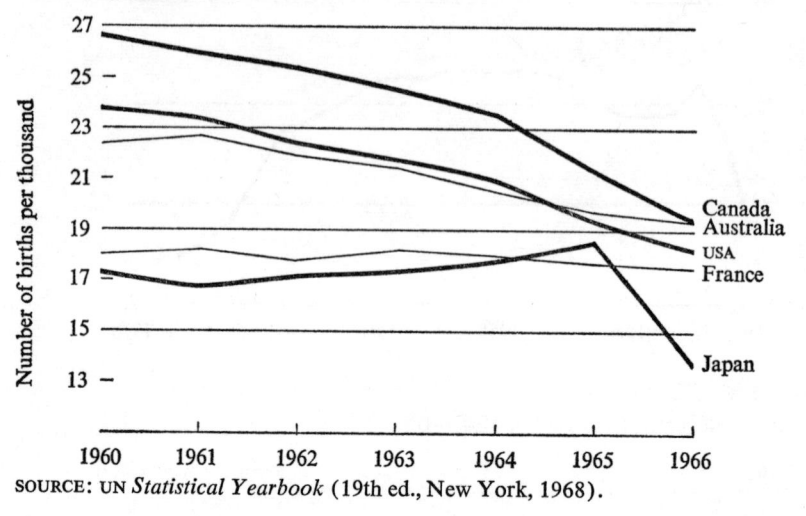

Canada
Australia
USA
France
Japan

1960   1961   1962   1963   1964   1965   1966

SOURCE: UN *Statistical Yearbook* (19th ed., New York, 1968).

since it remained uniformly low throughout the period. Religious influences are considered to account for an otherwise incomprehensible increase in Japan in 1965, followed by an extremely sharp decline to unprecedentedly low levels in 1966. These trends are illustrated in Chart 1-3.

AGE

Gross population figures can give only a very general idea of the nature of the problems that educational planners and administrators must deal with. A detailed age breakdown provides essential information about such factors as the total group requiring education at each level, the proportion in the active labour force in a position to contribute to the support of education, the proportion in the child-bearing group capable of contributing to school enrolment within a predictable period of time, and the proportion of older people who also draw on the productive capacities of the labour force.

Table 1-4 shows the population of Ontario by single years up to age twenty-four, and by five-year intervals thereafter, for the census years 1941, 1951, 1956, 1961, and 1966. The figures give a good idea of the extent of the school accommodation problem and the problem of finding enough teachers during the period. The number of six-year-olds, nearly all of whom might be considered to have been eligible for school attendance, mostly in grade 1, rose from 59,000 in 1941 to 137,000 in 1961, an increase of over 132 per cent. The same group reached a total of 155,000 in 1966, over 160 per cent higher than the number in the base year. The number of fourteen-year-olds, a large proportion of whom

TABLE 1-4

Population of Ontario by age, 1941–66 (numbers in thousands)

AGE GROUP	1941	1951	1956	1961	1966	AGE GROUP	1941	1951	1956	1961	1966
Under 1	59	106	132	155	138	19	69	65	68	80	123
1	56	103	132	150	141	20	69	67	70	78	106
2	64	102	127	149	155	21	70	69	71	77	97
3	60	104	121	145	157	22	61	70	73	76	95
4	59	100	116	141	155	23	61	72	75	77	96
5	59	84	122	140	160	24	63	74	77	79	91
6	59	82	118	137	155	25–29	316	387	417	423	434
7	58	80	113	135	155	30–34	287	351	439	460	447
8	62	80	108	132	153	35–39	268	341	391	469	473
9	63	74	102	130	147	40–44	250	302	361	397	469
10	66	69	96	127	150	45–49	233	268	312	361	391
11	64	66	90	125	141	50–54	214	247	269	310	353
12	65	64	84	121	139	55–59	182	210	236	258	293
13	65	63	80	114	132	60–64	150	182	194	219	244
14	65	62	76	106	126	65–69	116	155	167	180	199
15	65	62	73	99	122	70–74	86	116	134	146	159
16	68	62	70	91	118	75–79	55	70	83	98	109
17	67	63	68	85	118	80–84	30	38	44	53	63
18	69	64	68	82	120	85–89	11	16	19	23	28

SOURCE: DBS, *Census of Canada*, 1941, 1956, and 1966.

were in high school, approximately doubled between 1941 and 1966, rising from 65,000 to 126,000. Those in the eighteen-year group increased from 69,000 to 120,000, and those in the nineteen-year group by a slightly larger figure. These would be the young people eligible for teachers' colleges as well as for university entrance.

Particularly worth noting is the fact that, while the number of six-year-olds doubled between 1941 and 1956, the number in the eighteen- and nineteen-year groups actually decreased slightly. This kind of comparison helps to show why the teacher shortage was so acute in the elementary schools during the mid-1950s. During the same fifteen-year period the number of fourteen-year-olds rose only from 65,000 to 76,000, an increase of about 17 per cent. Up to this time increased high school enrolment was mainly a result of the rising proportion of young people attending.

These figures document the fairly obvious fact that a substantial fluctuation in birth rates, along with whatever further influence is exerted by the immigration of very young children, takes a long time to work its way through the system. In the post-war period, the responsible authorities had relatively little time to plan for the necessary expansion in the elementary schools. For those who were in a position to make any advance provision, there was a much more adequate warning as far as the secondary schools were concerned. And, by an extension of the same reasoning, the universities and such inadequate alternatives at the post-secondary level that existed during most of the period should have been even better prepared. But institutions at the secondary and post-secondary levels were confronted by a factor that did not affect the elementary schools: they had to estimate the increase in percentage of young people in the relevant age groups who would be likely to wish to attend. It usually proved easier to underestimate than to overestimate this percentage.

The changing percentages of the population in different age and sex groups during the same span of years are shown in Table 1-5. These figures emphasize the particularly dramatic increase in the younger groups in proportion to the rest of the population. Between 1941 and 1961 the number of boys under five years of age as a percentage of the total population rose from 4.00 to 6.08, and of girls from 3.87 to 5.79. There was a modest decline to 5.50 and 5.22 per cent for these respective sex groups between 1961 and 1966. The percentage of the population in the five-to-nine-year group rose throughout the period to a figure in 1966 that was nearly 40 per cent higher for boys and over 38 per cent higher for girls than it was in 1941. For both sexes the percentage was still increasing. The pattern for the ten-to-fourteen-year group was somewhat different. The percentage declined fairly sharply into the 1950s and did not pass the 1941 percentage until some time between 1956 and 1961. By 1966 the percentage of boys in this group was about 16 per cent greater than in 1941, and of girls about 14 per cent greater.

Figures from Table 1-5 provide additional evidence of the difficulties associated with the relationship between the potential school enrolment and the pool from which new teachers were largely recruited. For the elementary schools the teachers would come mainly from females in the latter part of the fifteen-to-nineteen group and perhaps also from the early part of the twenty-to-twenty-four group. Between 1941 and 1956 the percentage of females in the former of these groups fell from 4.41 to 3.16, a decline of 28 per cent, and for the latter from 4.23 to 3.38, a decline of about 20 per cent. The percentage between fifteen and nineteen increased by a modest 8.5 per cent between 1956 and 1961, and by about 23 per cent in the next five-year interval. The percentage in the twenty-to-twenty-four group continued to decline until after 1961, and then rose by about 11 per cent between 1961 and 1966, but remained far below the 1941 percentage.

GROSS POPULATION PROJECTIONS

At the beginning of the post-war period the educational system moved with relatively little foresight into the future. The experience of the depression years of the 1930s and the war years instilled rather deeply the impression that relative stability was the normal state of affairs. Some of the most influential projections of that period indicated the likelihood of static populations in the nations of the West, followed by a gradual decline. Canada looked forward at best to a moderate increase for the foreseeable future. It was not until the rapid rise was firmly established that statisticians had a base for projecting the same trend. For a time they

TABLE 1-5
Ontario population percentages by age and sex, 1941-66

AGE GROUP	1941 Male	1941 Female	1951 Male	1951 Female	1956 Male	1956 Female	1961 Male	1961 Female	1966 Male	1966 Female
0-4	4.00	3.87	5.73	5.46	5.93	5.70	6.08	5.79	5.50	5.22
5-9	4.04	3.92	4.45	4.24	5.32	5.11	5.54	5.28	5.65	5.41
10-14	4.35	4.23	3.60	3.47	4.03	3.85	4.87	4.64	5.05	4.83
15-19	4.54	4.41	3.48	3.38	3.26	3.16	3.58	3.43	4.38	4.23
20-24	4.32	4.23	3.85	3.82	3.37	3.38	3.05	3.15	3.46	3.51
25-29	4.22	4.11	4.14	4.28	3.92	3.80	3.42	3.35	3.09	3.14
30-34	3.84	3.72	3.78	3.86	4.01	4.10	3.75	3.62	3.26	3.17
35-39	3.67	3.41	3.76	3.66	3.62	3.61	3.73	3.79	3.44	3.35
40-44	3.39	3.22	3.37	3.21	3.43	3.26	3.21	3.16	3.35	3.40
45-49	3.15	2.99	3.01	2.82	2.98	2.80	2.95	2.84	2.81	2.81
50-54	2.91	2.75	2.75	2.64	2.57	2.41	2.53	2.44	2.57	2.51
55-59	2.48	2.32	2.30	2.28	2.21	2.17	2.10	2.04	2.11	2.10
60-64	1.99	1.96	1.99	1.98	1.76	1.83	1.73	1.77	1.72	1.79
65-69	1.52	1.55	1.68	1.69	1.51	1.59	1.38	1.51	1.34	1.52
70-74	1.09	1.17	1.19	1.33	1.17	1.31	1.07	1.27	1.01	1.27
75-79	0.68	0.77	0.71	0.82	0.71	0.83	0.71	0.86	0.67	0.89
80 and over	0.52	0.64	0.55	0.73	0.55	0.74	0.56	0.79	0.57	0.87

SOURCE: DBS, *Census of Canada*, 1941, 1951, 1956, and 1966.

were uncertain whether to treat the large number of births that followed the return of the servicemen as a temporary phenomenon or as the beginning of a genuine trend toward larger families. When they concluded that the latter was the correct interpretation, some of them carried matters too far and spoke of the family of three, four, or more children as a predictable concomitant of prosperity. Thus many of the projections produced in the early part of the 1960s overestimated the birth rate by a considerable amount.

The difficulty of forecasting population growth has been particularly great in Canada because of the generally large amount of immigration, and because of its irregularity from year to year. Major fluctuations have resulted from variations in economic conditions, with their consequent influence on official immigration policy, as well as from variations in the economic, social, and political climate in the countries from which the newcomers originate. Most of the projections have been presented in the form of alternatives based on different assumptions about immigration. This kind of evasion may help to keep the producer of the statistics from being too grossly in error, but it does not help the educational decision-maker, who is unlikely to have any sound basis for selecting among the proffered alternatives.

Three successive sets of population projects for Ontario are shown in Table 1-6: the first by the Royal Commission on Canada's Economic Prospects in 1957, the second by the Ontario Department of Economics and Development in 1964, and the third by the Metropolitan Toronto Planning Board in 1968. Comparisons among projections for five-year intervals are made somewhat complicated by differing practices among statisticians; some of them give figures for the census years while others choose the years that are divisible by five.

The three sets show a successive scaling down of the estimates of the rate of population growth. At a maximum rate of immigration, the earliest projections had Ontario's population passing the ten million mark by 1980. At a comparable rate of immigration (assuming that if all of Canada got 100,000 immigrants, Ontario would get 60,000), the most recent set of projections would have the province reach the same point five years later. The middle set makes the smallest allowance for immigration, while the most recent makes the largest. Taking the Metropolitan Toronto Planning Board's figures based on a migration rate of 60,000 a year, Ontario may expect an increase in population of approximately 34 per cent between 1971 and 1986 as compared with about 40 per cent during the previous fifteen-year period.

The kind of educational challenge Canada has faced during the last few years and is expected to face in the next decade in comparison with that of other developed countries is indicated by figures produced in an Economic Council of Canada study reported in 1967, and shown in Table 1-7. The figures presented in this table take immigration into account, as

TABLE 1-6
Successive population projections for Ontario (numbers in thousands)

AGENCY MAKING PROJECTIONS AND DATE	ASSUMPTION RE MIGRANT RATE		1970	1971	1975	1976	1980	1981	1986
Royal Commission on Canada's Economic Prospects (Gordon Report), November 1957	Net migration to Canada	50,000 75,000 100,000	7,320 7,590 7,860		8,120 8,540 8,910		9,140 9,620 10,100		
Ontario Department of Economics and Development (Report of Economics Branch), December 1964	Net migration to Ontario	10,000 30,000		7,528 7,788		8,335 8,753		9,292 9,891	10,388 11,167
Metropolitan Toronto Planning Board, September 1968	Net migration to Ontario	40,000 60,000 80,000	7,355 7,438 7,521	7,454 7,559 7,664	7,896 8,092 8,288	8,023 8,243 8,463	8,253 8,933 8,613	8,777 9,123 9,470	9,622 10,104 10,585

SOURCE: Metropolitan Toronto Planning Board, Research Division, *Metropolitan Plan Review, Report No. 2, Appendix, Population Projections 1966–2001, Metropolitan Toronto Planning Area, Ontario and Canada*, September 1968. Mimeographed.

TABLE 1-7
Estimated population growth in selected countries, 1965–80 (numbers in millions)

COUNTRY	POPULATION, 1965	POPULATION GROWTH, 1965–80 No.	Per cent
Britain	54.4	6.1	11
CANADA	19.6	5.5	28
France[a]	48.2	5.6	12
Germany (West)	58.2	4.2	7
Italy	52.2	6.2	12
Sweden	7.7	1.0	13
United States	193.3	50.1	26

SOURCE: Economic Council of Canada, *Staff Study*, No. 19, *Population, Family, Household and Labour Force Growth to 1980*, by Wolfgang M. Illing with technical contributions by Y. Kasahara, Frank T. Denton, and M.V. George (Ottawa: Queen's Printer, 1967); reproduced with the permission of Information Canada.

[a]Excluding migration 1965–80.

well as the birth rate. Between 1965 and 1980 Canada's absolute increase, at about 5.5 million, is expected to be only slightly under 6.1 million estimated for Britain, even though the 1965 base for Canada was only a little more than one-third that for Britain. Similarly, the absolute increases for Canada and France were expected to be of comparable size, even though France's population was about two and one-half times that of Canada in 1965. Canada's rate of population growth was estimated at four times that of West Germany, although only a little greater than that of the United States.

PROJECTED AGE DISTRIBUTION

Projections of population by one-year age intervals up to twenty-four and by five-year intervals for the whole age range for the period between 1971 and 1991 are given in Table 1-8. These show a steady increase in each age group up to five, but a dip in the numbers from age six to age eleven in 1976, carrying through to the immediately higher ages in 1981 as the same group proceeds. These are the children born during the mid-1960s of the relatively small numbers between twenty and thirty-four, the most productive childbearing years. This was the generation born during the period of low fertility in the 1930s and early 1940s. As a result of this phenomenon, the taxpayers may count on at least one influence contributing to restraint on the rising costs of education as the dip affects the five- to-nine-year range about 1976. By the middle 1970s and through most of the 1980s, a second wave of lesser relative dimensions is expected to build up and gradually subside. Presumably the major distortions in the age distribution will ultimately disappear unless, as is not at all

TABLE 1-8

Projected population of Ontario by age, 1971-91 (numbers in thousands)

AGE GROUP	1971	1976	1981	1986	1991	AGE GROUP	1971	1976	1981	1986	1991
Under 1	141	163	186	200	204	0-4	666	762	878	970	1,006
1	135	156	179	196	201	5-9	755	675	770	886	978
2	132	151	175	194	201	10-14	779	764	684	779	895
3	129	148	171	191	201	15-19	698	788	773	694	789
4	129	144	167	189	201	20-24	618	716	806	791	712
5	137	141	163	185	200	25-29	508	640	738	828	813
6	150	137	158	181	198	30-34	451	525	656	754	843
7	155	134	154	177	196	35-39	457	461	534	665	762
8	157	131	150	173	193	40-44	476	460	464	538	668
9	156	131	146	169	191	45-49	467	473	458	462	535
10	162	139	143	165	187	50-54	384	457	464	450	454
11	157	152	139	160	183	55-59	340	370	440	447	434
12	157	157	136	156	179	60-64	275	319	347	413	419
13	154	159	133	152	175	65-69	220	248	288	313	373
14	149	158	133	148	171	70-74	169	187	211	245	267
15	152	164	141	145	166	75-79	122	130	144	163	189
16	143	158	154	141	162	80-84	70	80	85	95	108
17	141	159	159	138	157	85 and over	40	45	52	57	64
18	134	156	160	135	154						
19	128	151	160	135	150	TOTAL	7,494	8,099	8,792	9,548	10,307
20	124	155	166	143	147						
21	121	146	161	157	144						
22	122	144	163	162	142						
23	124	138	160	165	139						
24	127	133	156	164	140						

SOURCE: Ontario, Department of Treasury and Economics, Economic Planning Board.

NOTES:
1 Net immigration estimated at 30,000 per year.
2 Death rates assumed to decline in all age groups except those from five to twenty-four.
3 Fertility rates assumed level after 1967.

impossible, some new catastrophe or drastic social change upsets the pattern.

The population dip will begin to affect those in the post-secondary level age groups, that is, between eighteen and twenty-four, by 1986, but during most of the period up to that time a steadily rising number must be expected. Young people in the same age group must also be regarded as potential entrants into the labour force, although the age range at which employment will begin will depend a great deal on changing conditions of work as well as on the type and amount of educational preparation required for job opportunities. Despite some irregularities, a steady increase in the numbers in the higher age categories may be expected. The number between sixty-five and sixty-nine should rise by nearly 70 per cent between 1971 and 1991, while the twenty-to-twenty-four age group is increasing by only about 15 per cent. It is a question whether young people will be in danger of being crushed by the gerontocracy, or whether they will be highly valued because of their scarcity, during the 1990s.

The projections of the percentages of the total population by age group and sex produced by the Metropolitan Toronto Planning Board are shown in Table 1-9. When compared with the actual percentages given in Table 1-5, they indicate the sharpness of the reduction in the under-four age group between 1966 and 1971, also noted in Table 1-8 in terms of absolute numbers. For boys the percentage in this group is expected to drop from 5.50 to 4.08, and for girls, from 5.22 to 3.85. The beginning of the next dip can be detected in the declining percentage in the under-four group from 1986 on. It corresponds to the group of potential parents around age twenty who will have entered school in the 1970s. Although the projected absolute numbers in the post-secondary and initial employment age groups hold up fairly well, as has been noted, during the late 1980s and early 1990s the percentage at that age will reach a relatively low ebb. The low percentage of the group in their forties and fifties during the early 1980s once again identifies those born during the Great Depression and the Second World War.

GROSS IMMIGRATION

The arrival of large numbers of newcomers has been a central aspect of population growth in Ontario during the post-war period. During this time the province has received somewhat over half the total settling in the entire country. It is doubtful that many of the immigrants have chosen this particular destination in order to take advantage of its educational facilities, or even that they have given this factor much conscious consideration in making their choice.

There have been two immediate and obvious consequences of immigration for education: 1 / school enrolments have been greatly swelled and 2 / special provisions have been needed to ensure that immigrant children, particularly those without an adequate knowledge of English,

TABLE 1-9
Projected Ontario population percentage by age and sex, 1971–96

AGE GROUP	1971 Male	1971 Female	1976 Male	1976 Female	1981 Male	1981 Female	1986 Male	1986 Female	1991 Male	1991 Female	1996 Male	1996 Female
0–4	4.08	3.85	4.46	4.22	5.30	5.02	5.48	5.20	5.14	4.87	4.74	4.50
5–9	5.22	4.94	3.89	3.65	4.16	3.92	4.90	4.63	5.11	4.83	4.84	4.58
10–14	5.33	5.11	4.90	4.65	3.62	3.41	3.85	3.64	4.56	4.31	4.79	4.54
15–19	4.78	4.56	4.98	4.74	4.51	4.25	3.34	3.13	3.59	3.36	4.27	4.01
20–24	4.23	4.13	4.55	4.36	4.66	4.45	4.22	3.98	3.19	3.00	3.44	3.23
25–29	3.51	3.53	4.18	4.06	4.38	4.19	4.45	4.24	4.07	3.84	3.15	2.95
30–34	3.13	3.09	3.48	3.42	4.00	3.83	4.16	3.93	4.24	4.00	3.93	3.67
35–39	3.16	3.05	3.02	2.95	3.27	3.20	3.73	3.55	3.89	3.67	4.01	3.77
40–44	3.24	3.17	2.96	2.87	2.78	2.74	3.00	2.95	3.43	3.29	3.61	3.43
45–49	3.06	3.16	2.95	2.94	2.66	2.64	2.50	2.51	2.72	2.72	3.13	3.06
50–54	2.52	2.60	2.74	2.91	2.60	2.67	2.34	2.39	2.22	2.30	2.44	2.51
55–59	2.24	2.30	2.20	2.37	2.35	2.61	2.23	2.40	2.03	2.17	1.95	2.11
60–64	1.77	1.90	1.88	2.07	1.81	2.10	1.93	2.31	1.85	2.14	1.70	1.96
65–69	1.37	1.59	1.41	1.68	1.47	1.79	1.42	1.82	1.53	2.01	1.48	1.88
70–74	0.99	1.28	1.02	1.33	1.03	1.38	1.07	1.47	1.04	1.50	1.13	1.67
75–79	0.66	0.94	0.65	0.96	0.66	0.99	0.67	1.03	0.70	1.10	0.69	1.14
80 and over	0.58	0.94	0.57	0.98	0.55	0.98	0.54	0.99	0.55	1.04	0.58	1.11

SOURCE: Metropolitan Toronto Planning Board, Research Division, *Metropolitan Plan Review, Report No. 2, Appendix, Population Projections 1966–2001*, Metropolitan Toronto Planning Area, Ontario and Canada, September 1968. Mimeographed.

TABLE 1-10
Immigration to Canada and Ontario, 1946-69
(numbers in thousands)

YEAR	IMMIGRATION Canada	Ontario	YEAR	IMMIGRATION Canada	Ontario
1946	72	30	1958	125	64
1947	64	36	1959	107	56
1948	125	62	1960	104	54
1949	95	49	1961	72	37
1950	74	39	1962	75	37
1951	194	105	1963	93	49
1952	164	86	1964	113	61
1953	169	90	1965	147	80
1954	154	83	1966	195	108
1955	110	58	1967	223	117
1956	165	91	1968	184	96
1957	282	147	1969	162	86

SOURCE: Canada, Department of Manpower and Immigration, *Immigration Statistics*.

may be integrated into the school and into the cultural environment. Immigration has of course had much broader and more diffuse educational implications, many of which have not been assessed in any deliberate or exact fashion. Its influence on the development of the economy, for example, has had unidentified effects on the ability and willingness of the public to pay for education, and on interest in education of particular types and at various levels. Any cultural changes produced by the immigrants' retention of some of their former attitudes and life styles, even as they are assimilated into the dominant culture, are particularly subtle and hard to define.

Figures for post-war immigration into Canada as a whole and Ontario in particular are shown in Table 1-10. Information is given for each specific year to show the great fluctuations within relatively brief time spans. For example, the peak of approximately 147,000 reached in 1957 was over two and one-half times the 58,000 figure of two years earlier, and about four times the 37,000 who arrived in 1961, just four years later. For a time it was widely theorized that immigration would make a declining contribution to population increase, but a fairly large influx in some recent years has changed the prospect. In the final analysis, the number depends largely on the policies adopted by the federal government and to a lesser extent on those of the provincial government. Unlimited numbers of immigrants are no doubt available from some parts of the world if they are not excluded by educational or racial barriers, and if someone finances their passage. Given a policy of selecting those with a reasonable chance of economic success, the situation is less predictable.

Immigration figures may be compared with the numbers resulting from natural increase, as shown in Table 1-2. In 1955 immigration was 58,000

CHART 1-4
Number of immigrants to Ontario, 1946–69

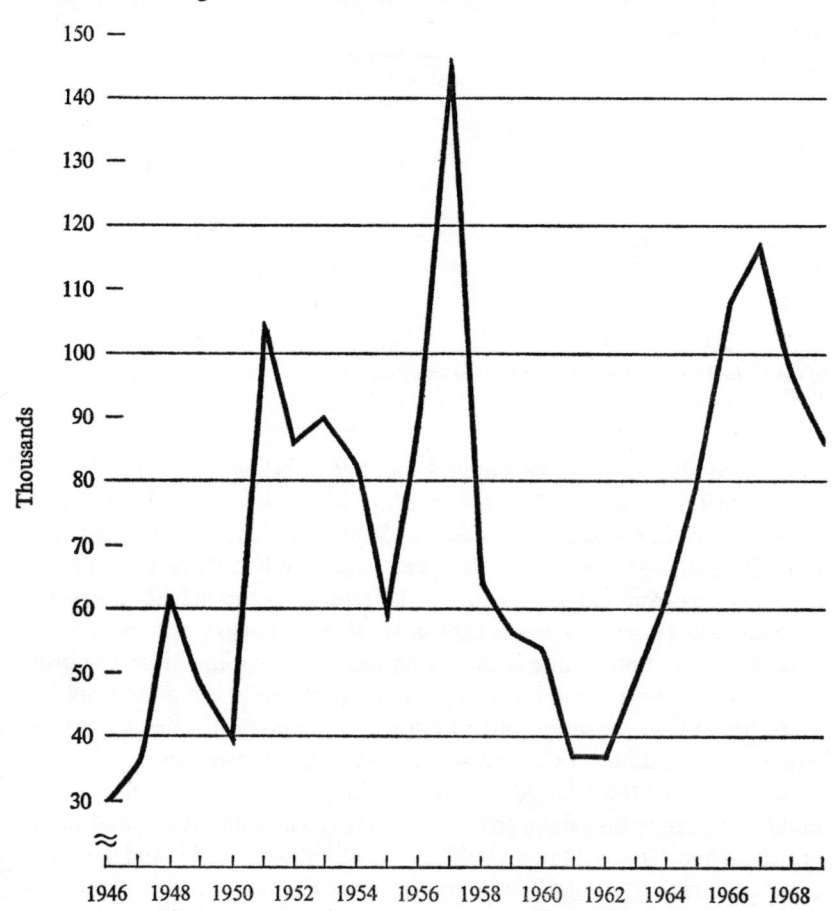

and natural increase 94,000; in 1957 the corresponding figures were 147,000 and 102,000; in 1961, 37,000 and 107,000; and in 1967, 117,000 and 74,000. These comparisons show how irregular the relationship has been between the two figures. Some generalizations are, however, possible for the post-war period as a whole.[1]

Between 1947 and 1966 immigration to Canada averaged 131,350 per year, thus contributing a total of over 2.6 million for the twenty-year period. During the same interval approximately one million people left Canada. The net gain thus averaged about 80,000 per year. In the same period Ontario gained an average of about 67,000 people from other countries, adding up to a total of 1.34 million. On the assumption that the loss to other countries was about the same for Ontario as for Canada as a whole, the net gain from external sources was in the neighbourhood of 42,000 per year, totalling about 840,000 for the twenty years.

TABLE 1-11
Immigration to the United States, 1941-67
(numbers in thousands)

YEAR	NUMBER	ANNUAL RATE PER 1,000 POPULATION
1941-50	1,035	0.7
1951-60	2,515	1.5
1961	271	1.5
1962	284	1.5
1963	306	1.6
1964	292	1.5
1965	297	1.5
1966	323	1.6
1967	362	1.8

SOURCE: US Bureau of the Census, *Statistical Abstract of the United States: 1968* (89th ed.; Washington, DC, 1968).

Ontario also gained a substantial number of people as a result of migration within Canada. The average number added to the population from this source has been estimated at 13,000 per year, constituting a total of about 260,000 over the twenty-year period. When these are added to the net gains from external sources, the total is in the neighbourhood of 1.25 million people, or more than a third of Ontario's population gain from 1947 to 1966. While it can by no means be assumed that the province's natural population increase would have been at the same level had there been no immigration, it can hardly be supposed that a comparable expansion could have occurred without this major infusion.

Some idea of the relative impact of immigration on the United States and Canada may be gained from Table 1-11. The total number of immigrants to the United States was 2,515,000 between 1951 and 1960, as compared with 1,574,000 to Canada. Thus Canada, with a population ranging between one-twelfth and one-tenth of the population of the United States, took approximately 60 per cent as many immigrants. For the period between 1961 and 1967 American and Canadian immigration totals were respectively 2,135,000 and 918,000, the latter constituting about 43 per cent of the former. In relative terms, immigration into the United States was roughly 1.5 per thousand; into Canada as a whole, 4 per thousand; and into Ontario, 6 per thousand in 1961. The comparable rates in 1964 were 1.5, 6, and 9 respectively, and in 1967, 1.8, 11, and 16.

ORIGIN OF IMMIGRANTS

The distribution of immigrants according to country of origin has a great deal to do with their impact on the educational system. The relevant factors revolve around the extent to which their home culture differs from that in the new environment. In order to understand the immigrant's problems, one needs to know his feelings about family cohesion; his views

TABLE 1-12

Population of Ontario by place of birth, 1941–61 (numbers in thousands)

YEAR	BORN IN ONTARIO No.	Per cent	BORN ELSEWHERE IN CANADA No.	Per cent	BORN OUTSIDE CANADA No.	Per cent	TOTAL POPULATION No.	Per cent
1941	2,830	74.7	225	5.9	733	19.4	3,788	100.0
1951	3,338	72.6	410	8.9	850	18.5	4,598	100.0
1961	4,305	69.0	578	9.3	1,353	21.7	6,236	100.0

SOURCE: DBS, *Census of Canada*, 1941, 1951, and 1961.

about the responsibilities of members of one generation to those of another; his opinion about what constitutes acceptable public behaviour on the part of males and females at different age levels; his recreational and aesthetic interests; his clothing preferences; his acceptance of responsibilities toward the immediate community, the municipality, the province, and the nation; and other such factors. Sociologists still have not completed a description of the Canadian milieu into which those coming from other cultural environments must fit, and are a long way from producing an adequate delineation of the characteristics of the immigrant groups. Even if such information were available, it would be impossible to give it more than passing recognition in the present context.

From the point of view of the school, the most immediate question has usually been whether or not the child could be effectively taught in English. To an increasing extent, as French becomes a language of instruction in more areas of the province, it will be realistic to add "or in French." It may in some cases be useful to define three categories: 1 / those whose native language is the same as the language of instruction; 2 / those who have studied the language of instruction as a second language; and 3 / those with no significant knowledge of the language of instruction. This division is meaningful on the assumption that those in the first category are likely to have a higher degree of competence than those in the second, although in individual cases the reverse may be true.

Unfortunately there are no adequate statistics to indicate the exact extent of the language problem among Ontario immigrants, either at the age of school attendance or beyond. The best that can be done is to make some rough deductions from available information on the origins of the population. As a first step, Table 1-12 indicates the number and percentage of the Ontario population according to three categories of place of origin: those born in Ontario, those born elsewhere in Canada, and those born outside the country. Unfortunately, data could be obtained only for ten-year census intervals, although it is a reasonable guess that trends established in the 1941–61 period continued into or through the 1960s. The percentage of Ontario-born citizens declined during the period from 74.7 to 69.0. The major part of the change was, however,

TABLE 1-13

Percentages of immigrants to Ontario from various sources, 1959–68

SOURCE	1959	1960	1961	1962	1963	1964	1965	1966	1967	1968
British Isles	19.4	21.8	19.2	25.3	33.3	31.9	31.3	38.7	32.9	23.7
Australia and New Zealand	1.1	1.1	1.5	1.6	1.4	1.4	1.3	1.4	1.9	1.9
West Indies	0.9	1.0	1.4	2.1	2.4	1.9	2.0	2.0	4.3	4.9
Austria	1.4	2.1	1.7	1.2	0.9	1.0	1.0	1.2	1.3	4.2
France	0.7	1.1	1.2	0.9	0.9	1.2	1.2	1.2	1.1	1.6
Germany	9.6	10.8	9.2	7.7	7.6	5.5	6.2	4.6	5.4	5.3
Greece	3.3	3.6	4.3	4.0	3.9	3.3	3.5	3.5	5.3	4.8
Italy	29.0	23.2	24.0	20.6	17.2	20.9	23.2	20.2	16.8	14.1
Netherlands	5.2	5.6	2.9	2.6	2.2	1.9	1.8	1.8	1.8	1.8
Portugal	4.4	5.2	4.5	4.3	4.3	5.3	4.5	4.7	5.6	5.6
Scandinavia	1.5	1.4	0.9	1.2	1.1	0.9	0.8	0.8	0.9	1.0
Yugoslavia	1.2	1.0	1.6	1.5	1.1	1.5	1.2	1.1	1.3	3.4
Other European	1.0	1.4	1.7	1.6	1.2	1.7	1.6	1.5	1.7	2.9
Africa	0.4	0.7	1.2	0.9	0.9	1.1	0.7	0.9	1.1	1.3
Asia	1.9	1.2	1.4	1.6	1.6	1.5	4.6	4.4	6.4	8.0
Middle East	1.6	1.7	1.2	1.6	1.6	2.8	1.4	1.4	1.8	2.3
Central and South America	1.7	1.8	2.3	1.9	2.2	2.4	2.0	1.6	1.8	1.9
United States	8.8	9.0	13.4	13.7	10.8	8.7	7.7	6.4	6.0	8.5
Others	6.9	6.3	6.4	5.7	5.4	5.1	4.0	2.6	2.6	2.8
TOTAL	100.0	100.0	100.0	100.0	100.0	100.0	100.0	100.0	100.0	100.0

SOURCE: Canada, Department of Manpower and Immigration, *Immigration Statistics*.

attributable to the increase in the percentage from elsewhere in Canada, which rose from 5.9 to 9.3. The percentage of foreign-born increased only from 19.4 to 21.7. Thus the relative extent of the burden of assimilating the foreign-born does not appear to have increased greatly. This generalization of course has limited value unless it is related to the age distribution of the immigrants, their ability to use the language of the community, and other factors.

Table 1-13 shows the countries or broader geographical regions from which most of the immigrants came during the period between 1959 and 1968. It may be assumed that those from the British Isles, Australia, New Zealand, the West Indies, and the United States would have little difficulty with the language. The percentage from the British Isles rose from 19.4 in 1959 to 38.7 in 1966, and then declined to 23.7 in 1968; that from Australia and New Zealand together was never more than 1.9; that from the West Indies rose fairly steadily from 0.9 to 4.9; and that from the United States fluctuated considerably, reaching a high point of 13.7 in 1962 and a low of 6.0 in 1967. The percentage from all these sources together was 30.2 in 1959, 48.5 in 1966, and 39.0 in 1968.

It is perhaps hardly less risky to assume that the immigrants from Africa and Asia were familiar with the language of the Ontario community in which they chose to settle, although often as the language of the school only, rather than of the home and school. The negligible proportion coming from Africa would largely have been educated in English or French. English was a familiar language to most of those arriving from Asia, a large proportion of whom originated in India, Pakistan, and Hong Kong. The percentage from Asia was low until 1964, rising from 1.5 in that year to 8.0 in 1968.

Only rather vague speculation is possible about the remainder of the immigrants. The adults intending to enter many of the possible occupations generally had to know something of the predominant language in order to demonstrate the capacity to support themselves, although those who were sponsored by relatives did not have to meet such a test. But even a working knowledge of the language often left plenty of room for upgrading in adult classes. Families often consisted of parents who could speak English and of children who could not, and the failure of the latter to hear English spoken in the home compounded the difficulties faced by the school. In terms of language problems, adolescents from certain countries such as the Netherlands and the Scandinavian countries, where the schools concentrated with particular effectiveness on foreign languages, were often at a considerable advantage.

AGE OF IMMIGRANTS

The age distribution of immigrants to Ontario from outside the country has been very different from that of the population as a whole. Percentages by five-year age categories are given in Table 1-14 for the years from 1958 to 1968. Comparison with Table 1-5 shows how heavily the immigrant group has been weighted in favour of youth. The percentage in the under-four category has hovered around 9, rising substantially higher and then declining again in the recent period, while the comparable percentage in the same category in the whole population has normally varied between 5 and 6. During the ten-year period covered by the table the percentage in the range between five and nineteen, from which the elementary and secondary school enrolment comes, has varied consistently between 22 and 24. The comparable range for the population in general has been about 12 to 15. In very rough terms, it may be said that newly-arrived immigrants have included between one and one-half and twice as many children as the entire population who might be considered eligible for elementary and secondary school education. The proportion who actually took advantage of educational opportunities would correspond closely during the period of compulsory attendance. What happened to those beyond that age is uncertain.

During the same period the percentage of the new arrivals in what might be called the early productive years has exceeded that in the population at large by an even greater amount. In the age group between twenty and twenty-four, the percentage among the immigrants has varied above and below 19, as compared with a figure between 3 and 4.5 in the general population. Comparable percentages for the twenty-five to

TABLE 1-14
Percentages of immigrants from outside Canada to Ontario by age, 1958–68

YEAR	AGE GROUP												
	0–4	5–9	10–14	15–19	20–24	25–29	30–34	35–39	40–44	45–49	50–54	55–59	60–64	65–69	70 and over	Total
1958	9.0	8.1	6.0	9.2	19.8	15.6	10.3	6.6	3.7	3.5	2.6	2.0	1.5	1.1	1.0	100.0
1959	8.8	8.0	6.2	8.9	19.3	15.5	10.4	6.9	3.7	3.6	2.7	2.2	1.6	1.1	1.1	100.0
1960	8.5	7.5	6.0	8.8	20.8	15.8	10.3	6.8	3.5	3.2	2.7	2.1	1.6	1.2	1.2	100.0
1961	8.3	7.3	6.2	9.2	20.5	15.5	9.5	6.7	3.8	3.0	2.8	2.2	1.9	1.6	1.5	100.0
1962	8.9	7.7	5.8	8.9	19.4	16.2	10.2	6.8	3.9	2.7	2.4	2.0	2.0	1.5	1.6	100.0
1963	9.6	7.8	5.8	8.6	18.8	16.8	10.8	7.1	4.2	2.1	2.1	1.9	1.6	1.4	1.4	100.0
1964	10.0	8.4	6.2	8.9	17.4	16.2	10.5	6.9	4.5	2.4	2.3	2.1	1.6	1.3	1.3	100.0
1965	10.6	8.8	6.2	8.8	17.3	16.3	10.4	7.0	4.3	2.4	2.2	1.9	1.5	1.2	1.1	100.0
1966	11.0	9.3	6.1	8.0	18.1	16.4	10.4	7.1	4.5	2.5	2.0	1.6	1.2	0.9	0.9	100.0
1967	9.6	8.4	5.4	7.4	20.3	18.3	11.0	6.6	4.0	2.5	1.7	1.6	1.3	1.0	0.9	100.0
1968	8.9	7.9	5.2	8.1	21.7	17.9	10.3	6.2	3.7	2.3	1.7	1.7	1.8	1.3	1.3	100.0

SOURCE: Canada, Department of Manpower and Immigration, *Immigration Statistics*.

twenty-nine age group have been around 16 for the immigrants and from about 3 to 4.5 for the general population. Only for those in their forties do the percentages approach equality. Immigrants constitute a very small relative percentage of the total population in the higher age groups.

It would be impossible to estimate with any degree of accuracy the extent to which the burden placed on the schools by immigration has been balanced by the greater proportion of the adults in the productive age groups as compared with the population in general. A valid judgment would depend not only on a knowledge of the use made of educational facilities, but also of the kinds of economic contributions to the economy made by adults and the extent to which the relative absence of older people relieved the community of a burden of support at that end of the age scale.

LABOUR FORCE STATUS OF POPULATION
There are several major aspects of the labour force that have important implications for education. It is rather obvious that the smaller the percentage of the total population in the labour force, the more productive the individual must be in order to sustain a given standard of living for the population as a whole. For those of the non-workers who are too young to work, formal educational facilities must be provided; for those who are too old, other types of services are in demand. A relatively young labour force requires rapidly increasing provision for part-time education, whether in night school, within industry, or in some other form. While warnings have been issued for many years that a successful career in almost any field will eventually demand continuous upgrading or preparation for changes in function, many older workers still manage to get by on what they learned in their youth. But the differences in the consumption of part-time education according to age are almost certain to diminish, in line with predictions.

The proportion of the labour force without employment has growing implications for education as governments at different levels become more involved in training and retraining. The assumption of the cost of maintenance of the unemployed and their families could become a serious public burden in periods of severe and prolonged depression, thus restraining expenditure for other purposes, including education. The implications of unemployment for the state of the economy have, of course, much broader implications than this rather obvious one.

Trends in the employment of women are important for a number of reasons. Other things being equal, a rising proportion of women in the labour force naturally means a positive contribution to the economy. If the birth rate remains constant, there is a growing demand for certain services such as nursery schools. If it falls, the implications for schools are clear. The effect of the mother's outside employment on the welfare of the family may be desirable or undesirable, depending on a variety of accompanying circumstances. The tendency to attribute delinquency to the fact that the mother does not look after the house on a full-time basis has been modified considerably in the light of certain studies conducted in recent years.

The percentage of the total population in the labour force for each individual year between 1946 and 1968 is shown in Table 1-15, with separate figures by sex. The percentage for men declined from 31.4 in 1946 to 26.8 in 1964; there was a slight rise to 27.2 in 1968. The decline during the period as a whole is attributable mainly to the relative increase in numbers at the lowest age levels and to a tendency for the period of formal education to be prolonged. By the late 1960s the relatively large numbers born in the immediate post-war period were flowing into the labour force. As far as women were concerned, there was an appreciable decline after the war, the percentage of 10.2 in 1946 falling to 9.3 in 1953, after which there was a fairly regular increase to 13.1 in 1968. While the low point in the 1950s paralleled the high birth rate, it would be difficult to disentangle cause and effect. The net result of the declining proportion of men and the increasing proportion of women in the labour force has meant an over-all percentage of 40.3 in 1968 which was only slightly below that of 42.1 in 1947. The low point of 38.2 per cent was reached in 1962–3.

Table 1-16 follows the common practice of showing the number in the labour force as a percentage of the population aged fourteen and over, even though it might seem more satisfactory to use age sixteen, the end of compulsory attendance at school, as the line of demarcation. The percentage of males in the labour force from this group declined from a high point of 86.3 in 1949 to 79.2 in 1968. Since the percentage of males over sixty years of age showed no substantial change during the period, this decline largely reflects the tendency of boys to remain in school longer, a factor which is related to the availability of employment for youth. The change appears somewhat more dramatic if one examines the rising percentage of males *not* in the labour force. This percentage increased from 13.7 in 1949 to 20.8 in 1968.

Among women, the percentage in the labour force fell from 26.9 in 1946 to 25.8 in 1948 and 1950, and then began a steady rise, reaching 36.9 in 1968. This increase of approximately 43 per cent obviously indicates a social change of considerable importance. The figures in Table 1-16 emphasize the fact that the increase in employment among women has counteracted the decline among men. The total of both sexes aged fourteen and over in the labour force rose from 55.7 per cent in 1946 to 57.7 in 1968.

Table 1-16 also shows the percentage of the population aged fourteen and over who were actually employed during the same period. The rather regular decline in male employment over the entire period tends to obscure the relatively difficult years of the late 1950s and early 1960s. The situation shows up more clearly when one examines the percentage considered to be in the labour force who were not employed. This percentage, for

TABLE 1-15
Ontario labour force in relation to total population by sex, 1946–68[a] (numbers in thousands)

YEAR	MALES No. in labour force	MALES Percentage of total population in labour force	FEMALES No. in labour force	FEMALES Percentage of total population in labour force	TOTAL No. in labour force	TOTAL Percentage of total population in labour force
1946	1,285	31.4	417	10.2	1,702	41.6
1947	1,341	32.1	419	10.0	1,760	42.1
1948	1,364	31.9	413	9.7	1,777	41.6
1949	1,388	31.7	427	9.8	1,815	41.5
1950	1,395	31.2	430	9.6	1,825	40.8
1951	1,426	31.0	444	9.6	1,870	40.6
1952	1,454	30.4	454	9.5	1,908	39.9
1953	1,487	30.1	461	9.3	1,948	39.4
1954	1,526	29.8	496	9.7	2,022	39.5
1955	1,545	29.3	514	9.8	2,059	39.1
1956	1,587	29.4	560	10.4	2,147	39.8
1957	1,644	29.2	594	10.5	2,238	39.7
1958	1,674	28.8	589	10.1	2,263	38.9
1959	1,690	28.3	612	10.2	2,302	38.5
1960	1,714	28.0	663	10.8	2,377	38.8
1961	1,717	27.5	684	11.0	2,401	38.5
1962	1,725	27.2	697	11.0	2,422	38.2
1963	1,751	27.0	724	11.2	2,475	38.2
1964	1,780	26.8	776	11.7	2,556	38.5
1965	1,817	26.8	798	11.8	2,615	38.6
1966	1,869	26.8	850	12.2	2,719	39.0
1967	1,929	27.0	906	12.8	2,835	39.8
1968	1,984	27.2	951	13.1	2,935	40.3

[a] Calculated from figures supplied by the Ontario Regional Office, Canada, Department of Manpower and Immigration; DBS, *Population 1921–66*, publication no. 92-511, 1968.

TABLE 1-16
Percentages of population of Ontario 14 years of age and over by labour force status, 1946–68[a]

YEAR	MEN Labour force Employed	Unemployed	TOTAL	Not in labour force	WOMEN Labour force Employed	Unemployed	TOTAL	Not in labour force	TOTAL Labour force Employed	Unemployed	TOTAL	Not in labour force
1946	82.9	2.6	85.5	14.5	26.3	*	26.9	73.1	54.2	1.3	55.7	44.3
1947	84.4	1.5	85.9	14.1	26.2	*	26.6	73.4	55.1	0.8	56.1	43.9
1948	84.6	1.4	86.0	14.0	25.2	*	25.8	74.2	54.7	0.7	55.7	44.3
1949	84.2	2.1	86.3	13.7	25.7	*	26.2	73.8	54.8	1.0	56.0	44.0
1950	83.5	2.2	85.7	14.3	25.4	*	25.8	74.2	54.1	1.1	55.4	44.6
1951	84.7	1.4	86.1	13.9	25.7	*	26.2	73.8	54.8	0.7	55.8	44.2
1952	83.4	2.0	85.4	14.6	25.7	*	26.1	73.9	54.2	1.0	55.4	44.6
1953	83.1	2.1	85.2	14.8	25.6	*	25.9	74.1	54.1	1.0	55.2	44.8
1954	81.5	3.7	85.2	14.8	26.5	0.6	27.1	72.9	53.7	2.2	55.9	44.1
1955	81.5	3.0	84.5	15.5	26.9	0.6	27.5	72.5	53.9	1.8	55.7	44.3
1956	82.7	2.3	85.0	15.0	29.0	*	29.4	70.6	55.6	1.2	56.9	43.1
1957	81.5	3.3	84.8	15.2	29.5	0.6	30.1	69.9	55.3	2.0	57.3	42.7
1958	79.1	5.2	84.3	15.7	28.1	1.0	29.1	70.9	53.4	3.0	56.4	43.6
1959	79.3	4.3	83.6	16.4	28.8	0.8	29.6	70.4	53.8	2.5	56.3	43.7
1960	78.0	5.2	83.2	16.8	30.4	1.0	31.4	68.6	53.9	3.1	57.0	43.0
1961	76.9	5.2	82.1	17.9	30.8	1.1	31.9	68.1	53.6	3.1	56.7	43.3
1962	77.4	4.0	81.4	18.6	30.9	1.0	31.9	68.1	53.8	2.4	56.2	43.8
1963	77.8	3.4	81.2	18.8	31.6	0.9	32.5	67.5	54.4	2.1	56.5	43.5
1964	77.8	2.8	80.6	19.4	33.2	0.9	34.1	65.9	55.1	1.8	56.9	43.1
1965	77.9	2.2	80.1	19.9	33.3	0.8	34.1	65.9	55.3	1.4	56.7	43.3
1966	77.6	2.1	79.7	20.3	34.4	0.8	35.2	64.8	55.7	1.5	57.2	42.8
1967	76.7	2.6	79.3	20.7	35.3	1.0	36.3	63.7	55.7	1.8	57.5	42.5
1968	76.2	3.0	79.2	20.8	35.7	1.2	36.9	63.1	55.7	2.0	57.7	42.3

*Negligible.
[a]Calculated from figures supplied by the Ontario Regional Office, Canada, Department of Manpower and Immigration.

CHART 1-5
Percentages of men and women aged fourteen and over in the labour force, 1946–68

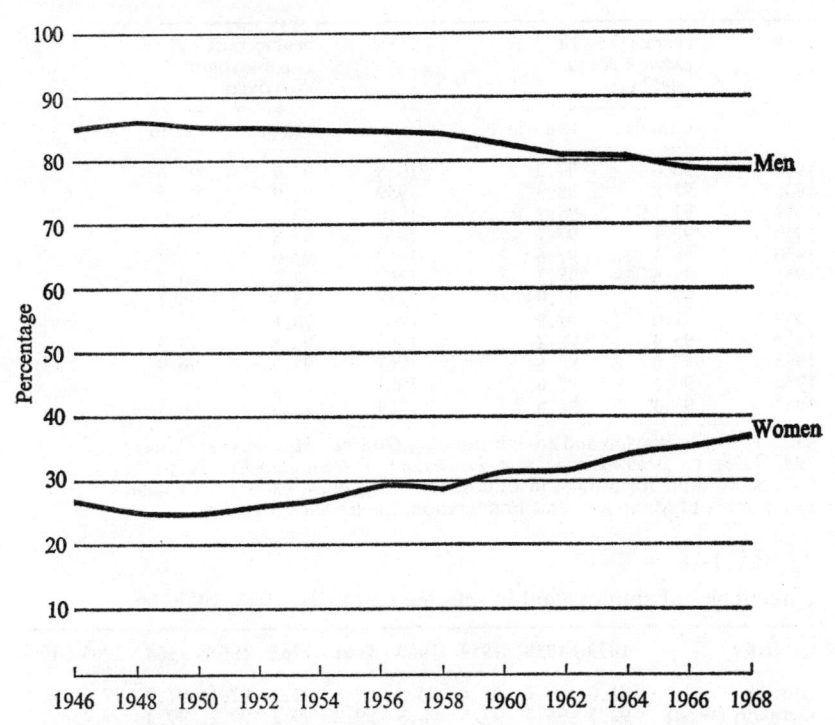

most of the period hovering around 2 or 3, rose to a high point of 5.2 in 1958, 1960, and 1961. Economic difficulties during this period also show up in Table 1-17, which gives the percentage, not of the whole population over a certain age, but of the labour force, who were employed. The same table shows that Ontario uniformly had a higher percentage of the labour force employed than did Canada as a whole. This fact is considered to be an effective refutation of the claim, heard with decreasing frequency, that immigrants take jobs away from the native population. Unemployment among women has been negligible throughout the period.

The period of high unemployment at the beginning of the 1960s saw the initiation of the Federal-Provincial Technical and Vocational Training Agreement, which included, in Program 5, an attempt to improve existing arrangements for enhancing the employability of those without jobs. Considerable apprehension was expressed at that time that unemployment would be a problem of ever-increasing proportions because of the changes resulting from automation. The apparent improvement after that must be explained in part, as we have seen, by the greatly increased retention rate of educational institutions. While it would of course be impossible to say how many of those who remained in school could not have found work

TABLE 1-17
Percentages of labour force employed in Canada and Ontario, 1946-69

YEAR	PERCENTAGE OF LABOUR FORCE EMPLOYED		YEAR	PERCENTAGE OF LABOUR FORCE EMPLOYED	
	Canada	Ontario		Canada	Ontario
1946	96.6	97.2	1958	92.9	94.6
1947	97.8	98.3	1959	94.0	95.5
1948	97.7	98.3	1960	93.0	94.6
1949	97.1	97.7	1961	92.8	94.5
1950	96.4	97.6	1962	94.0	95.7
1951	97.6	98.3	1963	94.5	96.2
1952	97.1	97.9	1964	95.3	96.7
1953	97.0	97.9	1965	96.1	97.5
1954	95.4	96.2	1966	96.4	97.5
1955	95.6	96.8	1967	95.9	96.9
1956	96.6	97.6	1968	95.2	96.5
1957	95.4	96.6	1969	95.3	96.8

SOURCE: Cecily Watson and Joseph Butorac, *Qualified Manpower in Ontario 1961-1986*, I: *Determination and Projection of Basic Stocks* (Toronto: Ontario Institute for Studies in Education, 1968), p. 24, Table 13; Canada, Department of Manpower and Immigration, *Immigration Statistics*.

TABLE 1-18
Percentages of employment in selected countries, 1953, 1958-66

COUNTRY	1953	1958	1959	1960	1961	1962	1963	1964	1965	1966
Austria	91.0	94.9	95.4	96.5	97.3	97.3	97.1	97.3	97.3	97.5
Germany (West)	92.5	96.5	97.6	98.8	99.2	99.3	99.2	99.3	99.4	99.3
Italy	91.2	93.4	94.4	95.8	96.5	97.0	97.5	97.3	96.4	96.1
Japan	98.7	98.6	98.5	98.9	99.0	99.1	99.1	99.2	99.2	99.1
Kenya				96.2	95.2	97.7	94.9	91.9	92.3	92.6	92.9
United Kingdom	98.3	98.0	97.8	98.4	98.5	98.0	97.6	98.2	98.5	98.5
United States	97.1	93.2	94.5	94.5	93.3	94.5	94.3	94.8	95.5	96.2

SOURCE: United Nations, *Statistical Yearbook: 1967* (19th ed.; New York, 1968).

had they joined the labour force at an earlier age, the role of the schools and colleges as unemployment relief agencies should not be discounted.

The employment situation in Canada in general and in Ontario in particular may be appraised in relation to the experience of other countries. Table 1-18 shows employment rates for Austria, West Germany, Italy, Japan, Kenya, the United Kingdom, and the United States for 1953 and 1958-66. During the 1950s the first three of these had not entirely recovered from the effects of the war, but during the 1960s they all had uniformly high employment rates. In West Germany, as in the United Kingdom, and more particularly in Japan, unemployment has been a negligible factor. The situation in the United States has been more like that of Ontario, with unemployment varying between a little less than 3 per cent to a little less than 7. Kenya, an example of a country at an earlier stage of development, has had somewhat higher rates.

TABLE 1-19

Percentages of Ontario labour force by occupational groups, 1951 and 1961

OCCUPATIONAL GROUP	1951	1961
Professional	7.5	10.0
Proprietary and managerial	8.0	8.1
Clerical	13.0	14.7
Financial	0.7	1.0
Commercial	6.3	7.2
Service	9.5	12.4
personal	6.8	9.3
Agricultural	10.8	7.2
Fishing, hunting, and trapping	0.2	0.1
Logging	0.9	0.5
Mining and quarrying	1.1	1.1
Manufacturing and mechanical	21.4	18.4
Construction	5.5	5.0
Transportation	7.3	6.9
Labouring	6.8	5.1
Not stated	1.0	2.3

SOURCE: DBS, *Census of Canada*, 1961, *Historical Tables*, Volume 3, 1-1, Table 3.

Dependable statistics on the distribution of the labour force among various occupations are obtained only during each decennial census. The figures in Table 1-19 apply only to 1951 and 1961. The information is thus of only moderate value for understanding the current period. It is fairly reasonable to assume, however, that the trends in most of the occupational categories continued during or throughout the decade of the sixties.

In 1951 the largest groups were in manufacturing and mechanical, and in clerical, service, and agricultural occupations. By 1961 the proportion in the professional had exceeded that in the agricultural occupations. Between the two census years the major increases were in the professional and service occupations, while definite decreases were registered in agricultural, fishing, hunting, trapping, logging, manufacturing and mechanical, transportation, and labouring occupations.

STATUS OF IMMIGRANTS IN THE LABOUR FORCE

The percentages of immigrants entering the labour force in Ontario each year between 1956 and 1968 are shown in Table 1-20. These figures varied from a high of 53.8 in 1956 to a low of 47.9 in 1961, rising again to 53.1 in 1967. During the same period, the comparable percentage for the entire population, as shown in Table 1-15, never rose above 40 until 1968.

Table 1-21 shows the distribution of working immigrants to Ontario by intended occupational groups between 1946 and 1968. There is of course no way of determining what occupations they actually settled into, but it is commonly assumed that most of them did as they intended. Since the

TABLE 1-20
Percentages of immigrants entering the labour force in Ontario, 1956–68

YEAR	PERCENTAGE ENTERING LABOUR FORCE
1956	53.8
1957	52.0
1958	49.5
1959	49.2
1960	50.7
1961	47.9
1962	48.3
1963	48.5
1964	48.9
1965	49.6
1966	49.4
1967	53.1
1968	52.0

SOURCE: Canada, Department of Manpower and Immigration, *Immigration Statistics*.

occupational categories are defined somewhat differently from those in Table 1-19, only very general comparisons can be made with the occupational distribution of the labour force in the population as a whole. Despite such difficulties, some useful comparisons are possible. The percentages of immigrants by intended occupation over the 1946–52 period may be examined in relation to the occupational distribution of the working population in 1951. This comparison shows considerably fewer of the immigrants going into professional and technical occupations than the 7.5 per cent of the working population counted as professionals. Only a negligible proportion of the immigrants planned to enter managerial and official occupations as compared with 8.0 per cent of the working population in proprietary and managerial positions. Clerical and financial occupations claimed about twice the proportion of the general population as of the immigrant group. By the same comparison, service and transportation occupations were attracting relatively few immigrants. On the other hand, over twice the proportion of immigrants were headed for agriculture, fishing, and logging as were thus occupied in the general population, and a relatively large proportion were drawn to construction and unskilled labour. The percentage of the immigrants planning to go into manufacturing and mechanical occupations was 24.2, as compared with the population percentage of 21.4.

Comparisons on the basis of the situation in 1961 show some considerable changes. The proportion of working immigrants in professional and technical occupations was much higher than the proportion of the general population. The percentage destined for managerial and official occupations had risen to 2.4. The proportions of the two groups in clerical and

TABLE 1-21
Percentages of immigrants to Ontario by intended occupational groups, 1946–68[a]

OCCUPATIONAL GROUP	1946–52	1953–55	1956	1957	1958	1959	1960	1961	1962	1963	1964	1965	1966	1967	1968
Professional and technical	3.9	10.0	9.8	10.1	10.2	11.2	11.9	16.8	20.7	19.3	18.5	18.4	19.7	22.5	27.5
engineers	0.8	2.2	1.8	1.9	1.4	1.2	1.1	1.3	2.5	2.6	2.4	2.4	2.8	2.8	2.8
health professionals	1.9	0.9	1.0	0.9	1.4	1.5	1.8	2.7	8.0	7.4	6.0	5.2	4.9	5.3	6.8
teachers		2.7	2.7	2.8	3.3	3.9	3.8	5.4	3.0	2.7	3.0	3.2	3.3	4.5	6.6
others									2.4	2.0	2.0	2.0	2.3	2.8	3.6
Managerial and official	6.9	1.7	0.9	0.7	1.5	1.4	1.5	2.4	2.9	2.5	2.1	2.0	2.0	2.2	2.0
Clerical		9.2	11.7	12.7	10.9	10.5	11.4	13.0	14.0	13.9	13.8	13.4	13.3	13.9	13.6
Finance		0.2	0.3	0.3	0.3	0.3	0.2	0.2	0.5	0.2	0.1	0.2	0.2	0.3	0.5
Sales	4.2	3.6	4.4	4.8	3.3	3.8	4.1	3.5	3.0	3.1	3.3	3.3	3.2	2.5	2.8
Service	5.9	13.5	13.6	11.0	17.4	17.3	15.7	18.1	15.6	12.6	10.7	9.8	8.0	8.7	9.8
Agriculture, fishing, logging	22.3	13.4	8.2	6.7	8.5	10.1	10.6	6.8	4.9	4.9	3.9	3.3	3.4	2.9	2.5
Mining	1.7	0.4	1.4	1.2	0.6	0.5	1.2	0.3	0.3	0.3	0.2	0.2	0.3	0.2	0.4
Manufacturing and mechanical	24.2	21.0	22.2	26.0	17.9	15.6	17.4	16.2	19.6	24.1	23.8	25.0	26.7	24.4	25.7
Construction	9.1	10.0	10.9	11.3	9.3	8.2	8.2	7.5	7.8	8.7	9.4	10.0	10.8	9.8	9.4
Transportation	2.4	1.8	1.6	2.3	1.2	1.3	1.5	1.1	1.0	0.9	1.0	1.2	1.3	1.0	0.8
Communications		0.5	0.8	0.9	0.6	0.5	0.7	0.5	0.4	0.4	0.4	0.4	0.5	0.4	0.4
Unskilled labourers	11.8	13.6	13.7	11.5	17.5	18.6	15.1	13.4	9.1	8.9	12.2	12.2	9.6	9.9	4.5
Occupation not stated	7.6	1.1	0.5	0.5	0.8	0.7	0.5	0.2	0.2	0.2	0.6	0.6	1.0	1.3	0.1
TOTAL	100.0	100.0	100.0	100.0	100.0	100.0	100.0	100.0	100.0	100.0	100.0	100.0	100.0	100.0	100.0

Calculated from figures supplied by Canada, Department of Manpower and Immigration, *Immigration Statistics*.

financial occupations were approaching equality. Agriculture, fishing, and logging had ceased to attract a disproportionate number of immigrants, although construction and unskilled labour continued to do so. The percentages headed for the last two categories were 7.5 and 13.4 respectively, as compared with 5.0 and 5.1 of the general population. Only 1.1 per cent of immigrants planned to enter transportation occupations, where 6.9 per cent of the labour force were engaged. The percentage of immigrants headed for manufacturing and mechanical occupations was now below that of the general population, although it rose considerably after 1961.

LANGUAGE

While changes in the distribution of the population by mother tongue are not entirely attributable to the rate of immigration and the sources from which the immigrants come, there is, of course, a close relationship between the two. Table 1-22 shows the situation, both for the entire population and for various age groups, in the census years 1941, 1951, and 1961. Those who claimed English as their mother tongue remained a fairly constant percentage between 1941 and 1951, and then declined during the next ten-year interval from 81.7 per cent to 77.5 per cent. The level of immigration from Britain, which was higher during the immediate postwar period than in more recent years, helps to explain the maintenance of the earlier language balance until after 1951. The proportion whose mother tongue is English has presumably continued to decline since 1961. During the twenty-year period covered by the table, the percentage claiming French as their mother tongue declined from 7.6 to 6.8, a proportionately greater decrease than that for English.

Among the various age groups there are two main patterns for those claiming English as their mother tongue. Up to age nineteen, the percentage rose substantially between 1941 and 1951, and then fell by 1961, but remained higher than in 1941. Above nineteen, there was a regular and substantial decline from 1941 through 1951 to 1961. The decline in those whose mother tongue was French was largely manifested in the younger age groups rather than in the older, and was in evidence between 1941 and 1951, even when the over-all percentage for all age groups remained relatively constant. The recent extension of opportunities for education in French cannot, of course, affect the identity of a child's mother tongue but may be expected to prevent some school-age young people from abandoning French as the language of the home, and thus ensure that their children claim it as a mother tongue.

The percentage of those of all ages whose mother tongue was other than English or French declined slightly between 1941 and 1951, and then rose by about 44 per cent in the next ten years. The change was very pronounced between the ages of twenty-five and thirty-four, corresponding to the large percentage of immigrants in that group. The percentage speaking "other" languages also rose very sharply among those presumed to be the

TABLE 1-22
Percentages of population of Ontario by mother tongue and age, 1941-61

AGE GROUP	1941 MOTHER TONGUE			1951 MOTHER TONGUE			1961 MOTHER TONGUE		
	English	French	Other	English	French	Other	English	French	Other
0-4	81.1	10.5	8.4	87.2	7.7	5.1	83.2	6.5	10.3
5-9	80.2	10.2	9.6	85.2	8.8	6.0	84.3	6.6	9.1
10-14	80.2	9.5	10.3	83.3	9.2	7.5	82.9	6.8	10.3
15-19	79.8	9.0	11.2	81.0	9.4	9.6	80.6	8.2	11.2
20-24	81.4	8.3	10.3	79.3	9.0	11.7	73.6	8.6	17.8
25-34	80.9	7.7	11.4	79.4	7.8	12.8	69.6	7.7	22.7
35-44	77.1	6.6	16.3	79.8	7.1	13.1	72.8	6.8	20.4
45-54	80.9	5.7	13.4	76.6	6.2	17.2	75.4	6.5	18.1
55-64	84.9	5.1	10.0	81.3	5.4	13.3	74.0	5.8	20.2
65-69	87.1	5.3	7.6	84.4	5.0	10.6	79.0	5.2	15.8
70 and over	88.5	4.9	6.6	87.8	4.7	7.5	84.0	4.7	11.3
TOTAL	81.1	7.6	11.3	81.7	7.4	10.9	77.5	6.8	15.7

SOURCE: DBS, *Census of Canada*, 1941, 1951, and 1961.

CHART 1-6
Ontario population by mother tongue, 1941–61

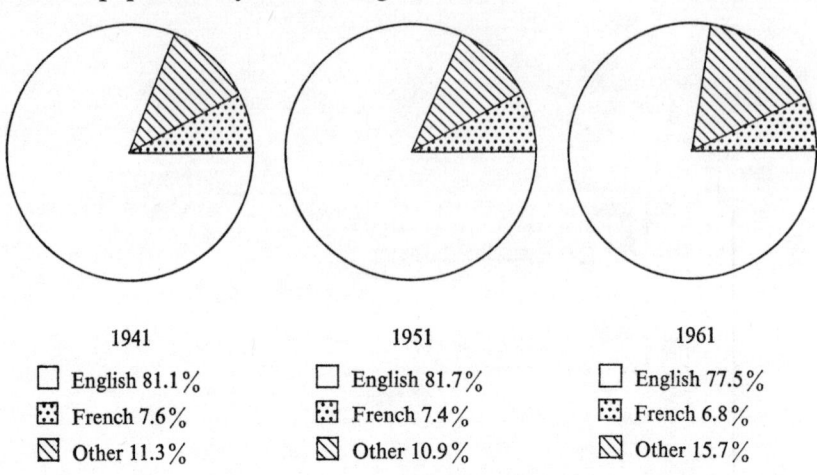

1941	1951	1961
☐ English 81.1%	☐ English 81.7%	☐ English 77.5%
▦ French 7.6%	▦ French 7.4%	▦ French 6.8%
▧ Other 11.3%	▧ Other 10.9%	▧ Other 15.7%

children of the same group, more than doubling below age five, and increasing by 50 per cent among those between five and nine.

EDUCATIONAL LEVEL

Statistics on the educational level of the population of Ontario have been scanty. Table 1-23 gives, for 1960 and 1965, the percentage in five age groups in three categories of educational achievement: those who had completed elementary school or less, those who had completed some high school, and those who had completed high school or gone further. Two types of comparisons may be made: among age groups and between years. There was a very substantial difference between the extreme age groups, representing a span of approximately fifty years. While 20.8 per cent of the fourteen-to-nineteen-year group had gone no further than the end of elementary school in 1960, no fewer than 70.6 per cent of those aged sixty-five and over fell in the same category. Five years later the comparable percentages were 16.4 and 67.1. For the intervening age groups, the percentage fell steadily. Among those from fourteen to nineteen, between four and five times as many had some high school education in both 1960 and 1965 as in the sixty-five-and-over group. The third educational level category is not really valid for the youngest age group, since those in the earlier part of the age range would hardly have had a chance to complete high school, much less go beyond. Among those aged twenty to twenty-four, 30.0 per cent fell into this category in 1960, as compared with 14.3 per cent of those sixty-five and over; in 1965 the respective percentages were 35.1 and 15.2. Evidently there was more change among the three educational levels in the lower age groups than there was in the higher between 1960 and 1965.

TABLE 1-23
Population of Ontario 14 years of age and over by age and level of education, 1960 and 1965 (numbers in thousands)

LEVEL OF EDUCATION	YEAR	AGE GROUP 14-19 No.	Per cent	20-24 No.	Per cent	25-44 No.	Per cent	45-64 No.	Per cent	65 and over No.	Per cent
Completed elementary school or less	1960	105	20.8	99	26.2	597	35.7	595	54.3	326	70.6
	1965	109	16.4	69	16.4	534	31.4	575	46.6	337	67.1
Some high school	1960	358	70.9	165	43.8	641	38.3	272	24.8	70	15.1
	1965	516	77.8	204	48.3	704	41.5	374	30.3	89	17.7
Completed high school or more	1960	42	8.3	113	30.0	436	26.0	228	20.8	66	14.3
	1965	37	5.6	148	35.1	461	27.1	285	23.1	76	15.2
TOTAL	1960	505	100.0	377	100.0	1,674	100.0	1,095	100.0	462	100.0
	1965	663	100.0	422	100.0	1,698	100.0	1,233	100.0	502	100.0

SOURCE: DBS (71-505), *Special Labour Force Studies*, No. 1.

Table 1-24 indicates the educational level of the population by sex for the same two years. In both years the level was higher for the females in the three basic categories. For 1965, however, the percentage of males who had some university education or a degree was 10.2 as compared with 6.9 for females. At lower educational levels the discrepancy between the sexes narrowed somewhat between 1960 and 1965.

Comparisons are often made between the educational level of the population of the United States and that of Canada, to the latter's considerable disadvantage. The situation as it existed in 1965 is shown in Table 1-25. It may come as a surprise to many people, who assume that Canada had been rapidly catching up before that time, that there was a much greater difference in the proportion at the lowest educational level in the younger age groups of the respective countries than there was in the higher age groups. Approximately three times as many Canadians as Americans between twenty and twenty-four years of age had gone no further than the end of elementary school, while the respective percentages of those aged sixty-five and over were 69.7 and 63.7, and of those aged fifty-five to sixty-four, 61.1 and 45.7.

In the twenty-to-twenty-four-year age group, 18.7 per cent of Americans had some high school education or less, as compared with 37.5 per cent of Canadians. This discrepancy progressively narrowed from one age group to another until the respective percentages reached 20.6 and 18.3 in the fifty-five-to-sixty-four age group. Among those between twenty and twenty-four, 24.1 per cent of Canadians had a complete high school education or less as compared with 44.3 per cent of Americans. This discrepancy increased in the next higher age group, and then declined only moderately up to age sixty-four. In almost all of the age groups, more than twice as many Americans as Canadians had some university education or a university degree.

It would of course be a mistake to apply these findings indiscriminately to Ontario in 1970. At least in the youngest age groups, the difference in favour of the Americans should have been substantially reduced. On the other hand, discrepancies in the higher age groups will probably remain for decades, despite the best that adult education programs can do. Those responsible for such programs might well look upon the situation as a challenge calling for a supreme effort.

GEOGRAPHICAL DISTRIBUTION

Chart 1-7 shows the population densities in various zones of the province in 1966, and thus gives a rough indication of where the most serious problems of isolation are found. It is evident that, quite apart from urban concentrations, the great imbalance in settlement constitutes one of the major difficulties in providing for educational services and in coming as close as possible to the realization of equal opportunity for all.

As indicated on the map, the areas of greatest population density are

TABLE 1-24
Population of Ontario 14 years of age and over by sex and level of education, 1960 and 1965 (numbers in thousands)

LEVEL OF EDUCATION	1960 MALE No.	Per cent	FEMALE No.	Per cent	TOTAL No.	Per cent	1965 MALE No.	Per cent	FEMALE No.	Per cent	TOTAL No.	Per cent
Completed elementary school or less	903	44.5	819	39.3	1,722	41.9	843	37.9	780	34.0	1,623	35.9
Some high school	717	35.3	789	37.9	1,506	36.6	912	41.0	974	42.5	1,886	41.8
Completed high school	234	11.5	361	17.3	595	14.5	242	10.9	380	16.6	622	13.8
Some university education or degree	177	8.7	113	5.5	290	7.0	228	10.2	158	6.9	386	8.5
Completed high school or more	411	20.2	474	22.8	885	21.5	470	21.2	538	23.5	1,008	22.3
TOTAL	2,031	100.0	2,082	100.0	4,113	100.0	2,225	100.0	2,292	100.0	4,517	100.0

SOURCE: DBS (71-505), *Special Labour Force Studies*, No. 1.

TABLE 1-25
Comparison of certain age groups in Canada and the United States by percentage at each level of education, 1965

| AGE GROUP | COUNTRY | LEVEL OF EDUCATION ||||||||||||
| | | Completed elementary school or less ||| Some high school ||| Completed high school ||| Some university or university degree |||
		M	F	Total	M	F	Total	M	F	Total	M	F	Total
20-24	Canada	25.1	21.9	23.5	37.6	37.2	37.5	18.8	29.4	24.1	18.5	11.5	14.9
	US	9.3	6.7	8.0	17.7	19.6	18.7	39.0	49.1	44.3	34.0	24.6	29.0
25-34	Canada	37.5	31.7	34.5	33.8	36.6	35.3	15.8	22.5	19.2	12.9	9.2	11.0
	US	14.4	12.4	13.3	17.1	20.0	18.6	38.9	47.1	43.2	29.6	20.5	24.9
35-44	Canada	42.7	39.2	40.9	31.2	32.4	31.8	14.1	21.2	17.7	12.0	7.2	9.6
	US	22.2	17.6	19.8	19.8	20.6	20.2	32.2	44.3	38.6	25.8	17.5	21.4
45-54	Canada	49.9	44.1	47.0	26.2	30.5	28.4	13.6	18.4	16.0	10.3	7.0	8.6
	US	32.9	28.5	30.7	20.1	19.9	20.0	27.9	35.9	32.0	19.1	15.7	17.3
55-64	Canada	63.2	58.9	61.1	19.4	21.8	20.6	9.3	13.6	11.4	8.1	5.7	6.9
	US	48.8	42.9	45.7	18.0	18.6	18.3	17.9	23.6	20.9	15.3	14.9	15.1
65 and over	Canada	72.6	67.1	69.7	13.9	16.4	15.2	7.8	12.3	10.2	5.7	4.2	4.9
	US	67.4	60.8	63.7	10.5	13.8	12.4	11.5	14.8	13.3	10.6	10.6	10.6

SOURCE: DBS (71-505), *Special Labour Force Studies*.

Characteristics of the Ontario population 79

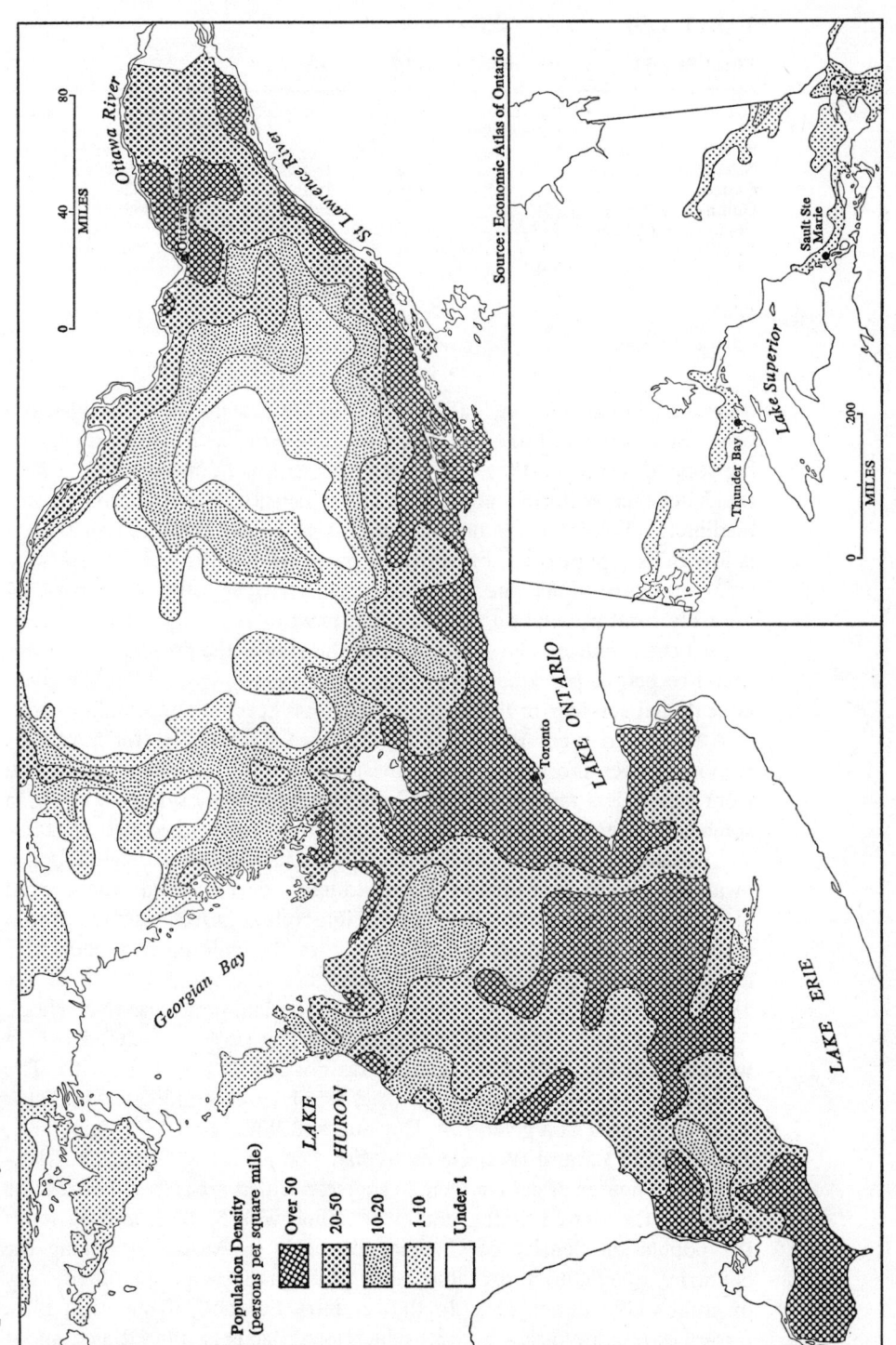

Population density in Ontario, 1966

Population Density (persons per square mile)
- Over 50
- 20-50
- 10-20
- 1-10
- Under 1

Source: Economic Atlas of Ontario

TABLE 1-26

Population density in selected countries, 1966

COUNTRY	INHABITANTS PER SQUARE KM.	COUNTRY	INHABITANTS PER SQUARE KM.
Australia	2	Ireland (Northern)	105
Canada	2	Italy	172
China (Mainland)	74	Japan	267
England and Wales	318	Kenya	17
France	90	Scotland	66
Germany (East)	158	USA	21
Germany (West)	232	USSR	10
India	164		

SOURCE: UNESCO, *Statistical Yearbook: 1967* (5th ed.; Paris, 1968).

a small area in the Ottawa Valley, including Ottawa, and much of the shore of the St Lawrence, Lake Ontario, and Lake Erie, with stretches extending some distance north of Toronto as far as Lake Simcoe and north of the Kitchener-Waterloo area. The lower density of population in immediately adjoining areas does not necessarily mean that the countryside is less thickly populated, but in some cases reflects the absence of large cities and towns. As one proceeds north, however, the proportion of the truly rural population declines, and most of the people are clustered in the urban centres. The greater part of the area of the province has fewer than two people per square mile. The provision of anything like adequate educational services in the north has at times seemed almost impossible.

Attempts to meet the needs of this area have called forth varying responses over the years. The provision of daily transportation to and from school is a matter of major importance to many school boards. In some cases where such a solution is out of the question because of excessive distance or cost, assistance has had to be supplied for room and board away from home. For many years up to half a dozen railway cars moved along the northern lines, offering brief intervals of direct instruction as a respite from long periods of home study for the children of section men and trappers. Departmental correspondence courses appeared in the 1920s, in part to serve the needs of those who had no access to a school.

The problem of meeting the needs of a few people scattered over a wide area is one that many nations do not have to contend with. The population density of certain countries as of 1966 is indicated in Table 1-26. In an area of a given size, England and Wales had 159 inhabitants, Japan had 133.5 and West Germany had 116 for every Canadian. Overall density figures of course include sparsely settled areas in countries like the USSR, the United States, and even China, with 5, 10.5, and 37 times the population density of Canada. But only in Australia, among the countries referred to in the table, is the problem of low population density of comparable dimensions. In that country the lack of sufficient local resources in many areas to meet educational needs is offered as a major reason for the establishment of a centralized educational system. Recent moves to decentralize control in Ontario have had to be modified to allow for the special situation in the north.

Population shifts and varying rates of population growth have meant an uneven distribution of the burden of maintaining educational facilities. Areas of slow growth, population stability, or even population loss have been left with comparatively little apparent need for further accommodation. Many a rural community has been slow to abandon its small schools in favour of central facilities that could provide a much better quality of service simply because of the existence of what appeared to be perfectly adequate buildings. Also, in the central core of certain urban areas as, for example, in the city of Toronto, older buildings have served long after they have begun to act as a serious hindrance to educational progress because the newly settled suburbs, with no schools at all, have demanded priority. Because so many communities have been able to begin with a relatively clean slate, the way has been left open for many innovations that might not otherwise have been possible. While new approaches in buildings are not always accompanied by improved education, there is likely to be a positive relationship between the two.

Population shifts have had a considerable influence on educational finance. It has been found necessary to allow for the "growth need" factor in administering the system of provincial grants to school boards. While variations in wealth among communities would call for compensating grants to equalize opportunity even in a relatively stable and immobile population, the major population shifts in recent years have undoubtedly greatly strengthened the need for provincial intervention.

The extent of the population growth in counties and "census divisions," or territorial districts, is shown in Table 1-27. The actual population of the counties was an important consideration when these units were chosen as the basis for the school divisions established in 1969. Their extreme variations in population constituted one of the disadvantages associated with the decision. The differences in their rate of growth promise to make these variations even more extreme in the future. For example, Haliburton County, with the smallest population, has tended to change very little since 1941. On the other hand, Waterloo County, which had the largest population of any county without a separate urban board of education within its borders, grew from about 99,000 to about 217,000, or by approximately 119 per cent, between 1941 and 1966.

The relative extent of population growth in the counties and districts between 1941 and 1966 is shown in Chart 1-8. These units are categorized in four growth-rate groups according to whether the rate was 1 / less than 10 per cent, 2 / between 10 and 40 per cent, 3 / between 50 and 99 per cent, and 4 / 100 per cent or more. Those in the first group, comprising the counties of Bruce, Dundas, Glengarry, Grey, and Prescott, and the territorial districts of Manitoulin, Parry Sound, and Timiskaming,

TABLE 1-27
Population of Ontario by county or census division, 1941–66 (numbers in thousands)

COUNTY OR CENSUS DIVISION	1941	1951	1956	1961	1966	COUNTY OR CENSUS DIVISION	1941	1951	1956	1961	1966
Algoma	52	64	82	111	114	Muskoka	22	25	25	27	28
Brant	57	73	78	84	91	Nipissing	43	51	60	70	74
Bruce	42	41	42	43	43	Norfolk	36	43	46	50	51
Carleton	202	242	283	353	407	Northumberland	31	33	38	42	45
Cochrane	81	84	87	96	97	Ontario	66	87	108	136	171
Dufferin	14	15	16	16	17	Oxford	51	59	65	70	76
Dundas	16	16	17	17	17	Parry Sound	30	27	28	30	28
Durham	25	30	36	40	45	Peel	32	56	83	112	172
Elgin	46	55	59	63	62	Perth	50	53	55	57	60
Essex	174	217	247	258	281	Peterborough	47	61	68	76	82
Frontenac	54	66	77	88	97	Prescott	25	26	26	27	27
Glengarry	19	18	19	19	18	Prince Edward	17	19	21	21	22
Grenville	16	17	21	23	23	Rainy River	19	22	25	27	26
Grey	57	59	61	62	63	Renfrew	55	67	78	90	89
Haldimand	22	24	26	28	30	Russell	17	18	19	21	21
Haliburton	7	8	8	9	8	Simcoe	87	106	127	141	149
Halton	28	44	68	107	141	Stormont	41	48	56	58	60
Hastings	63	74	84	93	94	Sudbury	81	110	142	166	174
Huron	44	49	52	54	54	Thunder Bay	85	105	123	138	144
Kenora	33	39	47	52	54	Timiskaming	51	50	50	51	47
Kent	66	79	85	89	96	Victoria	26	27	28	30	31
Lambton	57	75	90	102	108	Waterloo	99	126	149	177	217
Lanark	33	36	38	40	41	Welland	94	123	150	165	179
Leeds	36	39	43	47	49	Wellington	59	67	76	85	94
Lennox and Addington	18	20	22	24	25	Wentworth	207	266	316	359	394
Lincoln	65	89	112	127	146	York	952	1,177	1,441	1,733	2,018
Manitoulin	11	11	11	11	11						
Middlesex	127	162	191	221	250	Total Ontario	3,788	4,598	5,405	6,236	6,961

SOURCE: DBS, *Census of Canada*, 1941, 1956, and 1966.

Characteristics of the Ontario population 83

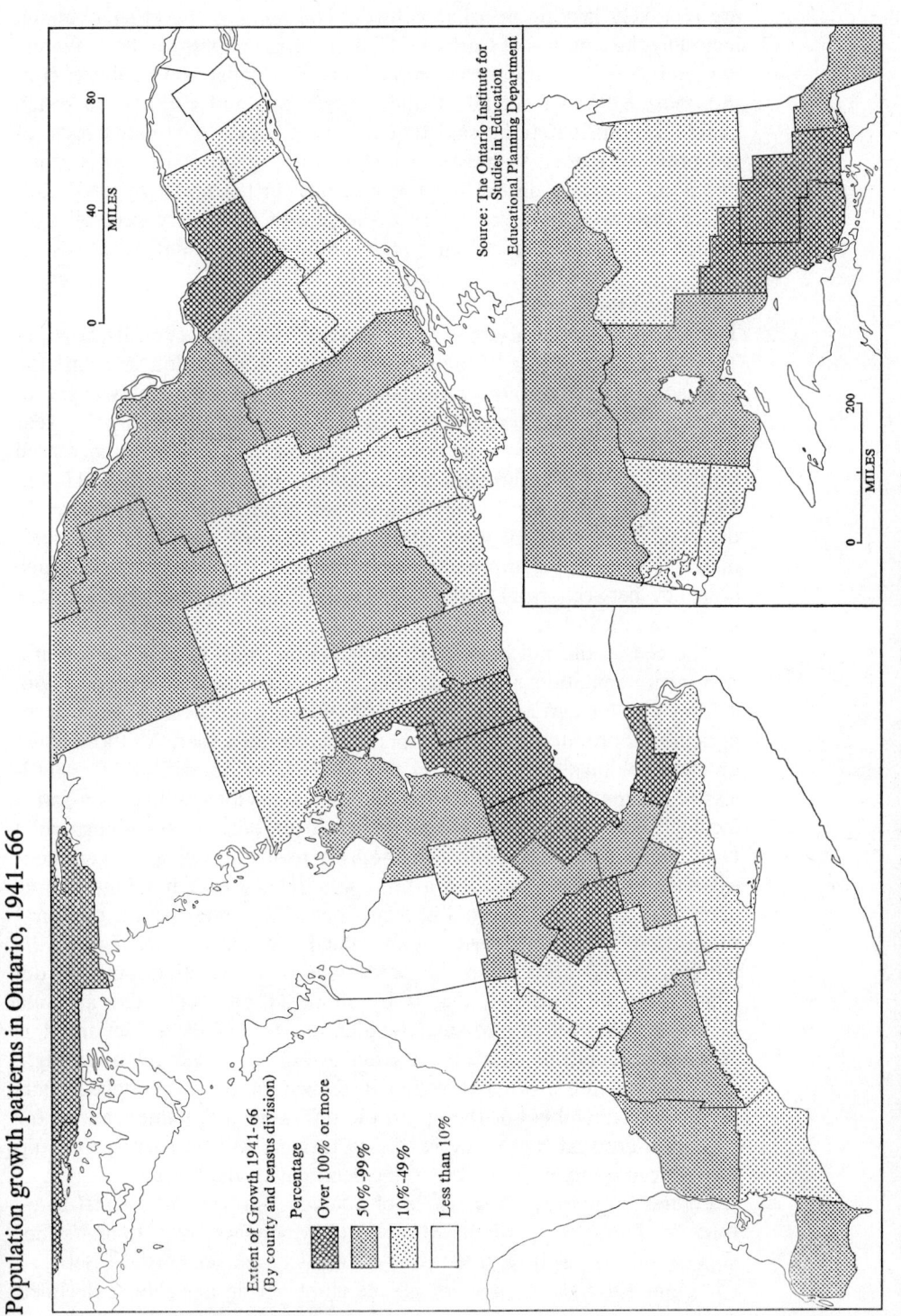

Population growth patterns in Ontario, 1941–66

Extent of Growth 1941-66
(By county and census division)
Percentage
- Over 100% or more
- 50%-99%
- 10%-49%
- Less than 10%

Source: The Ontario Institute for Studies in Education Educational Planning Department

NOTE: The names of the counties and territorial districts are shown on Chart 1-10, on page 90.

are relatively lacking in urban centres. The units at the other extreme, including the counties of Carleton, Halton, Lincoln, Ontario, Peel, Waterloo, and York, and the territorial districts of Algoma and Sudbury, contain most, although not all, of the larger towns and cities. As a rough generalization, it may be said that the most heavily populated parts of the province tended to have the highest rates of growth. This is really just a commentary on the rural-urban shift. In the northern territories, where the population was sparsest, the growth rates were generally, although not always, higher than in the southern rural counties.

THE RURAL-URBAN SHIFT

The extent of the rural-urban shift between 1941 and 1966 is shown in Table 1-28. According to the Census of Canada definition, the "urban" classification includes the population of cities, towns, and villages of 1,000 and over, whether incorporated or not. During the twenty-five year period, the percentage of the population in the urban category increased from 61.7 to 80.4. The shift was relatively greater between 1941 and 1951 than in subsequent years. In absolute numbers the actual decline in the rural population between 1941 and 1966 was only from approximately 1,449,000 to approximately 1,368,000; that is, the growing discrepancy between rural and urban populations was due largely to the increase in the latter.

The census did not distinguish between the rural farm and the rural non-farm populations until 1956. For census purposes in 1961 and 1966, a farm was an agricultural holding of one or more acres with sales of agricultural products of $50 or more in the previous year. All those living on such holdings were placed in the "rural farm" classification, regardless of occupation. Thus the population considered to be living on farms included some who derived their income from other occupations, while farm operators who lived in neighbouring towns and villages were considered to be urban. In 1956 a farm was defined as a holding of three acres or more in size or a holding from one to three acres with agricultural production during the previous year valued at $250 or more. During the ten-year period after 1956 the percentage of the farm population declined from 11.7 to 6.9, that is by about 41 per cent. The absolute decrease was from approximately 632,000 to 482,000. The trend is expected to continue, since the average age of farmers is relatively high, and the application of technology will reduce the need for replacements as the older members of the group die off. Among the implications for education are that higher levels of skill training will be needed to equip the reduced number of farmers in the economy of the future.

Figures applying to the whole of Canada, supplied in an article by John R. Nicholson, federal Minister of Manpower and Immigration, indicate the nation-wide trend over a somewhat longer period.[2] Between 1948 and 1964 the number of people employed in agriculture declined

TABLE 1-28
Rural and urban population trends in Ontario, 1941–66 (numbers in thousands)

YEAR	RURAL FARM		RURAL NON-FARM		TOTAL RURAL		URBAN		TOTAL	
	No.	Per cent	No.	Per cent	No.	Per cent	No.	Per cent	No.	Per cent
1941					1,449	38.3	2,339	61.7	3,788	100.0
1951					1,222	26.6	3,376	73.4	4,598	100.0
1956	632	11.7	670	12.4	1,302	24.1	4,103	75.9	5,405	100.0
1961	506	8.1	907	14.5	1,413	22.7	4,824	77.3	6,237	100.0
1966	482	6.9	886	12.7	1,368	19.6	5,593	80.4	6,961	100.0

SOURCE: DBS, *Census of Canada*, 1941, 1956, and 1966.

from 1,095,000 to 628,000. That is, about 30,000 individuals were leaving agricultural employment each year.

The rural-urban migration has presented two major types of problems: those involving the provision of physical facilities for new urban and suburban communities and those involving the creation of educational programs that meet the needs of a predominantly urban population. In some respects the problems have been completely unlike those in many of the underdeveloped or semi-developed countries. These latter often present the most striking contrasts between the complex organization and sophisticated way of life in the cities and the primitive existence of the villages. Those who move from the villages to the cities face what is almost a different world. They must learn how to use all the amenities of city life, how to take advantage of transportation systems, and how to express, and even to identify, their need for health, educational, and recreational services. A move from the countryside or a small village in Ontario does require some readjustments but, while there is no close counterpart in the city to actual farm work, in many cases the transfer does not even call for a change in occupation. Although the entire urban population faces great problems in adapting to changing environmental conditions, those of non-urban origin, with some exceptions, are not at an extreme disadvantage.

Ontario urban centres grew at varying rates between 1941 and 1966, the latest year for which population figures could be obtained at the time of writing. The relevant information for forty of the largest incorporated centres, as well as Metropolitan Toronto, is shown in Table 1-29. During the twenty-five year span so many of the centres had their boundaries changed that it is impossible to make any exact comparisons of their rate of population growth. But it is evident from a glance at the figures that a large proportion of them at least doubled their population. In many cases the rate of growth was relatively modest until 1951 or 1956, and then accelerated quickly. In others the increase has been relatively steady. Metropolitan Toronto's expansion took place in the suburbs while at times the city itself lost population. The growth in Burlington, where boundary changes obscure the situation somewhat, reflects the overflow from Hamilton, the second largest city in the province. Oakville's location within commuting distance of Toronto accounts for much of its phenomenal growth.

INCOME

Ontario's post-war educational expansion has occurred during a period of steadily increasing provincial and per capita personal income. Provincial income rose from approximately $3,656 million in 1945 to an estimated $24,900 million in 1969, or by over 581 per cent, as shown in Table 1-30. Between 1945 and 1969 per capita annual income rose from $914 to about $3,341, or by over 266 per cent. The rate of increase was

TABLE 1-29
Population in largest urban units in Ontario, 1941-66 (numbers in thousands)

URBAN UNIT	1941	1951	1956	1961	1966	URBAN UNIT	1941	1951	1956	1961	1966
Barrie	10	13	17	21	24[a]	Ottawa	155	202	222	268	291
Belleville	16	20	21	31	33	Owen Sound	14	16	17	17[a]	18
Brantford	32	37	52[a]	55[a]	60[a]	Pembroke	11	12	15	17[a]	16
Brockville	11	12	14[a]	18[a]	19	Peterborough	25	38	43[a]	47[a]	56[a]
Burlington	4	6	9	47[a]	66[a]	Port Arthur	24	31	38	45	48
Chatham	17	21	22[a]	30[a]	32[a]	Port Colborne	7	8	14[a]	15	18[a]
Cornwall	14	17	18	44[a]	46[a]	St Catharines	30	38	40[a]	84[a]	97
Dundas	5	7	10[a]	13[a]	16	St Thomas	17	18	19[a]	22[a]	23
Eastview	8	14	19	25	24	Sarnia	19	35	43	51	54
Fort William	30	35	39	45	48	Sault Ste Marie	26	32	37	43[a]	74[a]
Galt	15	19	24[a]	28[a]	33[a]	Stratford	17	19	20[a]	20[a]	23[a]
Guelph	23	27	34[a]	40[a]	51[a]	Sudbury	32	42	46	80[a]	85[a]
Hamilton	166	208	240[a]	274[a]	298[a]	Timmins	29	28	28	29	29
Kingston	30	33	47[a]	54	59	Toronto	667	676	668	672	664
Kitchener	36	45	60[a]	74[a]	93[a]	Metropolitan Toronto	910	1,210	1,502	1,824	2,158
London	78	95	102[a]	170[a]	194	Waterloo	9	12	16[a]	21[a]	30[a]
Niagara Falls	20	23	24	22	57[a]	Welland	12	15	16	36[a]	40
North Bay	16	18	21[a]	24[a]	24	Whitby	6	7	10	15	17
Oakville	4	7	10	10	53	Windsor	105	120	122[a]	114[a]	192[a]
Orillia	10	12	14	15[a]	15	Woodstock	12	16	18[a]	20	24[a]
Oshawa	27	42	50	62	78						

SOURCE: DBS, *Census of Canada*, 1941, 1951, 1956, 1961, and 1966.

[a] Indicates a change in municipal boundaries since the preceding census; population totals are based on areas as incorporated at each of these dates.

TABLE 1-30
Income level in Ontario, 1945–69

YEAR	PERSONAL INCOME		YEAR	PERSONAL INCOME	
	Total $ million	Per capita dollars		Total $ million	Per capita dollars
1945	3,656	914	1964	14,057	2,120
1950	5,285	1,182	1965	15,444	2,275
1955	7,918	1,504	1966	16,986	2,440
1960	11,023	1,804	1967	18,758	2,624
1961	11,490	1,843	1968[a]	20,340	3,065
1962	12,252	1,929	1969[a]	24,900	3,341
1963	13,099	2,021			

SOURCE: Ontario, Department of Treasury and Economics, *Ontario Statistical Review 1968*, July 1969.

[a]Estimate of Ontario, Department of Treasury and Economics.

TABLE 1-31
Average constant dollar income in Ontario, 1950–69[a]

YEAR	BASED ON 1949 CONSUMER PRICE INDEX	YEAR	BASED ON 1949 CONSUMER PRICE INDEX
1950	1,149	1964	1,576
1955	1,292	1965	1,640
1960	1,409	1966	1,696
1961	1,426	1967	1,761
1962	1,478	1968	1,795
1963	1,527	1969	2,061

[a]Calculated from figures in Ontario, Department of Treasury and Economics, *Ontario Statistical Review 1968*, June 1969.

more rapid in the early 1950s than in the late 1940s, declined in the late 1950s, and accelerated again during the 1960s.

A considerable part of the increased per capita income was of course eaten up by inflation. For example, the rise from $1,182 in 1950 to $3,341 in 1969 represented an increase of $2,159, that is, of 183 per cent. When adjusted by the consumer price index for Canada, however, the actual increase in constant dollars according to 1949 values was only 79 per cent, according to the figures in Table 1-31. This increment was sufficient, of course, to provide for a substantial increase in goods and services, including education. Demand for the latter has been shown to be relatively elastic.

Table 1-32 shows the extent to which per capita consumption expenditure varied in 1967 according to the different regions of the province. The area covered by each of these regions is shown on Chart 1-10. The Georgian Bay region was at the bottom, with $1,451, which was only about 60.7 per cent of the $2,389 figure for the Metropolitan region. Also

TABLE 1-32

Consumption expenditure per capita by economic region of Ontario, 1967 (in dollars)

REGION	PER CAPITA EXPENDITURE
Eastern Ontario	1,802
Georgian Bay	1,451
Lake Erie	1,917
Lake Ontario	1,519
Lake St Clair	1,965
Metropolitan	2,389
Mid-Western Ontario	1,919
Niagara	2,198
Northeastern Ontario	1,591
Northwestern Ontario	1,660
Province	2,039

SOURCE: Ontario, Department of Treasury and Economics, *Ontario Economic Review*, VI, September/October 1968.

CHART 1-9
Per capita income in Ontario, 1945–69

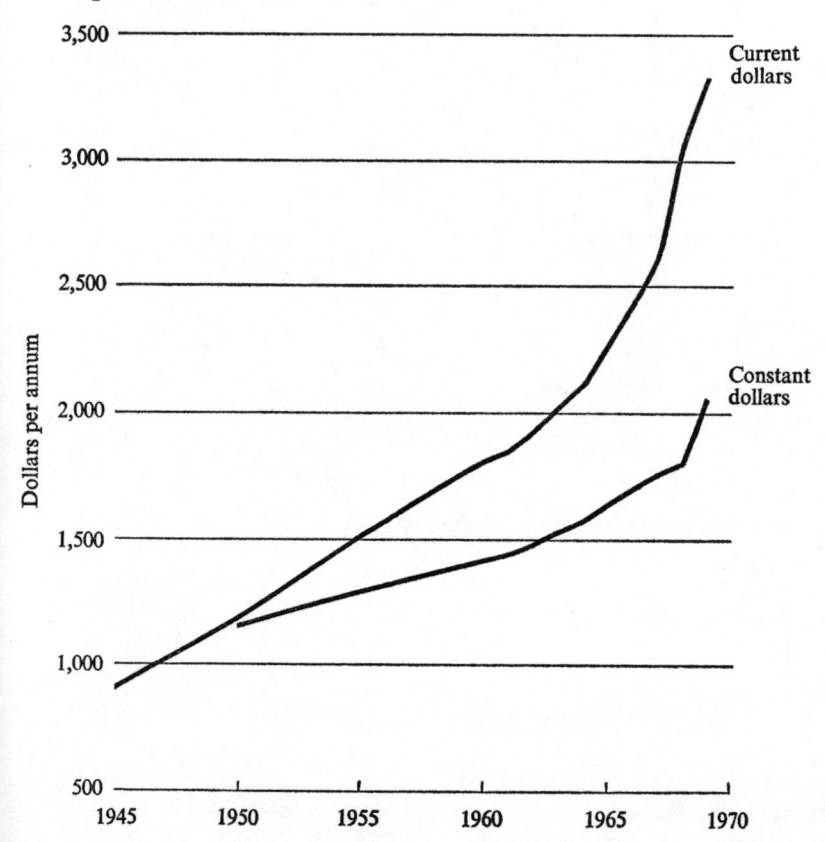

90 The expansion of the educational system

CHART 1-10
The economic regions of Ontario

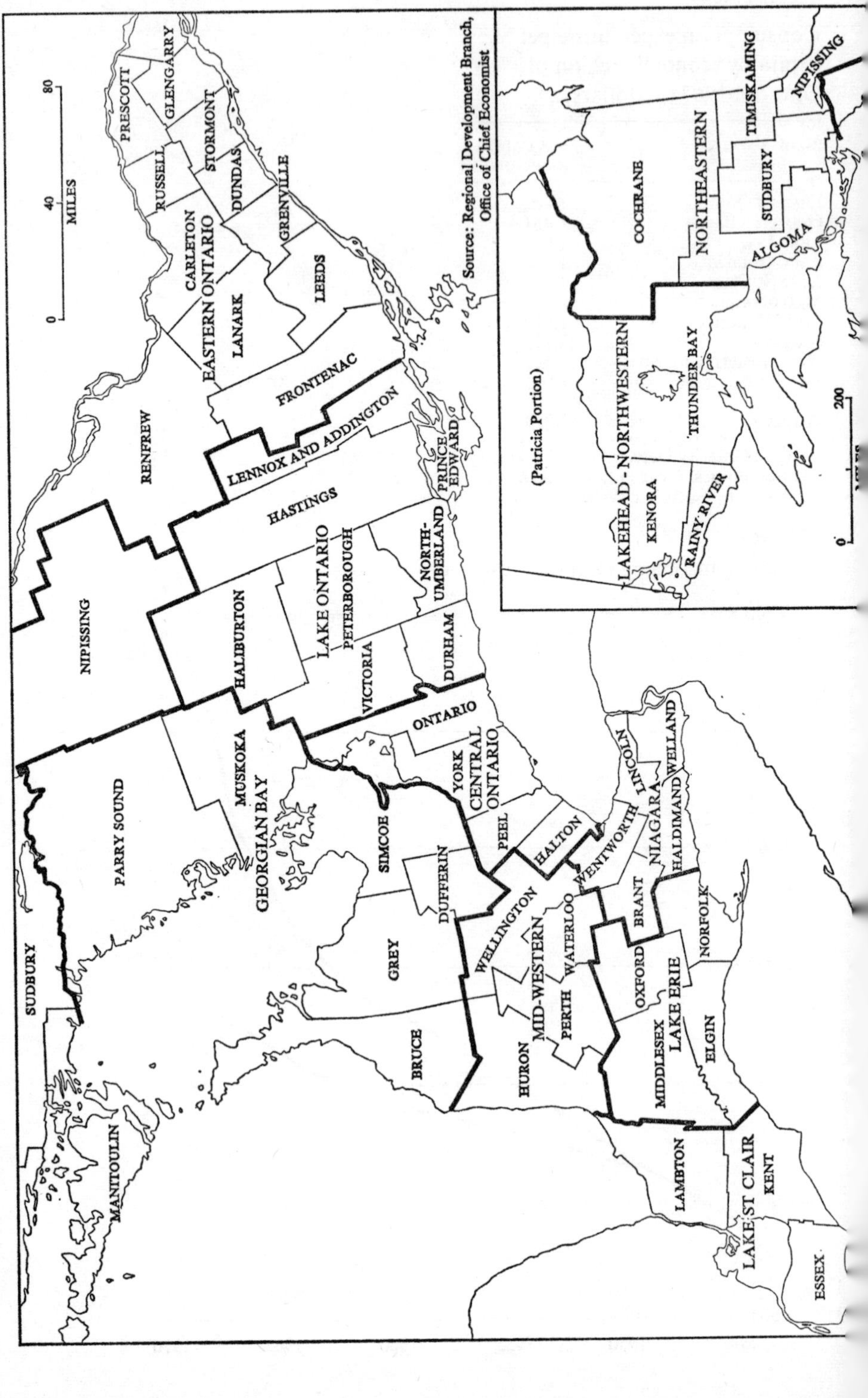

TABLE 1-33

Average income per person in Canadian provinces and territories, 1960–7 (in dollars)

PROVINCE OR TERRITORY	1960	1961	1962	1963	1964	1965	1966	1967
Newfoundland	882	934	955	1,006	1,065	1,173	1,287	1,424
Prince Edward Island	990	962	1,047	1,103	1,234	1,370	1,376	1,532
Nova Scotia	1,166	1,197	1,252	1,298	1,370	1,485	1,575	1,790
New Brunswick	1,048	1,064	1,110	1,153	1,259	1,376	1,475	1,658
Quebec	1,310	1,383	1,454	1,509	1,614	1,755	1,885	2,069
Ontario	1,804	1,843	1,932	2,031	2,134	2,295	2,454	2,624
Manitoba	1,543	1,513	1,688	1,683	1,801	1,919	2,054	2,317
Saskatchewan	1,477	1,222	1,695	1,867	1,683	1,966	2,238	2,183
Alberta	1,554	1,595	1,703	1,747	1,795	1,976	2,215	2,372
British Columbia	1,779	1,813	1,892	1,986	2,087	2,281	2,438	2,579
Yukon and Northwest Territories	1,389	1,324	1,282	1,359	1,390	1,500	1,561	1,795
Canada	1,535	1,564	1,688	1,743	1,827	1,988	2,144	2,313

SOURCE: DBS, National Accounts, Production and Productivity Division (13-201), *National Accounts Income and Expenditure* (1966, 1967).

NOTE: The figures for Ontario were obtained from a different source from those in Table 1-30.

low on the scale were the Lake Ontario and the Northeastern Ontario regions. Second to the Metropolitan region at the high-expenditure extreme was the Niagara region. In a general way the distribution followed local expenditure for educational purposes, although the degree of correspondence was by no means close.

Ontario has regularly had the highest per capita income of any of the Canadian provinces. Throughout the period between 1960 and 1967, as indicated on Table 1-33, British Columbia followed close behind, with the three Prairie provinces trailing somewhat, and changing their relative positions from year to year. The four Atlantic provinces had the lowest income, with Nova Scotia consistently in the lead and Newfoundland at the bottom. In 1960 the figure for Newfoundland was only 48.9 per cent of that for Ontario; by 1967 it had risen to a little more than 54 per cent. Thus in this case the cliché that the rich get richer and the poor get poorer did not apply.

Table 1-34 makes it possible to carry the comparison further. It shows the per capita income in certain states of the United States, including some of the most and some of the least prosperous, for five-year intervals from 1950 on, and for 1966 and 1967. Since the amounts are in American dollars, comparisons must be very general. During the late 1950s the Canadian dollar fluctuated up to a value of $1.05 in terms of its American counterpart, and was subsequently reduced to approximately $0.92.

In rough terms per capita dollar income in Ontario has been approximately 80 per cent of that in the United States as a whole throughout the period. It has ranged from about 63 per cent in 1950 to about 70 per

TABLE 1-34

Per capita income in certain states of the United States, 1950–67 (in dollars)

STATE	1950	1955	1960	1965	1966	1967
California	1,852	2,313	2,710	3,261	3,457	3,660
Georgia	1,034	1,375	1,639	2,174	2,379	2,513
Illinois	1,825	2,243	2,650	3,302	3,532	3,725
Massachusetts	1,633	2,026	2,459	3,067	3,271	3,488
Michigan	1,700	2,183	2,324	3,060	3,269	3,393
New York	1,873	2,283	2,746	3,286	3,497	3,726
North Carolina	1,037	1,313	1,561	2,060	2,277	2,396
Ohio	1,620	2,081	2,334	2,845	3,056	3,212
Pennsylvania	1,541	1,889	2,242	2,750	2,968	3,149
South Carolina	893	1,181	1,377	1,855	2,052	2,167
Texas	1,349	1,667	1,925	2,350	2,542	2,704
West Virginia	1,065	1,326	1,594	2,034	2,176	2,341
United States	1,496	1,876	2,215	2,760	2,963	3,137

SOURCE: US Bureau of the Census, *Statistical Abstract of the United States: 1968* (89th ed.; Washington, DC, 1968), p. 322, No. 468.

cent in 1967 of that in New York, which has been consistently at or near the top among the American states. California and Illinois have been comparable to New York, and Massachusetts and Michigan have been a comparatively short distance behind. Ontario has been at a level close to that of Texas, and well ahead of such states as Georgia and North and South Carolina.

TWO

Enrolment in schools and in courses sponsored by the Department of Education

HISTORICAL BACKGROUND

In 1830 approximately 10,000 pupils out of a total population of 200,000 in Upper Canada were enrolled in the common schools. According to an estimate by Phillips, between one-third and two-thirds of the children in the various provinces, presumably including Upper Canada, received from twelve to twenty-four months of schooling.[1] Thus there was obviously much less need for accommodation for a given level of enrolment than there is today.

The subsequent period was one of very rapid expansion. The Royal Commission estimated common school enrolment at 96,000 in 1845 and at 446,000 in 1871, a rate of increase that was about twice that of the population. During the same period the school year was lengthened from less than eight to over eleven months, and the ordinary period of schooling was extended to about five years.[2] With a large proportion of children enrolled, subsequent growth more closely paralleled that of the population. In 1890 there were about half a million pupils out of a population of approximately 2,114,000. Only about half of these, however, were in attendance on the average day.[3]

According to a review by Phillips of the situation in 1891, about seven-eighths of the pupils who managed to get through the first reader survived to reach the fourth, which was roughly the level of grades 7 and 8. There were about 85,000 of these, with perhaps between 35,000 and 40,000 in the senior fourth. Approximately 22,000 wrote the high school entrance examinations, and 12,000 passed. The collegiate institutes and high schools had an enrolment of 19,000 at this stage, which was between four and five times the number enrolled at the grammar schools thirty years earlier. Of the total number of students at the secondary level, about 15,000 were in form I, and a mere 85 in form IV. About 500 matriculated, mostly at the junior or form III level.[4]

The percentage of those proceeding to secondary school was less than 8 per cent in 1901, although it continued to rise. The passage of *The Adolescent School Attendance Act*, which went into operation in 1921, contributed to a rapid subsequent increase. By 1931 16.6 per cent of provincial school enrolment was at the secondary level, and by 1937 more than 18 per cent.[5] The improvement in average daily attendance was particularly noticeable in vocational courses, where it rose from 2,771 in 1919–20 to 35,130 in 1939–40.[6]

What Phillips called a phenomenal increase occurred in secondary enrolment across Canada between 1921 and 1948. The number doing work at that level rose from 84,000 to 278,000, while elementary school enrolment declined. As contributory causes, he listed "greater wealth, smaller families, less need for immediate wage earning, more need in business for educated employees, fewer jobs in depression years, new secondary school courses of utilitarian value, more consideration of pupils' interests and needs, and the cumulative effect of a growing appreciation of the value of education in successively better-educated generations."[7]

OVER-ALL ENROLMENT IN PUBLICLY SUPPORTED ELEMENTARY AND SECONDARY SCHOOLS

Some of the most basic facts about Ontario education in the post-war period are presented in Table 2-1, which shows enrolment in public and Roman Catholic separate elementary schools and in secondary schools between 1945–6 and 1969–70. During that time total enrolment at all levels increased from 664,780 to 1,986,796, a percentage increase of 198.9. Between 1945–6 and 1950–1 the percentage increase was 11.8; between 1950–1 and 1955–6, 39.7; between 1955–6 and 1960–1, 33.8; between 1960–1 and 1965–6, 25.2; and between 1965–6 and 1969–70, 14.3. (The last interval, consisting of only four years, is of course not directly comparable with the others.) It is clear from these figures that the period has been one of expansion that is most unlikely to be duplicated in the future.

The actual enrolment increase by five-year intervals in the post-war period was as follows: 1945–6 to 1950–1, 78,617; 1950–1 to 1955–6, 294,779; 1955–6 to 1960–1, 350,987; 1960–1 to 1965–6, 349,618; and for the four-year interval 1965–6 to 1969–70, 248,015. Thus, although the greatest rate of increase occurred in the 1950s, the number added to the enrolment was almost as great between 1960–1 and 1965–6 as between 1955–6 and 1960–1. The average annual increase in enrolment during the same intervals was as follows: 1945–6 to 1950–1, 15,723; 1950–1 to 1955–6, 58,956; 1955–6 to 1960–1, 70,197; 1960–1 to 1965–6, 69,924; and 1965–6 to 1969–70, 49,603.

By far the greatest numerical increase was at the elementary school level, as might be expected from the greater grade span covered, as well as from the greater proportion of the age groups included. The total elementary school enrolment grew from 545,007 in 1945–6 to 1,456,117 in 1969–70, a percentage increase of 167.2. The numbers added by five-year intervals were as follows: between 1945–6 and 1950–1, 67,175; between 1950–1 and 1955–6, 251,432; between 1955–6 and 1960–1, 262,774; between 1960–1 and 1965–6, 193,655; and between 1965–6

TABLE 2-1

Enrolment in elementary and secondary schools of Ontario, 1945–70

YEAR	ELEMENTARY[a]			SECONDARY[b]	ELEMENTARY AND SECONDARY
	Public	Roman Catholic separate	TOTAL[c]		
1945–6	436,709	108,298	545,007	119,773	664,780
1946–7	441,333	108,877	539,012	123,846	662,858
1947–8	453,116	111,413	550,035	123,085	673,120
1948–9	469,517	115,507	571,459	125,234	696,693
1949–50	493,532	122,687	592,726	127,250	719,976
1950–1	508,364	127,253	612,182	131,215	743,397
1951–2	544,483	134,177	654,506	133,556	788,062
1952–3	588,344	146,668	712,892	141,091	853,983
1953–4	620,446	162,738	768,397	148,744	917,141
1954–5	643,951	174,208	821,736	160,166	981,902
1955–6	676,246	187,368	863,614	174,562	1,038,176
1956–7	706,319	205,577	911,896	185,605	1,097,501
1957–8	747,236	223,881	971,117	203,525	1,174,642
1958–9	784,167	243,431	1,027,598	222,075	1,249,673
1959–60	817,880	263,769	1,081,649	237,576	1,319,225
1960–1	843,737	282,651	1,126,388	262,775	1,389,163
1961–2	861,715	301,338	1,163,053	299,177	1,462,230
1962–3	880,198	316,831	1,197,029	331,578	1,528,607
1963–4	901,830	331,334	1,233,164	364,210	1,597,374
1964–5	925,068	353,405	1,278,473	395,301	1,673,774
1965–6	949,374	370,669	1,320,043	418,738	1,738,781
1966–7	976,900	387,971	1,364,871	436,026	1,800,897
1967–8	1,002,555	402,497	1,405,052	463,736	1,868,788
1968–9	1,021,676	408,914	1,430,590	500,807	1,931,397
1969–70	1,042,561	413,556	1,456,117	530,679	1,986,796

SOURCE: Reports of the Minister of Education of Ontario.

[a]Including grades 9 and 10 in separate schools, and auxiliary.
[b]Including non-graded students.
[c]Net enrolment used from 1945–54 accounts for the discrepancy in the totals.

and 1969–70, 136,074.* The percentage increase for these intervals were respectively 12.3, 41.1, 30.4, 17.2, and 10.3.* Thus, the relative increase was greatest in the first half of the 1950s and the absolute increase in the latter half of the decade. Both the relative and the absolute increase declined sharply in the 1960s. These trends reflect the changing age structure of the population, as indicated in Tables 1-4 and 1-5.

The growth of enrolment was much greater in the Roman Catholic separate than in the public elementary schools. The increase in the former between 1945–6 and 1969–70 was from 108,298 to 413,556, a percentage increase of 281.9, and in the latter from 436,709 to 1,042,561, a percentage increase of 138.7. In 1945–6 the number enrolled in Roman

*The fact that these figures are based on a four-year interval, and are thus not strictly comparable with the others in the series should be kept in mind.

CHART 2-1
Enrolment in Ontario elementary and secondary schools, 1945–70

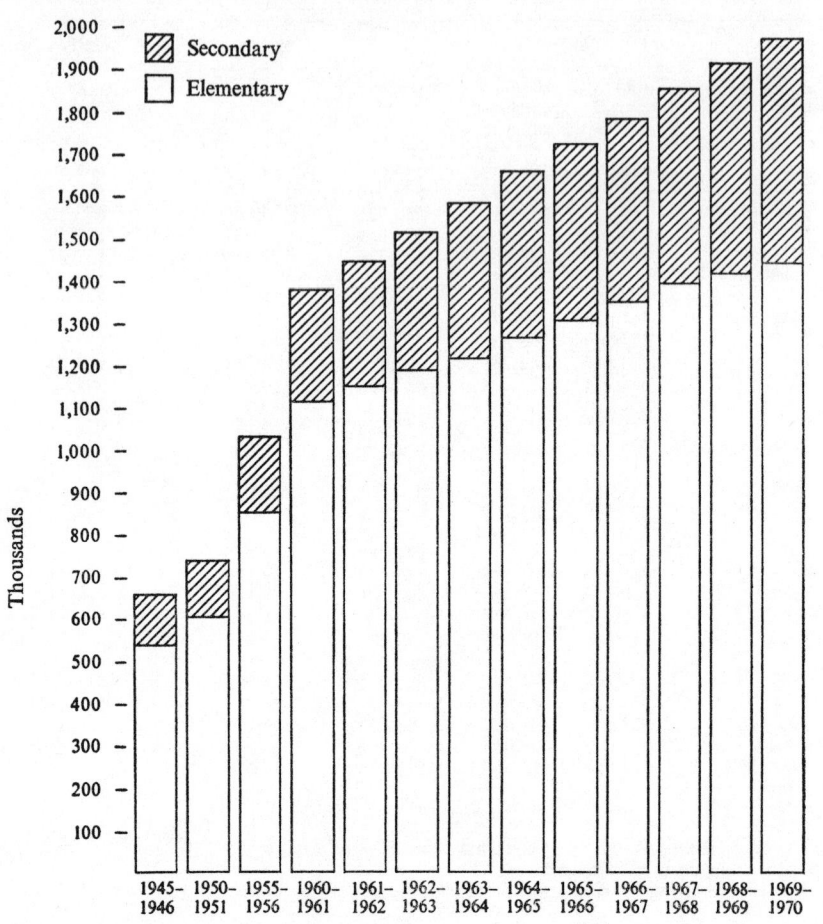

[Bar chart showing enrolment in thousands from 1945–1946 through 1969–1970, with stacked bars for Secondary (hatched) and Elementary (white). Y-axis labeled "Thousands" from 100 to 2,000.]

Catholic separate schools constituted 19.9 per cent of the total elementary school enrolment; the corresponding figure for 1950–1 was 20.8; for 1955–6, 21.7; for 1960–1, 25.1; and for 1969–70, 28.4. Thus the large increase in the proportion of children attending separate schools has occurred in the 1960s. The relationship is illustrated diagrammatically in Chart 2-2.

Secondary school enrolment has increased much more sharply in relative terms than has that in elementary schools. During the 1945–6 to 1969–70 interval, the absolute increase was from 119,773 to 530,679, or 410,906, and the percentage increase was 343.1. For successive five-year intervals, the numerical and percentage increases were as follows: from 1945–6 to 1950–1, 11,442, or 9.6 per cent; from 1950–1 to 1955–6, 43,347, or 33.0 per cent; from 1955–6 to 1960–1, 88,213 or 50.5 per cent; and from 1960–1 to 1965–6, 155,963, or 59.4 per cent.

CHART 2-2
Enrolment in public elementary and Roman Catholic separate schools in Ontario, 1945–70

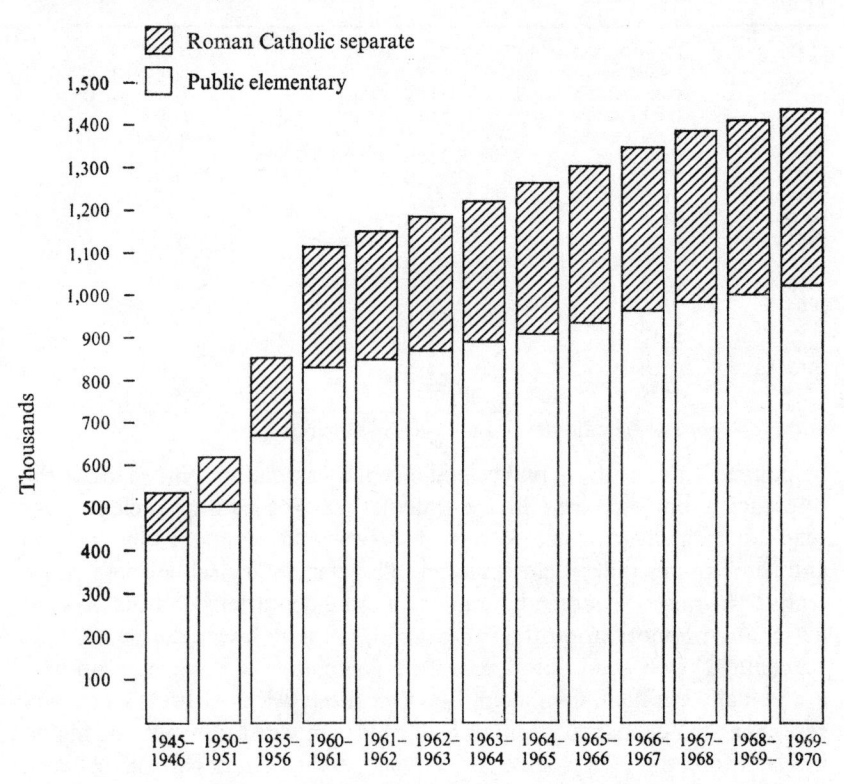

From 1965–6 to 1969–70, the increase was 111,941, or 26.7 per cent. Up to 1960 the increase was considered to reflect mainly the growing interest in and value placed on education. The Reorganized Program, or Robarts Plan, has been given credit for adding an extra incentive after 1962.

The fact that rising enrolment has involved a strong shift toward the secondary level has had important implications for educational expenditure. Since the cost per secondary student, particularly in technical and vocational courses, has been much greater than that per elementary pupil, financial investment has had to increase at a much greater rate, even allowing for inflation, than over-all enrolment figures might suggest. The effect of the change in balance between the two levels has been felt strongly in terms both of capital and of operating expenditure.

The relationship between actual school enrolment and the number in the age group from which most of the attendance is drawn at each of the elementary and secondary school levels is shown in Table 2-2. For the benefit of those who are not familiar with the approach involved, it may

TABLE 2-2

School enrolment in Ontario as percentages of certain age groups, 1950–69

YEAR	ELEMENTARY SCHOOL ENROLMENT AS PERCENTAGE OF POPULATION AGED 5–14 YEARS	SECONDARY SCHOOL ENROLMENT AS PERCENTAGE OF POPULATION AGED 15–19 YEARS	SCHOOL ENROLMENT AS PERCENTAGE OF TOTAL POPULATION
1950–1	87.8	41.0	16.6
1955–6	91.7	51.1	19.7
1960–1	94.0	62.6	22.8
1961–2	91.8	68.5	23.4
1962–3	92.0	71.0	24.1
1963–4	92.2	72.4	24.6
1964–5	93.1	73.2	25.2
1965–6	93.4	73.3	25.6
1966–7	93.5	72.8	25.9
1967–8	93.8	74.0	26.1
1968–9	93.4	77.1	26.4

SOURCE: Reports of the Minister of Education of Ontario.

be pointed out that the actual attendance may extend on both sides of the reference group involved in the calculation. For example, elementary school enrolment may include some four-year-olds in junior kindergarten and some pupils older than fourteen. The elementary school percentage tends to be raised as more children enrol in kindergartens. A trend toward automatic promotion, on the other hand, tends to lower the figure. The percentage given is not the same as the percentage of the age group who are actually enrolled. Confusion between these two measures is not very serious at the elementary school level, but can cause difficulty at higher levels. More than one person has made a direct comparison between university enrolment as a percentage of the eighteen-to-twenty-one-year-old group and the percentage of the same age group actually enrolled.

The fluctuations for elementary schools between 1950–1 and 1968–9 are not of great significance. The rise from 87.8 to 91.7 per cent between 1950–1 and 1955–6 was probably mainly a reflection of increased kindergarten enrolment, and the decline from 94.0 to 91.8 between 1960–1 and 1961–2 must have resulted from the provision in the latter year of more opportunities in secondary schools for those who might otherwise have been retained in grade 8. At the secondary level the increase from 41.0 to 77.1 per cent in eighteen years was phenomenal, and reflects great credit on Ontario society and the Ontario government. Even though it may be reasoned that successive increments become more difficult to add, the annual increase in percentage points was very nearly as great in the 1960s as in the previous decade. While levels of attendance attained in the United States suggest that further improvement is possible, a practical limit is likely to be reached within the next few years. There is a feeling in some quarters that the percentage may be about 82 by 1975.

The last column of Table 2-2 provides an illustration of the increasing extent to which Ontario society has devoted its efforts to school-level formal education. Both increased attendance rates and the rising proportion of the population at the eligible age levels have contributed to the jump from 16.6 per cent to 26.4 per cent in school between 1950–1 and 1968–9. If the figures for post-secondary enrolment are considered as well, they add up to an extraordinary social transformation.

ENROLMENT TRENDS IN CANADA AS A WHOLE

According to the *Fourth Annual Review* of the Economic Council of Canada,[8] Canada's total school population approximately doubled during the 1950s and the first half of the 1960s, rising from approximately 2.7 to 5.4 million. The increase was about one million in the second half of the 1950s and again in the first half of the 1960s. In the former period two-thirds of the increase was at the elementary school level, while in the second about 40 per cent of it was at the secondary school level. A much smaller advance was anticipated for the period after 1965–6, with perhaps a million being added between that year and 1975–6. All but a small part of the increase was expected to occur at the secondary and post-secondary levels. A small decline in the total elementary school enrolment was foreseen for the early 1970s. Secondary school enrolment was expected to rise much more slowly than it had up to 1965. Between 1951–2 and 1965–6 the percentage of the fourteen-to-seventeen year age group enrolled in secondary school had risen from 46 to 80. (It should be noted that these percentages are not directly comparable to those in Table 2-2, applying to Ontario, because the age group is different.) The report predicted that this percentage would rise to 92 by the mid-1970s, approximately equalling the current figure in the United States.

ENROLMENT IN PUBLICLY SUPPORTED ELEMENTARY SCHOOLS

Grade distribution in public elementary schools
Since the growth in enrolment in the public elementary schools has not been smooth, the balance among grades has tended to shift from one period of time to another. The result has been more administrative problems than might otherwise have been expected. Immediately after the post-war bulge reached the schools in the early 1950s, there was a relatively large increase in the demand for classes and teachers at the kindergarten and primary levels. As time went on, a more even distribution among grades was restored.

The grade distribution for public elementary schools for 1945–6, 1950–1, 1955–6, and each subsequent year to 1969–70 is shown in Table 2-3. For 1950–1 only the enrolment for grades 1 to 3 and for grades 4 to 6 combined is available. The enrolment bulge had not reached grade 1 in 1950–1, but by 1955–6 was felt strongly in grade 3, and to a lesser extent in grade 4. By 1960–1 it was beginning to affect the secondary

TABLE 2-3
Grade distribution in public elementary schools, 1945–70

YEAR	Kindergarten	1	2	3	4	5	6	7	8	Auxiliary
1945-6	24,389	61,374	53,662	49,328	48,543	50,339	48,612	46,075	47,081	4,361
1950-1	37,416			202,408[a]			166,543[a]	49,346	45,441	4,633
1955-6	57,022	96,339	91,229	91,685	76,529	67,163	65,189	65,067	59,338	5,765
1956-7	61,341	97,179	92,173	89,500	85,696	79,099	67,351	64,901	61,874	6,665
1957-8	67,685	101,479	94,028	90,829	86,274	88,637	79,388	67,862	62,457	7,864
1958-9	71,896	107,041	96,423	91,692	86,469	88,622	87,593	79,823	65,441	8,602
1959-60	75,057	109,972	101,798	93,910	87,165	88,649	87,724	87,767	76,384	9,055
1960-1	77,479	113,007	104,476	98,376	89,293	89,296	87,994	88,596	84,158	10,666
1961-2	80,116	113,269	106,627	100,953	93,529	91,376	88,863	89,611	85,132	11,667
1962-3	82,745	114,929	107,050	103,104	96,240	95,559	90,830	90,072	86,439	12,738
1963-4	85,823	117,165	108,961	104,124	98,731	98,525	95,021	92,166	87,168	13,055
1964-5	88,677	119,433	110,230	106,226	99,833	101,078	98,553	96,928	89,247	14,211
1965-6	92,881	121,752	112,371	107,448	101,674	102,455	101,135	100,203	93,586	15,797
1966-7	96,109	124,405	115,517	110,352	104,326	104,517	103,108	103,571	97,672	17,246
1967-8	101,293	125,120	117,385	112,889	107,575	106,774	105,124	104,779	100,773	20,829
1968-9	106,874	124,240	117,971	114,264	109,595	109,324	107,010	106,246	102,372	23,754
1969-70	116,914	123,804	117,726	115,076	112,257	112,156	110,489	108,662	103,839	21,613

SOURCE: Reports of the Minister of Education of Ontario.

[a] Three consecutive grades.

schools. At that time the increase from the lower to the higher elementary grades was fairly regular. By 1968-9 the number entering grade 1 had begun to decline slightly, although a definite decrease in public school enrolment was still in the future.

Grade distribution in Roman Catholic separate schools
The grade distribution in the Roman Catholic separate schools has tended to be different from that in the public schools. Both the increasing number of children in the relevant age group and the growing proportion enrolling in the separate schools have contributed to the relatively large number in the lower as compared with the higher elementary grades. In 1945-6, for example, there were about 64.1 per cent as many pupils in grade 8 as in grade 1. The corresponding percentage for 1955 was 52.7, as compared with 61.6 for the public schools. In 1960-1 the comparable percentages were 61.4 and 74.5; in 1965, 64.9 and 76.9; and in 1969-70, 82.3 and 83.9. The shift toward the separate schools has contributed not only to a disproportionately large number in their lower grades but toward a leveling out of the grade distribution in the public schools as well.

The rapid growth in kindergarten classes in the separate schools is particularly evident in Table 2-4. These classes were virtually non-existent in 1945. Between 1950-1 and 1960-1 enrolment increased from 2,381 to 15,714, or by 560.0 per cent; between 1960-1 and 1969-70 it rose to 41,451, a further increase of 163.8 per cent. The number in auxiliary classes increased much more rapidly than the general enrolment after 1960. The percentage increase between 1960-1 and 1969-70 was 483.9, as compared with 46.6 in the total enrolment.

Age-grade distribution
The Department of Education has made it a practice to publish an age-grade table for public school enrolment only at intervals of five or six years. Those for 1949-50, 1955-6, 1960-1, and 1966-7 are reproduced with no important change in Tables 2-5, 2-6, 2-7, and 2-8. There have been certain differences in practice over the years. The sex classification has, for example, been dropped in Table 2-8. Also, enrolment for 1966-7 is given for September, while for previous years it is given as of June. Table 2-6 for 1955-6 groups together the three grades of the Primary Division and those of the Junior Division. Those for 1949-50 and 1955-6 (Tables 2-5 and 2-6) carry the distribution through grade 13, while the others stop at grade 10.

The tables show an interesting variation in average or median age. In 1949-50 the average age of grade 1 beginners was 6.4 years. Even if the repeaters, who constituted a little more than 10 per cent of the total, and whose average age was 7.5, were taken into account, the over-all average would not have been more than about 6.5 years. In 1960-1 the median age for grade 1 was 7.0 years. The apparent decline to 6.4 years by

TABLE 2-4
Grade distribution in Roman Catholic separate schools, 1945-70

YEAR	GRADE Kindergarten	1	2	3	4	5	6	7	8	Auxiliary
1945-6	272	16,306	13,711	13,362	12,350	12,765	11,879	10,836	10,444	613
1950-1	2,381			52,209[a]			43,469[a]	11,935	10,824	619
1955-6	7,707	27,659	26,133	24,814	21,539	19,826	18,061	17,172	14,588	649
1956-7	8,939	30,014	27,413	26,781	24,200	23,442	19,547	18,294	15,833	678
1957-8	9,388	32,226	29,679	28,062	26,280	26,225	23,146	19,595	17,035	660
1958-9	11,017	34,880	31,567	29,582	27,689	27,677	25,996	22,972	18,313	743
1959-60	13,546	36,593	34,000	31,457	29,258	29,093	27,428	25,878	21,528	852
1960-1	15,714	39,284	35,621	33,469	31,410	29,947	28,813	26,764	24,103	1,111
1961-2	18,917	40,812	37,858	34,973	33,164	31,953	29,455	28,498	25,355	1,387
1962-3	21,580	42,305	39,646	37,034	34,639	33,825	31,354	29,273	26,975	1,630
1963-4	23,474	44,642	40,765	38,828	36,426	35,138	33,331	30,768	27,583	2,098
1964-5	30,493	45,723	43,178	40,211	38,222	36,971	34,317	32,986	29,276	3,115
1965-6	35,151	47,577	43,861	42,317	39,834	38,613	36,140	33,951	30,890	3,912
1966-7	37,895	48,934	45,887	43,414	41,774	39,944	38,067	36,066	32,454	4,931
1967-8	38,766	48,396	46,973	44,589	42,872	41,656	39,248	37,829	34,560	6,586
1968-9	39,930	47,253	46,872	46,059	43,911	42,371	41,173	39,054	36,490	7,166
1969-70	41,451	45,893	45,730	45,764	45,339	43,425	42,373	40,965	37,783	6,487

SOURCE: Reports of the Minister of Education of Ontario.

[a]Three consecutive grades.

TABLE 2-5
Age-grade distribution of enrolment, 1949-50

Age on June 1, 1950		Under 5	5	6	7	8	9	10	11	12	13	14	15	16	17	18	19	20	21+	TOTALS–SEX	TOTALS–GRADE	AVERAGE AGE	GRADE PERCENTAGE
Kindergarten	Boys	332	6,514	5,387	90	12	1	1												12,336	24,006	5.4	3.2
	Girls	330	6,373	4,889	68	8	1													11,670			
Kindergarten–Primary	Boys	115	3,303	3,526	285	24	3	2												7,258	14,083	5.5	1.8
	Girls	102	3,268	3,223	202	27	3													6,825			
Grade 1 (Beginners)	Boys	3	923	21,744	18,147	1,545	227	58	26	14	7	8		1						42,703	82,643	6.4	12.2
	Girls	8	931	20,904	16,668	1,179	161	45	16	11	11	3	1	2						39,940			
Grade 1 (Repeaters)	Boys		4	378	2,902	2,180	493	135	55	27	13	8	4							6,201	9,806	7.5	1.3
	Girls		1	289	1,740	1,202	247	79	24	15	7		1							3,605			
Grade 2	Boys		1	512	17,206	18,325	5,058	1,391	362	137	55	30	7	2						43,086	81,764	7.7	11.0
	Girls		1	909	17,925	15,800	3,080	667	186	62	29	13	3	2	1					38,678			
Grade 3	Boys			8	801	13,517	15,476	5,457	1,877	706	272	111	41	1	4					38,273	72,790	8.8	9.8
	Girls			12	1,283	14,739	13,639	3,371	1,035	274	103	36	16	7	2					34,517			
Grade 4	Boys				16	1,381	11,901	13,167	5,684	2,323	914	322	116	30	5	1				35,860	69,066	9.9	9.3
	Girls				30	2,080	13,532	12,132	3,573	1,249	395	164	41	6	3	1				33,206			
Grade 5	Boys					30	1,829	10,474	12,551	6,012	2,753	1,129	390	88	8	2	1			35,267	68,340	10.9	9.2
	Girls					78	2,682	12,335	11,535	4,105	1,593	526	177	38	2	1	1			33,073			
Grade 6	Boys						69	1,786	10,004	11,495	5,913	2,899	1,047	242	21	3				33,479	64,835	11.9	8.7
	Girls						74	2,603	11,725	10,719	3,994	1,561	537	129	14					31,356			
Grade 7	Boys							81	1,727	8,607	10,155	5,622	2,821	730	58	3	1			29,808	58,873	12.9	7.9
	Girls							128	2,728	10,584	9,555	4,108	1,579	349	28	3				29,065			
Grade 8	Boys								115	1,847	8,013	10,120	5,939	2,160	216	15	8			28,433	57,268	13.8	7.7
	Girls								174	2,877	10,125	9,934	4,313	1,280	119	11	1			28,835			
Grade 9	Boys									144	2,084	7,260	8,153	4,249	1,196	160	29	6	3	23,286	48,024	15.2	6.5
	Girls									247	3,101	9,262	8,351	3,092	569	95	7	1	1	24,738			
Grade 10	Boys									2	189	1,847	5,662	5,591	2,679	701	101	10	11	16,797	35,981	16.0	4.9
	Girls									12	299	2,853	7,800	6,065	1,847	278	28	5	2	19,184			
Grade 11	Boys										6	1,847	1,312	3,599	3,677	1,542	450	47	17	10,768	22,559	16.4	3.0
	Girls										7	120	2,130	5,021	3,492	802	130	23	15	11,791			
Grade 12	Boys											4	86	1,033	3,129	2,738	1,121	283	83	8,479	17,631	17.4	2.3
	Girls											8	167	1,635	3,891	2,619	1,670	126	39	9,152			
Grade 13	Boys											1	2	67	841	2,167	1,901	746	203	5,927	10,187	18.3	1.3
	Girls												12	124	997	1,860	1,002	204	61	4,260			
TOTALS	Boys	450	10,745	31,555	39,447	37,014	32,551	32,403	31,318	30,373	29,481	25,580	17,795	11,834	7,334	3,611	1,092	317	377,961			
	Girls	440	10,574	30,226	37,916	35,113	31,361	31,008	30,150	29,220	28,635	25,128	17,750	10,964	5,670	1,841	360	118	359,895			
TOTALS		890	21,319	61,781	77,363	72,127	68,482	63,411	61,468	59,593	58,116	50,708	35,545	22,798	13,004	5,452	1,452	435	737,856			
PERCENTAGE – YEARS		.1	2.8	8.4	10.5	9.8	9.3	8.7	8.6	8.3	8.1	7.9	6.9	4.8	3.1	1.8	.7	.2	(.05)				

Bold face within table denotes ideal age spread.

SOURCE: Report of the Minister of Education of Ontario, 1950.

TABLE 2-6
Age-grade distribution of enrolment, 1955-6

Age on June 1, 1956		Under 6	6	7	8	9	10	11	12	13	14	15	16	17	18	19	20	21+	TOTALS–SEX	TOTALS–GRADES	MEDIAN AGE	GRADE PERCENTAGE
Kindergarten	Boys	18,613	14,082	254	28	3	5						1						32,985	64,533		6.3
	Girls	17,901	13,418	200	19	6	2												31,548			
Primary division (Gr. 1, 2, 3)	Boys	626	31,835	54,755	53,967	33,286	7,929	2,188	636	256	86	22	9	3	1				185,599	353,496	8.1	34.3
	Girls	677	30,670	52,156	50,596	27,546	4,599	1,143	321	112	49	18	7	1	1			1	167,897			
Junior division (Gr. 4, 5, 6)	Boys	1	2	12	2,010	24,118	37,490	37,524	24,896	10,541	3,981	1,149	162	21	5	3			141,912	274,662	11.1	26.7
	Girls			37	2,883	27,524	38,386	35,428	19,693	6,185	1,927	587	79	11	6	1			132,750			
Grade 7	Boys					2	60	2,146	14,066	15,224	6,723	2,429	352	31	3	3	2		41,041	80,778	13.1	7.8
	Girls			2	1	4	68	3,170	16,670	13,925	4,335	1,366	177	17	1		1		39,737			
Grade 8	Boys						2	84	2,442	13,179	13,061	5,926	1,462	164	17	3	2	3	36,346	72,946	14.0	7.1
	Girls					1		122	3,738	15,856	12,155	3,872	763	83	7	2	2	1	36,600			
Grade 9	Boys							2	140	2,572	11,102	12,130	6,275	1,614	226	34	6	14	34,116	67,969	15.0	6.6
	Girls							5	184	3,916	13,308	11,556	4,155	648	66	9	4	2	33,853			
Grade 10	Boys						1	1	3	155	2,199	8,252	8,435	3,818	1,006	173	33	36	24,114	49,303	16.0	4.8
	Girls							1		237	3,264	10,812	8,164	2,297	353	50	7	4	25,189			
Grade 11	Boys										90	1,706	5,803	5,456	2,285	551	83	48	16,022	31,744	16.9	3.1
	Girls									2	170	2,608	7,206	4,568	1,029	124	11	4	15,722			
Grade 12	Boys										3	1,465	4,321	3,967	1,601	408	164	12,024	23,998	17.8	2.3
	Girls										3	95	2,144	5,502	3,238	765	131	59	11,974			
Grade 13	Boys											2	937	4,321	2,475	2,069	794	296	6,652	10,793	18.7	1.0
	Girls											5	119	1,164	1,934	779	109	31	4,141			
TOTALS–SEX	Boys	19,239	45,917	55,021	56,006	57,411	45,488	41,945	42,183	41,927	37,245	31,711	24,042	16,365	9,985	4,437	1,328	561	530,811			
	Girls	18,579	44,090	52,395	53,499	55,080	43,056	39,869	40,606	40,234	35,211	30,956	22,815	14,291	6,635	1,730	264	101	499,411			
TOTALS		37,818	90,007	107,416	109,505	112,491	88,544	81,814	82,789	82,161	72,456	62,667	46,857	30,656	16,620	6,167	1,592	662		1,030,222		
AGE PERCENTAGES		3.7	8.7	10.4	10.6	10.9	8.6	7.9	8.1	8.0	7.0	6.1	4.5	3.0	1.6	0.6	0.2	0.1				100.0
JUNIOR AUXILIARY PUPILS	Boys	4	6	46	190	380	475	480	521	485	500	358	90	18	7	5	1	6	3,572		12.3	
	Girls		3	26	84	214	232	270	278	247	285	192	67	11	3	1	1		1,914	5,486		
TOTALS		4	9	72	274	594	707	750	799	732	785	550	157	29	10	6	2	6				
SPECIAL INDUSTRIAL PUPILS	Boys								17	175	248	248	115	20	1	1			824		14.9	
	Girls							5	40	160	176	219	128	9	3				742	1,566		
Totals								5	57	335	424	467	243	29	4	1						
SUMMARY	Boys	19,243	45,923	55,067	56,196	57,791	45,963	42,425	42,721	42,587	37,993	32,317	24,247	16,403	9,993	4,442	1,329	567	535,207			
	Girls	18,579	44,093	52,421	53,583	55,294	43,288	40,144	40,924	40,641	35,672	31,367	23,010	14,311	6,641	1,732	266	101	502,067			
GRAND TOTALS		37,822	90,016	107,488	109,779	113,085	89,251	82,569	83,645	83,228	73,665	63,684	47,257	30,714	16,634	6,174	1,595	668		1,037,274		

SOURCE: Report of the Minister of Education of Ontario, 1956.

Enrolment in schools and courses 105

TABLE 2-7
Age-grade distribution of enrolment, 1960-1

Age on June 1, 1961		Under 6	6	7	8	9	10	11	12	13	14	15	16	17	18	19	20	21+	TOTAL-SEX	GRADE OR DIVISION TOTAL	GRADE OR DIVISION PER-CENTAGE	MEDIAN AGE
Kindergarten K & K.P.	Male Female	21,848 20,957	17,512 16,308				2												39,688 37,496	77,184	9.2	
Grade 1	Male Female	230 314	27,845 26,653	26,094 23,077	2,932 1,717	414 230	87 48	37 24	15 13	6 3		1 2	1	2			1		57,667 52,086	109,753	13.1	7.0
Grade 2	Male Female	1 4	512 679	22,901 23,679	24,617 31,434	4,559 2,395	903 434	179 97	73 24	28 7	3 3	3 4	2	1		1			53,792 48,761	102,553	12.2	8.1
Grade 3	Male Female		12	782 1,192	19,728 21,365	22,090 19,444	5,586 3,251	1,412 717	308 183	119 50	33 16	7 7	4 2	2 1				1	50,071 46,241	96,312	11.5	9.1
Total primary division	Male Female	231 318	28,357 27,344	49,777 47,948	47,277 44,516	27,063 22,069	6,576 3,733	1,628 838	396 220	153 60	49 23	11 13	6 3	5 1		1	1	1	161,530 147,088	308,618	36.8	8.0
Grade 4	Male Female			8 16	1,491 2,102	17,714 19,546	19,898 17,417	6,045 3,594	1,836 906	538 235	175 72	52 16	8 7	1 1	2	1	1		47,767 43,914	91,681	10.9	10.1
Grade 5	Male Female				30 35	1,793 2,631	16,898 18,967	17,812 16,598	6,628 3,982	2,420 1,159	678 350	185 80	33 22	1 4					46,478 43,828	90,306	10.8	11.1
Grade 6	Male Female				1	36 30	1,904 2,847	15,917 17,935	17,287 16,113	6,913 4,301	2,614 1,354	618 268	90 48	12 6	1			2	45,394 42,903	88,297	10.5	12.2
Total junior division	Male Female			8 16	1,522 2,137	19,543 22,207	38,700 39,231	39,774 38,127	25,751 21,001	9,871 5,695	3,467 1,776	855 364	131 77	13 11	2 1	1	1	2	139,639 130,645	270,284	32.2	11.1
Grade 7	Male Female						17 59	1,908 2,978	15,028 17,388	16,949 15,846	7,983 4,937	2,412 1,286	470 184	59 19	7 2	6	1	21	44,862 42,699	87,561	10.5	13.2
Grade 8	Male Female						1	32 47	1,999 2,986	14,548 17,334	16,884 16,196	6,241 4,042	1,739 846	192 109	22 8	4 4	2 2	2 35	41,665 41,610	83,275	10.0	14.1
Grade 9	Male Female								1 6	20 41	63 52	48 57	37 26	13 6	3			1	183 191	374		15.0
Grade 10	Male Female									2	5 5	16 22	23 28	27 4	3 2	1			76 63	139		16.4
TOTAL BY SEX	Male Female	22,079 21,275	45,869 43,652	50,075 48,176	48,830 46,667	46,612 44,281	45,295 43,024	43,342 41,990	43,175 41,601	41,541 38,978	28,451 22,989	9,583 5,784	2,406 1,164	309 150	34 16	11 6	5 3	26 36	427,643 399,792			
TOTAL, 1961		43,354	89,521	98,251	95,497	90,893	88,319	85,332	84,776	80,519	51,440	15,367	3,570	459	50	17	8	62	827,435		98.7	
TOTAL, 1956		31,023	71,153	85,174	88,739	69,478	64,240	65,115	64,514	54,046	31,388	11,392	2,451	283	54	38	27	49	639,164			
AUXILIARY		1	54	140	430	856	1,243	1,328	1,573	1,623	1,705	1,268	433	89	37	1		1	10,783		1.3	
GRAND TOTAL		43,355	89,575	98,391	95,927	91,749	89,562	86,660	86,349	82,142	53,145	16,635	4,003	548	87	18	9	63	838,218			
AGE PERCENTAGE, 1961		5.2	10.7	11.7	11.5	10.9	10.7	10.3	10.3	9.8	6.3	2.0	0.5	0.1							100.0	
AGE PERCENTAGE, 1956		4.8	11.1	13.2	13.8	10.9	10.1	10.2	10.1	8.5	5.0	1.9	0.4								100.0	

SOURCE: Report of the Minister of Education of Ontario, 1961.

TABLE 2-8
Age-grade distribution of enrolment, 1966-7

Age of pupils on Sept. 30, 1966	Under 5	5	6	7	8	9	10	11	12	13	14	15	16	17	18	19	20	21	22+	TOTAL ALL AGES	PER CENT OF GRAND TOTAL	MEDIAN AGE
Junior Kindergarten	3,071	110	3																	3,184	.3	4.5
Senior Kindergarten	23,043	68,852	987	40	3															92,925	9.5	5.3
Grade 1	7	27,081	86,357	9,947	875	120	12	5	1											124,405	12.7	6.4
Grade 2		14	21,713	78,612	13,138	1,763	214	37	20											115,517	11.8	7.5
Grade 3			52	20,232	71,788	15,118	2,664	383	81	5	1									110,352	11.3	8.5
Grade 4			1	232	19,279	64,800	15,699	3,546	603	23	11	14	2							104,326	10.7	9.5
Grade 5				2	794	21,702	60,054	16,648	4,378	120	30	31	1							104,517	10.7	10.5
Grade 6					4	1,261	22,020	56,275	17,247	733	174	149	21	17	2					103,108	10.6	11.5
Grade 7						8	1,320	22,675	53,776	4,742	789	892	110	56	9	1				103,571	10.6	12.5
Grade 8							4	1,457	21,594	19,093	5,678	5,578	639	4						97,672	10.0	13.5
Grade 9								3		49,247	19,087	12	8	2						55		14.8
Grade 10										9	1	11	8							22		15.9
Auxiliary	14	60	291	668	1,334	1,828	2,246	2,501	2,703	2,293	1,834	776	592	63	14	3	3		23	17,246	1.8	11.9
TOTAL	26,135	96,117	109,404	109,733	107,215	106,600	104,833	103,530	100,403	76,265	27,624	7,463	1,381	142	25	4	3		23	976,900	100	
PER CENT OF GRAND TOTAL	2.7	9.8	11.2	11.2	11.0	10.9	10.7	10.6	10.3	7.8	2.8	.8	.1								100	

SOURCE: Report of the Minister of Education of Ontario, 1966.

1966–7 can largely be accounted for by the fact that age was recorded eight months earlier in the year. Thus the real average was about the same or slightly higher in 1966–7 than in 1960–1. Children beginning grade 1 thus averaged half a year older in the 1960s than in 1949–50.

Some indirect clues can also be gained with respect to acceleration and retardation practices by comparisons within and among tables. For example, as shown in Table 2-5, the average ages for pupils in grades 2 and 6 respectively in 1949–50 were 7.7 and 11.9 years, a difference of 4.2 years. It is of course impossible to deduce from these figures alone to what extent acceleration of some pupils balanced retardation of others. In 1960–1 the comparable medians for the same grades were 8.1 and 12.2, and in 1966–7, 7.5 and 11.5, as shown in Tables 2-7 and 2-8 respectively. Thus the average loss of one-fifth of a year over the span of four grades disappeared between 1949–50 and 1966–7. The difference may not have been as great as it seemed because of the possibility that rounding errors in the averaging process worked in opposite directions.

Table 2-5, for 1949–50, indicates specifically what was considered the "ideal age spread" for each grade, covering a span of two years. With progress from the lower to the higher grades, an increasing proportion fell outside this ideal spread. The proportion of those older than the ideal age increased more than that of the younger. It is a question whether certain extreme cases were correctly placed or represented statistical errors. We may wonder, for example, about the nineteen-year-old girl who was in grade 2. The thirteen-year-old boy who apparently enrolled in grade 12 must have been not only intellectually precocious, but also unusually fortunate in attending a school that had a sufficiently flexible administrative policy to allow him to study at that level. Within the so-called ideal spread of two years, the boys were consistently in the majority of the older group, while up to the end of grade 12 the girls were in a majority in the younger group. Also, girls were in a substantial majority among those considered younger than the ideal age, and in a minority among those above that age.

Table 2-6, for 1955–6, does not provide as useful information about elementary school enrolment because of the grouping of grades at that level. Again speculation is in order about the three boys aged respectively eight, nine, and ten who were enrolled in grade 10, and about the five-year-old girl who was in the Junior Division. The age spread in each grade in 1966–7, as shown in Table 2-8, was less than that for earlier years. Such a phenomenon might be considered to reflect, at least in part, the extension of the policy of keeping pupils with their peers rather than of promoting solely on the basis of achievement.

Bilingual elementary schools
The period of major expansion in enrolment in bilingual elementary schools was before 1960. Between 1945–6 and 1960–1 the increase was

TABLE 2-9
Enrolment in publicly supported bilingual elementary schools, 1945-70

YEAR	PUBLIC	ROMAN CATHOLIC SEPARATE	TOTAL	YEAR	PUBLIC	ROMAN CATHOLIC SEPARATE	TOTAL
1945-6			45,418	1964-5	2,700	87,610	90,310
1950-1	4,200	48,387	52,587	1965-6	2,354	88,241	90,595
1955-6	5,376	61,090	66,466	1966-7	2,455	90,771	93,226
1960-1	3,673	80,312	83,985	1967-8	2,459	92,145	94,604
1961-2	3,579	82,568	86,147	1968-9	2,336	87,858	90,194
1962-3	3,186	84,841	88,027	1969-70	2,354	88,043	90,397
1963-4	3,088	85,450	88,538				

SOURCE: Reports of the Minister of Education of Ontario.

from 45,418 to 83,985, or in the order of 85 per cent. During the 1960s there was comparatively little change. Throughout the period an overwhelming proportion of the bilingual enrolment was in Roman Catholic separate schools. In 1950-1 the percentage was 92.0; in 1960-1, 95.6; and in 1969-70, 97.4.

Enrolment by type of board

Enrolment in public elementary and Protestant separate schools operated by each type of school board for 1955-6 and from 1960-1 to 1968 is shown in Table 2-10. Contrary to the usual practice of combining for statistical purposes the very small number of children attending Protestant separate schools with those attending public elementary schools, this group is shown separately in the table. Figures are not given for 1969-70 because the school board reorganization for that year changed the situation completely.

One of the salient features of the table is the large proportion of pupils attending schools under the control of boards of education. Between 1955-6 and 1960-1 the percentage rose from 43.7 to 46.6, and between 1960-1 and 1968, to 53.8. Between 1964-5 and 1965-6, when the remaining school sections were combined and the township school area became the smallest unit of school administration, the percentage of the total enrolment under township boards increased from 19.7 per cent to 26.4. Enrolment under what were labeled "other public school area boards: rural" fell from 7.2 per cent to .05 per cent. For the years 1955-6 and 1961-2 the reports of the minister combined rural and urban public school area boards. Enrolment in the latter declined while that under boards of education increased as certain urban areas formed boards of education. The provision for the voluntary formation of county and district school area boards after 1965 resulted in a comparatively small change in the set-up. Enrolment under boards operating schools on Crown lands fluctuated but did not change drastically during the period. The railway car schools were dropped after 1965-6.

TABLE 2-10
Enrolment in public elementary and Protestant separate schools operated by each type of school board, 1955-68

TYPE OF SCHOOL BOARD	1955-6	1960-1	1961-2	1962-3	1963-4	1964-5	1965-6	1966-7	1967-8	1968
Boards of education	295,555	393,351	424,114	442,290	456,561	473,969	494,584	522,379	537,912	549,401
County school area boards								9,435	14,654	25,316
District school area boards								1,699	9,610	12,376
Township school area boards	145,623	169,856	163,434	164,679	172,461	182,632	250,511[a]	243,218	243,831	241,443
Other public school area boards										
urban	226,727	179,277	262,351	183,468	186,032	188,901	185,802	185,578	180,925	175,763
rural		89,263		77,277	73,743	66,245	4,831	4,370	5,783	5,160
Boards operating schools on Crown lands[b]	7,902	11,699	11,560	12,241	12,798	13,102	13,421	10,041	9,636	12,023
Protestant separate school boards	236	239	217	211	195	177	186	180	204	194
Others[c]	168	52	39	32	40	42	39			
TOTAL	676,246[d]	843,737	861,715	880,198	901,830	925,068	949,374	976,900	1,002,555	1,021,676

SOURCE: Reports of the Minister of Education of Ontario.

[a]Including county school area boards.
[b]Military and Hydro schools.
[c]Railway school cars.
[d]Includes 35 students under Roman Catholic Separate School Boards.

Enrolment by type of municipal organization

Enrolment in all elementary schools, both public and Roman Catholic separate, by type of municipality, is shown in Table 2-11. According to the classification scheme used in the reports of the minister, unorganized townships were separated from rural townships after 1964–5. The boroughs established in Metropolitan Toronto in 1967 absorbed most of the former enrolment in urban townships, and the rest was classified under rural townships in 1968–9. The main features of changing enrolment by type of municipality were the increase of 39.2 per cent in cities between 1960–1 and 1969–70, the rather slow increase in towns, and the stable enrolment in villages and rural townships.

ENROLMENT IN PUBLICLY SUPPORTED SECONDARY SCHOOLS

Grade distribution

Tables 2-12 and 2-13 show the grade distribution in publicly supported secondary schools by numbers and percentages respectively for the period between 1950–1 and 1969–70. In the early part of that period increasing retention rates tended to keep the grade distribution in relative balance, even though the number entering grade 9 began to rise rapidly after 1953. From about 1957 on, a gradual shift toward the upper grades set in. Between 1958–9 and 1969–70 the percentage in grade 13 rose from 6.5 to 8.7, and that in grade 12 from 14.1 to 18.3. During the same period the percentage in grade 10 decreased from 26.8 to 24.5, and that in grade 9 from 33.8 to 27.2. That is, the rising retention rate in the higher grades more than compensated for the constantly increasing number entering grade 9.

Enrolment by course, branch, and program

Because of the introduction of the Reorganized Program or Robarts Plan, 1962–3 represents a watershed in terms of courses, branches, and programs offered in the secondary schools. The grade 9 students of that year were actually enrolled in the new program, which was thereafter introduced in successive grades a year at a time. The official statistics, however, use the old categorization scheme for all grades in 1962–3, and the new one for all grades thereafter. The artificiality of this approach must be kept in mind in any interpretation of quantitative or numerical trends during the transition period.

Before the introduction of the new program, as indicated in Table 2-14, most of the students were enrolled in the General, Commercial, and Technical (labeled "Industrial" before 1959) courses. The overwhelming majority at this stage were in the General course, although the percentage declined from 75.7 in 1955–6 to 69.8 in 1962–3. The Federal-Provincial Technical and Vocational Training Agreement and the Reorganized Program were soon to accelerate this trend. During the 1955–6 to 1962–3 period, the number in the Commercial course approximately doubled,

TABLE 2-11
Enrolment in elementary schools in each type of municipality, 1960-70

TYPE OF MUNICIPALITY	1960-1	1961-2	1962-3	1963-4	1964-5	1965-6	1966-7	1967-8	1968-9	1969-70
Cities	409,091	443,521	455,920	478,078	492,705	512,761	542,511	555,653	563,125	569,544
Boroughs								228,993	233,146	238,520
Towns	184,896	190,053	201,288	202,955	209,826	216,193	216,703	214,810	247,963	254,767
Villages	43,495	44,058	44,043	46,391	46,786	50,806	48,026	46,159	50,696	50,249
Urban townships	192,725	192,433	206,402	211,596	228,404	242,011	248,432	42,140		
Rural townships	284,482	281,428	277,135	281,346	287,650	269,668	283,917	292,616	311,071[a]	320,088
Unorganized townships						13,797	12,737	12,512	12,566	12,384
Crown lands	11,699	11,560	12,241	12,798	13,102	14,807	12,545	12,169	12,023	10,565
TOTAL	1,126,388	1,163,053	1,197,029	1,233,164	1,278,473	1,320,043	1,364,871	1,405,052	1,430,590	1,456,117

SOURCE: Reports of the Minister of Education of Ontario.

[a] Urban and rural combined.

TABLE 2-12
Enrolment in secondary schools by grade, 1950–70

YEAR	GRADE 9	10	11	12	13	TOTAL
1950–1	46,191	33,886	22,931	17,576	9,457	130,041
1951–2	46,085	35,384	23,833	18,300	8,827	132,429
1952–3	49,549	36,946	25,321	19,245	8,975	140,036
1953–4	51,858	39,477	26,458	20,441	9,472	147,706
1954–5	55,887	42,262	29,133	21,713	9,981	158,976
1955–6	61,911	45,251	31,489	23,846	10,799	173,296
1956–7	66,354	48,640	32,830	25,041	11,487	184,352
1957–8	72,063	53,654	37,177	26,769	12,547	202,210
1958–9	74,604	59,109	41,718	31,058	14,278	220,767
1959–60	76,598	60,829	45,552	34,792	16,267	234,038
1960–1	88,607	64,783	47,833	38,697	18,447	258,367
1961–2	100,988	76,290	52,681	42,266	21,482	293,707
1962–3	103,866	86,012	61,733	46,776	23,750	322,137
1963–4	103,526	90,817	70,302	55,731	26,262	346,638
1964–5	105,899	93,453	77,922	64,418	32,770	374,462
1965–6	110,997	96,299	80,710	67,282	37,692	392,980
1966–7	117,582	100,710	83,963	70,625	35,007	407,887
1967–8	124,067	108,789	88,988	75,214	36,472	433,530
1968–9	131,082	117,425	98,585	82,371	40,087	469,550
1969–70	135,420	122,181	105,836	90,956	43,569	497,962

SOURCE: Reports of the Minister of Education of Ontario.

TABLE 2-13
Percentage of total enrolment in each secondary school grade, 1950–70

YEAR	GRADE 9	10	11	12	13	TOTAL
1950–1	35.5	26.1	17.6	13.5	7.3	100.0
1951–2	34.8	26.7	18.0	13.8	6.7	100.0
1952–3	35.4	26.4	18.1	13.7	6.4	100.0
1953–4	35.2	26.7	17.9	13.8	6.4	100.0
1954–5	35.2	26.6	18.3	13.6	6.3	100.0
1955–6	35.7	26.1	18.2	13.8	6.2	100.0
1956–7	36.0	26.4	17.8	13.6	6.2	100.0
1957–8	35.6	26.5	18.4	13.2	6.3	100.0
1958–9	33.8	26.8	18.8	14.1	6.5	100.0
1959–60	32.7	26.0	19.5	14.8	7.0	100.0
1960–1	34.3	25.1	18.5	15.0	7.1	100.0
1961–2	34.4	26.0	17.9	14.4	7.3	100.0
1962–3	32.2	26.7	19.2	14.5	7.4	100.0
1963–4	29.8	26.2	20.3	16.1	7.6	100.0
1964–5	28.3	25.0	20.8	17.2	8.7	100.0
1965–6	28.3	24.5	20.5	17.1	9.6	100.0
1966–7	28.8	24.7	20.6	17.3	8.6	100.0
1967–8	28.7	25.1	20.5	17.3	8.4	100.0
1968–9	27.9	25.1	21.0	17.5	8.5	100.0
1969–70	27.2	24.5	21.3	18.3	8.7	100.0

SOURCE: Calculated from reports of the Minister of Education of Ontario.

TABLE 2-14
Enrolment in secondary schools by course, 1955–63

YEAR	COURSE General	Commercial	Commercial special	Industrial	Technical[a]	Home Economics	Art	Special courses[b]	TOTAL[c]
1955-6	131,236	24,658		15,479		1,385	538		173,296
1956-7	140,975	25,481		16,589		726	581		184,352
1957-8	155,641	27,304		18,169		515	581		202,210
1958-9	170,263	29,014		20,366		465	659		220,767
1959-60	181,337	29,248	1,887		20,516	412	638	2,220	236,258
1960-1	200,368	32,345	2,182		22,343	365	764	3,050	261,417
1961-2	227,018	36,550	2,227		26,618	499	795	4,062	297,769
1962-3	230,516	50,512	2,962		37,165	334	648	7,969	330,106

SOURCE: Reports of the Minister of Education of Ontario.

NOTE: This table includes students in a small number of Junior High and Senior Public Schools.

[a]Including approved two-year trade courses.
[b]Including full-time, non-diploma, ungraded courses: e.g., pre-vocational, academic vocational, special trade, art, and similar courses.
[c]Not including special industrial students.

rising from a little over 14 per cent to over 15 per cent of the total. The beginning of the practice of listing enrolment in the Special Commercial course separately in 1959–60 tends to obscure a small relative increase in the regular Commercial course after that date.

After 1958–9 enrolment under the heading "Industrial" was shown under "Technical" and "Special courses." The latter included a number of ungraded, non-diploma courses. Between 1959–60 and 1962–3 the enrolment in these courses increased by nearly 260 per cent. During the same four-year interval the number in Technical courses almost doubled. There was a rather sharp decline in the Home Economics course and a fairly steady enrolment in the Art course.

Table 2-15 shows the distribution of enrolment in grades 9 to 13 by branch and program to 1968–9, and by branch only in 1969–70. Since enrolment in the Occupational program and in various special ungraded courses is not included, the totals in the final column are considerably lower than those in Table 2-1. Beginning in 1968–9, grade 13 enrolment was no longer differentiated according to branch. For the sake of tracing trends from previous years, students in this grade have been treated as if they were in Arts and Science. Such a procedure corrects the anomalous decrease in the number in the Five-year Arts and Science program between 1967–8 and 1968–9.

Table 2-15 and Chart 2-3 indicate that the Arts and Science branch continued to attract the majority of the graded students. The percentage, however, declined from 65.4 per cent in 1963–4 to 57.2 per cent of the total of graded students in 1969–70. The percentage in Business and Commerce, on the other hand, increased from 19.7 to 21.7. The greatest gain among the three branches was in Science, Technology, and Trades, where the percentage rose from 15.0 to 21.0. A change in balance among the three branches was one of the main purposes of the reorganization and, in the light of these figures, showed signs of being realized.

The minister made an assessment of the way the situation seemed to be changing in 1964.

When the three-branch reorganized programme was announced, concern was expressed in some quarters that there was little use in setting up the two vocational streams – business and commerce; and science, technology and trades – and in providing technical class accommodation in new buildings across the province under the federal-provincial agreement, because parents would be insistent that their children follow the traditional university preparatory course – arts and science. Happily, Mr. Chairman, this has not been the case. A survey last September, covering 22 representative high school districts, showed the situation to be as follows: Of pupils entering Grade 10 in September, 1963, 46 per cent were headed for the arts and science branch; 28 per cent planned to enter the business and commerce branch; and 26 per cent planned to enter the science, technology and trades branch.

TABLE 2-15
Enrolment in secondary schools by branch and program, 1963-70

YEAR	ARTS AND SCIENCE				BUSINESS AND COMMERCE					SCIENCE, TECHNOLOGY, AND TRADES					UN-GRADED	GRAND TOTAL
	5-year	4-year	2-year	TOTAL	5-year	4-year	2-year	1-year	TOTAL	5-year	4-year	2-year	1-year	TOTAL		
1963-4	218,271	7,911	355	226,537	13,012	49,569	2,575	2,988	68,144	12,741	36,715	2,466	35	51,957		346,638
1964-5	221,177	13,094	216	234,487	15,031	58,166	2,534	3,599	79,330	15,793	42,745	2,085	22	60,645		374,462
1965-6	218,711	18,371	160	237,242	18,324	65,555	2,577		86,456	19,087	47,978	2,217		69,282		392,980
1966-7	216,605	19,918		236,523	21,046	70,313	2,746		94,105	22,238	52,744	2,277		77,259		407,887
1967-8	223,162	21,591		244,753	22,004	76,902	2,572		101,478	25,586	58,802	2,911		87,299		433,530
1968-9	199,252	25,120	41	264,500[a]	25,178	80,125	2,202		107,505	29,821	64,469	3,255		97,545		469,550
1969-70				247,718[a]					93,889					90,999	65,356	497,962

SOURCE: Reports of the Minister of Education of Ontario.

[a]The grade 13 enrolment of 40,087 in 1968-9 and 43,569 in 1969-70 is included in the respective totals; distribution by branch was no longer, strictly speaking, applicable.

116 The expansion of the educational system

CHART 2-3
Percentage of secondary school enrolment in Ontario in each branch, 1963–70

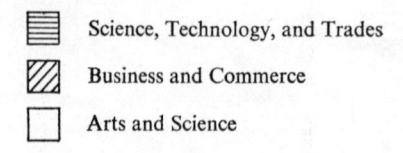

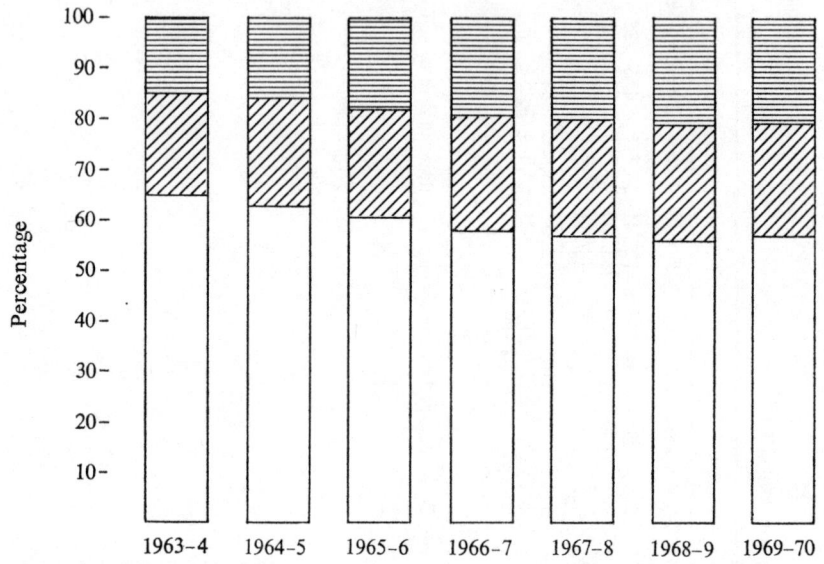

▤ Science, Technology, and Trades
▨ Business and Commerce
☐ Arts and Science

[Bar chart showing percentages for years 1963–4, 1964–5, 1965–6, 1966–7, 1967–8, 1968–9, 1969–70, with Percentage on the y-axis from 0 to 100]

NOTE: All grade 13 students of 1968–9 and 1969–70 are treated as Arts and Science students.

Of the total enrolment in the secondary schools, approximately 40 per cent of the students are enrolled in vocational courses. Since many schools do not separate Grade 9 students into the various branches, but offer a more or less common course under the arts and science branch, the percentage who are actually and potentially vocational is likely somewhat higher than 40 per cent. This distribution of students is evidence that the variety of opportunity now being offered in the secondary schools of the province is being welcomed by parents and pupils alike. The fact that the vocational courses have a strong academic content, and that their pupils graduate with not only a marketable skill, but with a good general education, has contributed to this change in attitude towards vocational instruction.[9]

The survey to which Davis referred suggested a greater shift away from the Arts and Science branch than was apparently occurring in the province as a whole.

The former General course was almost the only route by which students

CHART 2-4
Percentage of secondary school enrolment in Ontario in each program, 1963–9

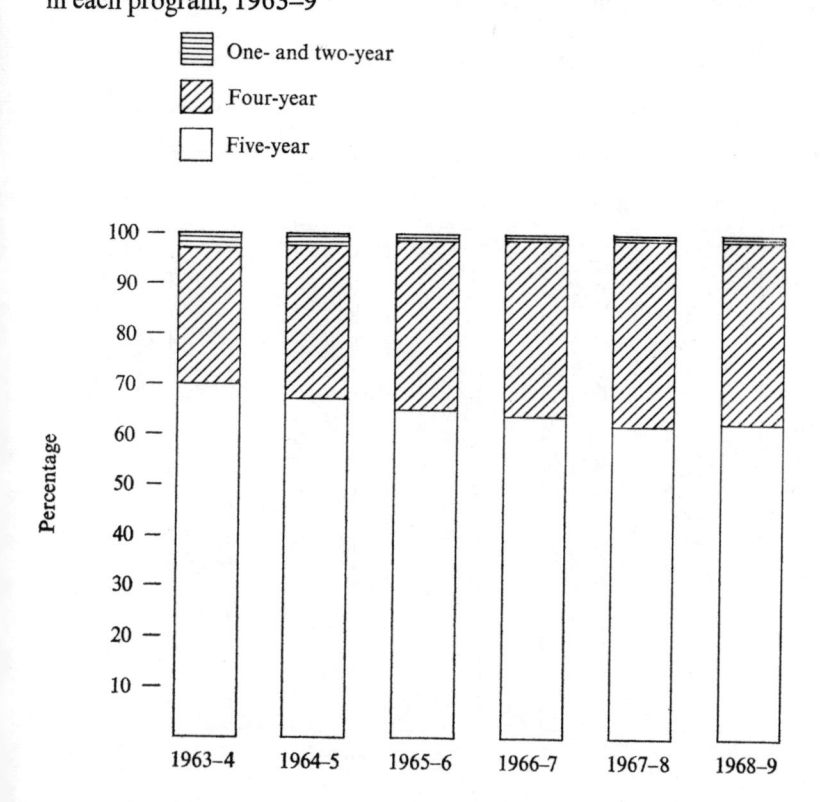

One- and two-year
Four-year
Five-year

could proceed to university. It was originally intended that the Reorganized Program would provide alternative routes to the same goal through the Business and Commerce and the Science, Technology, and Trades branches. Table 2-16 reveals that this objective was not attained to any real extent up to 1967–8. While the grade 13 enrolment increased from 11.9 per cent in 1963–4 to 16.1 per cent in 1967–8 in the five-year program of the Arts and Science branch, the corresponding percentages for Business and Commerce were 0.5 and 0.7, and for Science, Technology, and Trades, 2.1 and 1.6.

The original intention was that there would be three programs within each branch: the five-year, four-year, and two-year programs. The two-year program never caught on at all in the Arts and Science branch. In the other two branches a relatively small proportion of students have been enrolled in it. Even if the students taking the one-year courses (mainly Special Commercial students in Business and Commerce up to 1964) are grouped with the two-year students, they together constituted at most fewer than 3 per cent of the total between 1963–4 and 1968–9. Those who

CHART 2-5
Percentage of secondary school enrolment in Ontario in each branch and program, 1963-9

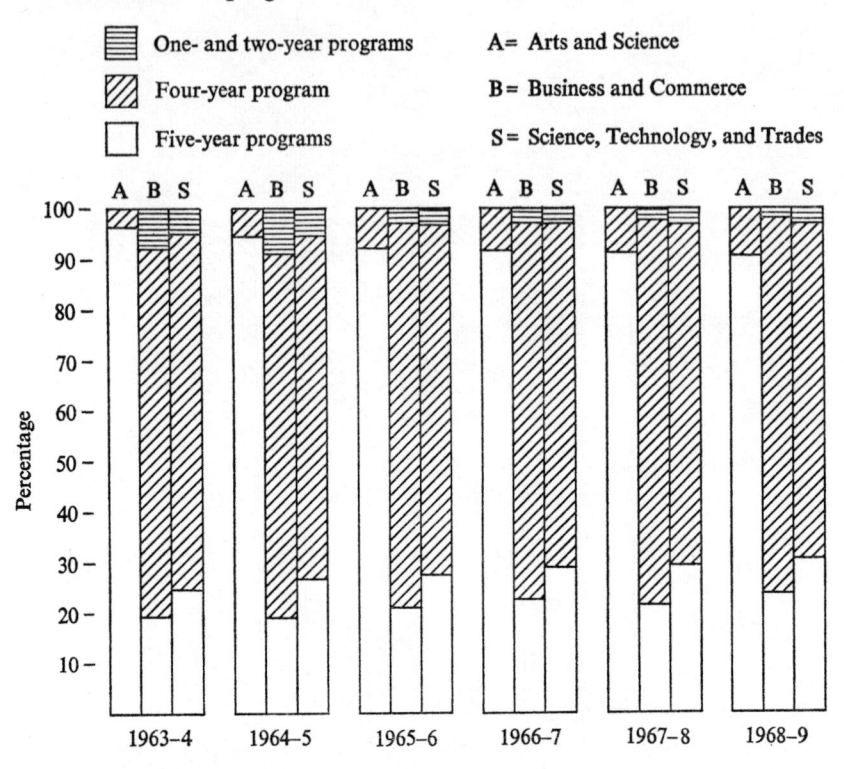

- One- and two-year programs
- Four-year program
- Five-year programs

A = Arts and Science
B = Business and Commerce
S = Science, Technology, and Trades

did not go into the five-year and four-year programs went to a large extent into ungraded programs.

Enrolment by grade, branch, and program
In the Arts and Science branch, the great majority of those in the five-year program continued to the end of grade 12, as indicated by the grade distribution in Table 2-16. In most years from 1963 on, the percentage of the enrolment in grade 12 was between 70 and 80 per cent of that in grade 9. Grade 13 had 11.9 per cent of the enrolment of the total in the five grades in 1963, 14.7 per cent in 1964, and 17.1 per cent in 1965, after which the percentage declined slightly. The increasing availability and attractiveness of programs that could be entered at the end of grade 12, particularly those offered by the colleges of applied arts and technology, are assumed to account for this decline.

In the other two branches, a large percentage of those in the five-year program in 1963-4 withdrew from it by the end of grade 9, and most of the rest by the end of grade 10. For that year the enrolment in grades 11, 12, and 13 in Business and Commerce constituted only 7.5 per cent of the

Enrolment in schools and courses 119

TABLE 2-16
Enrolment in five-year programs in Ontario secondary schools by branch and grade, 1963–9

YEAR	BRANCH	GRADE 9 No.	Per cent	10 No.	Per cent	11 No.	Per cent	12 No.	Per cent	13[a] No.	Per cent	TOTAL No.	Per cent
1963–4	Arts and Science	54,183	24.8	45,067	20.7	51,382	23.5	41,708	19.1	25,931	11.9	218,271	100.0
	Business and Commerce	8,127	62.4	3,915	30.1	567	4.4	342	2.6	61	0.5	13,012	100.0
	Science, Technology, and Trades	7,374	57.9	3,964	31.1	737	5.8	396	3.1	270	2.1	12,741	100.0
1964–5	Arts and Science	55,466	25.1	44,054	19.9	42,742	19.3	46,444	21.0	32,471	14.7	221,177	100.0
	Business and Commerce	7,807	51.9	4,595	30.6	2,162	14.4	406	2.7	61	0.4	15,031	100.0
	Science, Technology, and Trades	7,168	45.4	4,870	30.8	2,868	18.2	673	4.3	214	1.3	15,793	100.0
1965–6	Arts and Science	56,004	25.6	44,095	20.2	41,498	19.0	39,676	18.1	37,438	17.1	218,711	100.0
	Business and Commerce	8,472	46.2	5,078	27.7	3,054	16.7	1,660	9.1	60	0.3	18,324	100.0
	Science, Technology, and Trades	7,744	40.6	5,190	27.2	3,657	19.1	2,302	12.1	194	1.0	19,087	100.0
1966–7	Arts and Science	56,167	25.9	44,510	20.5	41,893	19.3	39,497	18.4	34,538	15.9	216,605	100.0
	Business and Commerce	9,712	46.2	5,691	27.0	3,341	15.9	2,213	10.5	89	0.4	21,046	100.0
	Science, Technology, and Trades	9,164	41.2	5,810	26.1	3,815	17.2	3,069	13.8	380	1.7	22,238	100.0
1967–8	Arts and Science	57,476	25.6	46,564	21.0	42,798	19.2	40,428	18.1	35,896	16.1	223,162	100.0
	Business and Commerce	9,528	43.3	6,105	27.7	3,580	16.3	2,634	12.0	157	0.7	22,004	100.0
	Science, Technology, and Trades	10,365	40.5	6,853	26.8	4,504	17.6	3,445	13.5	419	1.6	25,586	100.0
1968–9	Arts and Science	60,713	30.5	49,554	24.9	46,165	23.1	42,820	21.5			199,252	100.0
	Business and Commerce	10,397	41.3	6,961	27.7	4,565	18.1	3,255	12.9			25,178	100.0
	Science, Technology, and Trades	11,487	38.5	8,381	28.1	5,685	19.1	4,268	14.3			29,821	100.0

SOURCE: Reports of the Minister of Education of Ontario.

[a] The grade 13 enrolment of 40,087 is not included in the total for 1968–9; distribution by branch and program not applicable.

total. The corresponding percentage for Science, Technology, and Trades was 11.0. This was the traditional pattern that had prevailed in the Commercial and Technical courses, which had not yet been phased out in those grades. Signs of a change were evident from 1964–5 on. The percentage of the total five-year program enrolled in grade 11 more than tripled in both branches between 1963–4 and 1964–5, and a comparable increase occurred in grade 12 between 1964–5 and 1965–6 as the Reorganized Program students reached those grades in succession. In subsequent years the increase in the percentages in the same two grades was not very great.

When grade 13 enrolment ceased to be categorized according to branch and program in 1968–9, the percentage distribution of Arts and Science enrolment among the grades was affected drastically. Thus the figures in Table 2-16 for that year are not really comparable to those of the preceding years. If the 40,087 grade 13 students are arbitrarily assigned to that branch, the percentages for grades 9 to 13 are respectively 25.4, 20.7, 19.3, 17.9, and 16.7. These represent little change from the previous year.

The relatively small enrolment assigned to the four-year program in the Arts and Science branch in 1963–4, before the General course had been phased out in the upper grades, was concentrated in grades 9 and 10, as shown in Table 2-17. Between 1963–4 and 1964–5 the grade 11 enrolment in this program and branch increased from 4.8 per cent of that in all four grades to 42.9 per cent. The corresponding increase for the same successive years was from 20.5 to 24.6 per cent in Business and Commerce, and from 19.2 to 23.7 in Science, Technology, and Trades. Between 1963–4 and 1965–6 the percentage of the four-year enrolment registered in grade 12 increased from 11.9 to 16.6 and from 11.1 to 16.1 in these two branches respectively. The distribution of enrolment among grades in the four-year program subsequently remained in a state of relative equilibrium.

Enrolment in special or ungraded courses in secondary schools for the years 1963–4 to 1969–70 is shown in Table 2-18. There was an increase in enrolment in the Occupational program from 9,922 in 1963–4 to 15,000 in 1965–6, after which the number changed little from year to year. The special vocational program showed a slow increase up to 1967–8, and nearly doubled in the subsequent year.

Retention

The retention rate in secondary schools can be determined by taking the percentage of each successive year's enrolment surviving in the following year. The situation for those starting in 1951–2, and in the years between 1956–7 and 1964–5, is shown in Table 2-19. The percentage surviving from each grade to the succeeding one showed a progressive increase during that period. Thus, by 1968–9 10 per cent more survived from grade 9 to grade 10, 21 per cent more of the original group survived to

TABLE 2-11

Enrolment in four-year programs in Ontario secondary schools by branch and grade, 1963–9

YEAR	BRANCH	GRADE 9 No.	Per cent	10 No.	Per cent	11 No.	Per cent	12 No.	Per cent	TOTAL No.	Per cent
1963–4	Arts and Science	2,683	33.9	4,695	59.3	379	4.8	154	2.0	7,911	100.0
	Business and Commerce	15,331	31.0	18,158	36.6	10,177	20.5	5,903	11.9	49,569	100.0
	Science, Technology, and Trades	12,828	34.9	12,767	34.8	7,032	19.2	4,088	11.1	36,715	100.0
1964–5	Arts and Science	2,609	19.9	4,590	35.1	5,624	42.9	271	2.1	13,094	100.0
	Business and Commerce	16,926	29.1	19,321	33.2	14,303	24.6	7,616	13.1	58,166	100.0
	Science, Technology, and Trades	13,428	31.4	13,825	32.4	10,148	23.7	5,320	12.5	42,721	100.0
1965–6	Arts and Science	2,353	12.8	4,918	26.8	6,064	33.0	5,036	27.4	18,371	100.0
	Business and Commerce	18,750	28.6	20,749	31.6	15,199	23.2	10,857	16.6	65,555	100.0
	Science, Technology, and Trades	14,633	30.5	14,420	30.0	11,209	23.4	7,716	16.1	47,978	100.0
1966–7	Arts and Science	2,495	12.5	5,008	25.1	6,653	33.4	5,762	29.0	19,918	100.0
	Business and Commerce	20,617	29.3	21,804	31.0	16,496	23.5	11,396	16.2	70,313	100.0
	Science, Technology, and Trades	16,492	31.3	15,799	29.9	11,765	22.3	8,688	16.5	52,744	100.0
1967–8	Arts and Science	2,113	9.8	5,485	25.4	7,260	33.6	6,733	31.2	21,591	100.0
	Business and Commerce	22,743	29.6	23,638	30.7	17,771	23.1	12,750	16.6	76,902	100.0
	Science, Technology, and Trades	18,847	32.1	17,656	30.0	13,075	22.2	9,224	15.7	58,802	100.0
1968–9	Arts and Science	3,736	14.9	6,073	24.2	8,038	32.0	7,273	28.9	25,120	100.0
	Business and Commerce	22,340	27.9	24,284	30.3	19,226	24.0	14,275	17.8	80,125	100.0
	Science, Technology, and Trades	19,607	30.4	19,476	30.2	14,906	23.1	10,480	16.3	64,469	100.0

SOURCE: Reports of the Minister of Education of Ontario.

TABLE 2-18
Enrolment in Ontario secondary schools in special or ungraded courses, 1963–70

YEAR	COURSE				TOTAL	TOTAL, GRADES 9–13	GRAND TOTAL
	One-year	Occupational program	Special vocational	Other			
1963–4		9,922	5,177	2,473	17,572	346,638	364,210
1964–5		12,474	6,187	2,178	20,839	374,462	395,301
1965–6	4,073	15,000	5,947	738	25,758	392,980	418,738
1966–7	3,963	15,876	7,860	440	28,139	407,887	436,026
1967–8	2,836	17,974	8,484	912	30,206	433,530	463,736
1968–9	1,596	14,428	14,455	778	31,257	469,550	500,807
1969–70	993	15,569	15,132	1,023	32,717	497,962	530,679

SOURCE: Reports of the Minister of Education of Ontario.

grade 11, 22 per cent more to grade 12, and 13 per cent more to grade 13. The percentage proceeding from grade 13 to university more than doubled. Of course these comparisons can be misleading. The increase between grades 9 and 10 could not be very great because the survival rate was already 79 per cent. A gain of 10 percentage points represents a very creditable improvement. The greater part of this gain, as of that at other grade levels, occurred in the 1960s.

Between 1955–6 and 1967–8 the percentage of the original grade 9 group who received the Ontario Secondary School Honour Graduation Diploma increased from 12 to 25. The percentage of those enrolled in grade 13 who received the diploma rose from 57 to 78 between those two years, an increase which was partly accounted for by the adoption of the practice of granting the diploma to private school candidates. The success rate dipped somewhat in 1966–7, the last year of the grade 13 departmental examinations.

Another way of looking at the retention question is demonstrated in Table 2-20, which shows the percentage of the number enrolled in elementary school and in each grade of secondary school who withdrew without completing the year. Figures are shown for 1955–6 and for the years between 1958–9 and 1968–9. During this period the reduction in the withdrawal rate in the elementary school, where attendance was compulsory for nearly all children, was from 1.5 per cent to an insignificant 0.4 per cent. It was in the secondary grades that major changes were recorded. The percentage of withdrawals or retirements from grade 9 fell from 16.0 to 2.3; from grade 10, from 21.8 to 4.8; from grade 11, from 18.1 to 4.8; from grade 12, from 40.3 to 21.8; and from grade 13, from 25.2 to 8.8. These figures suggest a decrease in the attractiveness of immediate employment opportunities that might tempt students to abandon their school year.

The reasons why students left the school system, either during the year or after completing a particular program, are shown in Table 2-21 for the

TABLE 2-19

Estimated progress of students through Ontario secondary schools, 1951-69, by percentage of grade 9 enrolment in each subsequent year

STARTING YEAR	GRADE 9	GRADE 10	GRADE 11	GRADE 12	GRADE 13	FINAL YEAR	HONOUR GRADUATION DIPLOMA	INTENDED TO ENTER UNIVERSITY
1951-2	100	79	51	42	21	1955-6	12	7
1956-7	100	81	57	48	25	1960-1	13	9
1957-8	100	82	57	49	27	1961-2	15	10
1958-9	100	81	58	51	29	1962-3	16	11
1959-60	100	84	62	55	31	1963-4	17	12
1960-1	100	85	62	56	33	1964-5	19	12
1961-2	100	84	62	57	34	1965-6	23	14
1962-3	100	86	68	59	31	1966-7	21	14
1963-4	100	89	70	62	32	1967-8	21	14
1964-5	100	89	72	64	34	1968-9	25	16

SOURCE: Reports of the Minister of Education of Ontario.

TABLE 2-20
Percentages of retirements from Ontario schools according to grade level, 1955–69

YEAR	PERCENTAGE OF RETIREMENTS FROM					
	Elementary school	Grade 9	Grade 10	Grade 11	Grade 12	Grade 13
1955–6	1.5	16.0	21.8	18.1	40.3	25.2
1958–9	1.3	12.7	16.3	15.5	33.4	21.5
1959–60	1.2	13.4	16.6	16.1	34.1	20.9
1960–1	1.1	11.9	16.2	15.1	32.4	19.2
1961–2	1.0	9.2	13.6	12.5	29.5	17.5
1962–3	1.0	9.7	13.7	13.1	32.4	20.5
1963–4	1.0	9.2	12.5	11.5	31.3	18.8
1964–5	0.7	6.8	11.2	10.3	29.3	18.7
1965–6	0.7	4.5	8.7	8.4	25.8	15.3
1966–7	0.5	4.3	8.3	8.3	31.6	16.2
1967–8	0.4	3.0	6.5	6.3	27.6	12.7
1968–9	0.4	2.3	4.8	4.8	21.8	8.8

SOURCE: Reports of the Minister of Education of Ontario.

years between 1959–60 and 1967–8. The three general categories of reasons are employment, unemployment, and further training. Those who left Ontario and those who withdrew because of physical disability are included under the heading "other reasons." During the nine years covered in the table, the percentage who left to take jobs fell from 40.8 to 26.6. The period of regular decline was actually that after 1963–4. The relatively high level of unemployment in the labour force in general may account for the drop from 40.8 per cent in 1959–60 to 36.8 per cent in 1960–1, and improved economic conditions for the rise to 40.7 per cent in 1963–4. Among the types of employment for which withdrawals declined most sharply were agricultural (from 4.6 per cent in 1959–60 to 1.0 per cent in 1967–8) and service (from 6.2 per cent to 2.8 per cent). There was also a substantial decline in the "commercial, financial," "construction," and "transportation and communications" categories. The percentage going into manufacturing and mechanical occupations increased until 1963–4, and then remained fairly constant until 1967–8, when a sharp decline was recorded. The existence of a group who withdrew to enter "professional" occupations raises a question about the meaning attached to the term. A partial or complete high school education is not in itself usually regarded as adequate preparation for any profession according to common definitions.

The percentage recorded as unemployed rose slightly from 11.3 in 1959–60 to 12.1 in 1962–3, and fell sharply from 10.2 in 1963–4 to 6.6 in 1964–5, after which it remained fairly constant. It may be assumed that those in this group were eligible for and seeking employment. Girls withdrawing to engage in housework at home would fall in the "other reasons" category.

In the further training category, the pronounced and steady increase in

TABLE 2-21

Percentages of pupils leaving Ontario elementary and secondary schools for various reasons, 1959–68

DESTINATION	1959-60	1960-1	1961-2	1962-3	1963-4	1964-5	1965-6	1966-7	1967-8
EMPLOYMENT									
Agricultural	4.6	4.3	3.7	3.4	2.7	1.6	1.3	1.3	1.0
Clerical	10.7	9.7	10.7	10.6	11.5	12.3	12.5	10.8	9.3
Commercial, financial	4.1	3.8	3.4	3.3	3.5	1.9	2.1	2.1	2.0
Construction	1.3	1.1	1.1	1.2	1.2	1.0	1.0	*	*
Fishing, hunting, trapping, logging, mining	0.6	0.4	0.4	0.5	0.5	0.4	0.5	0.4	0.4
Labouring occupations	6.7	6.2	7.2	7.3	7.8	7.4	7.5	5.6	5.6
Manufacturing and mechanical	4.1	3.5	4.5	4.9	5.9	5.7	5.7	5.6	3.6
Professional	0.7	0.5	0.5	0.5	0.5	0.4	0.6	0.6	1.1
Proprietary and managerial	0.1	0.1	0.1	0.1	0.1	0.1	0.1	0.1	0.1
Service	6.2	5.9	6.4	6.4	5.3	4.6	3.6	3.7	2.8
Transportation and communications	1.7	1.3	1.5	1.5	1.7	1.5	1.6	1.2	0.7
Total	40.8	36.8	39.5	39.7	40.7	36.9	36.5	31.4	26.6
UNEMPLOYMENT	11.3	11.7	11.9	12.1	10.2	6.6	6.0	6.4	6.3
FURTHER TRAINING									
Agricultural schools	0.2	0.2	0.2	0.2	0.2	0.1	0.1	0.1	0.2
Business schools	2.3	2.1	1.9	1.7	1.5	1.3	1.0	0.7	0.4
Colleges of applied arts and technology								2.8	4.3
Pre-teachers' college summer course	0.2								
Private academic schools	8.8	9.3	9.7	8.1	7.2	6.7	5.5	5.1	5.5
Private trade schools	0.4	0.6	0.5	0.4	0.5	0.4	0.4	0.1	0.3
Provincial institutes of trades				0.2	0.4	0.4	0.4	0.2	
Provincial technical institutes	0.9	1.3	1.2	1.3	1.5	1.4	1.5	0.3	
Schools of nursing	2.0	2.4	2.3	2.2	2.1	2.1	1.8	1.7	1.8
Teachers' colleges	2.9	3.0	2.2	2.7	2.6	2.1	2.4	2.1	2.8
Universities	5.9	6.9	6.8	7.5	8.4	8.7	9.9	10.5	11.9
Other educational institutions	1.4	0.7	0.9	0.7	0.8	0.8	1.4	0.9	1.0
Total	25.0	26.5	25.8	25.0	25.2	24.0	24.4	25.2[a]	28.9[a]
OTHER REASONS	22.9	25.0	22.8	23.2	23.9	32.5	33.1	37.0	38.2
TOTAL LEAVING SCHOOL SYSTEM	100.0	100.0	100.0	100.0	100.0	100.0	100.0	100.0	100.0

SOURCE: Reports of the Minister of Education of Ontario.
[a] Included in the totals, further training at Ryerson Polytechnical Institute.
*Negligible.

TABLE 2-22
Enrolment in secondary schools operated by each type of school board, 1966-8

TYPE OF SCHOOL BOARD	1966-7	1967-8	1968
Collegiate institute and high school boards	196,114[a]	206,646	225,620
Continuation school boards	524	301	276
Boards of education	239,388	255,605	273,700
Boards operating schools on Crown lands		1,184	1,211
TOTAL	436,026	463,736	500,807

SOURCE: Reports of the Minister of Education of Ontario.

[a]Two of these boards operated schools on Crown lands.

the percentage going to university, which rose from 5.9 in 1959-60 to 11.9 in 1967-8, was one of the most striking trends. By 1967-8 4.3 per cent were enrolling in colleges of applied arts and technology. The development of these colleges contributed to the decline in enrolment in business schools. The percentage entering agricultural schools, private trade schools, and teachers' colleges fluctuated, but did not show a definite change in any particular direction. Schools of nursing attracted a declining percentage of the total.

Enrolment by type of board
Satisfactory data for enrolment by type of school board have been obtainable only for the three years between 1966 and 1969, as shown in Table 2-22. There was no important change in growth in schools controlled by collegiate institute and high school boards or by boards of education. Enrolment under continuation school boards had almost disappeared in the latter year.

Enrolment by type of municipal organization
Enrolment in secondary schools by type of municipality is shown for 1960-70 in Table 2-23, which follows the pattern of Table 2-11 for elementary school enrolment. During this period enrolment in cities more than doubled, that in towns rose by about 90 per cent, and that in villages rose by about 17 per cent. Again, the variations in classification of rural and urban townships obscure the situation, but it is nevertheless evident that enrolment in the former increased substantially.

NUMBERS OF CERTIFICATES GRANTED IN SECONDARY SCHOOLS

The Ontario Secondary School Honour Graduation Diploma (grade 13)
Table 2-24 shows the number of Ontario Secondary School Honour Graduation Diplomas issued between 1950 and 1969 by pattern of school attendance. The second column under "One-year attendance" indicates the number of students who wrote one or more grade 13 papers while

TABLE 2-23
Enrolment in secondary schools in each type of municipality, 1960-70

TYPE OF MUNICIPALITY	1960-1	1961-2	1962-3	1963-4	1964-5	1965-6	1966-7	1967-8	1968-9	1969-70
Cities	111,555	130,696	145,072	161,787	175,289	183,830	192,959	204,935	220,547	233,669
Boroughs								75,779	80,458	86,277
Towns	73,820	83,142	89,969	95,167	101,436	110,073	110,849	113,688	132,706	140,594
Villages	18,300	19,290	20,559	21,059	21,703	20,244	20,494	21,031	22,617	21,471
Urban townships	38,801	45,561	53,165	58,674	65,098	71,354	76,034	10,348	43,268[a]	47,412
Rural townships	20,299	20,488	22,813	27,523	31,775	32,002	34,447	36,771		
Unorganized townships						82	71			
Crown lands						1,153	1,172	1,184	1,211	1,256
TOTAL	262,775	299,177	331,578	364,210	395,301	418,738	436,026	463,736	500,807	530,679

SOURCE: Reports of the Minister of Education of Ontario.

[a] Rural and urban combined.

TABLE 2-24
Number of Ontario Secondary School Honour Graduation Diplomas issued by pattern of school attendance, 1950-69

YEAR	ONE-YEAR ATTENDANCE			TWO-YEAR ATTENDANCE			THREE-YEAR ATTENDANCE			PRIVATE STUDY	TOTAL
	All required papers in same year	Some required papers in another year	TOTAL	At same school	Part at other school	TOTAL	At same school	Part at other school	TOTAL		
1950	3,123	618	3,741	1,148	167	1,315	40	14	54		5,110
1955	3,841	672	4,513	915	111	1,026	6	6	12		5,551
1960	6,308	655	6,963	1,821	285	2,106	8	1	9		9,078
1961	7,616	675	8,291	2,053	309	2,362	27	15	42		10,695
1962	8,247	978	9,225	2,015	345	2,360	20	20	40		11,625
1963	9,113	999	10,112	2,694	431	3,125	25	23	48		13,285
1964	10,708	1,180	11,888	2,529	378	2,907	32	16	48		14,843
1965	17,240	1,439	18,679	3,682	506	4,188	52	42	94	18	22,979
1966	21,828	1,511	23,339	4,339	749	5,088	51	43	94	44	28,565
1967	21,467	1,633	23,100	2,599	743	3,342	38	20	58	42	26,542
1968											32,492
1969											34,748

SOURCE: Reports of the Minister of Education of Ontario.

enrolled in grade 12, or in some cases in grade 11, but who were enrolled in grade 13 for only one year. Those whose attendance is spread over two or three years have generally been considered to be inferior students, although there have, of course, been many exceptions. Because of the general trend, however, the universities have been inclined to adopt the practice of requiring a higher average for admission to certain programs when standing has been attained in this way.

There was a percentage increase of 63.5 in diplomas granted between 1955 and 1960. During the 1960s the greatest year-to-year numerical and percentage increases were between 1964 and 1965 and between 1965 and 1966. In the former case the number rose from 14,843 to 22,979, a percentage increase of 54.8; and in the latter to 28,565, a percentage increase of 24.3. In other words, the number of diplomas awarded almost doubled in the two-year period from 1964 to 1966. The temporary decline of the following year corresponded to the end of the grade 13 departmental examinations. The reduction in the number of grade 13 papers failed during the following year was reflected in a substantial increase in the number of diplomas awarded. The diversion of considerable numbers of students to the colleges of applied arts and technology who would otherwise have proceeded to grade 13 acted as a restraining influence on the number of diplomas awarded after 1967, even though the total continued to increase moderately.

There was a markedly increasing tendency during the 1950s for students to obtain their diplomas with one year of attendance in grade 13, either by taking all the required papers in a single year or by taking one or more along with a regular grade 11 or 12 program. In 1950, 1955, and 1960 the respective percentages in this group were 83.5, 85.1, and 90.6. By 1965 the percentage had reached 92.3, after which there was little change. This development was paralleled by a marked decline in the percentage in the one-year group taking one or more grade 13 papers in grade 11 or 12. For 1950, 1955, 1960, and 1967, the respective percentages were 16.5, 14.9, 9.4, and 7.1. These trends appear to indicate a move toward greater uniformity rather than flexibility. Recent organizational and curricular changes encourage an expectation that the trend will be reversed.

The percentage of students obtaining a diploma after spending two or more years in grade 13 naturally declined in direct relation to the number taking only one year. There was a sharp numerical and percentage decline, the percentage falling from 17.8 to 12.6 in the two-year group between 1966 and 1967. Those who obtained a diploma after three years of attendance constituted only an insignificant proportion of the total during the period under review. The majority of these fairly consistently obtained the required credits through attendance at more than one school.

Grade 13 examinations
The numbers of grade 13 examination papers written and passed each

130 The expansion of the educational system

TABLE 2-25
Number of papers written and number and percentage passed in the grade 13 examinations, 1950–69

YEAR	NO. OF PAPERS WRITTEN	NO. OF PAPERS PASSED	PERCENTAGE OF PAPERS PASSED	YEAR	NO. OF PAPERS WRITTEN	NO. OF PAPERS PASSED	PERCENTAGE OF PAPERS PASSED
1950	86,360	68,554	79.38	1960	148,485	119,478	80.46
1951	84,005	67,936	84.18	1961	171,520	141,004	82.21
1952	81,761	68,826	79.57	1962	189,595	150,849	79.56
1953	82,300	64,709	78.62	1963	207,700	170,630	82.15
1954	86,460	71,756	82.99	1964	234,283	188,898	80.63
1955	90,209	72,831	80.74	1965	221,205	166,757	75.39
1956	98,685	79,770	80.83	1966	234,431	198,375	84.62
1957	105,028	85,412	81.32	1967	176,808	150,593	85.17
1958	113,853	90,928	79.86	1968[a]	185,773	171,840	92.50
1959	128,693	101,060	78.53	1969[a]	196,118	183,441	93.54

SOURCE: Reports of the Minister of Education of Ontario.

[a] For 1968 and 1969 the figures indicate the number of marks submitted by the schools, and the number and percentage of passing marks.

year between 1950 and 1967 are given in Table 2-25. For 1968 and 1969 the table indicates the number of marks submitted by the schools, with the number and percentage of passing marks. The percentage of passes does not, as many people have supposed, give an indication of the variations in the quality of performance of grade 13 students. Up to and including 1967, it indicated rather the degree of success of those who set the papers, worked out the marking schemes, and adjusted the distributions of marks in order to attain a predetermined objective. If 80 per cent passed on all papers considered together, the result was regarded as reasonable. A difficulty occurred in 1965, when the percentage of passes fell to 75.39. This phenomenon coincided with the introduction of the practice of counting the teacher's mark for 25 per cent of the final total. The story of what happened at that time is told in volume v, chapter 15. Obviously no chance of an adverse political reaction was taken during the next two years, when the percentage of passes rose above 85. When the schools were given the responsibility in 1968 of determining final standing in whatever way they saw fit, the percentage of successes rose to 92.50, and in 1969 reached 93.54. This occurrence called forth some critical comments about what was happening to standards, although any direct comparison of the results of 1967 with those of 1968 is a doubtful proposition.

Table 2-26 shows the percentage passing each of the most frequently written grade 13 papers from 1964 to 1967 and the percentage of students awarded passing marks by the schools in 1968 and 1969. In 1965 a single paper was substituted for the two formerly offered in each of the languages; in 1966 a single biology paper was substituted for the separate papers in botany and zoology; and in 1967 the papers referred to as Math A and Math B were offered instead of separate papers in algebra, geometry, and trigonometry and statics. Separate papers were, however, continued for the benefit of those who had taken only one biology subject or only one or two of the mathematics offerings under the older scheme. The small number who wrote these subjects after the new procedures were introduced were mostly not among the best candidates, and a relatively high percentage of them failed.

The table shows that there was a very substantial variation in the number of candidates who passed each paper over the six-year period. The effects of the high failure rate affecting most papers in 1965 was mitigated by an unusually lenient policy on appeals. The high rate of success in 1966 and 1967, and most particularly in 1968 and 1969, was especially evident with respect to the language papers.

The Ontario Secondary School Graduation Diploma (grade 12)
Tables 2-27 and 2-28 show the numbers of Ontario Secondary School Graduation Diplomas awarded during each year of the 1960s. Up to 1965 grade 12 students continued to graduate from the courses existing before the Reorganized Program had been fully introduced, even though, for

TABLE 2-26
Percentages of certain Ontario grade 13 examination papers passed, 1964–9

PAPER	PERCENTAGE PASSED					
	1964	1965	1966	1967	1968[a]	1969[a]
English Composition	82.5					
English Literature	81.4					
English		73.2	87.7	85.6	94.9	96.0
History	76.8	70.8	79.9	82.1	93.3	95.0
Geography	73.1	75.3	79.3	82.4	94.7	95.0
Algebra	79.5	78.6	84.1	76.7	83.0	90.0
Geometry	82.8	78.2	83.5	77.4	79.4	97.0
Trigonometry and Statics	78.7	76.8	83.4	76.8	89.9	
Introduction to Analysis (Math A)				84.6	88.0	89.0
Algebra (Math B)				89.4	91.9	93.0
Botany	79.5	72.1	77.2			
Zoology	77.3	72.3	81.3			
Biology			84.7	85.6	93.1	94.0
Physics	80.9	80.5	85.0	89.9	89.4	91.0
Chemistry	79.9	76.4	81.7	84.1	91.1	92.0
Latin Authors	82.7					
Latin Composition	83.5					
Latin		79.3	90.7	87.6	95.9	97.0
French Authors	81.6					
French Composition	81.8					
French		73.3	87.2	86.9	94.1	94.0
Littérature Française	79.4					
Composition Française	81.6					
Français		70.9	81.7	82.3	96.6	98.0
German Authors	84.0					
German Composition	83.4					
German		79.6	89.3	91.7	96.5	97.0

SOURCE: Reports of the Minister of Education of Ontario.

[a]For 1968 and 1969 the figures indicate the percentage of passing marks submitted by the schools for each subject.

TABLE 2-27
Number of Ontario Secondary School Graduation Diplomas issued, 1960–5

COURSE	1960	1961	1962	1963	1964	1965
General						
Three-option	5,951					
Four-option	14,151	18,932	20,839	22,718	27,394	31,151
Five-option	3,927	5,380	5,800	6,865	8,549	10,504
Six-option	227	311	290	368	428	456
Total General	24,256	24,623	26,929	29,951	36,371	42,111
General Technical				11	24	57
Technical	1,785	2,050	2,257	2,400	2,876	3,888
Art	73	82	100	100	119	217
Commercial	4,118	4,432	4,945	5,594	6,951	9,102
Home Economics	55	56	59	67	64	141
TOTAL	30,287	31,243	34,290	38,123	46,405	55,516

SOURCE: Reports of the Minister of Education of Ontario.

TABLE 2-28

Number of Ontario Secondary School Graduation Diplomas issued to graduates of the Reorganized Program, 1966-9

PROGRAM AND BRANCH	1966	1967	1968	1969[a]
FIVE-YEAR PROGRAM				
Arts and Science	36,776	38,046	40,356	40,779
Business and Commerce	1,162	1,709	2,177	2,352
Science, Technology, and Trades	1,607	2,090	2,758	3,256
TOTAL	39,545	41,845	45,291	46,387
Four options	26,668	27,923	29,998	30,882
Five options	12,245	13,305	14,766	14,825
Six options	626	610	520	655
Seven options	6	7	7	25
FOUR-YEAR PROGRAM				
Arts and Science	4,552	5,169	6,152	6,195
Business and Commerce	11,635	12,045	13,211	13,309
Science, Technology, and Trades	6,065	6,917	7,775	8,618
TOTAL	22,252	24,131	27,138	28,122
BOTH PROGRAMS				
Arts and Science	41,328	43,215	46,508	46,974
Business and Commerce	12,797	13,754	15,388	15,661
Science, Technology, and Trades	7,672	9,007	10,533	11,874
TOTAL	61,797	65,976	72,429	74,509

SOURCE: Reports of the Minister of Education of Ontario.

[a]The number of options was raised by one because history became an optional rather than an obligatory subject.

purposes of convenience, enrolment in all grades was classified in the new branches after 1962-3.

Corresponding to enrolment, the number of diplomas awarded in the General course constituted an overwhelming proportion of the total, although the percentage declined from 80.1 in 1960 to 78.6 in 1963 and to 75.9 in 1965. What this declining percentage meant was that alternative programs were exerting an increasing attraction even before those who were admitted to grade 9 had an opportunity to choose among the three branches set up under the Reorganized Program. The three-option diploma was not awarded after 1960. During the subsequent period the proportion taking the minimum of four options declined from 76.9 per cent in 1961 to 74.0 per cent in 1965. More than two and one-half times as many students received five-option diplomas in 1965 as in 1960, even though the total number of diplomas issued increased by only 73.6 per cent.

During the same period the number of Technical and General Technical diplomas increased from 1,785 to 3,945, that is, from 5.9 to 7.1 per cent of the total, while the number of Commercial diplomas increased from 4,118 to 9,102, or from 13.6 to 16.4 per cent of the total. Although Art

TABLE 2-29
Number of Certificates of Standing issued to students successfully completing grades 9 and 10 of the two-year program in Ontario secondary schools, 1964–9

YEAR	CERTIFICATES
1964	953
1965	1,604
1966	1,388
1967	1,685
1968	1,780
1969	1,888

SOURCE: Reports of the Minister of Education of Ontario.

diplomas showed a very large percentage increase, the number remained insignificant. Home Economics diplomas remained a minor and declining percentage of the total until 1965, when there was a sudden jump to 141, as compared with 64 during the previous year.

As indicated in Table 2-28, and again following enrolment trends, the percentage of diplomas in the Arts and Science branch of the five-year program continued to decline. The percentages for the four successive years from 1966 to 1969 were 93.0, 90.9, 89.1, and 87.9. During the same period the percentage of diplomas in the Business and Commerce branch rose from 2.9 to 5.1, and that in the Science, Technology, and Trades branch from 4.1 to 7.0. In the four-year program approximately half of the diplomas were awarded to students in the Business and Commerce branch, somewhat over 20 per cent in the Arts and Science branch, and between 25 and 30 per cent in the Science, Technology, and Trades branch. In both the five-year and four-year programs together, the percentages of diplomas awarded in the Arts and Science branch for the four respective years were respectively 66.9, 65.5, 64.2, and 63.0; in the Business and Commerce branch, 20.7, 20.8, 21.2, and 21.0; and in the Science, Technology, and Trades branch, 12.4, 13.7, 14.5, and 15.9.

Certificates of Standing in two-year program
Under the Reorganized Program it was made possible for students completing the two-year program to receive Certificates of Standing after 1964. The number of these awarded in that and each subsequent year to 1969 is shown in Table 2-29. Although there was an increase from 953 to 1,604 between 1964 and 1965, the figures remained fairly stable thereafter. As enrolment trends have also shown, this program did not exert any great appeal to students. The end of grade 10 has seemed less and less satisfactory as a terminal point for formal schooling. Those who

TABLE 2-30
Enrolment in private schools in Ontario by level of instruction, 1963–70

LEVEL OF INSTRUCTION OFFERED IN SCHOOL	1963–4	1964–5	1965–6	1966–7	1967–8	1968–9	1969–70
Elementary	6,901	7,694	8,434	10,116	12,318	11,907	12,347
Elementary and secondary	13,033	12,908	11,953	12,169	11,447	11,499	11,937
Secondary	23,475	22,953	22,762	23,259	19,151	18,174	18,325
Roman Catholic	19,223	19,938	19,892	20,767	*	15,905	*
Other	4,252	3,015	2,870	2,492	*	2,269	*
Other		77	77	528	70	24	48
TOTAL ENROLLED	43,409	43,632	43,226	46,072	42,986	41,604	42,657

SOURCE: Reports of the Minister of Education of Ontario.
*Not available.

have not seemed destined to go at least to the end of grade 12 have been increasingly channeled into ungraded programs.

ENROLMENT IN PRIVATE SCHOOLS

Enrolment in private schools, as shown in Table 2-30 for the years 1963–4 to 1969–70, is categorized under the following headings: elementary, elementary and secondary (both levels offered in the same school), secondary, and other (including ungraded schools). The total number enrolled in private schools declined from 43,409 in 1963–4 to 42,657 in 1969–70. Private school enrolment constituted 2.7 per cent of total enrolment in publicly supported elementary and secondary schools in 1963–4 and 2.1 per cent in 1969–70. There was an absolute decline in every category except in schools offering elementary grades only, where enrolment rose from 6,901 in 1963–4 to 12,347 in 1969–70. These figures constituted 15.9 and 28.9 per cent of total private school enrolment, and an insignificant percentage of enrolment in public and separate elementary schools. The increase has been attributed, among other factors, to growing affluence and to apprehension among certain parents about organizational, instructional, and curricular changes in the publicly supported system. The decline in private school enrolment at higher levels has been ascribed to higher costs and to the wholesale movement of French-speaking students and teachers in some communities from private schools into the public system. Enrolment in Roman Catholic private secondary schools constituted 81.9 per cent of that in all private secondary schools in 1963–4, and 87.5 per cent in 1968–9.

Table 2-31 indicates enrolment between 1963–4 and 1969–70 in private schools categorized as boys', girls', and co-educational schools, and in each case subcategorized according to whether they catered to day pupils, to boarders only, or to both. Enrolment in schools for boys only and for girls only declined over the period in roughly the same proportions.

TABLE 2-31
Enrolment in private schools in Ontario by type of school, 1963-70

TYPE OF SCHOOL		1963-4	1964-5	1965-6	1966-7	1967-8	1968-9	1969-70
Boys' schools	Day pupils only	4,345	5,145	5,597	5,920	3,862	4,148	4,445
	Boarders only	897	836	637	557	479	432	441
	Day pupils and boarders	6,909	5,639	5,051	5,153	4,638	3,974	3,881
	Total	12,151	11,620	11,285	11,630	8,979	8,554	8,767
Girls' schools	Day pupils	6,005	5,554	5,529	5,332	4,963	4,687	4,738
	Boarders only[a]	45	373	44	302	80	29	29
	Day pupils and boarders	5,529	7,246	7,080	5,312	3,589	2,840	2,468
	Total	11,579	13,173	12,653	10,946	8,632	7,556	7,235
Co-educational schools	Day pupils only	16,069	16,699	17,296	19,640	21,866	22,736	23,738
	Boarders only	115	140	132	168	24	5	55
	Day pupils and boarders	3,495	2,000	1,860	3,688	3,485	2,753	2,862
	Total	19,679	18,839	19,288	23,496	25,375	25,494	26,655
GRAND TOTAL		43,409	43,632	43,226	46,072	42,986	41,604	42,657

SOURCE: Reports of the Minister of Education of Ontario.

[a] There is no official explanation for the implausible fluctuations in numbers from year to year, except possibly a failure of certain schools to report consistently.

TABLE 2-32

Enrolment in private schools in Ontario by grade, 1963–70

	1963–4	1964–5	1965–6	1966–7	1967–8	1968–9	1969–70
Kindergarten	1,045	610	45[a]	1,926[b]	2,109	2,139	2,529
Grade 1	1,602	1,699	1,745	2,041	1,994	2,078	2,128
2	1,445	1,655	1,781	1,799	2,018	1,932	2,036
3	1,542	1,489	1,690	1,823	1,806	1,942	1,961
4	1,332	1,603	1,527	1,683	1,826	1,790	2,000
5	1,359	1,506	1,774	1,669	1,811	1,851	1,907
6	1,282	1,430	1,614	1,787	1,711	1,829	1,896
7	1,437	1,629	1,723	1,830	1,950	1,891	2,053
8	1,497	1,520	1,732	1,742	1,921	2,028	1,968
9	5,179	4,487	4,093	4,606	2,524	2,146	2,081
10	4,567	4,004	3,671	4,016	2,280	2,038	2,018
11	9,445	9,223	9,134	8,646	8,666	8,077	7,747
12	7,973	8,133	7,922	7,859	7,873	6,998	7,185
13	3,130	3,801	4,149	3,956	4,092	4,264	4,629
Ungraded	574	843	626	689	405	601	519
TOTAL	43,409	43,632	43,226	46,072	42,986	41,604	42,657

SOURCE: Reports of the Minister of Education of Ontario.

[a]Excluding pupils under age 6 on the first school day of September 1965.
[b]From 1966–7 junior and senior kindergarten.

In 1963–4 the percentage of the grand total enrolled in boys' schools was 28.0, and in 1969–70, 20.6. The corresponding percentages for girls' schools were 26.7 and 17.0. The percentage in co-educational schools rose from 45.3 to 62.5 over the same period.

There was a strong tendency for enrolment in schools for day pupils only to increase as a percentage of the total. The figures for 1963–4 and 1969–70 were 35.8 and 50.7 per cent respectively for boys' schools; 51.9 and 65.5 per cent respectively for girls' schools; and 81.7 and 89.1 per cent respectively for co-educational schools. Most of the remaining enrolment has been consistently in schools for both day pupils and boarders, with very few students attending schools for boarders only.

The grade distribution for private schools from 1963–4 to 1969–70 is shown in Table 2-32. There are some peculiarities in the way kindergarten enrolment was reported in certain years. From 1966–7 on it is evident that the proportion enrolled at this level was high in comparison with the publicly supported schools. The tendency for enrolment in elementary school grades to increase and that in secondary school grades to decline is brought out clearly in this table. Contrary to the trend in other secondary school grades, however, enrolment in grade 13 increased from 3,130 in 1963–4 to 4,629 in 1969–70.

ENROLMENT IN SPECIAL SCHOOLS

Schools for the blind and deaf
The Ontario School for the Blind at Brantford and the Ontario Schools for the Deaf at Belleville and Milton are the chief facilities provided by

138 The expansion of the educational system

TABLE 2-33
Enrolment in schools for the blind and deaf operated by the Department of Education, 1950-70

YEAR	BLIND	DEAF
1950-1	176	345
1955-6	180	382
1960-1	227	512
1961-2	236	543
1962-3	240	549
1963-4	245	673
1964-5	251	710
1965-6	247	757
1966-7	256	800
1967-8	257	838
1968-9	261	897
1969-70	250	960

SOURCE: Reports of the Minister of Education of Ontario.

TABLE 2-34
Enrolment in schools operated by the Retarded Children's Authorities, 1965-8

YEAR	BOYS	GIRLS	TOTAL
1965-6	1,892	1,472	3,364
1966-7	2,080	1,673	3,753
1967-8	2,358	1,848	4,206
1968	2,546	1,981	4,527

SOURCE: Reports of the Minister of Education of Ontario.

the Department of Education for the blind and deaf. These schools are operating in the face of a trend to place as many of the handicapped as possible in a relatively normal environment. As shown in Table 2-33, the enrolment of the blind increased from 176 to 227 between 1950-1 and 1960-1, an increase of 29.0 per cent, and to 261 in the next eight years, a further increase of 15.0 per cent. There was a slight decline between 1968-9 and 1969-70. Reflecting the establishment of the second school at Milton, enrolment of the deaf rose more quickly. The increase was from 345 to 512 between 1950-1 and 1960-1, amounting to 48.4 per cent; and to 960 in 1968-9, a further 87.5 per cent.

Schools for the retarded
Although figures on which valid comparisons can be based are available only for the four-year period between 1965 and 1968, Table 2-34 gives some indication of the scale of operations of the Retarded Children's Education Authorities. Enrolment increased by more than a third during the

period. The school boards assumed complete responsibility for these children in 1969.

ENROLMENT IN CORRESPONDENCE COURSES OFFERED
BY THE DEPARTMENT OF EDUCATION

The post-war period has been characterized by a shift in the Department of Education toward the provision of an increasing number of direct services to supplement its administrative and supervisory responsibilities. A description of those departmental agencies providing such service is given in volume II, chapter 2. Among the oldest of the measures taken to supplement the school program is the provision of correspondence courses, which were first offered in 1926.

In 1950 only academic courses were offered at the elementary and secondary school levels. During that same year the province signed an agreement with the federal government by which the latter subsidized the development and administration of vocational correspondence courses. Similar arrangements were made with other provinces, and there was provision for making the service available across the country.

The enormous increase from 1,446 enrolled in the courses in 1950 to 48,153 in 1968–9 was by no means reflected in every part of the program. From 945 English-speaking children taking courses at the elementary school level in 1950, the number shrank to 175 in 1963, and then gradually rose again. Working against a numerical increase in this area has been the extension of regular school facilities, obviating the need for home study. On the other hand, there has been some increase in the number of children living abroad for various periods of time who have needed to keep up with the Ontario program. The bilingual program at the same level has never involved a large group. Between 1950 and 1955 the enrolment fell from 202 to 55. After a continued decline to a low of 11, the number again began to rise, reaching 66 in 1968–9.

The move toward upgrading the level of skills in the labour force has meant that many adults have first had to establish an academic foundation in the basic subjects. An increasing number have chosen the correspondence course route, either in the absence of, or in preference to, more formal instruction. From an enrolment of 45 in 1950, the number increased slowly until 1964, and then much more rapidly during the next two years. The improvement in the quality of the courses probably had a good deal to do with their increased drawing power. The *Adult Occupational Training Act* of 1967, which provided up to one year's living maintenance for a course in academic school subjects, offered an alternative that might be expected to reduce interest in correspondence courses covering the same ground. The reduced enrolment in vocational or trades correspondence courses between 1966–7 and 1967–8 might be attributed to the operation of the same act.

The really impressive enrolment increases have been registered in the

TABLE 2-35
Active enrolment in Department of Education correspondence courses, 1950-69

YEAR	ELEMENTARY GRADES					SECONDARY GRADES			GRAND TOTAL
	Children: Grades 1-8		Adult courses	TOTAL		Academic	Trades	TOTAL	
	English	Bilingual							
1950	945	202	45	1,192		254		254	1,446
1955	554	55	155	764		1,525	74	1,599	2,363
1960	299	20	234	553		3,059	91	3,150	3,703
1961	250	19	308	577		4,083	88	4,171	4,748
1962	198	11	359	568		5,583	82	5,665	6,233
1963	175	19	614	808		10,550	68	10,618	11,426
1964	277	34	814	1,125		13,213	102	13,315	14,440
1964-5	454	44	2,227	2,725		22,376	208	22,584	25,309
1965-6	683	38	3,197	3,918		27,658	281	27,939	31,857
1966-7	519	40	2,883	3,442		31,375	317	31,692	35,134
1967-8	650	55	3,019	3,724		40,643	214	40,857	44,581
1968-9	900	66	3,801	4,767		43,023	363	43,386	48,153

SOURCE: Reports of the Minister of Education of Ontario.

NOTE: Figures prior to 1964-5 are active enrolment on November 30 each year. Beginning in 1964-5, gross figures are shown for the period July 1 to June 30.

CHART 2-6
Enrolment in adult elementary school level correspondence courses provided by the Ontario Department of Education, 1960-9

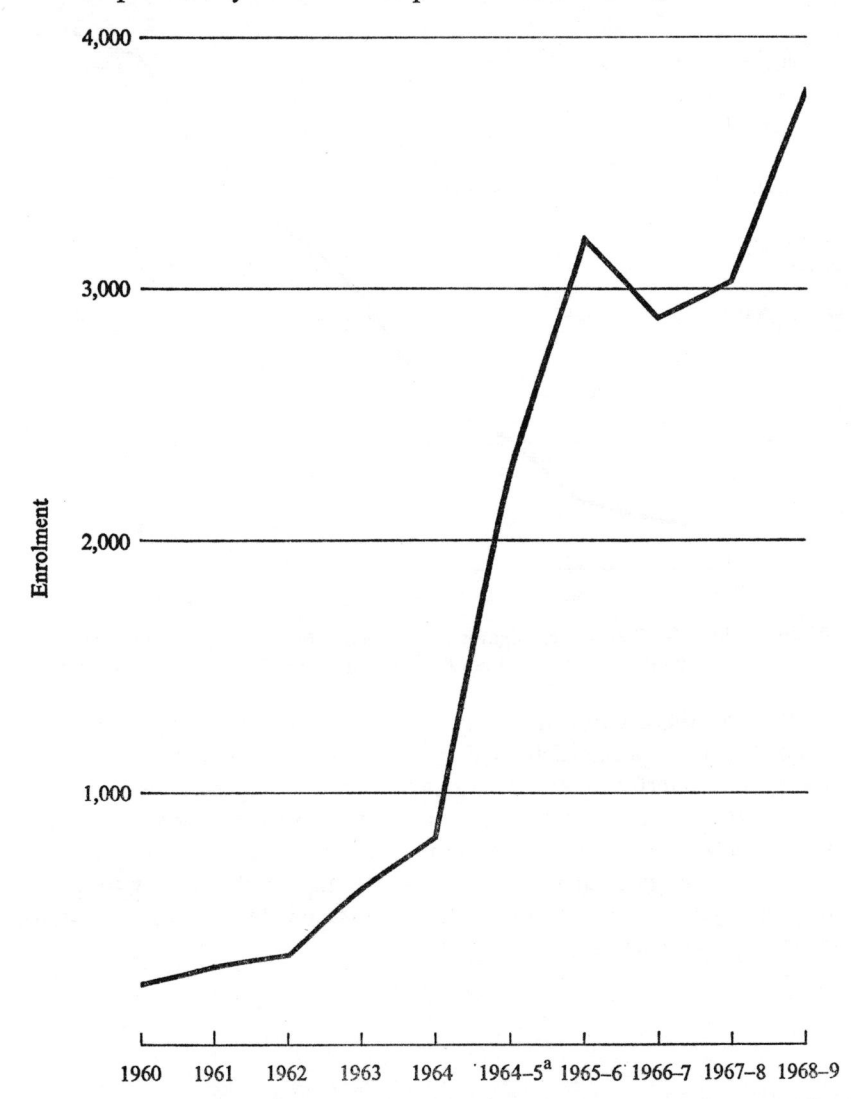

1960 1961 1962 1963 1964 1964-5[a] 1965-6 1966-7 1967-8 1968-9

[a]Beginning in 1964-5, enrolment figures were obtained by counting all those enrolled at any time during the year rather than the number enrolled on one specific date.

academic courses in the secondary grades. From 254 in 1950, this enrolment grew to 43,386 in 1968-9. Between 1962 and 1963 alone the numbers nearly doubled, and up until 1967-8 the average increase was more than six thousand a year. The change in the procedure for recording enrolment in 1964-5 had the effect of inflating the figures, since it involved

CHART 2-7
Enrolment in academic secondary school correspondence courses provided by the Ontario Department of Education, 1960–9

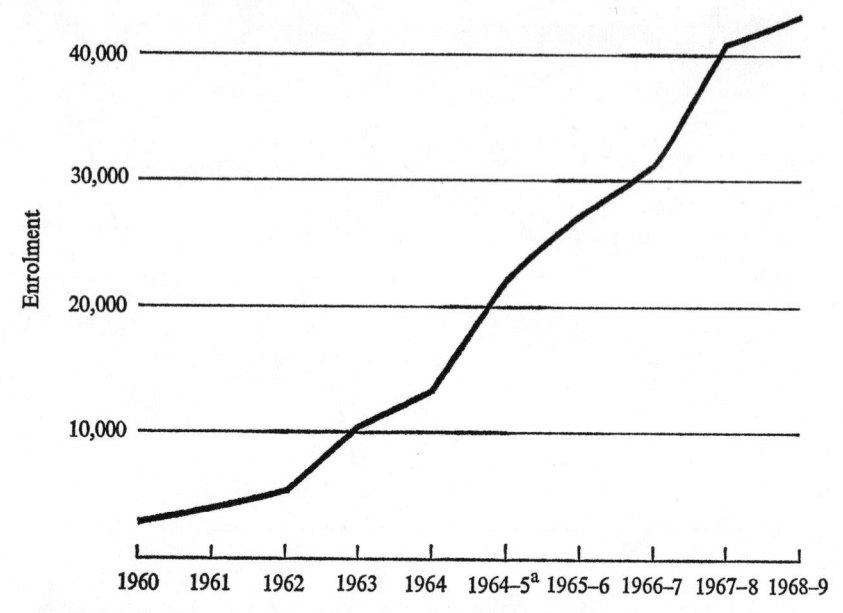

[a]Beginning in 1964–5, enrolment figures were obtained by counting all those enrolled at any time during the year rather than the number enrolled on one specific date.

counting all those enrolled at any time during the year instead of the number on one specific date. This modification does not, over the long run, greatly interfere with an interpretation of the general trend. The impressive increase in enrolment at this level, like that among adults at the elementary level, is evidence of the desire for occupational upgrading. The *Adult Occupational Training Act* is not, apparently, tending to draw too many people away from academic correspondence courses at the secondary school level.

THREE

Educational institutions

ELEMENTARY SCHOOLS

Gross number
Although the post-war period has seen a great deal of school building, there has also been a considerable decline in the number of elementary school buildings in actual use. This change, of course, reflects the rapid abandonment of small schools, particularly those with only one or two classrooms. As shown in Table 3-1, the total number of buildings in use decreased from 6,852 in 1945–6 to 4,356 in 1969–70. This decline did not take place until after 1960–1, when the number reached 7,052. An examination of the figures for public elementary and Roman Catholic separate schools reveals that the number of the former declined over a considerably longer period. In fact, the number of Roman Catholic separate schools reached a peak of 1,430 in 1964–5, and then declined only slightly, reaching 1,343 in 1969–70. The large increases in enrolment for the most part more than compensated for the trend toward increasing size of schools.

Schools operating kindergartens
Statistics on the number of schools operating kindergartens are not available for the entire post-war period. Table 3-2 indicates the increase for both public elementary and Roman Catholic separate schools between 1955–6 and 1969–70. The number of public schools offering this service increased steadily from 937 at the beginning of the period to 2,082 in 1969–70, a percentage increase of 122.2. The increase among Roman Catholic separate schools has been much greater in relative terms, rising from 191 in 1955–6 to 1,010 in 1969–70, or by 428.8 per cent. A large number of kindergartens were added to these schools in the 1963–5 period, reflecting the more substantial grant assistance that was provided by the Ontario Foundation Tax Plan.

Size of schools
The number of public elementary schools classified according to enrolment during the period from 1960–1 to 1969–70 is shown in Table 3-3. Among the most obvious trends during the period was the rapid decrease in the number of very small schools. There were 104 schools in 1961–2

TABLE 3-1
Number of publicly supported elementary schools, 1945–70

YEAR	PUBLIC AND PROTESTANT SEPARATE	ROMAN CATHOLIC SEPARATE	TOTAL	YEAR	PUBLIC AND PROTESTANT SEPARATE	ROMAN CATHOLIC SEPARATE	TOTAL
1945–6	6,015	837	6,852	1964–5	4,859	1,430	6,289
1950–1	5,899	947	6,846	1965–6	4,285	1,422	5,707
1955–6	5,948	1,091	7,039	1966–7	3,806	1,391	5,197
1960–1	5,696	1,356	7,052	1967–8	3,381	1,380	4,761
1961–2	5,522	1,412	6,934	1968–9	3,136	1,366	4,502
1962–3	5,375	1,419	6,794	1969–70	3,013	1,343	4,356
1963–4	5,133	1,425	6,558				

SOURCE: Ontario, Department of Education, Statistical Unit, "Public School Enrolment," September, 1967.

TABLE 3-2
Number of publicly supported elementary schools operating kindergartens, 1955–70

YEAR	PUBLIC	ROMAN CATHOLIC SEPARATE	TOTAL	YEAR	PUBLIC	ROMAN CATHOLIC SEPARATE	TOTAL
1955–6	937	191	1,128	1965–6	1,539	782	2,321
1960–1	1,267	383	1,650	1966–7	*	*	*
1961–2	1,327	463	1,790	1967–8	1,716	873	2,589
1962–3	1,370	501	1,871	1968–9	1,857	939	2,796
1963–4	1,413	542	1,955	1969–70	2,082	1,010	3,092
1964–5	1,565	682	2,247				

SOURCE: Reports of the Minister of Education of Ontario.

*Not available.

with an enrolment of fewer than 10, and only 7 in 1969–70. Between 1960–1 and 1969–70 the number of those enrolling between 10 and 29 pupils fell from 1,989 to 87, and of those with 30 to 49 pupils from 1,024 to 111. The number of schools in the next category, with between 50 and 99 pupils, was cut by more than 60 per cent. A particularly sharp decline in the number of very small schools occurred in 1965–6, at the time when the township school areas were established as the smallest administrative units, consolidating the remaining school sections.

During the decade the number of schools with an enrolment between 100 and 199 remained almost constant, while the number above that size increased by 47.9 per cent. The increase in numbers was fairly uniform among the larger size categories: that is, among schools with an enrolment above 200, there was no definite trend toward larger size. A very small proportion had an enrolment of more than 1,000, and the number increased only slightly between 1960–1 and 1969–70.

No Roman Catholic separate school had an enrolment under 10 after 1967–8, as indicated in Table 3-4. From 1960–1 to 1969–70 the number

TABLE 3-3
Number of public elementary schools by enrolment, 1960-70

ENROLMENT	1960-1	1961-2	1962-3	1963-4	1964-5	1965-6	1966-7	1967-8	1968-9	1969-70
0-9	101	104	90	89	75	33	17	7	9	7
10-29	1,989	1,883	1,769	1,571	1,383	954	604	327	150	87
30-49	1,024	911	845	739	624	481	348	211	140	111
50-99	647	612	608	591	553	480	425	353	302	249
100-149	284	302	300	295	305	321	300	278	262	226
150-199	222	226	231	257	255	264	257	239	229	219
200-299	385	398	421	446	463	472	502	529	528	525
300-399	336	354	347	343	356	397	411	468	490	502
400-499	246	268	268	285	304	306	334	329	373	390
500-699	284	282	312	328	337	359	373	399	407	463
700-999	139	145	148	152	159	176	186	195	202	195
1,000 and over	39	37	36	37	45	42	49	46	44	39
TOTAL	5,696	5,522	5,375	5,133	4,859	4,285	3,806	3,381	3,136	3,013

SOURCE: Reports of the Minister of Education of Ontario.

TABLE 3-4
Number of Roman Catholic separate schools by enrolment, 1960–70

ENROLMENT	1960–1	1961–2	1962–3	1963–4	1964–5	1965–6	1966–7	1967–8	1968–9	1969–70
0–9	12	11	13	8	10	4	3	1		
10–29	158	147	137	115	96	75	46	25	24	11
30–49	131	130	105	94	74	61	44	37	27	20
50–99	214	214	216	218	195	178	150	139	116	93
100–149	138	162	168	173	182	173	167	172	164	156
150–199	130	144	139	135	137	148	151	123	132	130
200–299	208	204	225	247	267	278	287	317	323	344
300–399	164	183	184	189	210	222	236	240	253	252
400–499	111	112	121	122	120	133	145	142	141	150
500–699	67	80	81	89	97	99	112	128	126	128
700–999	17	18	22	27	36	45	45	49	50	51
1,000 and over	6	7	8	8	6	6	5	7	10	8
TOTAL	1,356	1,412	1,419	1,425	1,430	1,422	1,391	1,380	1,366	1,343

SOURCE: Reports of the Minister of Education of Ontario.

TABLE 3-5
Number of publicly supported elementary schools using French as a language of instruction, 1955–70

YEAR	PUBLIC	ROMAN CATHOLIC SEPARATE	TOTAL	YEAR	PUBLIC	ROMAN CATHOLIC SEPARATE	TOTAL
1955–6	73	478	551	1963–4	39	461	500
1956–7	72	499	571	1964–5	30	443	473
1957–8	71	498	569	1965–6	16	409	425
1958–9	65	517	582	1966–7	14	389	403
1959–60	64	504	568	1967–8	13	372	385
1960–1	58	509	567	1968–9	11	335	346
1961–2	52	505	557	1969–70	9	320	329
1962–3	41	491	532				

SOURCE: Reports of the Minister of Education of Ontario.

TABLE 3-6
Number of teaching areas in publicly supported elementary schools using French as a language of instruction, 1955–69

YEAR	PUBLIC	ROMAN CATHOLIC SEPARATE	TOTAL	YEAR	PUBLIC	ROMAN CATHOLIC SEPARATE	TOTAL
1955–6	196	1,966	2,162	1962–3	129	2,850	2,979
1956–7	133	2,133	2,266	1963–4	124	2,941	3,065
1957–8	133	2,215	2,348	1964–5	106	3,080	3,186
1958–9	136	2,395	2,531	1965–6	88	3,026	3,114
1959–60	137	2,589	2,726	1966–7	85	3,179	3,264
1960–1	140	2,670	2,810	1967–8	80	3,251	3,331
1961–2	136	2,744	2,880	1968–9	82	3,255	3,337

SOURCE: Reports of the Minister of Education of Ontario.

with between 10 and 29 pupils decreased from 158 to 11, the number with between 30 and 49 from 131 to 20, and the number with between 50 and 99, from 214 to 93. Beyond that enrolment the number increased in every category of size. In both public elementary and Roman Catholic separate schools, the largest concentration of schools was consistently in the 200–299 enrolment category.

Schools using French as a language of instruction
Available statistics on the number of schools using French as a language of instruction between 1955–6 and 1969–70 are shown in Table 3-5. The very pronounced decline in the number of public elementary schools in this category, from 73 in 1955–6 to 9 in 1969–70, was relatively much greater than the decrease in enrolment, as noted in Table 2-9. In the Roman Catholic separate schools the decline in the number of schools of the same type was accompanied by a substantial increase in enrolment, indicating the same trend toward the closing of small schools that was evident among elementary schools in general. Table 3-6, giving the num-

ber of "teaching areas" or classrooms where French was used for instructional purposes up to 1968-9, helps to confirm the nature of the change. The decrease in public school teaching areas between 1955-6 and 1968-9 was from 196 to 82, while the increase in such areas in Roman Catholic separate schools was from 1,966 to 3,255. There has been comparatively little change in either type of school since 1965-6.

Schools by type of board

The number of public elementary and Protestant separate schools operated by each type of school board between 1955-6 and 1968 is shown in Table 3-7. During that period the number of such schools under boards of education increased from 632, or 10.6 per cent of the total, to 1,165, or 37.1 per cent of the total. In 1968, however, the majority of public elementary school pupils attended these schools, as was pointed out in Table 2-10. As indicated also by enrolment, the increase in the number of schools operated by county and district school area boards during the period when their formation was merely encouraged rather than made mandatory was not great enough to change the situation drastically. The number of schools operated by township school area boards rose from 1,927 in 1964-5 to 2,629 in 1965-6 as a result of the organizational changes of the latter year. There was a corresponding drop from 1,362 to 103 schools under "rural" boards. The fact that the number under township school area boards fell by almost 25 per cent between 1965-6 and 1966-7 indicates that these boards lost no time in closing down many of the small schools that came under their control. During the period under consideration the number of schools operated by "other public school boards: urban" decreased while they experienced a very substantial increase in enrolment, as observed in Table 2-10. The Protestant separate school boards, with three schools up to 1961-2 and two thereafter, were more of a curiosity than a factor of any importance.

School boards of each type

The number of school boards of the types shown in Table 3-7 are given in Table 3-8 for the years 1960-8. The number of boards of education remained fairly constant during the eight-year period, occasionally rising or falling by one or two as a new one was formed or an existing one dissolved. The number of township school area boards increased until 1964-5, when a peak of 634 was reached, and then declined to 432 in 1968. The number of urban public school boards other than boards of education was reduced to about half its 1960-1 total by 1968. Most of the rural boards of course disappeared in 1965.

After the school board reorganization was completed with the formation of the Board of Education for Ottawa, Eastview, and Rockcliffe Park on January 1, 1970, the numbers of boards of different types were as follows: there was a board of education for each of the thirty-eight

TABLE 3-7

Number of public elementary and Protestant separate schools operated by each type of school board, 1955–68

TYPE OF SCHOOL BOARD	1955–6	1960–1	1961–2	1962–3	1963–4	1964–5	1965–6	1966–7	1967–8	1968
Boards of education	632	813	890	921	949	977	1,010	1,098	1,138	1,165
County school area boards								108	90	107
District school area boards								12	57	64
Township school area boards	2,691	2,401	2,226	2,168	2,012	1,927	2,629[a]	1,985	1,524	1,250
Other public school boards	2,596		2,372							
Urban		551		555	560	561	506	493	478	460
Rural		1,895		1,695	1,577	1,362	103	81	71	62
Boards operating schools on Crown land[b]	21	30	28	31	30	28	33	27	21	26
Protestant separate school boards	3	3	3	3	3	2	2	2	2	2
Others[c]	5	3	3	2	2	2	2	2		
TOTAL	5,948	5,696	5,522	5,375	5,133	4,859	4,285	3,806	3,381	3,136

SOURCE: Reports of the Minister of Education of Ontario.

[a]Including one county school area board.
[b]Military and Hydro schools.
[c]Railway school cars.

Educational institutions 149

TABLE 3-8
Number of school boards of each type operating public elementary and Protestant separate schools, 1960-8

TYPE OF SCHOOL BOARD	1960-1	1961-2	1962-3	1963-4	1964-5	1965-6	1966-7	1967-8	1968
Boards of education	52	52	54	53	53	53	53	50	51
County school area boards						1	10	12	15
District school area boards							2	13	16
Township school area boards	556	565	570	601	634	596	545	469	432
Other public school boards									
Urban	261	260	252	259	250	170	172	155	138
Rural	1,862	1,789	1,644	1,541	1,330	97	78	61	51
Boards operating schools on Crown lands[a]	22	20	23	22	20	23	20	15	16
Protestant separate school boards	3	3	3	3	2	3	2	2	2
TOTAL	2,756	2,689	2,546	2,479	2,289	942	882	777	721

SOURCE: Reports of the Minister of Education of Ontario.

[a]Military and Hydro schools.

administrative counties of southern Ontario, one for each of the three defined cities of Hamilton, London, and Windsor; one for each of the six municipalities of Metropolitan Toronto; one for the Ottawa region; and twenty-eight for divisions in northern Ontario as defined in Regulation 283/68, for a total of seventy-six. There were thirty Roman Catholic separate school boards for combined zones in southern Ontario and eighteen in northern Ontario established in 1969, and one for Ottawa and Eastview established on January 1, 1970, for a total of forty-nine. All but a very small proportion of the pupils of the province were under the jurisdiction of these 125 boards. There remained approximately 110 additional boards to administer schools in sections and zones in remote areas, on Crown lands, and in hospitals and treatment centres.

Schools by type of municipal organization
The number of elementary schools, both public and Roman Catholic separate, located in cities showed a substantial increase from 980 in 1960–1 to 1,420 in 1969–70, an increase of 44.9 per cent, as shown in Table 3-9. A total of 412 schools were included in the boroughs of Metropolitan Toronto in 1967–8, reducing the number in urban townships from 469 in 1966–7 to 104 in 1967–8. Schools in towns increased moderately in numbers during the eight-year period. By far the greatest change in relation to municipal units was the drop in the number of schools in rural townships. In interpreting figures such as those in Table 3-9, it should of course be kept in mind that some of the fluctuations in numbers of schools in different categories resulted from changes in municipal boundaries, rather than simply the opening of new schools and the closing of old ones.

SECONDARY SCHOOLS

Gross number
Because of the method of classifying secondary schools in the minister's reports of the immediate post-war years, it is impossible to make any meaningful comparison between that and the later period. Table 3-10 indicates the situation in 1955–6 and in successive years from 1960–1 on. There was a modest increase in the number of collegiate institutes from sixty-two in 1955–6 to eighty-six in 1968–9. In the same period the number of composite schools more than doubled, rising from twenty-two to forty-four. The continuation schools, which had numbered 194 in 1945–6, were down to 50 in 1955–6, and almost disappeared in little more than a decade. There were 212 high schools in 1955–6 and 378 in 1968–9, an increase of 78.3 per cent. The number of vocational schools remained fairly constant throughout the period.

Size of schools
Like the small elementary schools of the province, the small secondary schools showed a tendency to disappear rapidly during the 1960s, as indi-

TABLE 3-9
Number of elementary schools by type of municipality, 1960–70

TYPE OF MUNICIPALITY	1960–1	1961–2	1962–3	1963–4	1964–5	1965–6	1966–7	1967–8	1968–9	1969–70
Cities	980	1,085	1,109	1,169	1,200	1,257	1,336	1,364	1,391	1,420
Boroughs								412	425	439
Towns	589	611	637	636	649	682	641	634	708	701
Villages	208	214	215	225	221	313	208	199	195	184
Urban townships	465	440	449	444	462	472	469	104	1,624[a]	1,465
Rural townships	4,780	4,556	4,353	4,054	3,729	2,740	2,342	1,880		
Unorganized townships						206	172	144	133	124
Crown lands	30	28	31	30	28	37	29	24	26	23
TOTAL	7,052	6,934	6,794	6,558	6,289	5,707	5,197	4,761	4,502	4,356

SOURCE: Reports of the Minister of Education of Ontario.

[a]Combined rural and urban.

TABLE 3-10
Number of publicly supported secondary schools in Ontario by type of school, 1955–69

TYPE OF SCHOOL	1955–6	1960–1	1961–2	1962–3	1963–4	1964–5	1965–6	1966–7	1967–8	1968–9
Collegiate institute	62	77	82	81	76	79	82	84	85	86
Composite school	22	34	38	37	38	42	41	44	47	44
Continuation school	50	22	21	15	13	10	10	7	4	4
High school[a]	212	272	281	298	313	325	338	359	368	378[b]
Vocational school	22	20	20	21	28	25	23	24	24	36[b]
Junior vocational school					2	2	5	5	7	5
TOTAL	368	430[c]	447[c]	457[c]	470	483	499	523	535	553

SOURCE: Reports of the Minister of Education of Ontario.

[a]Including junior high schools.
[b]The difference in numbers between 1967–8 and 1968–9 appears to be partly a result of differences in classification.
[c]Including senior public schools.

cated in Table 3-11. While there were twenty-seven with an enrolment below 100 in 1960–1, there were only four in 1969–70. During the same period the number with an enrolment between 100 and 199 fell from fifty-six to twenty-four. In each larger category of the table up to 500–699, there was at least a small decline. Above that point the number of schools in each category increased substantially. While in 1960–1 there were eighteen schools with an enrolment of 1,500 or over, there were fifty-two such schools in 1969–70. The trend toward larger schools may be attributed to such factors as a desire to provide a more diversified program and a variety of facilities, and the availability of larger numbers of students within a given attendance area. Teachers also like to work in schools where a reasonable degree of specialization is possible.

Bilingual schools
Certain Ontario secondary schools have long offered French for French-speaking students at a more advanced level than that for English-speaking students. In recent years this version of the language has been labeled "Français" to distinguish it from the program taken by English-speaking students. Naturally it is available only in the schools where there is a reasonable proportion of French-speaking students, and thus sufficient demand to make its provision a viable proposition. These schools are found in the eastern and north-eastern parts of the province. As shown in Table 3-12, their number declined from fifty-six in 1950–1 to thirty-three in 1955–6. Obviously the reason was that the smaller schools offering the program were disappearing, since enrolment in Français classes increased from 2,370 to 3,326, or by over 40 per cent, in the same five-year period. From that time on, the number of schools involved remained almost constant until 1964–5, and then rose to forty-one in 1966–7, after which figures were inaccessible. The extent to which the program has flourished is indicated by the increase in enrolment from 2,370 in 1950–1 to 21,590 in 1969–70.

In 1965–6 secondary schools were authorized to offer instruction in history, geography, and Latin through the medium of French. In 1966–7 there were fifteen schools offering instruction in French to 2,424 students of geography, twenty-three schools similarly offering instruction to 4,211 students of history, and nine schools offering instruction to 556 students of Latin. By 1968–9 French was being used to instruct 10,932 students in geography, 14,028 in history, and 3,044 in Latin.

Schools by type of municipal organization
Information available for use in the present volume makes possible a comparison of the number of schools under each type of municipal organization only from 1965–6 on. Table 3-13 shows a substantial increase from year to year in the number in cities, the beginning of a rising trend in boroughs since the appearance of these units in 1967, a relatively

TABLE 3-11
Number of publicly supported secondary schools in Ontario by enrolment, 1960–70

ENROLMENT	1960–1	1961–2	1962–3	1963–4	1964–5	1965–6	1966–7	1967–8	1968–9	1969–70
0–99	27	24	19	12	10	11	8	7	7	4
100–199	56	39	35	34	29	29	30	27	26	24
200–299	43	49	50	42	45	41	42	39	37	34
300–399	47	50	39	49	46	48	49	47	44	41
400–499	35	40	38	26	30	36	30	30	29	34
500–699	64	59	69	73	67	54	66	63	61	61
700–899	51	60	52	61	59	60	68	66	65	61
900–999	20	24	29	27	29	37	37	36	39	37
1,000–1,299	52	60	70	80	87	96	109	126	122	138
1,300–1,499	17	17	23	30	37	42	38	51	69	81
1,500–1,899	15	16	23	18	27	29	33	32	38	34
1,900 and over	3	9	10	18	17	16	13	11	16	18
TOTAL	430	447	457	470	483	499	523	535	553	567

SOURCE: Reports of the Minister of Education of Ontario.

TABLE 3-12
Number of publicly supported secondary schools offering Français and number of students enrolled, 1950–70

YEAR	NO. OF SCHOOLS	NO. OF STUDENTS
1950–1	56	2,370
1955–6	33	3,326
1960–1	31	4,830
1961–2	31	5,120
1962–3	30	5,602
1963–4	30	6,097
1964–5	30	7,005
1965–6	39	7,985
1966–7	41	8,739
1967–8		9,680
1968–9		16,984
1969–70		21,590

SOURCE: Reports of the Minister of Education of Ontario.

TABLE 3-13
Number of publicly supported secondary schools in Ontario by type of municipality, 1965–70

TYPE OF MUNICIPALITY	1965–6	1966–7	1967–8	1968–9	1969–70
Cities	155	171	185	201	212
Boroughs			84	87	91
Towns	148	148	144	155	157
Villages	51	51	47	41	38
Urban townships	78	86	9	67[a]	67
Rural townships	64	64	64		
Unorganized townships	1	1			
Crown lands	2	2	2	2	2
TOTAL	499	523	535	553	567

SOURCE: Reports of the Minister of Education of Ontario.

[a]Rural and urban townships combined.

constant number in towns, a decline in villages, and a fairly stable situation in rural townships until 1967–8. Most of the schools in the urban township classification appeared under "boroughs" in and after 1967–8.

School boards of each type
For recent years the reports of the Minister of Education have listed only three categories of boards operating secondary schools: collegiate institute and high school boards, boards of education, and continuation school boards. During the period between 1960–1 and 1968 the number in the first of these categories for the most part remained fairly constant, although a slight decline set in after 1965–6. The number of boards of

TABLE 3-14
Number of school boards of each type operating secondary schools, 1960-8

TYPE OF SCHOOL BOARD	1960-1	1961-2	1962-3	1963-4	1964-5	1965-6	1966-7	1967-8	1968
Collegiate institute and high school boards	192	193	196	191	196	197	188	181	177
Continuation school boards	22	17	15	11	10	9	7	4	4
Boards of education	51	51	53	52	51	51	51	48	49
TOTAL	265	261	264	254	257	257	246	233	230

SOURCE: Reports of the Minister of Education of Ontario.

education operating secondary schools followed much the same pattern. The number of continuation school boards, on the other hand, declined from twenty-two to four.

SCHOOL BUILDING

Few aspects of educational activity since the Second World War are more impressive than the number of building projects undertaken and the amount of funds invested in them. It may be true that, without a high quality of education going on within, the buildings would be no more than "bricks and mortar," or even worse, so many prisons for aspiring youth. Yet even Richard J. Needham could hardly deny that they are a powerful testimony of the Ontario citizen's faith in the virtues of formal education. During the period between 1945 and 1969 inclusive, no fewer than 8,287 elementary school projects were completed, providing places for nearly 1,333,000 pupils at an estimated cost of $1,193 million, and 1,427 secondary school projects, providing places for nearly 487,000 students, at an estimated cost of $1,115 million. The figures for individual years are shown in Table 3-15.

The building campaign did not get under way immediately after the war. For a time the scarcity of materials and the need to provide other services meant that many children had to continue their schooling in obsolete or temporary buildings. By the mid–1950s, however, construction of elementary schools had reached a high level. The number of pupil places provided each year fluctuated between 1958 and 1969, but did not follow a consistent upward or downward trend. Paralleling enrolment trends, the 1960s were much the most active period for the building of secondary schools. The phenomenal 174 projects recorded for 1963 reflected the attempt to take the fullest possible advantage of the maximum rate of federal subsidy for the building of vocational schools and additions thereto under the Federal-Provincial Technical and Vocational Training Agreement. The relative lull during the next two years was followed by two more years of conspicuous activity.

The extent of Ontario's response to the offer of federal assistance was a source of comment and, in some quarters, of astonishment. D.M. Cameron has observed that, in the first fiscal year in which the agreement applied, school boards initiated approved projects for the construction of 124 new vocational or composite schools, representing 90 per cent of all such projects in Canada. Cameron has also reported that the total cost of the projects, including a few involving trade schools or institutes of technology, amounted to over fifteen times the original estimate of the total expenditure for the six-year term of the agreement.[1]

Donald MacDonald commented on the success of the program in the Legislature in 1965.

We had an absolutely phenomenal expansion of the educational "plant" to be

TABLE 3-15
New schools and additions built in Ontario, 1945-69

| YEAR | ELEMENTARY SCHOOLS ||| SECONDARY SCHOOLS ||| TOTAL |
------	No. of projects	Additional pupil places	Estimated cost in $ thousands	No. of projects	Additional student places	Estimated cost in $ thousands	Estimated cost in $ thousands
1945	53	4,200	1,200	2	210	56	1,256
1946	89	6,500	2,600	9	670	303	2,903
1947	132	11,400	6,100	19	1,490	539	6,639
1948	155	18,400	10,900	27	4,240	4,470	15,370
1949	190	22,500	16,400	19	4,810	7,577	23,977
1950	198	27,300	17,500	29	8,850	13,142	30,642
1951	241	31,000	21,300	29	7,020	8,631	29,931
1952	217	40,740	29,600	31	10,240	14,240	43,840
1953	303	45,675	33,200	43	10,750	16,891	50,091
1954	396	57,400	33,700	58	13,880	17,689	51,389
1955	425	63,000	39,300	56	14,750	20,217	59,517
1956	379	60,100	37,700	46	14,080	17,285	54,985
1957	417	64,480	43,950	66	22,890	29,209	73,159
1958	451	74,735	51,085	58	18,750	26,081	77,166
1959	427	73,605	56,672	71	18,510	25,193	81,865
1960	529	78,750	59,938	72	26,480	39,169	99,107
1961	452	66,150	53,301	62	19,520	31,941	85,242
1962	395	58,500	50,704	105	36,730	82,114	132,818
1963	412	66,730	58,707	174	66,650	181,611	240,318
1964	457	77,385	71,145	46	17,430	40,023	111,168
1965	480	84,280	84,497	69	16,972	59,581	144,078
1966	471	82,145	92,707	116	55,975	150,093	242,800
1967	330	72,800	91,117	108	40,750	133,540	224,657
1968	355	77,742	114,417	56	28,457	101,950	216,367
1969	333	67,374	115,395	56	26,472	93,451	208,846

SOURCE: Reports of the Minister of Education of Ontario.

able to implement the objectives of the Robarts plan. It is rather interesting to realize that in 1960, in the whole of the province of Ontario, notwithstanding the fact that technical and vocational education had been introduced in our system back in the early 20s, after World War I, there were no more than 72 schools that provided technical or vocational education, secondary schools. Fourteen of them were purely vocational schools; 58 of them were composite schools that provided technical education along with the other range of subjects.

In the intervening five years, with availability of 75 per cent capital funds from Ottawa and their ready acceptance by this government, we have developed a plant until today – I believe my figures are at least roughly accurate – there are something like 237 of the 435 secondary schools in the province of Ontario that have facilities now to provide in whole or in part, technical or vocational education.[2]

In certain quarters, there was an understandable feeling that five years of a high level of activity in this area should have left few communities without vocational facilities to meet their needs. Robert Nixon subscribed to this view in 1967, in questioning the minister's assertion that it would require $100 million a year to continue the program. Davis replied that the facilities which had been built for occupancy and total utilization in 1967 had actually reached that point some time in 1965 or 1966, and that there were many applications for extensions to existing accommodation. In some places there was a particular interest in building junior vocational schools.[3]

Table 3-15 gives some indication of the variations in cost per pupil place over the years. In 1948 the average for elementary schools was $592; in 1958, $684, and in 1969, $1,713. The rates per secondary school student for the same years were respectively $1,054, $1,391, and $3,530. There is, of course, no indication of the balance between new construction and extensions to existing structures in the years among which these comparisons are made. It is nevertheless obvious that there has been a very substantial increase in construction costs. The two obvious reasons are the general increase in all building costs and the tendency to provide more elaborate school facilities.

PRIVATE SCHOOLS

Data on private schools are somewhat scanty in official records. Table 3-16 shows the number of these in operation between 1963–4 and 1969–70 in three categories: elementary, secondary, and elementary and secondary combined. The elementary schools consist of a group providing a particular religious orientation and a number of others offering programs contrasting in certain ways with those of the public system. The number of such schools at the elementary level increased from 62 in 1963–4 to 114 in 1969–70.

CHART 3-1
Estimated cost of school building projects in Ontario, 1945–69

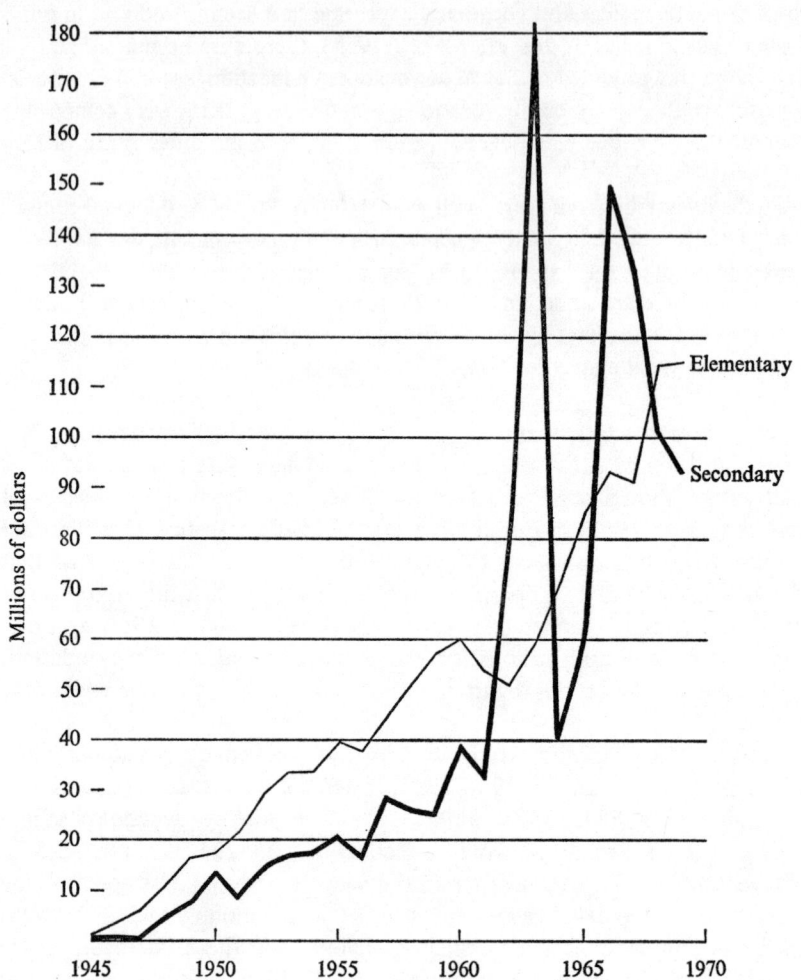

Private secondary schools consist of two main groups: Roman Catholic and independent schools. The total of both types was reduced from 135 in 1963–4 to 88 in 1969–70. As indicated in chapter 2, rising costs have made it difficult for many of them to carry on, while the acceptance of some of the French-speaking Roman Catholic high schools into publicly supported systems has reduced the number in that group.

Table 3-17 indicates the numbers of private schools in Ontario classified as boys', girls', and co-educational schools and subclassified according to whether they are for day pupils only, boarders only, or day pupils and boarders. Paralleling enrolment figures reviewed in chapter 2, the number

TABLE 3-16
Number of private schools in Ontario by level of instruction, 1963–70

LEVEL	1963–4	1964–5	1965–6	1966–7	1967–8	1968–9	1969–70
Elementary	62	69	74	80	93	98	114
Elementary and secondary	37	37	33	33	35	33	37
Secondary	135	130	124	119	108	93	88
Roman Catholic	102	104	98	94	*	72	*
Other	33	26	26	25	*	21	*
Other		2	2	5	2	1	2
Total number of schools	234	238	233	237	238	225	241

SOURCE: Reports of the Minister of Education of Ontario.

*Not available.

of boys' schools declined from forty-eight in 1963–4 to thirty-six in 1969–70; between the same years the number of girls' schools declined from fifty-two to thirty-two, while the number of co-educational schools increased from 134 to 173. There was little change in the numbers of boys' and girls' schools for day pupils only, and a rise in the number of co-educational schools in this category. The number of boys' schools for boarders only fell from eleven to five, and then rose to seven in 1969–70, while the number of girls' and co-educational schools of this type rose and fell, but remained insignificant throughout the period. There was a sharp decrease in the number of boys' and girls' schools for both day pupils and boarders, and a relatively constant number of co-education schools of this type.

In the five-year period private schools failed to show the same trend away from small schools that was evident in publicly supported schools. As indicated in Table 3-18, the number with an enrolment below 30 increased from twenty-seven to forty-eight. On the other hand, the number of those enrolling between 30 and 99 fell from seventy-two to fifty-seven. There was a small increase in the next category (100–299), followed by a decline, and little change in the next category (300–999). Throughout the period only one school had an enrolment of over 1,000.

PRIVATE VOCATIONAL SCHOOLS

Data on private vocational schools are not very up to date, the last obtainable for use in Table 3-19 being for 1967–8. The figures used, which were obtained from the Dominion Bureau of Statistics, do not correspond closely with those from other sources, presumably because of problems of classification and reporting. Regardless of differences, however, there is no doubt that the numbers of private business colleges have decreased from the early sixties. The number of private trade schools increased in the first few years of the decade, and then remained

TABLE 3-17
Number of private schools in Ontario by type, 1963–70

TYPE OF SCHOOL		1963–4	1964–5	1965–6	1966–7	1967–8	1968–9	1969–70
Boys' schools	Day pupils only	16	16	17	16	15	14	16
	Boarders only	11	11	9	8	6	5	7
	Day pupils and boarders	21	20	19	21	20	15	13
	Total	48	47	45	45	41	34	36
Girls' schools	Day pupils only	23	23	25	22	23	20	19
	Boarders only	1	4	2	4	3	1	1
	Day pupils and boarders	28	32	30	25	20	16	12
	Total	52	59	57	51	46	37	32
Co-educational schools	Day pupils only	115	116	114	121	133	139	155
	Boarders only	2	2	2	4	1	1	2
	Day pupils and boarders	17	14	15	16	17	14	16
	Total	134	132	131	141	151	154	173
GRAND TOTAL		234	238	233	237	238	225	241

SOURCE: Reports of the Minister of Education of Ontario.

TABLE 3-18
Number of private schools in Ontario by size, 1963–70

ENROLMENT	1963–4	1964–5	1965–6	1966–7	1967–8	1968–9	1969–70
0–29	27	27	21	24	28	30	48
30–99	72	74	76	62	82	57	57
100–299	87	92	91	103	106	93	87
300–999	47	44	44	47	41	44	48
1,000 and over	1	1	1	1	1	1	1
TOTAL	234	238	233	237	238	225	241

SOURCE: Reports of the Minister of Education of Ontario.

TABLE 3-19
Number of private vocational schools, 1960–8

YEAR	BUSINESS AND COMMERCE	TRADES	YEAR	BUSINESS AND COMMERCE	TRADES
1960–1	77	35	1964–5	61	70
1961–2	84	36	1965–6	57	63
1962–3	81	44	1966–7	48	71
1963–4	73	70	1967–8	44	84

SOURCE: Dominion Bureau of Statistics, *Survey of Vocational Education and Training*, publication no. 81-209.

TABLE 3-20
Number of schools of nursing in Ontario and enrolment, 1945–70

YEAR	NUMBER OF SCHOOLS	ENROL-MENT	YEAR	NUMBER OF SCHOOLS	ENROL-MENT
1945–6	62	3,947	1964–5	69	8,642
1950–1	61	4,914	1965–6	69	9,093
1955–6	60	5,994	1966–7	69	9,464
1960–1	61	7,055	1967–8	76	9,713
1961–2	62	7,826	1968–9	83	10,316
1962–3	62	8,256	1969–70	79	11,195
1963–4	63	8,465			

SOURCE: Figures supplied by the College of Nurses of Ontario.

fairly constant. Since 1967 the colleges of applied arts and technology have very drastically curtailed the operation of private institutions offering parallel courses.

SCHOOLS OF NURSING

Between 1945 and 1963, as indicated in Table 3-20, the number of schools of nursing remained almost constant, fluctuating between sixty and sixty-three. The enrolment rose steadily from 3,947 to 8,465 during that period, a percentage increase of 114.5. By 1969–70 there were seventy-nine such schools, with an enrolment of 11,195. Nursing educa-

164 The expansion of the educational system

CHART 3-2
Location of the universities of Ontario

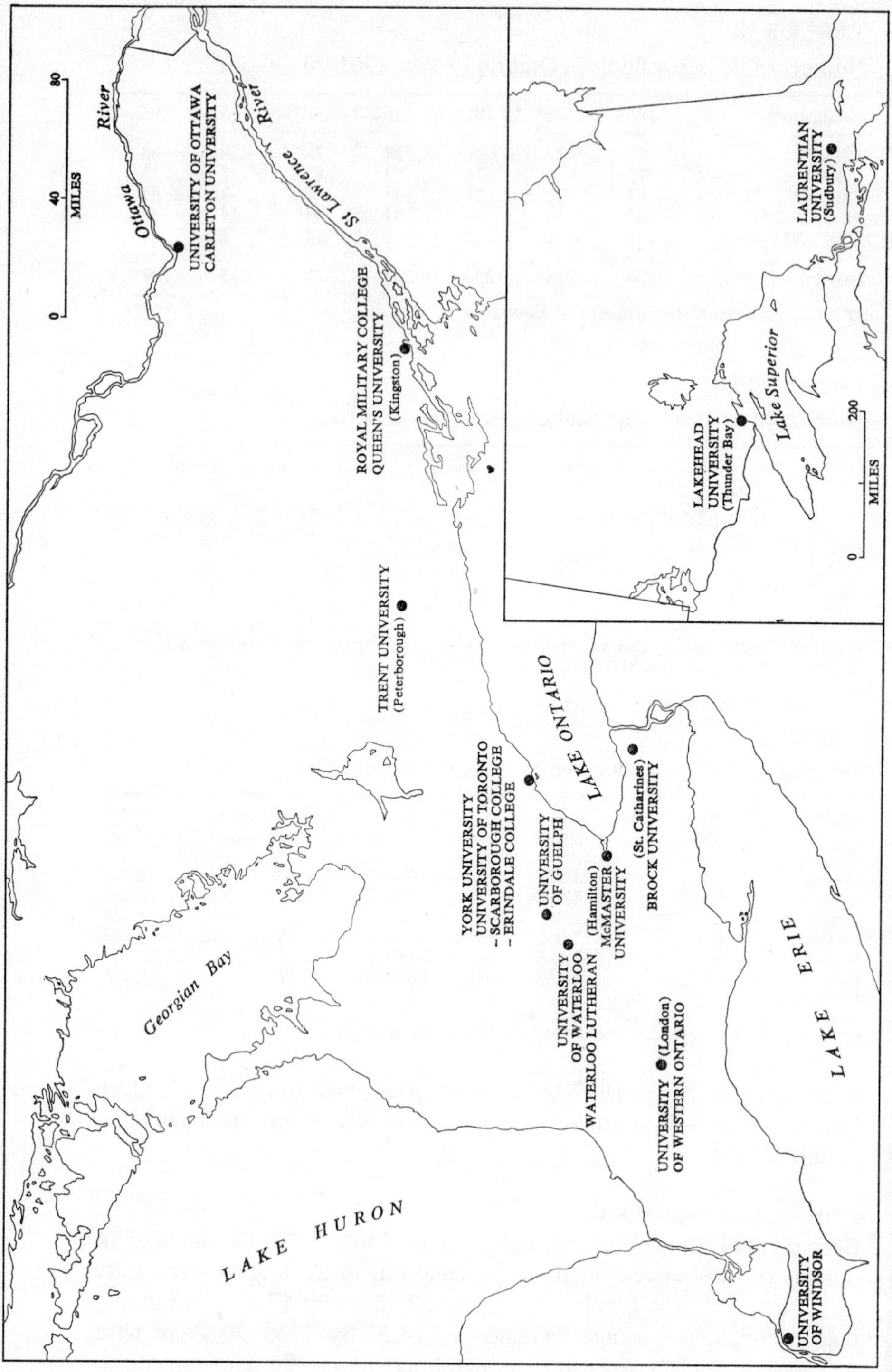

TABLE 3-21
Founding dates of the provincially assisted universities

FOUNDING DATE	UNIVERSITY
1964	Brock University
1942	Carleton University (as Carleton College)
1862	University of Guelph[a] (as the Ontario Veterinary College)
1946	Lakehead University[b] (as the Lakehead Technical Institute)
1913	Laurentian University of Sudbury[c] (as Sacred Heart College)
1857	McMaster University[d] (as the Canadian Literary Institute)
1849	University of Ottawa (as Bytown College)
1841	Queen's University
1827	University of Toronto (as King's College)
1963	Trent University
1957	University of Waterloo (as Waterloo College Associate Faculties)
1878	University of Western Ontario (as Western University)
1857	University of Windsor[e] (as Assumption College)
1959	York University

SOURCE: Report of the Minister of University Affairs of Ontario.

[a]Chartered as the University of Guelph in 1964.
[b]Given degree granting rights as the Lakehead College of Arts, Science, and Technology in 1962 and named Lakehead University in 1965.
[c]Chartered in 1960.
[d]Chartered as McMaster University in 1887.
[e]Chartered as the University of Windsor in 1963.

tion was undergoing a process of considerable change, as indicated in volume IV, chapter 19. The Minister of Health launched a campaign in 1965 to increase the number of graduating nurses to five thousand by 1971. The actual total of graduates in 1969 was 3,045, of whom 92 were from degree programs and 2,953 from diploma programs. The rate at which enrolment was increasing made it quite clear that there was no chance that the desired goal would be reached.

UNIVERSITIES

Table 3-21 gives the founding date of each of the provincially assisted universities or of the institution from which it evolved. The really senior ones, that is, those that had university status in the nineteenth century, are McMaster University, the University of Ottawa, Queen's University, the University of Toronto, and the University of Western Ontario. The University of Guelph and the University of Windsor also trace their antecedents back to the same period. Laurentian has traditions dating back to the early part of the twentieth century, as have the University of Waterloo and Waterloo Lutheran University, through Waterloo College. Of the recently created universities, only Brock and Trent are really "instant" institutions in the sense that they have neither evolved from others nor begun their existence in association with established universities.

INSTITUTES OF TECHNOLOGY,
ONTARIO VOCATIONAL CENTRES,
AND COLLEGES OF APPLIED ARTS AND TECHNOLOGY

Table 3-22 gives the name of each institute of technology, or technical institute, each institute of trades, and each Ontario vocational centre, along with its location, the date of its establishment, and an account of the change or changes in status it underwent during the period of its existence. Except for the former Lakehead Technical Institute, which became a full-fledged university in 1965, and the Ryerson Institute of Technology, which became the Ryerson Polytechnical Institute in 1964, all had been absorbed into colleges of applied arts and technology by 1968. The location of each of these colleges is shown on Chart 3-3.

LIBRARIES

Table 3-23 presents a certain amount of quantitative data about the development of public library facilities and services between 1960 and 1968. Considering the extent to which educational facilities and services expanded over the same period, the total number of volumes in all libraries showed a rather modest increase from a little under 7.5 million to a little over 11 million. Circulation of books and of all items increased by about the same relative amount. The average circulation of items per person of the population was under seven in 1968. The increase in the number of bookmobiles from eighteen in 1960 to fifty-three in 1967 represented a definite policy of attempting to improve services in remote areas. The increase in expenditure from $10,553,182 in 1960 to $28,937,850 in 1968, and from $1.82 to $4.28 per person, was fairly substantial in relative terms. It may be noted in this connection that the St John report referred to a claim made in the United States in 1965 that an expenditure of $4.47 per capita was needed to provide minimum service on the basis of costs at that time.[4] By this standard progress in Ontario was not impressive. The increase in the number of qualified librarians was also modest.

Municipal and county public libraries

Numbers of boards, volumes, and borrowers, and the circulation of all items in municipal and county public libraries in centres with a population of 10,000 and over are shown for the 1960–8 period in Table 3-24. There were sixty-four boards in 1960 and eighty-two in 1968. During the interval the number of volumes increased by 95.8 per cent, the number of borrowers by 52.6 per cent, and the circulation of all items by 79.4 per cent. Thus in all respects these libraries increased the extent of their activity to a greater extent than did libraries in general.

By way of contrast, municipal public libraries in centres with a population under 10,000 were relatively static, as shown in Table 3-25. The number of libraries and volumes showed comparatively little change. The

TABLE 3-22
Dates of establishment and changes in status of institutions for technological and trades training supported by the Department of Education

INSTITUTION	LOCATION	DATE OF ESTABLISHMENT	CHANGE IN STATUS
Lakehead Technical Institute	Port Arthur	1948	Renamed Lakehead College of Arts, Science and Technology in 1957; degree granting rights in 1962; designated Lakehead University in 1965.
Ryerson Institute of Technology	Toronto	1948	Became Ryerson Polytechnical Institute in 1964.
Eastern Ontario Institute of Technology	Ottawa	1957	Absorbed in Algonquin College of Applied Arts and Technology, 1967.
Northern Ontario Institute of Technology	Kirkland Lake	1962	Absorbed in Northern College of Applied Arts and Technology, 1967.
Provincial Institute of Mining	Haileybury	1945	Absorbed in Northern College of Applied Arts and Technology, 1967.
Provincial Institute of Textiles	Hamilton	1946	Became Hamilton Institute of Technology in 1956; absorbed in Mohawk College of Applied Arts and Technology, 1967.
Western Ontario Institute of Technology	Windsor	1958	Absorbed in St Clair College of Applied Arts and Technology, 1967.
Ontario Vocational Centre	London	1964	Absorbed in Fanshawe College of Applied Arts and Technology, 1967.
Ontario Vocational Centre	Ottawa	1964	Absorbed in Algonquin College of Applied Arts and Technology, 1967.
Ontario Vocational Centre	Sault Ste Marie	1965	Absorbed in Cambrian College of Applied Arts and Technology, 1967.
Provincial Institute of Automotive and Allied Trades	Toronto	1961	Absorbed in Centennial College of Applied Arts and Technology, 1967.
Provincial Institute of Trades	Toronto	1951	Absorbed in George Brown College of Applied Arts and Technology, 1968.
Provincial Institute of Trades and Occupations	Toronto	1961	Absorbed in George Brown College of Applied Arts and Technology, 1968.

SOURCE: Reports of the Minister of Education of Ontario.

168 The expansion of the educational system

CHART 3-3
Location of the colleges of applied arts and technology of Ontario

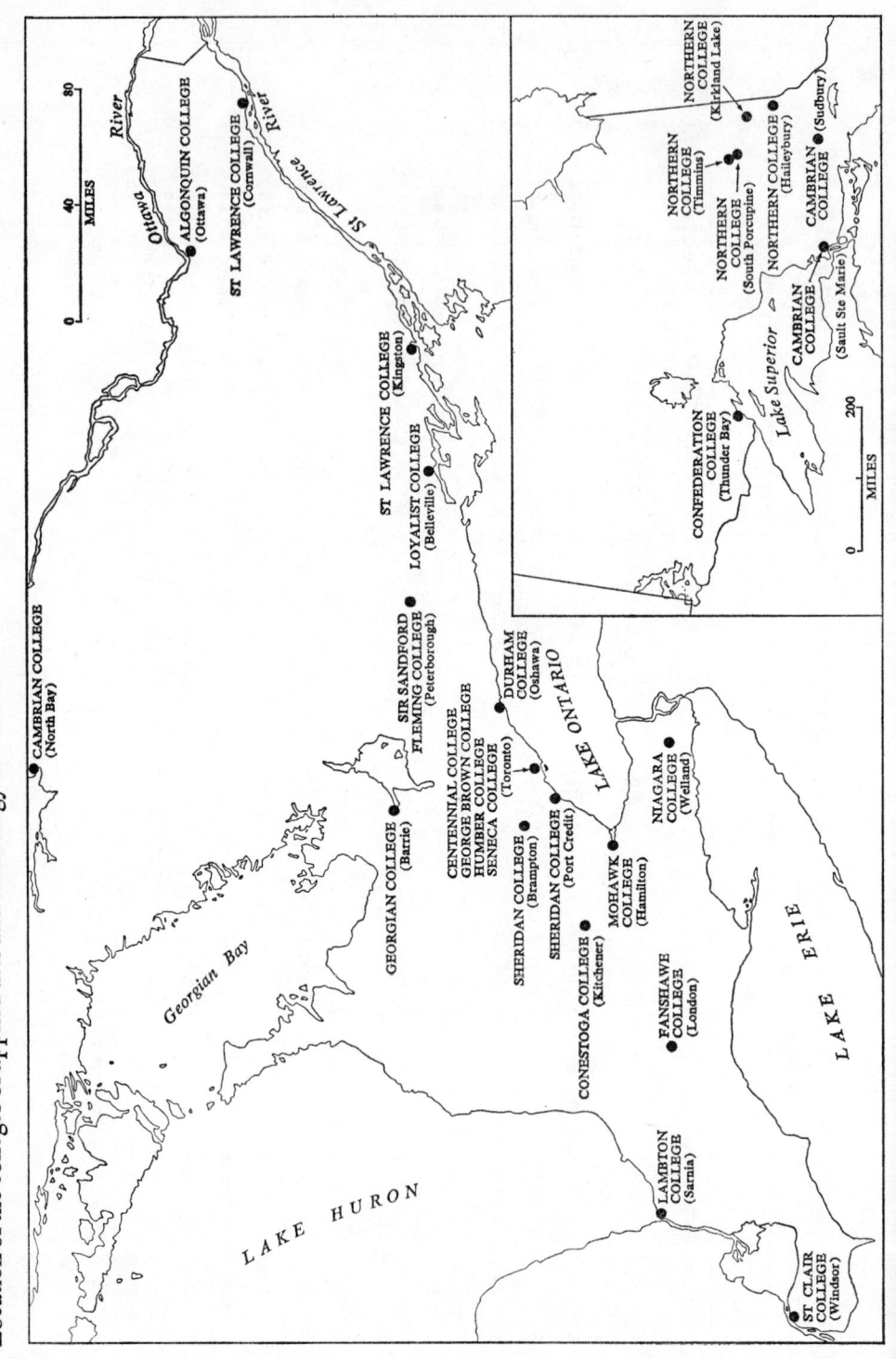

TABLE 3-23
General information about Ontario libraries, 1960-8

ITEM	1960	1961	1962	1963	1964	1965	1966	1967	1968
Total volumes – all libraries	7,438,035	7,811,095	8,427,165	8,507,073	8,965,070	10,059,800	9,667,286	10,434,865	11,110,602
Total circulation – books only	30,674,542	33,613,539	37,136,145	39,837,642	42,184,221	42,742,526	42,373,784	44,143,347	46,555,335
Total circulation – all items	31,961,582	35,510,980	38,543,615	41,980,425	43,997,325	44,736,479	44,634,036	46,460,076	48,963,244
Percentage of population served by municipal and county libraries	68.6	70.8	71.0	71.7	74.1	78.1	80.4	81.8	82.5
No. of bookmobiles operating	18	18	18	12	13	12	48	52	53	48
Total expenditure $	10,553,182	11,898,723	12,994,067	14,250,233	15,852,513	18,029,705	21,028,293	25,302,049	28,937,850
Expenditure per capita $	1.82	2.00	2.15	2.30	2.50	2.76	3.24	3.81	4.28
Certificates of Librarianship and Library Service A	31	31	37	38	34	36	31	33	30
B	342	355	373	417	436	481	484	493	524
C	91	75	84	88	74	76	79	77	74
D	14	28	30	34	36	46	49	60	62

SOURCE: Reports of the Minister of Education of Ontario; Ontario Department of Education Public Library Statistics.

TABLE 3-24
Stock and services of municipal and county public libraries in Ontario in centres with population 10,000 and over, 1960-8

YEAR	NO. OF BOARDS	NO. OF VOLUMES	NO. OF BORROWERS	CIRCULATION – ALL ITEMS
1960	64	4,735,176	1,288,338	24,208,090
1961	63	4,969,912	1,402,029	27,093,949
1962	63	5,646,172	1,526,187	29,346,335
1963	65	5,688,025	1,599,243	32,292,430
1964	68	6,090,891	1,673,779	33,894,989
1965	71	7,339,358	1,761,973	35,760,432
1966	75	7,535,368	1,875,580	37,828,319
1967	78	8,464,230	1,983,673	40,716,371
1968	82	9,270,148	1,965,691	43,439,435

SOURCE: Reports of the Minister of Education of Ontario; Ontario Department of Education Public Library Statistics.

NOTE: Statistics for the year ending December 31.

TABLE 3-25
Stock and services of municipal public libraries in Ontario in centres with population under 10,000, 1960-8

YEAR	NO. OF LIBRARIES	NO. OF VOLUMES	NO. OF BORROWERS	CIRCULATION – ALL ITEMS
1960	228	1,714,567	225,000	4,331,597
1961	238	1,825,457	230,000	4,773,891
1962	235	1,787,263	230,000	4,969,403
1963	238	1,870,102	273,241	5,100,931
1964	238	1,931,674	289,526	5,462,825
1965	217	1,874,400	296,358	5,292,094
1966	209	1,814,885	276,525	4,926,182
1967	230	1,970,635	292,836	5,743,705
1968	222	1,840,454	269,843	5,523,809

SOURCE: Reports of the Minister of Education of Ontario; Ontario Department of Education Public Library Statistics.

NOTE: Statistics for the year ending December 31.

number of borrowers reached its highest point in 1965, while circulation increased somewhat, although erratically, thereafter.

Regional libraries
The regions recognized for library purposes, which are shown on Chart 3-4, differ from other regional divisions of the province. Table 3-26 shows the growth in the number of member library boards between 1960 and 1968. These increased to 449 in 1965 and then declined to 304 after the regional organization was completely established in 1968. Between 1965 and 1966 a particularly large number of small library systems were amalgamated.

Regional library systems in Ontario

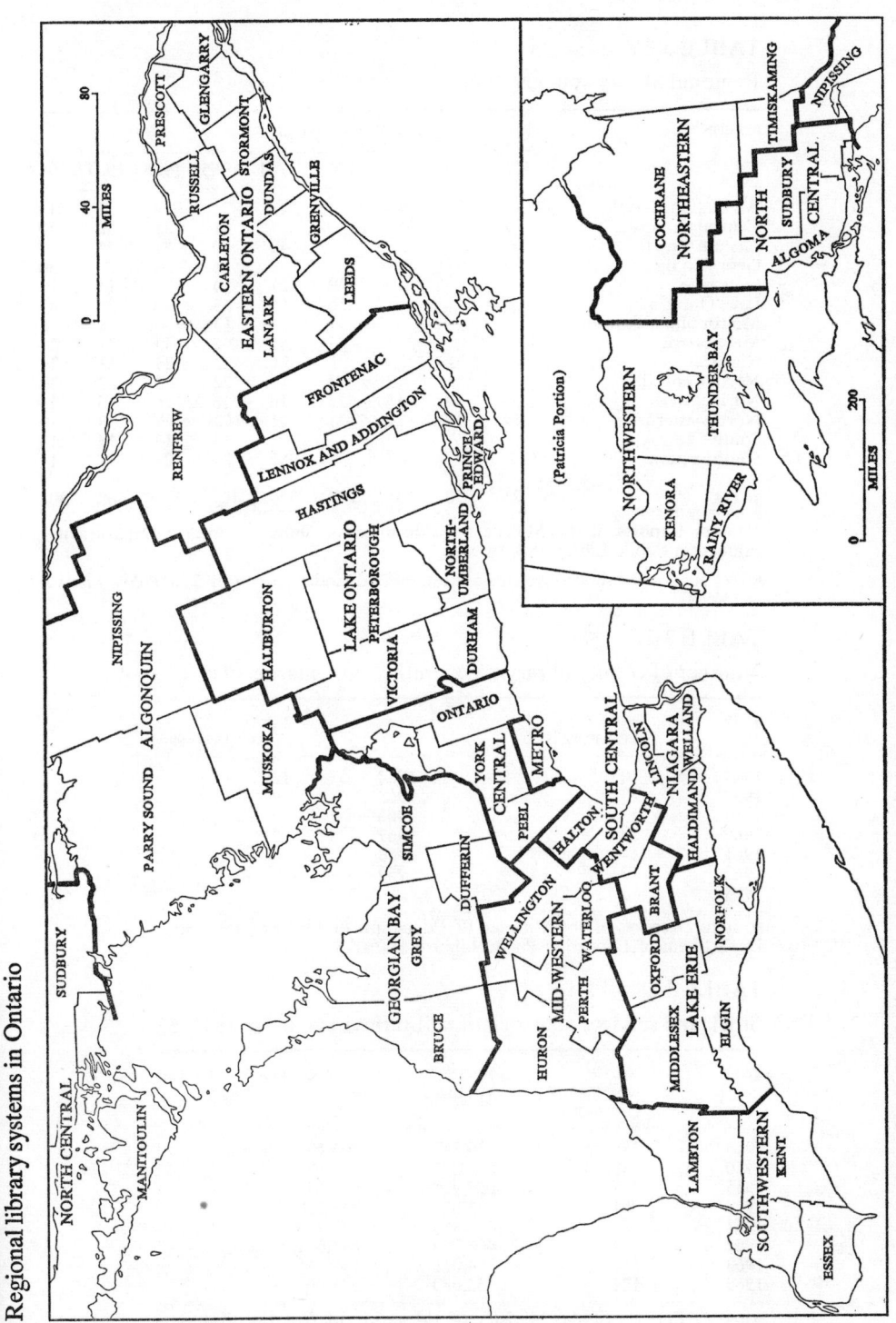

SOURCE: Special Research and Surveys Branch of the Ontario Department of Economics and Development.

172 The expansion of the educational system

TABLE 3-26
Regional library systems, 1966–8

REGION	NUMBER OF LIBRARY BOARDS								
	1960	1961	1962	1963	1964	1965	1966	1967	1968
Algonquin			13	13	21	21	14	14	14
Central Ontario						41	31	30	30
Eastern Ontario					49	50	35	36	39
Georgian Bay						56	29	29	30
Lake Erie				39	26	14	14	14	14
Lake Ontario				56	55	55	39	40	41
Metropolitan Toronto						13	6	6	6
Midwestern				65	65	65	30	24	24
Niagara			22	21	21	22	23	23	24
North Central		9	13	14	14	22	22	22	22
Northeastern	7	7	15	15	16	16	16	16	15
Northwestern	14	14	21	21	21	22	19	19	19
South Central						13	13	14	15
Southwestern			47	50	51	39	21	21	11
TOTAL	21	30	131	294	339	449	312	308	304

SOURCE: Reports of the Minister of Education of Ontario; Ontario Department of Education Public Library Statistics.

NOTE: Regional Library Systems are established under part III of *The Public Libraries Act*, 1966.

TABLE 3-27
Number of county library co-operatives in Ontario, 1945–69

YEAR	NO. OF CO-OPERATIVES	YEAR	NO. OF CO-OPERATIVES
1945	10	1964	12
1950	13	1965	9
1955	13	1966	4
1960	14	1967	2
1961	14	1968	
1962	13	1969	
1963	13		

SOURCE: Reports of the Minister of Education of Ontario; Ontario Department of Education Public Library Statistics.

TABLE 3-28
Stock and services of association libraries in Ontario, 1945–65

YEAR	NO. OF ASSOCIATION LIBRARIES	NO. OF VOLUMES	CIRCULATION – ALL ITEMS
1945	255	636,747	903,195
1950	251	664,273	953,180
1955	247	657,929	984,577
1960	201	476,676	723,526
1961	185	477,856	743,749
1962	173	408,209	691,081
1963	154	364,011	949,746
1965	122	352,680	531,967

SOURCE: Reports of the Minister of Education of Ontario; Ontario Department of Education Public Library Statistics.

County library co-operatives
As indicated in Table 3-27, county library co-operatives existed in relatively constant numbers from 1950 until 1964, after which they were rapidly phased out. They existed to provide member libraries within the county with extra services. The library regions were regarded as more satisfactory units for supplying this kind of assistance.

Association libraries
The association libraries represented an older type of service under the management of private associations. They tended to be inadequate, poorly maintained, open at infrequent and often inconvenient times, and able to continue operations only with the assistance of provincial grants. Although at one time they performed a valuable service, they tended in the period just before their final disappearance to stand in the way of the establishment of more adequate facilities. As indicated in Table 3-28, more than half of them disappeared between 1945 and 1965, the stock of books was reduced to a similar extent, and circulation declined by over 40 per cent.

FOUR

University enrolment and degrees awarded

BACKGROUND OF RECENT GROWTH

There were five active, degree-conferring universities in Ontario in 1939 – McMaster, Ottawa, Queen's, Toronto, and Western – with a full-time undergraduate enrolment of approximately 12,000, of whom about 7,000 were at Toronto. As seen in retrospect by the Committee of Presidents in 1963, the scope of their operations seemed very limited. They all offered three-year general and four-honours courses in arts and science. All had some connection with theological education; medicine was offered at Toronto, Queen's, and Western; engineering at Toronto and Queen's; nursing at Toronto, Ottawa, and Western; public health at Toronto and Western; and dentistry, pharmacy, architecture, forestry, and social work at Toronto. All of them offered graduate work to the MA, and Toronto to PhD in some fields. McMaster, Ottawa, Toronto, and Western had affiliated colleges, many of which were located in centres away from the campus, some outside the province, and most of a denominational character.[1]

With the return of the servicemen, large numbers of whom took advantage of opportunities that had been postponed or would not have been realized without Department of Veterans Affairs benefits, enrolment in all provincial universities more than doubled by 1949–50, and then declined to 21,700 in 1954–5. By that time the realization was beginning to dawn that a permanent upward trend had begun to develop. The high post-war birth rate had turned out to be not a temporary occurrence, to subside as soon as the effects of delayed family formation had become exhausted, but the beginning of a longer-lasting phenomenon. It was also becoming evident that a rising proportion of young people were seeking a university education to fit themselves for the new social and economic conditions that were developing.

Credit for first drawing attention to the dimensions of the developing problem is usually given to E.F. Sheffield who, at that time in the employ of the Dominion Bureau of Statistics, produced projections that were seriously discussed at the annual meeting of the National Conference of Canadian Universities held at Ottawa on November 12–14, 1956. In his paper entitled "The Expansion of Enrolment, 1955–1965," he forecast a doubling of Canadian university enrolment in the ten-year period. The universities themselves accepted the likelihood that the total Canadian enrolment of a little over 65,000 in 1955-6 would reach 123,573 by 1965-6. In considering the figures produced at the conference, C.T. Bissell, then President of Carleton University, attempted to assess certain regional and local prospects. He thought that, provided no restrictive or regulatory measures were adopted, enrolment in British Columbia and Central Canada would increase by well over 100 per cent in 1964-5.[2] As it turned out, the actual increase for Ontario was from 15,727 to 42,022, or 167.2 per cent, in provincially assisted universities between 1955-6 and 1964-5.

W.J. Dunlop, then Minister of Education, recognized that there would be an accommodation problem. On February 1, 1956, he reported to the Legislature as follows:

... I called a meeting last month, January 20, of the heads of the seven Ontario Universities and discussed with them a number of proposals designed to take care of the increasing enrolments which have already begun to be definitely noticeable. It was a most satisfactory conference and I found that the University authorities realize fully the magnitude and the urgency of the situation which will probably reach its peak in 1965 and will then continue at that level. It is not a tide of increasing enrolment but it will be a plateau. The University authorities readily undertook to consider carefully the several proposals which I made to them and we have agreed to have another conference in the very near future.[3]

The University of Toronto showed a considerable amount of foresight in initiating studies in the mid-fifties. In June 1956 the so-called Plateau Committee of the Senate received a report, prepared at its request, from Professor B.A. Griffith, who made five separate projections based on different assumptions. During the next four years actual enrolment figures for the university were extremely close to those projected on the assumption of a linearly increasing percentage of the age group between eighteen and twenty-one attending university. In 1960 Professor G.deB. Robinson undertook to secure a revision of the figures. He reported a projected enrolment for the University of Toronto for 1969-70 of 30,100. Of course the distribution of students among individual universities depended on the attitude of the institutions themselves and increasingly on that of the provincial government which, by its gradual assumption of overwhelming financial support, was inevitably assuming a powerful voice in determining the direction of expansion.

As President of the University of Toronto, Bissell appraised the prospects for the institution in 1959. Greatly underestimating the extent of growth in the immediate future, as most people were still doing, he foresaw an enrolment of 92,000 in all Ontario universities by 1975, a figure that was actually reached before the end of the 1960's. It appeared that at least 46,000 of the students would be in Metropolitan Toronto. Bissell asserted that the University of Toronto would be ready to accommodate 23,000 students in 1965, after which its numbers would remain constant. The remainder of the students from the area would have to look to other universities.[4] Presumably he had York in mind for a considerable part of that number. As things turned out, his estimate of the growth of enrolment at the University of Toronto in the immediate future was too high.

In 1960 Premier Frost was forecasting an enrolment of 90,000 by 1980. He was prepared to believe, however, that his projection was on the modest side. He remarked in the Legislature that, at the opening of the new campus at Carleton University, Bissell had told him that such was the case.[5]

Two years later the Committee of Presidents found grounds for an upward revision of the estimates on which previous planning had been based. According to earlier projections, total figures for 1965 and 1970 were 42,000 and 58,000 respectively. Now these were raised to 49,000 and 74,000 undergraduates alone. The more expansive and, as it turned out, realistic, appraisal of the situation owed a great deal to work done under the direction of R.W.B. Jackson of the Department of Educational Research of the Ontario College of Education.[6] Jackson presented six estimates to the presidents, who selected the assumptions that seemed to them most acceptable, and chose among the estimates accordingly. A careful check was made on subsequent developments and, when the figures for actual school enrolment were obtained, the forecasts were revised downward.[7]

E.F. Sheffield, operating under the auspices of the Canadian Universities Foundation and of the Association of Universities and Colleges of Canada, continued to update the forecasts for the whole of Canada. In 1964, on the basis of projected enrolment trends in the eighteen-to-twenty-four-year age group, he estimated that enrolment would increase by 240 per cent between 1962–3 and 1976–7.[8] He later found it necessary to make a further upward adjustment in these figures.

OVER-ALL ENROLMENT INCREASES

The actual enrolment growth in all Ontario degree-granting universities and colleges between 1951–2 and 1968–9 is shown in Table 4-1. In very approximate terms, it may be said that enrolment, after growing rather slowly between 1951–2 and 1955–6, increased by 50 per cent during the next five-year period and then almost tripled in the eight-year period up to 1968–9. The rate of increase in undergraduate enrolment was fairly steady from year to year. For graduates the rate was more rapid and a little less regular. Figures for part-time enrolment first became available in 1962–3, and since then part-time undergraduate enrolment has risen even more rapidly than full-time enrolment. Up to 1968–9 the percentage increase was about 176. Part-time graduate enrolment rose by a similar percentage during the same period.

TABLE 4-1
University and college enrolment in Ontario, 1951–69

YEAR	FULL-TIME UNDERGRADUATE	FULL-TIME GRADUATE	TOTAL FULL-TIME	PART-TIME UNDERGRADUATE	PART-TIME GRADUATE	TOTAL PART-TIME	TOTAL UNDERGRADUATE	TOTAL GRADUATE	GRAND TOTAL
1951–2	18,393	1,356	19,749						
1952–3	17,588	1,252	18,840						
1953–4	18,239	1,324	19,563						
1954–5	19,137	1,333	20,470						
1955–6	20,037	1,452	21,489						
1956–7	21,263	1,606	22,869						
1957–8	23,174	1,826	25,000						
1958–9	24,927	2,037	26,964						
1959–60	27,189	2,211	29,400						
1960–1	29,501	2,599	32,100						
1961–2	32,968	2,903	35,871	11,904	1,828	13,732	47,845	5,156	53,001
1962–3	35,941	3,328	39,269	15,763	1,812	17,575	55,753	6,013	61,766
1963–4	39,990	4,201	44,191	18,405	1,879	20,284	63,774	7,303	71,077
1964–5	45,369	5,424	50,793	20,317	2,066	22,383	72,441	8,925	81,366
1965–6	52,124	6,859	58,983	24,484	3,376	27,860	85,346	11,103	96,449
1966–7	60,862	7,727	68,589	26,982	4,047	31,029	96,289	13,829	110,118
1967–8	69,307	9,782	79,089	32,871	4,925	37,796	113,962	16,423	130,385
1968–9	81,091	11,498	92,589						

SOURCE: Dominion Bureau of Statistics (DBS), *Survey of Higher Education*, publication no. 81-204.

NOTE: The above table includes full-time enrolment at provincially assisted as well as other than provincially assisted universities and colleges.

CHART 4-1
Percentage increase in full-time undergraduate and graduate enrolment in the universities of Ontario, 1955–69

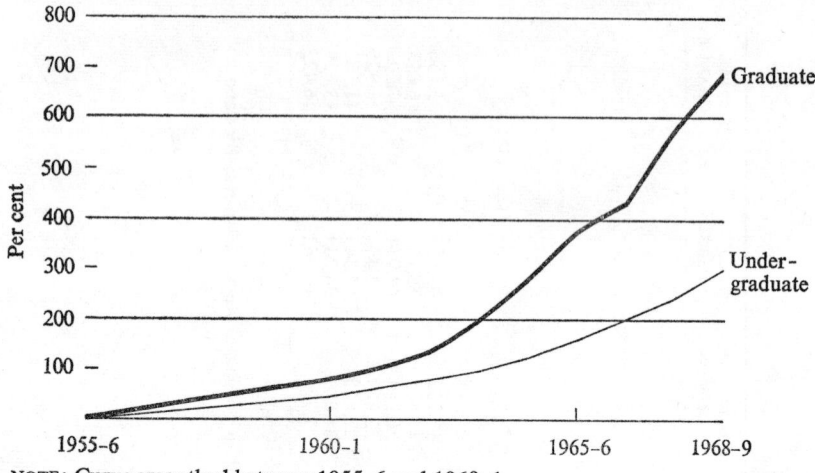

NOTE: Curve smoothed between 1955–6 and 1960–1.

PROPORTION OF RELEVANT AGE GROUP ENROLLED IN UNIVERSITY

Table 4-2 shows, for 1950–1 to 1967–8, the four-year cumulative enrolment in grade 13, the number in the age group from eighteen to twenty-one, the full-time undergraduate enrolment, and the undergraduate enrolment as a percentage of the grade 13 enrolment and of the eighteen-to-twenty-one age group. Undergraduate enrolment as a percentage of grade 13 enrolment fluctuated, reaching a low of 49.8 in 1951–2, a high of 56.5 in 1958–9, and another low of 49.0 in 1965–6. The significance of these figures is rather doubtful, since total enrolment in grade 13 has typically included a considerable number not preparing for enough papers to meet university requirements in any case. During the 1960s at least, few of those taking the nine(later seven) required papers and passing the examinations with sufficiently high standing did not actually proceed to university.

Undergraduate enrolment as a percentage of those aged eighteen to twenty-one followed a trend highlighted on Chart 4-2. The slight decline immediately after 1950 was caused by the disappearance of the last members of the older veteran group, and should not be interpreted as meaning that a smaller proportion of young people at the point of completing high school actually proceeded to university. It was one of Sheffield's particular contributions to point out that the existence of the veteran group was obscuring the trend toward a larger proportion of non-veteran enrolment from the relevant age group, a development that had been under way for some time. It is nevertheless evident that the prospect of expanding enrolment during the 1950s was based more on the evidence of a coming numerical increase in the relevant age group than on indica-

TABLE 4-2
Full-time undergraduate enrolment in Ontario universities in relation to 18–21 age group and grade 13 enrolment, 1950–68

YEAR	FOUR-YEAR CUMULATIVE GRADE 13 SEPTEMBER ENROLMENT	18–21 AGE GROUP	FULL-TIME UNDER- GRADUATE ENROLMENT	UNDERGRADUATE ENROLMENT AS A PERCENTAGE OF Grade 13 enrolment	18–21 age group
1950–1	38,378	268,000	20,621	53.7	7.7
1951–2	38,030	264,300	18,934	49.8	7.2
1952–3	37,450	267,500	18,868	50.4	7.1
1953–4	36,919	268,500	18,525	50.2	6.9
1954–5	36,731	271,100	19,881	54.1	7.3
1955–6	37,255	276,500	20,629	55.4	7.5
1956–7	39,227	282,500	21,765	55.5	7.7
1957–8	41,739	288,100	23,457	56.2	8.1
1958–9	44,814	296,500	25,304	56.5	8.5
1959–60	49,111	304,600	26,598	54.2	8.7
1960–1	54,579	310,640	28,787	52.7	9.3
1961–2	61,539	316,680	32,217	52.4	10.2
1962–3	70,474	336,600	35,177	49.9	10.5
1963–4	79,946	362,900	39,258	49.1	10.8
1964–5	89,941	384,600	44,487	49.5	11.6
1965–6	104,264	407,300	51,056	49.0	12.5
1966–7	120,474	444,919	59,564	49.4	13.4
1967–8	131,731	470,280	67,703	51.4	14.4

SOURCE: Cicely Watson and Saeed Quazi, *Ontario University and College Enrolment Projections to 1981/82 (1968 Projection)*, Enrollment Projections series, Number 4 (Toronto: The Ontario Institute for Studies in Education, 1969).

CHART 4-2
Full-time undergraduate enrolment in Ontario universities as a percentage of the 18–21 age group, 1950–68

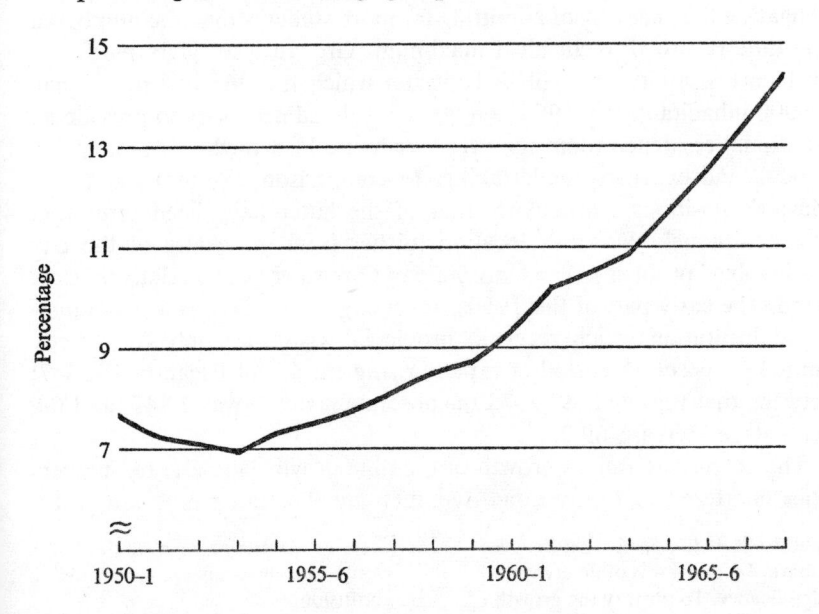

tions of a sharp proportionate increase. A linear projection of a rising curve of proportional attendance for that period produced a serious underestimate of later enrolment figures.

ENROLMENT AT INDIVIDUAL UNIVERSITIES

Full-time enrolment
Total full-time enrolment for 1955-6, and for each year from 1960-1 to 1969-70, is shown in Table 4-3 for each of the institutions that was financially assisted by the province during the 1960s. Enrolment trends are further illustrated by Charts 4-3, 4-4, and 4-5. In terms of size, the University of Toronto began and ended the decade in a class by itself. However, despite a sharp growth curve, accentuated in recent years by the development of Scarborough and Erindale Colleges, its percentage of the total declined from 43.5 to 24.4.

Of the other four "senior" universities, that is, those that were chartered in the nineteenth century, the University of Western Ontario has shown the greatest absolute growth. Its enrolment increased from 2,099 to 3,300 between 1955-6 and 1960-1, a percentage increase of 57.2, and from 3,300 in the latter year to 10,355 in the 1969-70, a percentage increase of 213.8. McMaster's growth rate was the most rapid of the group. It had 1,038 full-time students in 1955-6, 1,579 in 1960-1, and 7,309 in 1969-70, the percentage increases for the same intervals being 52.1 and 362.9. Queen's has experienced a much slower rate of growth. With 2,395 students in 1955-6, it had 296 more than Western, but in 1960-1 had fallen behind by 231 and in 1969-70 by 3,031. Size has had particularly little appeal to Queen's; in fact it has accepted as a public obligation the necessity of admitting far more students than the number at one time regarded as an ideal maximum. Growth also offers particular problems in a city as small as Kingston which in 1966 had fewer than 60,000 inhabitants. By 1968-9 it was considered necessary to provide an additional residence room for every student added to the enrolment – a difficult and expensive undertaking. In comparison, Western's and McMaster's positions, particularly that of the latter have been somewhat easier, although Western's location further from the centre of the city has involved problems. The University of Ottawa grew at a relatively slow rate in the early part of the 1960s, reflecting its position as a denominational institution which received provincial assistance only for strictly limited purposes. A period of rapidly rising enrolment began in 1966-7; between that year and 1969-70 the absolute increase was 2,847, and the percentage increase 69.2.

The extent and rate of growth of the nine provincially assisted universities chartered in the twentieth century are illustrated in Chart 4-4.*

*The basis of the distinction between Charts 4-3 and 4-4 is of no great significance. To portray the growth of fourteen institutions on a single chart would obviously have resulted only in confusion.

TABLE 4-3
Total full-time enrolment in provincially assisted universities in Ontario, 1955-70

UNIVERSITY	1955-6	1960-1	1961-2	1962-3	1963-4	1964-5	1965-6	1966-7	1967-8	1968-9	1969-70[a]
Brock						124	361	530	681	1,126	1,559
Carleton	500	1,158	1,582	1,964	2,278	2,729	3,068	3,724	5,167	5,972	6,535
Guelph[b]		1,452	1,564	1,642	1,762	1,927	2,414	3,298	4,357	5,149	5,827
Lakehead	41	172	220	224	315	466	833	1,183	1,585	2,029	2,436
Laurentian		183	260	272	364	556	938	1,129	1,459[c]	1,758[c]	1,999[c]
McMaster	1,038	1,579	1,858	2,142	2,625	3,312	3,779	4,648	5,191	6,280	7,309
Ottawa	1,469	2,646	3,052	3,247	3,517	3,838	3,873	4,116	4,880	6,156	6,963
Queen's	2,395	3,069	3,352	3,427	3,696	4,029	4,643	5,109	5,781	6,733	7,324
Toronto	7,330	12,082	12,050	12,750	13,967	15,207	16,835[d]	18,193[d]	19,975[e]	22,357[e]	24,059[e]
Trent						105	291	513	746	1,077	1,288
Waterloo	285	846	1,196	1,694	2,315	3,137	4,451	5,719	7,012	8,701	9,987
Western[f]	2,099	3,300	3,762	4,046	4,719	5,274	5,882	7,718	8,329	9,819	10,355
Windsor	570	1,185	1,414	1,575	1,816	1,986	2,387	2,812	3,317	4,214	5,187
York		76	216	305	511	795	1,491	2,659	3,735	5,924	7,807
TOTAL	15,727	27,748	30,526	33,288	37,885	43,485	51,246	61,351	72,215	87,295	98,635

SOURCES: Reports of the Minister of University Affairs of Ontario; DBS, *Survey of Higher Education*, publication no. 81-204.

NOTE: The above table includes undergraduate, graduate, preliminary, and diploma enrolment, and interns and residents in 1968-70.

[a] Projected.
[b] Until 1964-5 enrolment figures relate only to the former Ontario Agricultural College and the Ontario Veterinary College.
[c] Includes Algoma and Nipissing (79 and 50 in 1967-8; 108 and 54 in 1968-9; 140 and 60 in 1969-70 respectively).
[d] Includes Scarborough (191 in 1965-6; 502 in 1966-7).
[e] Includes Scarborough and Erindale (961 and 151 in 1967-8; 1,436 and 458 in 1968-9; 1,700 and 940 in 1969-70 respectively).
[f] Enrolment for affiliated and federated colleges not included prior to 1966-7.

CHART 4-3
Enrolment in five senior provincially assisted universities in Ontario, 1960–70

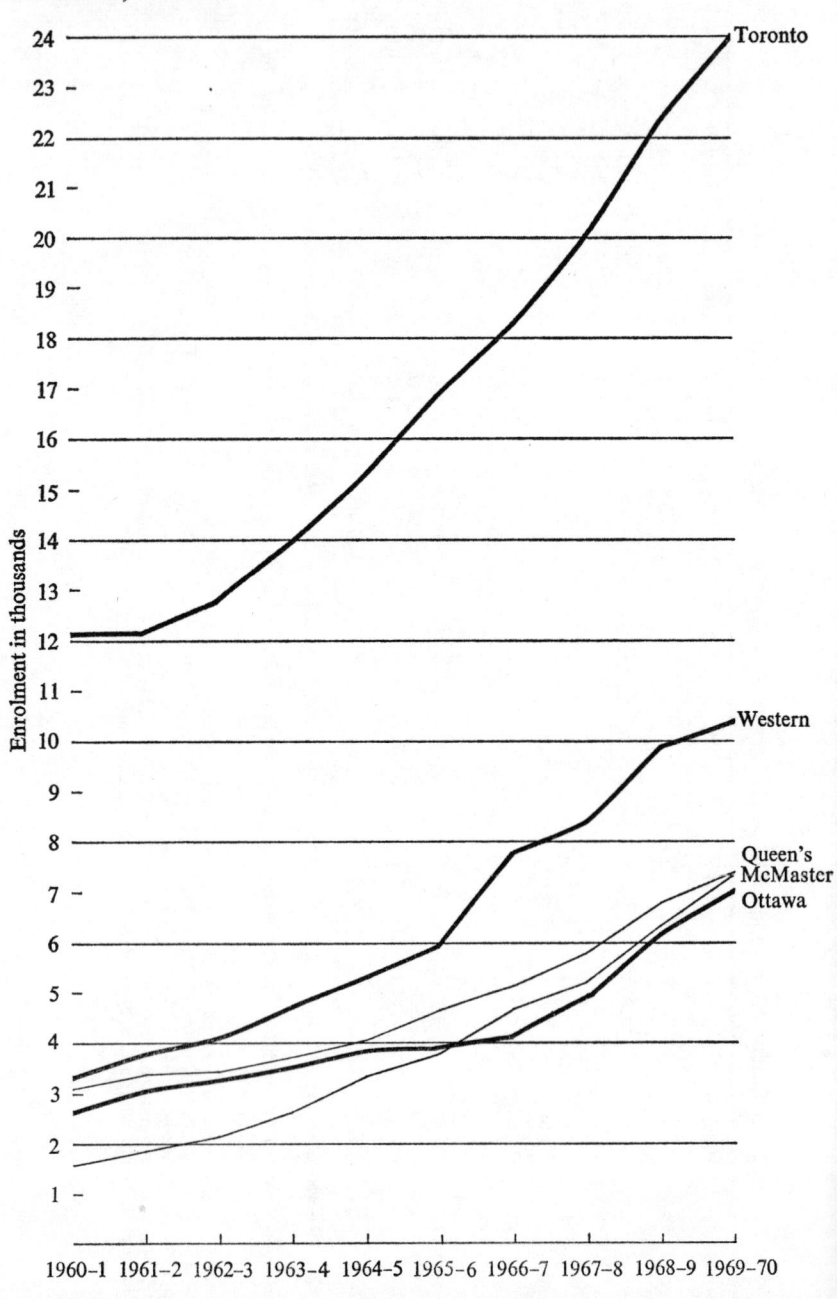

CHART 4-4
Enrolment in nine provincially assisted Ontario universities chartered in the twentieth century, 1960–70

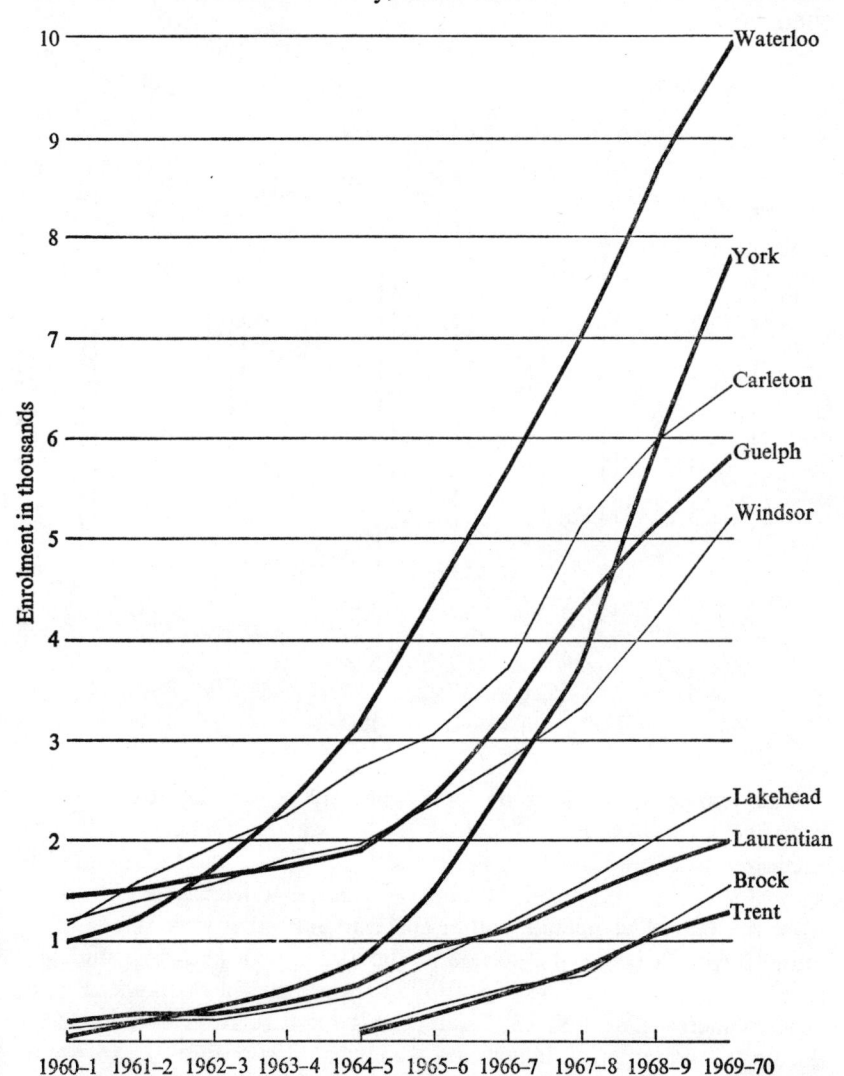

Two of these, Guelph and Windsor, date from the nineteenth century, although not, of course, as full-fledged universities. Their growth patterns were remarkably similar during the 1960s. Their respective enrolments were 1,452 and 1,185 in 1960–1 and 5,827 and 5,187 in 1969–70, representing percentage increases of 301.3 and 337.7. For both the period of rapid numerical and percentage growth occurred in the latter part of the decade. They received their present charters in 1964 and 1963 respectively.

184 The expansion of the educational system

CHART 4-5
Full-time enrolment at the University of Toronto as a percentage of full-time enrolment at all provincially assisted universities in Ontario, 1960-70

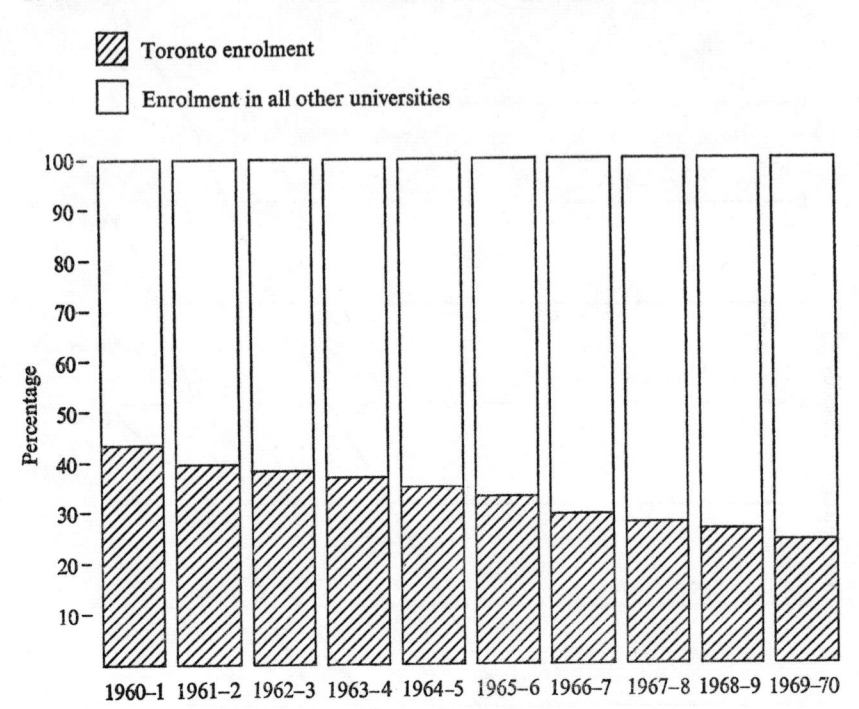

▨ Toronto enrolment

☐ Enrolment in all other universities

The two universities in the comparatively less settled parts of the province also show a very similar growth pattern. What was known successively as the Lakehead Technical Institute and the Lakehead College of Arts, Science, and Technology offered university-level courses from the period immediately after the war, but grew very slowly in its initial stages. It began the decade of the 1960s with only 172 students; thus its enrolment of 2,436 in 1969-70 represents a phenomenal percentage increase of 1,316.3. Laurentian's increase from 183 to 1,999 during the same period indicates a somewhat slower rate of expansion.

The three largest of the universities chartered in the twentieth century, Carleton, Waterloo, and York, show very rapid growth rates. During the early 1960s Waterloo's expansion was unique. Between 1960-1 and 1965-6 its enrolment rose from 846 to 4,451, a percentage increase of 426.1. Its figure of 9,987 at the end of the decade was 1,180.5 per cent of that at the beginning. The comparable figure for Carleton was 564.3 per cent. York was just beginning operations in 1960-1. Its initial growth rate was less rapid than generally expected, and only in 1965-6 did the recent sharp upward trend begin. With an enrolment of 5,924 in 1968-9, it was already as large as the second largest university in Ontario (Western) had been just three years earlier. The increasing number of potential students in Metropolitan Toronto who were not prepared to go outside the city for their education would have to be absorbed in the future largely by York and by Scarborough and Erindale Colleges, with the main campus of the University of Toronto near a limit.

Brock and Trent Universities recorded the smallest enrolment by a substantial margin after they began to accept students in 1964–5. Their growth patterns were very similar up to 1968–9, but in 1969–70 Brock spurted ahead. The area surrounding it is considered to have substantially greater growth potential, which may be expected to increase the difference between the two in the future.

Full-time undergraduate enrolment at Waterloo Lutheran University, not shown in the statistics provided by the Department of University Affairs, was 580 in 1960–1, and increased rapidly to 1,898 in 1964–5. At that time a policy of restricting the size of the entering class was adopted so that facilities would not be excessively strained. While it was intended that the number of undergraduates would not exceed 2,400, the total for 1968–9 was actually 2,441. By that time the Board of Governors had raised the permissible maximum to 2,500. In the same year the total number of students, full-time and part-time, enrolled for academic credit in all programs and courses was 7,957.

Undergraduate and graduate enrolments in the provincially assisted universities are shown in Tables 4-4 and 4-5 respectively for 1955–6 and for each year between 1960–1 and 1969–70. Undergraduate enrolment, generally speaking, followed an upward trend similar to that of total full-time enrolment. Graduate enrolment has been less stable and predictable. In the universities that were prepared for relatively rapid expansion, there were subsantial increases in 1964–5, when the provincial government's program of assistance to graduate students began to take effect. Toronto has continued to be predominant and there have been relatively rapid increases at Waterloo, McMaster, Carleton, and York. All the newer universities have entered the graduate field, although some on a very small scale.

To the extent that graduate enrolment has been a planned process, it has caused a certain amount of difficulty. The Committee to Study the Development of Graduate Programmes in Ontario Universities reported its attempt to get an estimate of provincial and national needs for higher graduates. The Ontario Economic Council had been dubious about the process of manpower prediction. The committee described the situation as follows.

Existing estimates are of two main kinds – those which predict the need for university teachers and industrial scientists as a function of predicted enrolment and output, and those put forward by the various specialized professions

TABLE 4-4
Total full-time undergraduate enrolment at provincially assisted universities in Ontario, 1955-70

UNIVERSITY	1955-6	1960-1	1961-2	1962-3	1963-4	1964-5	1965-6	1966-7	1967-8	1968-9	1969-70[a]
Brock						124	361	530	679	1,119	1,540
Carleton	492	965	1,361	1,664	1,925	2,263	2,556	3,229	4,464	5,139	5,531
Guelph[b]		1,145	1,230	1,275	1,403	1,498	1,893	2,639	3,655	4,419	4,950
Lakehead	41	102	107	100	160	269	431	747	1,053	1,491	1,758
Laurentian		183	260	272	364	556	938	1,129	1,429[c]	1,718[c]	1,959[c]
McMaster	972	1,446	1,686	1,912	2,310	2,902	3,256	4,001	4,412	5,152	5,830
Ottawa	1,361	1,807	2,010	2,117	2,472	2,649	2,683	2,951	3,327	4,363	5,100
Queen's	2,307	2,839	3,068	3,121	3,335	3,571	4,120	4,494	5,032	5,665	6,107
Toronto	6,443	9,951	9,844	11,273	11,964	12,902	13,743[d]	14,559[d]	16,236[e]	17,732[e]	19,004[e]
Trent						102	285	512	742	1,073	1,285
Waterloo	285	731	1,022	1,549	2,089	2,812	3,917	5,001	6,123	7,584	8,744
Western[f]	1,898	2,949	3,357	3,582	4,147	4,492	5,035	6,742	7,270	8,551	8,903
Windsor	568	998	1,181	1,336	1,529	1,679	2,027	2,344	2,972	3,811	4,725
York		76	216	305	511	784	1,453	2,540	3,509	5,575	7,293
TOTAL	14,367	23,192	25,342	28,506	32,209	36,603	42,698	51,418	60,903	73,392	82,729

SOURCE: Reports of the Minister of University Affairs of Ontario; DBS, *Survey of Higher Education*, publication no. 81-204.

[a]Projected.
[b]Until 1964-5 enrolment figures relate only to the former Ontario Agricultural College and the Ontario Veterinary College.
[c]Includes Algoma and Nipissing (79 and 50 in 1967-8; 108 and 54 in 1968-9; 140 and 60 in 1969-70 respectively).
[d]Includes Scarborough (191 in 1965-6; 502 in 1966-7).
[e]Includes Scarborough and Erindale (961 and 151 in 1967-8; 1,436 and 458 in 1968-9; 1,700 and 940 in 1969-70 respectively).
[f]Enrolment for affiliated and federated colleges not included prior to 1966-7.

TABLE 4-5
Total full-time graduate enrolment at provincially assisted universities in Ontario, 1955–70

UNIVERSITY	1955–6	1960–1	1961–2	1962–3	1963–4	1964–5	1965–6	1966–7	1967–8	1968–9	1969–70[a]
Brock									2	7	19
Carleton	8	50	31	87	148	217	268	281	408	517	614
Guelph[b]		103	109	121	131	154	206	250	360	402	542
Lakehead									6	27	43
Laurentian											
McMaster	66	133	172	230	315	410	523	647	779	1,050	1,354
Ottawa	108	320	404	513	490	632	610	477	746	877	1,023
Queen's	88	222	284	306	361	458	523	609	721	838	950
Toronto	887	2,131	2,206	1,477	2,003	2,305	3,092	3,142	3,257	3,454	3,810
Trent						3	6	1	4	4	3
Waterloo		22	42	69	153	302	512	702	884	1,109	1,243
Western[c]	201	351	405	464	572	782	847	955	1,029	1,061	1,256
Windsor	2	40	68	75	123	145	178	223	208	270	314
York						11	38	119	226	349	514
TOTAL	1,360	3,372	3,721	3,342	4,296	5,419	6,803	7,406	8,630	9,965	11,685

SOURCES: Reports of the Minister of University Affairs of Ontario; DBS, *Survey of Higher Education*, publication no. 81-204.

[a] Projected.
[b] Until 1964–5 enrolment figures relate only to the former Ontario Agricultural College and the Ontario Veterinary College.
[c] Enrolment for affiliated and federated colleges not included prior to 1966–7.

with respect to their own fields. Neither sort is satisfactory for the purpose of wise planning of graduate education. The demographically-based predictions of the first sort yield only very broad answers, and do not get down to cases, especially as regards specializations. Internal professional estimates usually reflect the optimism of the present practitioners. It is difficult, for example, for a chemist not to feel that Ontario is going to need a lot more chemists in the near future.[9]

Part-time enrolment
Part-time enrolment has developed according to patterns that are quite different from those of undergraduate enrolment. York's Atkinson College, for example, has flourished to such an extent that the number of part-time students has exceeded the number studying full-time at that university. This phenomenon has no doubt eased what would have otherwise been much greater pressure on the University of Toronto. As shown in Table 4-6, part-time undergraduate enrolment reached 6,941 at York in 1968–9, as compared with 8,621 on the three campuses at Toronto, while the estimated figures for 1969–70 were 8,878 and 8,965 respectively. Among other universities with a relatively strong orientation in the direction of part-time offerings were Carleton, which began as an institution for that type of study, McMaster, Ottawa, Queen's, Western, and Windsor. The northern universities, Lakehead and Laurentian, were also filling a need in their areas. Nipissing College, an affiliate of Laurentian, had an enrolment consisting largely of part-time students.

ENROLMENT BY TYPE OF PROGRAM
Only a relatively small proportion of students in the provincially assisted universities have enrolled in programs other than regular degree programs. The preliminary year, the equivalent of Ontario grade 13, has not particularly flourished in recent years; it is ordinarily offered to accommodate those for whom it is considered inconvenient to obtain grade 13 standing, particularly those from outside the province. In 1964–5 there were 991 such students in those of the fourteen of the provincially assisted universities that offered the course. Ottawa had 537, followed by Carleton, with 249, Windsor, with 164, and Waterloo, with 23. For 1967–8, 1968–9, and 1969–70 the numbers at Carleton were respectively 294, 311, and 384; at Ottawa, 561, 428, and 340; at Windsor, 115, 113, 123; at Laurentian, 30, 40, and 40. The number at Western was 21 during each of the three years, while the program disappeared at Waterloo.

There has been a growing tendency for the universities to offer diploma courses, although the enrolment in them remains a small percentage of the total. In 1964–5 Guelph had 275 diploma students, and Lakehead had 197 in technology courses. The total enrolment in diploma courses for all universities was 717 in 1965–6, 1,564 in 1966–7, 1,656 in 1967–8, 1,696 in 1968–9, and 1,888 in 1969–70. During the last of these years,

TABLE 4-6
Part-time enrolment in regular and summer sessions at provincially assisted universities in Ontario, 1966-70

UNIVERSITY	1966-7 Under-graduate	1966-7 Graduate	1967-8 Under-graduate	1967-8 Graduate	1968-9 Under-graduate	1968-9 Graduate	1969-70[a] Under-graduate	1969-70[a] Graduate
Brock	514		641		996		1,268	
Carleton	1,673	415	4,132	422	6,614	387	7,229	461
Guelph	142	86	180	63	323	115	313	68
Lakehead	846		1,515	8	2,068	34	2,150	18
Laurentian	1,468		1,711		2,216		2,450	
Algoma			350		759		971	
Nipissing			245		413		425	
McMaster	3,640	431	3,767	416	4,201	445	4,207	516
Ottawa	5,389	1,212	5,362	1,416	4,800	1,561	4,796	1,671
Queen's	3,789	128	3,542	153	3,837	137	4,111	162
Toronto-Main	5,481	1,167	5,957	1,281	7,384	1,408	7,595	1,474
Erindale	225		259		383		550	
Scarborough	446		818		854		820	
Trent	18	2	80		412		600	
Waterloo	665	56	619	115	787	225	1,029	193
Western	3,755	118	3,976	240	4,765	224	5,375	188
Windsor	2,216	124	3,188	99	3,884	182	4,290	207
York	3,846	309	5,280	490	6,941	384	8,878	324
TOTAL	34,113	4,048	41,622	4,703	51,637	5,102	57,057	5,282

SOURCE: Reports of the Minister of University Affairs of Ontario.

[a]Projected.

6 were at Carleton, 335 at Guelph, 635 at Lakehead, 290 at Ottawa, 117 at Queen's, 480 at Toronto, and 25 at Windsor.

In their study on student assistance Cook and Stager reviewed enrolment trends in university programs in all Ontario universities, whether provincially assisted or otherwise, between 1951–2 and 1968–9. During that time enrolment in arts and science increased from 43.8 to 63.8 per cent of the total. The corresponding percentages for engineering were 12.8 and 10.6; for agriculture, 1.9 and 1.0; for architecture 1.1 and 0.5; for commerce, 3.9 and 4.0; for dentistry, 2.1 and 0.7; for education, 2.2 and 2.5; for household science, 1.1 and 1.0; for law, 4.2 and 2.6; for medicine, 10.0 and 2.4; for nursing, 2.4 and 1.7; for pharmacy, 2.3 and 0.6; for physical and health education, 1.6 and 2.5; for theology, 2.4 and 1.2; and for others, 8.2 and 4.9.[10] In most cases, the upward or downward trend was consistent throughout the period. Engineering was a major exception in that it had 18.0 per cent of the total in 1956–7. Commerce also showed a sharp rise in the mid-fifties, followed by a decline to a figure close to that for 1951–2. Education was characterized by erratic increases and decreases.

Enrolment by program of study at the provincially assisted universities from 1964–5 to 1969–70 is shown in Table 4-7. The data have been taken from forms received by the Department of University Affairs. Certain changes have been made in the method of categorization used by that department in the tables as presented in the reports of the Minister of University Affairs. 1 / Figures for science, general science, and honours science have been combined, even though enrolment in honours science was reported separately from 1966–7 on. It appears that there were differences in interpretation of the terms from one university to another, and the validity of the distinctions is somewhat questionable. 2 / Students in library science, whether in the BLS or MLS program, have uniformly been classified as graduates. Reports from the universities have not followed the same practice consistently from year to year, sometimes classifying BLS students as undergraduates and sometimes as graduates. 3 / Figures for education students at the University of Toronto have not been included in the tables produced by the department. The courses are given at the Ontario Institute for Studies in Education, which comes under the jurisdiction of the Minister of Education rather than the Minister of University Affairs. Since the students concerned are in every essential way University of Toronto students working for Toronto degrees, they have been included in Table 4-7. 4 / The University of Ottawa reported its undergraduate students in philosophy under honours arts, and its graduate students in the same field under humanities in 1966–7. For the sake of consistency, these students have been reported in the same way for all years in Table 4-7. As a result of these modifications, the totals differ somewhat from those in tables produced by the Department of University Affairs.

Further investigation into the sources of information employed by the department has made it possible to make certain revisions in the figures in order to remove anomalies. Thus in a number of places the contents of the tables presented in the present volume do not correspond exactly with those in the report of the Minister of University Affairs. In most cases the changes are minor, and do not affect any general conclusions that may be drawn about enrolment or other trends.

Certain characteristic approaches used by the department should be noted. Humanities has been a comprehensive category for graduate studies, including a number of disciplines whose inclusion might be questioned even under the broadest definition of the term. The other major general category for graduate studies has been the physical and biological sciences. As graduate enrolment has increased markedly in certain specific fields, the latter have been assigned separate categories. In 1966–7 geography and mathematics were listed separately. Psychology has been treated as a separate field of graduate study since 1964–5. Also to be noted is the apparent variation in the way "other social sciences" have been reported from year to year. Such inconsistencies make it difficult to identify enrolment trends in these areas.

The combined total of students in general and honours arts increased from 44.6 per cent of undergraduate student enrolment in 1964–5 to 47.2 in 1966–7, and declined to 46.9 per cent in 1969–70. In 1967–8 the Department of University Affairs changed its method of recording the numbers in these fields of study. In order to improve the accuracy of comparisons between universities, students registered in honours during their first year of attendance were counted with general course students. Thus the figures in the University of Toronto were brought more into line with those in the other universities where students entered honours after their first, or even in some cases their second, year of attendance. This change accounts for the slight reduction in recorded honours enrolment in 1967–8. In the period just before that, the percentage of total undergraduate enrolment in general arts was on the increase, rising from 30.7 in 1964–5 to 35.4 in 1966–7. In 1969–70 it stood at 36.1 per cent. The percentage in honours arts declined from 13.9 in 1964–5 to 11.8 in 1966–7, and stood at 10.8 in 1969–70. The effect of the abolition of the old forms of general and honours courses at the University of Toronto in 1969–70, with whatever influence this change may have on other universities, makes future trends very difficult to predict.

While the number taking engineering at the undergraduate level rose from 4,950 in 1964–5 to 8,862 in 1969–70, the percentage of total undergraduate enrolment declined from 13.6 to 10.7. On the other hand, graduate engineering students numbered 1,769 in 1969–70, as compared with 648 in 1964–5, a percentage increase of 173.0. The number of undergraduate students taking science increased over the same period from 4,871 to 15,441, that is, by 217.0 per cent. The tendency for enrol-

TABLE 4-7
Full-time enrolment by program of study at provincially assisted universities, 1964–70

PROGRAM OF STUDY	1964–5 Under-graduate	1964–5 Grad-uate	1965–6 Under-graduate	1965–6 Grad-uate	1966–7 Under-graduate	1966–7 Grad-uate	1967–8 Under-graduate	1967–8 Grad-uate	1968–9 Under-graduate	1968–9 Grad-uate	1969–70[a] Under-graduate	1969–70[a] Grad-uate
Agriculture	844	135	767	138	762	70	796	128	844	136	914	171
Architecture	227	38	247	53	268	68	350	35	461	40	572	72
Arts, General[b]	11,189		14,182		18,119		22,175		27,171		29,801	
Arts, Honours[c]	5,090		6,083		6,042		5,953		7,308		8,871	
Child Study		16		15		24		16		30		35
Commerce, Business Administration	1,600	413	1,664	485	2,068	623	2,461	737	3,200	674	3,807	823
Dentistry	573	33	579	39	502	50	514	45	544	54	572	65
Education		56		70		134	36	296		287		355
Engineering	4,950	648	5,674	798	6,514	1,032	7,401	1,367	8,202	1,567	8,862	1,769
Fine and Applied Arts							41	19	249	26	389	33
Forestry	97	13	94	20	116	21	158	161	210	217	238	281
Geography						139						
Hospital Administration		5		13		20		52		67		62
Household and Food Sciences	399	10	464	8	608	9	689	11	800	35	894	47
Humanities		1,685		2,231		2,094		1,821		2,137		2,489
Hygiene and Public Health	101	80	114	101	180	119	5	74	1	95	3	107
Journalism	115	3	150	3		7	205	14	277	12	318	11
Law[d]	895	8	1,114	5	1,231	9	1,882[d]	47	2,102	12	2,412	18
Library Science[e]		142		182		238		297		332		384
Mathematics						285	842	326		444		548
Medicine	2,059	450	1,835	536	1,410	421	1,516	420	1,551	432	1,602	495

TABLE 4-7, continued

PROGRAM OF STUDY	1964-5 Under-graduate	1964-5 Graduate	1965-6 Under-graduate	1965-6 Graduate	1966-7 Under-graduate	1966-7 Graduate	1967-8 Under-graduate	1967-8 Graduate	1968-9 Under-graduate	1968-9 Graduate	1969-70[a] Under-graduate	1969-70[a] Graduate
Music	261	13	327	16	337	29	400	29	542	20	661	28
Nursing	939	10	923	9	935	14	973	12	1,029	3	1,167	5
Pharmacy	387	10	415	20	433	19	460	15	482	22	517	28
Physical and Biological Sciences		1,266		1,644		1,550		1,766		2,129		2,368
Physical and Health Education	689	28	701	7	862	9	1,652	11	2,366	15	2,995	18
Physical and Occupational Therapy	291	26	274	17		23	6	27	23	22	42	25
Pre-Medicine					579		871		459		776	
Psychology		177		159		490		521		588		704
Public Administration		66		68		59		61		72		94
Secretarial Science	125		135		146		143		150		625	
Science	4,871	17	6,425	20	9,743		11,143	595	14,516	827	15,441	1,030
Social Sciences – other		215	153	194		182	214	187	379	201	638	235
Social Work	355	19	286	22	268	34	66	38	270	37	278	48
Veterinary Medicine	439		91	1	63		259				46	
Unclassified												
Subtotal	36,496	5,582	42,697	6,874	51,186	7,772	61,211	9,128	73,136	10,533	82,441	12,348
TOTAL	42,078		49,571		58,958		70,339		83,669		94,789	

SOURCE: Reports of the Minister of University Affairs of Ontario.

[a] Projected.
[d] Arts – general and first year honours from 1967–8.
[c] Arts – upper year honours from 1967–8.
[b] Enrolment at Osgoode Hall Law School which became York Faculty of Law in 1968.
[e] Uniformly classified as graduate study.

ment in the health sciences, including medicine, dentistry, and nursing, to grow very slowly during the early and middle 1960s was in large measure attributable to lack of facilities. Although a major drive was begun to remedy this deficiency, as improved health services became an increasingly important social objective, the results have taken several years to become evident. Physical and health education has been a field of rapidly increasing popularity, with 689 students in 1964–5 and 2,995 in 1969–70.

The number of graduate students in psychology reached 704 in 1969–70, a percentage increase of 297.7 from 1964–5. After the practice of separate categorization was begun in 1966–7, the number in geography increased by 102.2 per cent by 1969–70, and the number in mathematics by 92.3 per cent. After a reduction caused by categorization changes, it appears that graduate enrolment in the humanities has increased fairly rapidly. There has been a similar trend in the physical and biological sciences, although a smaller increase was registered between 1968–9 and 1969–70 than in the humanities.

Tables 4-8 to 4-21 show the distribution of undergraduate students at each of the fourteen provincially assisted universities by program of study. As is true of Table 4-7, the data for which were obtained by summing the entries on the individual reports, the possibility of some differences in interpreting the program categories by different universities must be kept in mind.

Brock University

As shown in Table 4-8, Brock University reported only general arts students during its first year of operations in 1964–5, and added science students the next year. Enrolment in honours courses constituted 16.9 per cent of the total arts enrolment in 1969–70. Graduate enrolment in biological science rose from two in 1967–8 to nineteen in 1969–70.

Carleton University

Carleton has developed a fairly wide range of programs. Its general arts course has consistently accounted for somewhat more than half its total undergraduate enrolment. Comparatively few of its students have taken honours arts. The percentages of all undergraduates in honours arts for successive years from 1964–5 on were 3.1, 2.3, 5.9, 8.6, 8.8, and 8.8. Science has declined somewhat in popularity, constituting 20.0 per cent of total undergraduate enrolment in 1964–5 and 16.9 per cent in 1969–70. Engineering showed a sharp increase between 1964–5 and 1966–7, and a somewhat more moderate one in subsequent years. Commerce and journalism, for which Carleton is well known, have shown steady increases.

Among graduate programs, engineering has shown the rapid increase characteristic of Ontario universities in general. Public administration,

TABLE 4-8
Full-time enrolment by program of study at Brock University, 1964-70

PROGRAM OF STUDY	1964-5 Under-graduate	1964-5 Graduate	1965-6 Under-graduate	1965-6 Graduate	1966-7 Under-graduate	1966-7 Graduate	1967-8 Under-graduate	1967-8 Graduate	1968-9 Under-graduate	1968-9 Graduate	1969-70[a] Under-graduate	1969-70[a] Graduate
Arts, General[b]	124		281		402		267		588		805	
Arts, Honours[c]					13		209		118		164	
Physical and Biological Sciences			80		115		203	2	413	7	571	19
Subtotal	124		361		530		679	2	1,119	7	1,540	19
TOTAL	124		361		530		681		1,126		1,559	

SOURCE: Reports of the Minister of University Affairs of Ontario.

[a] Projected.
[b] Arts – general and first year honours from 1967-8.
[c] Arts – upper year honours from 1967-8.

TABLE 4-9
Full-time enrolment by program of study at Carleton University, 1964-70

PROGRAM OF STUDY	1964-5 Under-graduate	1964-5 Graduate	1965-6 Under-graduate	1965-6 Graduate	1966-7 Under-graduate	1966-7 Graduate	1967-8 Under-graduate	1967-8 Graduate	1968-9 Under-graduate	1968-9 Graduate	1969-70[a] Under-graduate	1969-70[a] Graduate
Architecture									32		70	
Arts, General[b]	1,211		1,373		1,577		2,356		2,794		2,920	
Arts, Honours[c]	71		59		192		385		454		485	
Commerce	156		182		196		262		229		244	
Engineering	261	26	307	21	412	41	470	62	511	72	591	90
Geography								3		9		11
Humanities		63		97		97		55		73		88
Journalism	93		125		158		179		249		289	
Mathematics						10		4		12		19
Physical and Biological Sciences		62		82		54		57		77		94
Psychology						20		16		28		35
Public Administration		66		68		59		61		72		77
Science	453		481		694		812		870		932	
Social Sciences - other								85		83		105
Social Work	18		29					65		91		95
Unclassified												
Subtotal	2,263	217	2,556	268	3,229	281	4,464	408	5,139	517	5,531	614
TOTAL	2,480		2,824		3,510		4,872		5,656		6,145	

SOURCE: Reports of the Minister of University Affairs of Ontario.

[a] Projected.
[b] Arts - general and first year honours from 1967-8.
[c] Arts - upper year honours from 1967-8.

one of the university's specialties, has remained relatively stable in absolute numbers. A result of the action of St Patrick's College in joining Carleton in 1967 has been the addition of a substantial number of graduate students in social work. Limited facilities have acted as a restraining influence on enrolment in this program.

The University of Guelph

Although it is a very new university in terms of independent status, and in terms of its arts programs, the University of Guelph has a long history as the Ontario Agricultural College, Macdonald Institute, and the Ontario Veterinary College, or, immediately before its university charter was granted in 1964, as the Federated Colleges, in affiliation with the University of Toronto. Its program, as indicated in Table 4-10, naturally reflects its earlier orientation. Agriculture and agricultural engineering as fields of study for a university degree are more than holding their own in absolute terms, but declining in relative importance. Their percentage of total undergraduate enrolment for each of the six respective years from 1964-5 on has been 56.3, 45.5, 33.7, 25.6, 22.4, and 21.9. This trend is an indication of the rapid development of a more diversified program, particularly of the increasing enrolment in arts. Most of the arts students have taken the general course, although the proportion in honours programs has increased since 1967-8. Science has attracted a fairly substantial proportion of the total enrolment. Among the fields of study particularly characteristic of the university, the course in food sciences has attracted increasing numbers of students, while the enrolment in veterinary medicine has remained fairly stable.

Lakehead University

In view of its relatively small enrolment, Lakehead University has offered a considerable range of programs. Until 1969-70 over half its students were in general arts, which, during the six years covered in Table 4-11, attracted 65.1, 59.1, 63.5, 55.7, 52.5, and 48.6 per cent of the enrolment respectively. Honours arts courses showed a marked increase in popularity after 1966-7. A substantial number of students have taken science. The remainder, in relatively small numbers, have been scattered among programs in business administration, engineering, forestry, and nursing. A beginning has been made in graduate programs in business administration, the humanities, the physical and biological sciences, psychology, and social sciences.

Laurentian University

In its earlier years, Laurentian University concentrated its efforts in a relatively small number of areas. Only general arts, science, commerce, and the initial stages in a program in engineering were offered in 1964-5. Nursing, physical and health education, and an undergraduate program in social work, the second in the province, were added in 1967-8. During

198 The expansion of the educational system

TABLE 4-10
Full-time enrolment by program of study at the University of Guelph, 1964-70

PROGRAM OF STUDY	1964-5 Under-graduate	1964-5 Graduate	1965-6 Under-graduate	1965-6 Graduate	1966-7 Under-graduate	1966-7 Graduate	1967-8 Under-graduate	1967-8 Graduate	1968-9 Under-graduate	1968-9 Graduate	1969-70[a] Under-graduate	1969-70[a] Graduate
Agriculture	844	135	767	138	762	70	796	128	844	136	914	171
Agricultural Engineering			95		128	18	139	21	146	20	169	24
Architecture, Landscape			8	2	24	4	37	1	44		51	
Arts, General[b]			225		566		1,138		1,256		1,527	
Arts, Honours[c]					45		124		335		357	
Business Administration	299		321		362	4	418	9	503	29	569	40
Food Sciences						1		2		3		6
Geography				2		38		43		46		61
Humanities								1				5
Mathematics												
Physical and Biological Sciences				41		77		99		107		140
Physical and Health Education					34		80	7	125	10	164	19
Psychology			191		450	4	664		896		444	
Science											470	
Secretarial Science												
Social Sciences – other								11		14		28
Textiles				1								
Veterinary Medicine	355	19	286	22	268	34	259	38	270	37	278	48
Subtotal	1,498	154	1,893	206	2,639	250	3,655	360	4,419	402	4,943	542
TOTAL	1,652		2,099		2,889		4,015		4,821		5,485	

SOURCE: Reports of the Minister of University Affairs of Ontario.

[a] Projected.
[b] Arts – general and first year honours from 1967-8.
[c] Arts – upper year honours from 1967-8.

TABLE 4-11
Full-time enrolment by program of study at Lakehead University, 1964-70

PROGRAM OF STUDY	1964-5 Under-graduate	1964-5 Grad-uate	1965-6 Under-graduate	1965-6 Grad-uate	1966-7 Under-graduate	1966-7 Grad-uate	1967-8 Under-graduate	1967-8 Grad-uate	1968-9 Under-graduate	1968-9 Grad-uate	1969-70[a] Under-graduate	1969-70[a] Grad-uate
Arts, General[b]	175		254		474		586		783		855	
Arts, Honours[c]	5		26		14		99		166		245	
Business Administration												20
Engineering	32		6		13		26		60	10	88	
Forestry			20		29		40		62		60	
Humanities			8	1	11		21		35		38	4
Mathematics								3		1		
Nursing			4		35		68	1	97		122	
Physical and Biological Sciences								2		6		9
Psychology										7		6
Science	57		112		171		213		288		350	
Social Sciences – other										3		4
Subtotal	269		430	1	747		1,053	6	1,491	27	1,758	43
TOTAL	269		431		747		1,059		1,518		1,801	

SOURCE: Reports of the Minister of University Affairs of Ontario.

[a] Projected.
[b] Arts – general and first year honours from 1967–8.
[c] Arts – upper year honours from 1967–8.

200 The expansion of the educational system

TABLE 4-12
Full-time enrolment by program of study at Laurentian University, including Algoma and Nipissing Colleges, 1964–70

PROGRAM OF STUDY	1964–5 Undergraduate	1965–6 Undergraduate	1966–7 Undergraduate	1967–8 Undergraduate	1968–9 Undergraduate	1969–70[a] Undergraduate
Arts, General[b]	416	731	808	993	1,026	1,079
Arts, Honours[c]			28	44	91	100
Commerce	32	52	76	83	133	149
Engineering	10	33	54	39	51	71
Nursing				13	30	43
Physical and Health Education				12	57	98
Science	98	122	163	221	284	324
Social Work				24	46	73
Other						22
TOTAL	556	938	1,129	1,429	1,718	1,959

SOURCE: Reports of the Minister of University Affairs of Ontario.

[a]Projected.
[b]Arts – general and first year honours from 1967–8.
[c]Arts – upper year honours from 1967–8.

that year enrolment in arts constituted 72.6 per cent of the total, and declined to 65.0 and 60.2 per cent in the next two years respectively.

McMaster University
As indicated in Table 4-13, enrolment in arts at McMaster fluctuated above and below 50 per cent of total undergraduate enrolment during the six-year period. Changes in program arrangements affecting physical and health education in 1967–8 make comparisons with earlier years of somewhat doubtful value. The number in that program increased from 435 to 718, or by 65.1 per cent, during the next two years. Among developments of interest are the large increases in engineering, business administration, and science. In the relatively large and rapidly increasing graduate program, the heaviest concentration has been in the physical and biological sciences, with large numbers also in business administration and engineering. There have also been rapid increases in the group consisting of the humanities, geography, mathematics, psychology, and other social sciences.

The University of Ottawa
The University of Ottawa has offered an extraordinary variety of programs in view of the size of its enrolment. As indicated in Table 4-14, the proportion in arts is relatively small, although as far as 1965–6 and 1967–8 are concerned, the number is reduced by the separate listing of undergraduate enrolment in social sciences, which would be combined

TABLE 4-13
Full-time enrolment by program of study at McMaster University, 1964–70

PROGRAM OF STUDY	1964-5 Under-graduate	1964-5 Graduate	1965-6 Under-graduate	1965-6 Graduate	1966-7 Under-graduate	1966-7 Graduate	1967-8 Under-graduate	1967-8 Graduate	1968-9 Under-graduate	1968-9 Graduate	1969-70[a] Under-graduate	1969-70[a] Graduate
Arts, General[b]	1,105		1,337		1,806		1,324		1,656		1,678	
Arts, Honours[c]	309		381		481		565		644		689	
Business Administration	99	18	58	43	53	56	282	93	243	176	313	220
Engineering	287	58	294	62	418	77	424	109	482	158	566	190
Fine Arts							30		38		55	
Geography						23		33		43		54
Humanities		75		118		162		125		185		245
Mathematics						22		23		31		54
Medicine												27
Music							14		26		20	
Nursing	75		84		92		103		110		28	
Physical and Biological Sciences		259		300		274		299		334		377
Physical and Health Education	75		81		97		435	51	540	38	718	62
Psychology						33						
Science	886		959		1,054		1,235		1,347	85	1,476	125
Social Sciences – other								46	66		160	
Social Work	66		62									
Unclassified												
Subtotal	2,902	410	3,256	523	4,001	647	4,412	779	5,152	1,050	5,813	1,354
TOTAL	3,312		3,779		4,648		5,191		6,202		7,167	

SOURCE: Reports of the Minister of University Affairs of Ontario.

[a] Projected.
[b] Arts – general and first year honours from 1967–8.
[c] Arts – upper year honours from 1967–8.

TABLE 4-14
Full-time enrolment by program of study at the University of Ottawa, 1964–70

PROGRAM OF STUDY	1964–5 Under-graduate	1964–5 Grad-uate	1965–6 Under-graduate	1965–6 Grad-uate	1966–7 Under-graduate	1966–7 Grad-uate	1967–8 Under-graduate	1967–8 Grad-uate	1968–9 Under-graduate	1968–9 Grad-uate	1969–70[a] Under-graduate	1969–70[a] Grad-uate
Arts, General[b]	566		703		796		816		1,352		1,678	
Arts, Honours[c]	78		243		224		188		451		597	
Commerce	290		248		272		376		382		420	
Education							36		53		55	
Engineering	159	46	108	45	204	44	252	56	337	110	340	105
Food Sciences	36		36		27		31	81	39	78	50	105
Geography						12		9		6		11
Hospital Administration		5		13		20		22		34		42
Humanities		140		197		191		245		292		337
Hygiene and Public Health	101		114									
Law	283	35	344	27	408	1	423	40	480	2	540	2
Library Science[d]						55		60		61		76
Mathematics						10				10		18
Medicine	304	20	329	22	264	36	275	52	268	59	270	68
Nursing	149		73		96		89		96		124	
Pharmacy					7							
Physical and Biological Sciences		101		127		74		115		125		137
Physical and Health Education	29		40		69		122	5	264	9	397	10
Pre-Medicine					203		97		109		110	
Psychology		177		159		89		81		95		100
Science	233	17	293	20	263		348	40	452	51	501	51
Social Sciences – other		71	153	75		69	214					
Social Work					63							
Unclassified	355											
Subtotal	2,583	612	2,684	685	2,896	601	3,267	806	4,283	932	5,082	1,062
TOTAL	3,195		3,369		3,497		4,073		5,215		6,144	

SOURCE: Reports of the Minister of University Affairs of Ontario.

[a] Projected.
[b] Arts – general and first year honours from 1967–8.
[c] Arts – upper year honours from 1967–8.
[d] Uniformly classified as graduate studies.

with arts in some other universities. Commerce and law have had a relatively strong appeal, and an increasing one in recent years. The number in medicine has increased at a steady, if unspectacular, rate. Education began to be listed as a field of study separate from psychology in 1967–8, corresponding to an organizational change made at that time. The separate listing of pre-medicine, begun in 1966–7, accounts for the apparent decline in enrolment in medicine for that year. Enrolment in nursing remained relatively stable for several years before beginning an upward trend in 1968–9. Among the most popular fields of graduate study were the humanities, the physical and biological sciences, and psychology. Graduate work in the professional schools such as engineering and medicine was also flourishing, and there was also a gradual increase in library science.

Queen's University
General and honours arts combined constituted 42.5, 43.7, 41.4, 42.4, 42.3, and 40.9 per cent of total undergraduate enrolment at Queen's in successive years from 1964–5 on. There was a marked reduction in the number counted in honours courses. Enrolment in these constituted 40.9, 40.8, 34.8, 19.0, 20.6, and 23.5 per cent of total arts enrolment in the six respective years. Engineering attracted almost as many students as did general arts before 1966–7, but substantially fewer after that. With an enrolment of 1,316 in 1969–70, Queen's had one of the largest of the province's faculties or schools of engineering. Law underwent a substantial increase in enrolment during the period under review. As at Ottawa, most of the apparent decline in enrolment in medicine in 1966–7 is to be attributed to the beginning of the separate listing of pre-medicine. The relative stability of physical and health education reflects the establishment of programs in this area in a number of the newer universities. Increased enrolment in graduate studies has been most evident in engineering, mathematics, medicine, the physical and biological sciences, psychology, and other social sciences. The first listing of a separate group of graduates under other social sciences in 1967–8 seems to account largely for the apparent drop in the humanities at that time.

The University of Toronto
The range and variety of programs offered by the University of Toronto is unique in the province, as indicated in Table 4-16. During successive years from 1964–5 on, enrolment in general and honours arts together has remained a relatively constant percentage of the total, ranging from 44.3 in 1964–5 to 45.4 in 1969–70. The percentages have been slightly higher than those at Queen's. The percentages in honours for 1964–5, 1965–6, and 1966–7 were respectively 52.8, 48.1, and 47.1. After the new method of classification was adopted in 1967–8, whereby honours students in their first year of attendance were counted with general stu-

TABLE 4-15
Full-time enrolment by program of study at Queen's University, 1964-70

PROGRAM OF STUDY	1964-5 Under-graduate	1964-5 Grad-uate	1965-6 Under-graduate	1965-6 Grad-uate	1966-7 Under-graduate	1966-7 Grad-uate	1967-8 Under-graduate	1967-8 Grad-uate	1968-9 Under-graduate	1968-9 Grad-uate	1969-70[a] Under-graduate	1969-70[a] Grad-uate
Arts, General[b]	897		1,066		1,214		1,728		1,905		1,912	
Arts, Honours[c]	620		736		647		406		493		587	
Commerce	134	48	158	50	165	62	231	62	327	72	400	95
Engineering	825	91	963	86	1,034	107	1,134	132	1,247	146	1,316	164
Fine and Applied Arts											15	
Geography						8		11		15		13
Humanities						163		127		163		179
Law	144		205		226		270		300		350	
Mathematics		168		193		27		34		49		4
Medicine	363	17	366	23	236	33	256	30	262	42	270	54
Music											20	44
Nursing	80		70		79		62		83		92	
Physical and Biological Sciences		134		171		166		189		208		218
Physical and Health Education	151		155		149		140		159		166	
Pre-Medicine					110		99		96		98	
Psychology						43		50		46		64
Public Administration												7
Science	357		401		634		706	86	793	97	821	108
Social Sciences – other												
Social Work											60	
Subtotal	3,571	458	4,120	523	4,494	609	5,032	721	5,665	838	6,107	950
TOTAL	4,029		4,643		5,103		5,753		6,503		7,057	

SOURCE: Reports of the Minister of University Affairs of Ontario.

[a] Projected.
[b]
[c] Arts – upper year honours from 1967-8.

dents, the percentage was much smaller. For 1967-8, 1968-9, and 1969-70, it was 29.5, 29.1, and 31.3 respectively.

Among other undergraduate programs, enrolment in architecture, commerce, engineering, forestry (until 1968-9), household and food sciences, law, music, nursing, pharmacy, physical and health education, and science has shown modest to substantial increases. Lesser growth has been registered in medicine and pre-medicine. Dentistry has shown a decline. Physical and occupational therapy was dropped as an undergraduate program after 1965-6. Among graduate programs there have been moderate or large increases in education, business administration, engineering, the humanities, music, the physical and biological sciences, and other social sciences.

Trent University
The undergraduate program at Trent University consisted of arts and science. Honours arts programs were reported in 1966-7, the third year in which the university was in operation. Honours enrolment has constituted the following percentages of the total in arts for that and the three subsequent years respectively: 35.5, 29.1, 26.3, and 30.7. There were a few graduate students in the humanities initially, and a small number later in the physical and biological sciences.

The University of Waterloo
The very rapid growth of enrolment at the University of Waterloo has continued to reflect early concentration on engineering and science. For successive years from 1964-5 on, engineering enrolment constituted 49.1, 43.8, 36.4, 35.7, 31.0, and 28.6 per cent of the total at the undergraduate level. The corresponding percentages for science were 18.5, 19.5, 34.9, 38.8, 40.4, and 40.6. For the six years under review, the enrolment in arts constituted the following percentages of undergraduate enrolment: 31.0, 35.3, 27.4, 21.1, 21.8, and 24.1. The establishment of a separate Faculty of Mathematics in 1967 was of course a major reason for the reduction in the proportion listed under arts. Enrolment in physical and health education has shown a very marked increase. Among graduate programs, expansion in engineering has been rapid, even for a field where substantial growth has been the rule. There has also been a major increase in the physical and biological sciences, in the humanities and, until 1969-70, in psychology.

The University of Western Ontario
The arts programs at the University of Western Ontario have attracted about the same proportion of the total undergraduate enrolment as at the other senior universities. Honours programs were not relatively as popular as at Queen's or Toronto during the period under review, constituting the following percentages of total arts enrolment in the six respective

206 The expansion of the educational system

TABLE 4-16
Full-time enrolment by program of study at the University of Toronto, including Erindale and Scarborough Colleges, 1964-70

PROGRAM OF STUDY	1964-5 Under-graduate	1964-5 Graduate	1965-6 Under-graduate	1965-6 Graduate	1966-7 Under-graduate	1966-7 Graduate	1967-8 Under-graduate	1967-8 Graduate	1968-9 Under-graduate	1968-9 Graduate	1969-70[a] Under-graduate	1969-70[a] Graduate
Architecture	227	38	239	51	244	64	277	34	289	40	289	72
Arts, General[b]	2,675		3,189		3,355		5,050		5,615		5,857	
Arts, Honours[c]	2,990		2,951		2,986		2,114		2,303		2,670	
Child Study		16		15		24		16		30		35
Commerce, Business Administration	391	82	368	112	397	138	408	151	410	147	478	170
Dentistry	573	33	579	39	494	50	499	45	496	54	493	65
Education		56		70		134		240		287		355
Engineering	1,524	274	1,612	354	1,828	397	2,059	519	2,248	532	2,410	555
Fine and Applied Arts									12	26	17	33
Forestry	97	13	86	20	105	21	137	19	175	48	200	60
Geography						27		43				
Hospital Administration								30		33		20
Household and Food Sciences	54	10	74	8	96	5	96	2	95	6	105	7
Humanities		738		1,000		1,100		947		896		1,025
Hygiene and Public Health		80		101		119	5	74	1	95	3	107
Law	329	8	386	5	408	8	422	6	409	5	412	5
Library Science[d]		107		155		182		192		222		240
Mathematics						79		97		100		115
Medicine	865	363	895	429	646	277	700	251	717	327	735	350
Music	177	13	216	16	215	29	233	29	315	19	382	23
Nursing	338		349		293		349		387		410	

Table 4-16, continued

PROGRAM OF STUDY	1964-5 Under-graduate	1964-5 Graduate	1965-6 Under-graduate	1965-6 Graduate	1966-7 Under-graduate	1966-7 Graduate	1967-8 Under-graduate	1967-8 Graduate	1968-9 Under-graduate	1968-9 Graduate	1969-70[a] Under-graduate	1969-70[a] Graduate
Pharmacy	387	10	411	20	426	19	460	15	482	22	517	28
Physical and Biological Sciences		457		556		509		550		585		595
Physical and Health Education	237		271		333		352		373		380	
Physical and Occupational Therapy	291	26	274	17	266	23	265	27	254	22	258	25
Pre-Medicine						66		66		59		75
Psychology	1,640		1,843		2,290		2,618		2,837		3,003	
Science[b]								234		299		330
Social Sciences – other[c]		144		194		182		102		104		110
Social Work[d]									97		150	
Subtotal	12,795	2,468	13,743	3,162	14,382	3,453	16,044	3,689	17,515	3,958	18,769	4,400
TOTAL	15,263		16,905		17,835		19,733		21,473		23,169	

SOURCE: Reports of the Minister of University Affairs of Ontario.

[a] Projected.
[b] Arts – general and first year honours from 1967–8.
[c] Arts – upper year honours from 1967–8.
[d] Uniformly classified as graduate studies.

TABLE 4-17
Full-time enrolment by program of study at Trent University, 1964–70

PROGRAM OF STUDY	1964-5 Under-graduate	1964-5 Grad-uate	1965-6 Under-graduate	1965-6 Grad-uate	1966-7 Under-graduate	1966-7 Grad-uate	1967-8 Under-graduate	1967-8 Grad-uate	1968-9 Under-graduate	1968-9 Grad-uate	1969-70[a] Under-graduate	1969-70[a] Grad-uate
Arts, General[b]	71		223		267		334		550		611	
Arts, Honours[c]		2		3	147		137		196		271	
Humanities												
Physical and Biological Sciences		1		3		1		4		4		3
Science	31		62		98		271		327		403	
Subtotal	102	3	285	6	512	1	742	4	1,073	4	1,285	3
TOTAL	105		291		513		746		1,077		1,288	

SOURCE: Reports of the Minister of University Affairs of Ontario.

[a] Projected.
[b] Arts – general and first year honours from 1967–8.
[c] Arts – upper year honours from 1967–8.

TABLE 4-18
Full-time enrolment by program of study at the University of Waterloo, 1964–70

PROGRAM OF STUDY	1964-5 Under-graduate	1964-5 Grad-uate	1965-6 Under-graduate	1965-6 Grad-uate	1966-7 Under-graduate	1966-7 Grad-uate	1967-8 Under-graduate	1967-8 Grad-uate	1968-9 Under-graduate	1968-9 Grad-uate	1969-70[a] Under-graduate	1969-70[a] Grad-uate
Architecture							36		96		137	
Arts, General[b]	683		844		1,181		1,069		1,390		1,633	
Arts, Honours[c]	188		540		191		226		261		476	
Commerce, Business Administration									101			
Engineering	1,381	108	1,717	175	1,822	270	2,185	321	2,350	403	2,501	447
Geography						14		26		34		48
Humanities		144		244		91		150		180		204
Mathematics						86		116		171		196
Physical and Biological Sciences		50		93		126		142		184		221
Physical and Health Education	41		52		60		232		325		443	
Psychology						115		129		137		127
Science	519		764		1,747		2,375		3,061		3,554	
Subtotal	2,812	302	3,917	512	5,001	702	6,123	884	7,584	1,109	8,744	1,243
TOTAL	3,114		4,429		5,703		7,007		8,693		9,987	

SOURCE: Reports of the Minister of University Affairs of Ontario.

[a] Projected.
[b] Arts – general and first year honours from 1967–8.
[c] Arts – upper year honours from 1967–8.

210 The expansion of the educational system

years: 19.3, 17.1, 13.0, 14.9, 14.8, and 15.5. Enrolment in engineering has increased rather slowly and has remained relatively small. Substantial increases have been recorded for household and food sciences, law, music, physical and health education, and science. Seemingly erratic fluctuations in enrolment in science have been caused by inconsistent classification of pre-medicine, which was counted with medicine in 1964–5 and with science in 1965–6, 1966–7, and 1968–9, and listed separately in 1967–8 and 1969–70. The relatively large number listed in medicine in 1964–5 is explained in the same way. Journalism and secretarial science have remained relatively stable, and nursing declined during the period as a whole. The largest graduate enrolment was in the physical and biological sciences, followed by business administration, with psychology and geography remaining fairly stable. The apparent sharp decline in graduate enrolment in medicine in 1968–9 and 1969–70 is attributable to a change in classification, by which other fields of specialization such as biochemistry were excluded.

The University of Windsor
Approximately half of the University of Windsor's enrolment has been in general arts since 1964–5, with honours courses attracting a modest additional number. For the six years up to 1969–70, the total in the two groups has constituted 56.6, 57.2, 55.6, 54.0, 52.6, and 50.0 per cent of undergraduate enrolment. Most of the remainder has been in business administration, engineering, and science. Enrolment in nursing has fluctuated, but failed to increase over the six-year period. A small number have been enrolled in the undergraduate program in social work since 1967–8. Physical and health education has shown a recent trend toward rapid growth. In the graduate field most of the students were concentrated in engineering, the humanities, the physical and biological sciences, psychology, and, recently, other social sciences.

York University
During its early years York University's enrolment was mainly confined to arts, with a relatively large percentage opting for honours programs as time went on. For the six successive years under review, the respective percentages of those in arts taking honours programs have been 18.8, 25.9, 24.0, 27.1, 23.9, and 25.5. Science has attracted rapidly increasing numbers since 1965–6. A large enrolment in law was acquired with the accession of Osgoode Hall in 1967–8. The largest groups of graduates have been in administration or business administration, the humanities, psychology, the physical and biological sciences, and other social sciences.

DEGREES AND DIPLOMAS AWARDED
Table 4-22 shows the number of undergraduate and graduate degrees of each type awarded by all Ontario universities, provincially assisted and

TABLE 4-19
Full-time enrolment by program of study at the University of Western Ontario, 1964-70

PROGRAM OF STUDY	1964-5 Under-graduate	1964-5 Graduate	1965-6 Under-graduate	1965-6 Graduate	1966-7 Under-graduate	1966-7 Graduate	1967-8 Under-graduate	1967-8 Graduate	1968-9 Under-graduate	1968-9 Graduate	1969-70[a] Under-graduate	1969-70[a] Graduate
Arts, General[b]	1,860		2,184		2,851		3,082		3,461		3,417	
Arts, Honours[c]	445		450		427		540		599		627	
Business Administration	343	255	408	266	627	294	542	318	709	175	802	205
Dentistry					8		15		48		80	
Engineering	256	18	278	14	291	27	303	52	370	75	395	95
Fine and Applied Arts												
Geography						54		31	60	46	90	55
Household and Food Sciences	10		33		123		144		163		170	
Humanities		285		284		189		77		106		135
Journalism	22	3	25	3	22	7	26	14	28	12	29	11
Law	139		179		189		202		254		290	
Library Science[d]						1		45		49		68
Mathematics						39		32		39		45
Medicine	527	50	245	62	264	75	285	87	304	4	307	6
Music	84		111		122		146		189	1	215	5
Nursing	219	10	222	9	247	14	171	12	165	3	175	5
Physical and Biological Sciences		153		202		198		227		376		404
Physical and Health Education	90	8	98	7	116	9	153	6	329	6	349	7
Physical and Occupational Therapy							6		23		42	
Pre-Medicine							410				310	
Psychology						48		42		49		55
Secretarial Science	125		135		146		143		150		155	
Science	372		667		1,309		1,097		1,696		1,447	
Social Sciences – other										123		163
Subtotal	4,492	782	5,035	847	6,742	955	7,265	1,034	8,548	1,064	8,900	1,259
TOTAL	5,274		5,882		7,697		8,299		9,612		10,159	

SOURCE: Reports of the Minister of University Affairs of Ontario.

[a] Projected.
[b] Arts – general and first year honours from 1967-8.
[c] Arts – upper year honours from 1967-8.
[d] Uniformly classified as graduate study.

TABLE 4-20
Full-time enrolment by program of study at the University of Windsor, 1964–70

PROGRAM OF STUDY	1964-5 Under-graduate	1964-5 Grad-uate	1965-6 Under-graduate	1965-6 Grad-uate	1966-7 Under-graduate	1966-7 Grad-uate	1967-8 Under-graduate	1967-8 Grad-uate	1968-9 Under-graduate	1968-9 Grad-uate	1969-70[a] Under-graduate	1969-70[a] Grad-uate
Arts, General[b]	804		992		1,177		1,372		1,801		2,090	
Arts, Honours[c]	147		167		127		234		202		271	
Business Administration	155	10	184	14	269	17	351	9	466	24	571	28
Engineering	215	27	247	41	294	51	356	70	398	83	443	99
Fine Arts							11		59	2	99	2
Geography												
Humanities		59		67		60		33	68	31	130	29
Law												
Mathematics						12	7	14	12	16	16	18
Music							118		61		91	
Nursing	78		125		93							
Physical and Biological Sciences		49		56		52		44		50		59
Physical and Health Education					4		88		144		164	
Psychology			5			31		32		39		46
Science	280		307		380		393		474		655	
Social Sciences – other								6		25		33
Social Work							42		126		195	
Subtotal	1,679	145	2,027	178	2,344	223	2,972	208	3,811	270	4,725	314
TOTAL	1,824		2,205		2,567		3,180		4,081		5,039	

SOURCE: Reports of the Minister of University Affairs of Ontario.

[a] Projected.
[b] Arts – general and first year honours from 1967–8.
[c] Arts – upper year honours from 1967–8.

University enrolment and degrees awarded 213

TABLE 4-21
Full-time enrolment by program of study at York University, 1964-70

PROGRAM OF STUDY	1964-5 Under-graduate	1964-5 Graduate	1965-6 Under-graduate	1965-6 Graduate	1966-7 Under-graduate	1966-7 Graduate	1967-8 Under-graduate	1967-8 Graduate	1968-9 Under-graduate	1968-9 Graduate	1969-70[a] Under-graduate	1969-70[a] Graduate
Administration							128	104	140	70		
Architecture											25	
Arts, General[b]	602		971		1,645		1,832		2,994		3,722	21
Arts, Honours[c]	139		339		520		682		942		1,277	77
Commerce, Business Administration						56						
Fine and Applied Arts									80		342	85
Geography								3		11	113	
Humanities		11		25				16		54		
Law					3		565[d]	1	591	5	690	7
Mathematics								4		16		24
Physical and Biological Sciences				13		19		36		66		92
Physical and Health Education							38		50		140	
Psychology						41		47		80		115
Public Administration												10
Science	43		143		375		829		778		960	83
Social Sciences – other								16		47	24	
Subtotal	784	11	1,453	38	2,540	119	4,074	227	5,575	349	7,293	514
TOTAL	795		1,491		2,659		4,301		5,924		7,807	

SOURCE: Reports of the Minister of University Affairs of Ontario.

[a] Projected.
[b] Arts – general and first year honours from 1967-8.
[c] Arts – upper year honours from 1967-8.
[d] Enrolment at Osgoode Hall Law School, which became York Faculty of Law in 1967-8.

TABLE 4-22
Number of degrees and diplomas of each type awarded by Ontario universities, 1955-69

DEGREE OR DIPLOMA	1955-6	1960-1	1961-2	1962-3	1963-4	1964-5	1965-6	1966-7	1967-8	1968-9
Degree or diploma at or below the bachelor's or first professional degree level										
Agriculture	78	107	137	117	130	174	143	154	160	127
Applied Science or Engineering	559	734	770	755	893	802	900	958	1,066	1,211
Architecture	21	23	37	24	25	32	30	34	47	39
Arts	2,000	2,945	3,464	3,997	4,630	5,427	5,987	7,504	8,860	10,568
Science (in Arts)	111	379	434	522	683	809	920	1,050	1,585	2,037
Commerce	189	285	272	289	324	347	347	417	424	418
Canon Law	2	4	5	4	3	2	3	2	2	5
Chiropractic	42	28	19	19	26	23	37	35	26	41
Dentistry	70	72	85	124	123	120	119	126	128	130
Education or Pedagogy	153	230	188	211	206	245	218	163	123	282
Fine and Applied Arts				18	19	21	15	24	28	37
Forestry	21	15	16	18	22	25	22	21	12	16
Household Science	35	41	65	61	73	64	84	102	99	124
Journalism	8	22	22	25	26	28	50	57	53	70
Law	244	305	260	249	298	315	400	469	520	517
Library Science	38	102	100	120	135	132	178	225	249	289
Medicine	307	297	312	303	276	288	320	298	345	369
Music	15	24	19	13	12	15	51	30	24	52
Nursing	66	140	136	143	181	213	316	380	383	332

TABLE 4-22, continued

DEGREE OR DIPLOMA	1955-6	1960-1	1961-2	1962-3	1963-4	1964-5	1965-6	1966-7	1967-8	1968-9
Occupational Therapy and Physiotherapy	83	46	54	76	77	105	79	85	89	95
Optometry	7	6	9	14	16	22	21	18	23	21
Pharmacy	66	65	73	87	84	99	92	66	92	91
Physical and Health Education	45	131	151	179	244	278	300	361	401	239
Social Work	67	67	56	88	81	89	89	2	3	
Theology (Roman Catholic)	183	91	90	98	93	104	80	104	155	131
Theology (Protestant)	151	93	129	119	110	135	106	141	148	82
Veterinary Science	59	41	44	53	58	58	63	74	65	62
Other		5	7	5	9	14	19	19		50
TOTAL	4,620	6,298	6,954	7,731	8,857	9,986	10,989	12,919	15,110	17,435
Degrees at the master's level										
Arts[a]	406	635	716	767	943	1,146	1,352	1,586	1,805	
Science	133	223	251	283	333	427	526	822	948	
Social Work	48	35	55	54	91	99	28	38	139	
TOTAL	587	893	1,022	1,104	1,367	1,672	1,906	2,446	2,892	
Doctorates (earned)	127	145	144	184	190	233	316	333	485	
Doctorates (honorary)	64	89	99	96	87	85	92	103	115	

SOURCE: DBS (81-211), *Survey of Higher Education, 1964-5*, October 1967, p. 45-52, Table 23; *1967-8*, May 1969, p. 47-54, Table 23.

[a]Includes M Comm, MBA, M Ed, M L Sc (MLS), LLM.

CHART 4-6
Percentage of undergraduate degrees awarded in each of five leading faculties in all Ontario universities, 1960–9

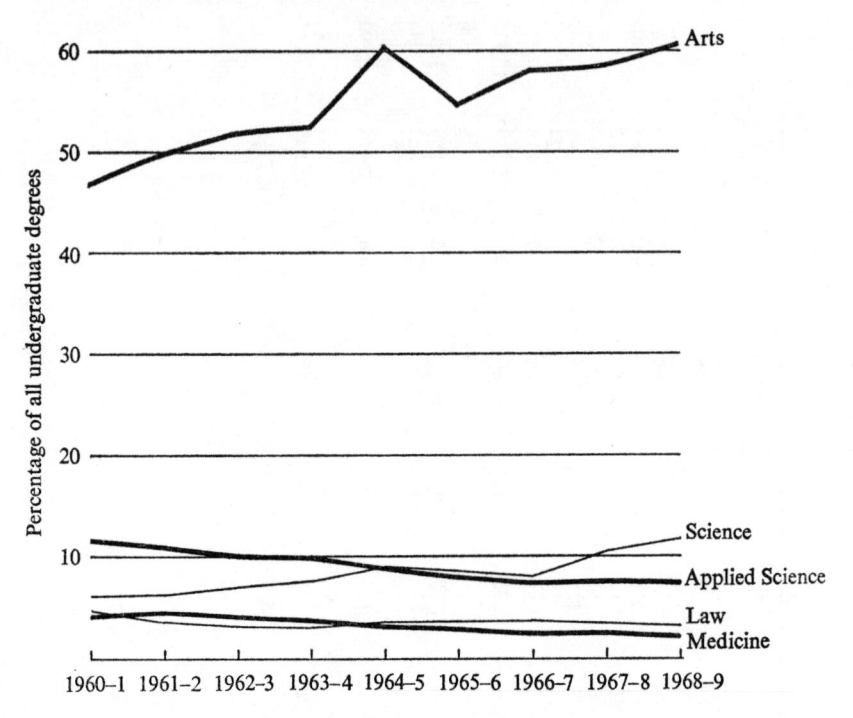

otherwise, in 1955–6 and between 1960–1 and 1968–9. At the beginning of the decade, 46.8 per cent of all undergraduate degrees were in arts. By 1962–3 this percentage had passed the 50 per cent mark, and by 1968–9 it was about 60.6 per cent. Paralleling enrolment trends, the growth of newer institutions tended to provide more opportunities for studies in arts than in some of the other areas. The trends in arts, applied science, science, law, and medicine are brought out in Chart 4-6. Of these, apart from arts, only in science was a substantially larger proportion of degrees awarded at the end of the period than at the beginning. After an initial dip, the proportion of law degrees leveled out. In medicine there were some years when even the absolute number of degrees awarded declined in relation to the previous year. Medical degrees constituted a continuously declining proportion of the total.

Among other types of degrees, those in library science and in physical and health education showed particularly marked increases. There were moderate or substantial increases in agriculture, architecture, commerce, dentistry, household science, journalism, nursing, optometry, and pharmacy. The trend was not, however, steadily upward in all these areas. Those that remained relatively stable during the period as a whole were

CHART 4-7
Percentage increase in undergraduate and graduate degrees awarded by all Ontario universities, 1960–8

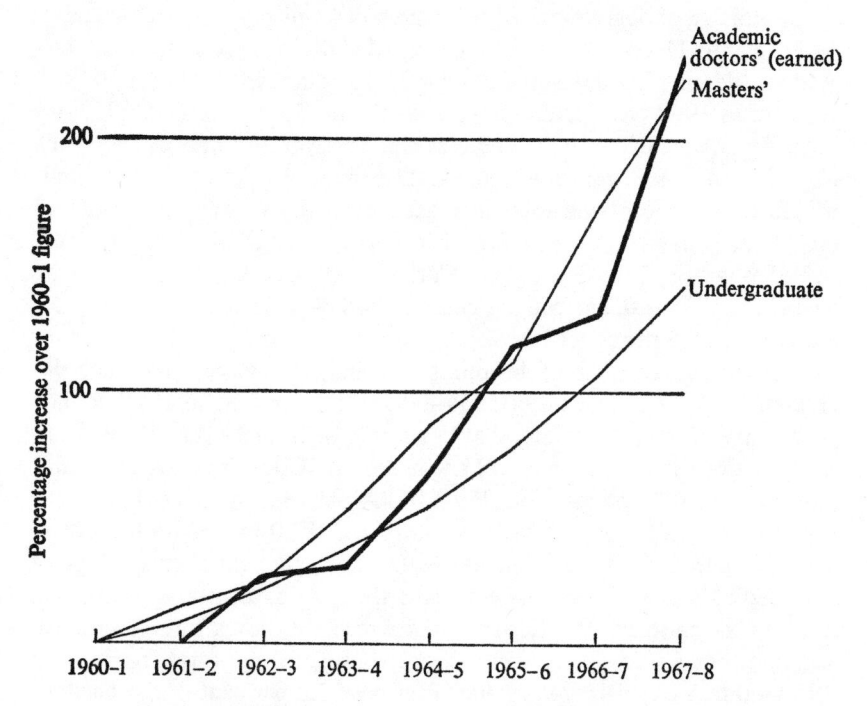

occupational therapy and physiotherapy, theology, and veterinary science. A decline was registered in chiropractic and forestry. The apparent decline in social work in 1966–7 resulted from the reclassification of the Bachelor of Social Work as a graduate degree when an undergraduate program was introduced. The decline in education degrees reflects the cessation of B Ed degree awards in the University of Toronto immediately after the founding of the Ontario Institute for Studies in Education.

The number of graduate degrees at the master's level rose from 893 in 1960–1 to 2,892 in 1967–8, a percentage increase of 223.9. The grouping together of the MA, the M Comm, the MBA, the M Ed, the M Sc, and the LLM in the official statistics makes the category such a comprehensive one that there seems little point in commenting on the general trend, except to observe that the rate of increase was less rapid than that in science. The number of earned doctorates rose from 145 to 485 between 1960–1 and 1967–8, a percentage increase of 234.5. The relatively small growth in the number of honorary degrees awarded suggests that the increasing number of universities, all presumably looking for distinguished figures to decorate their convocations, has not resulted in any wholesale lowering of the standards of selection.

The number of degrees awarded at each level by each of sixteen provincial universities is shown in Tables 4-23, 4-24, and 4-25 for certain years from 1959-60 to 1968-9. With the growth of the newer institutions, the proportion of degrees awarded by the senior universities has inevitably declined. The University of Toronto awarded 43.9 per cent of the undergraduate degrees in 1959–60, but only 33.3 per cent in 1964–5, and 25.1 per cent in 1968–9. Western's share fell from 15.8 per cent in 1959–60 to 12.4 per cent in 1968–9. The corresponding percentages for Queen's were 11.2 and 9.3, and for Ottawa, 11.5 and 8.0. On the other hand, McMaster's share of the total increased from 6.0 to 7.2 per cent, and that of the University of Windsor, or its predecessor, Assumption University of Windsor, from 3.5 to 5.0. Carleton awarded 2.4 per cent of the degrees in 1959–60, and 5.6 per cent in 1968–9. In the latter year Waterloo awarded 5.5 per cent of the total.

Toronto's share of the total number of masters' degrees awarded decreased from 59.0 per cent in 1959–60 to 45.5 per cent in 1968–9. The percentage of the total awarded at Western rose from 12.6 in 1959–60 to 15.4 in 1964–5, and declined to 11.5 in 1968–9. Queen's showed a similar pattern, with 6.4 per cent in 1959–60, 8.4 per cent in 1963–4, and 4.9 per cent in 1968–9. Ottawa's percentage was 13.0 in 1959–60, 15.8 in 1960–1, and 7.5 per cent in 1968–9. The actual number of degrees awarded rose in all these universities, although not always steadily from one year to another. At McMaster there was not only a large numerical increase, but also an increase in the percentage of the total from 2.6 in 1959–60 to 8.6 in 1968–9. In the latter year 7.2 per cent of the masters' degrees were awarded by Waterloo, 3.1 per cent by Carleton, 3.4 by Guelph, and 2.8 per cent by Windsor.

In 1959–60 Toronto awarded a large majority of the earned academic doctorates, with 63.8 per cent of the total; by 1968–9 the number awarded had risen from 74 to 192, but the percentage of the total for all universities had declined to 38.8. In 1959–60 most of the remainder were awarded by Ottawa (18.1 per cent) and Western (10.3 per cent). In 1968–9 the respective percentages for these two universities were 10.5 and 10.3. McMaster's percentage of the total rose during the same period from 4.3 to 10.7. Waterloo and Queen's each awarded 10.3 per cent of the total in 1968–9. Small contributions were made by Carleton, Guelph, Windsor, York, and Trent, while Brock, Lakehead, Laurentian, and Waterloo Lutheran had not yet entered the field.

PROJECTED ENROLMENT

Over-all
Since E.F. Sheffield's earliest projections of enrolment in the 1950s, an increasing number of agencies have been at work to refine the process. The results of their efforts have provided the essential basis for planning

TABLE 4-23

Number of bachelors' or first professional degrees conferred by individual colleges and universities in Ontario, 1959-69

COLLEGE OR UNIVERSITY	1959-60	1960-1	1963-4	1964-5	1966-7	1967-8	1968-9
Brock					39	115	136
Carleton	135	170	339	469	606	1,008	912
Guelph	162	196	251	266	316	539	833
Lakehead				45	148	148	295
Laurentian	47			104	206	311	337
McMaster	338	411	477	815	1,113	1,176	1,177
Ottawa	648	651	1,025	1,230	1,300	1,339	1,308
Queen's	629	730	784	883	1,131	1,178	1,526
Royal Military College[a]	53	50	191	190	179	199	169
Toronto[b]	2,477	2,717	3,217	3,300	3,563	3,739	4,115
Trent					75	90	93
Waterloo		16	178	333	447	873	899
Waterloo Lutheran	63	100	246	422	635	732	849
Western[b]	890	796	1,264	1,312	1,675	1,858	2,039
Windsor	198	250	379	455	631	803	825
York			83	76	294	717	889
TOTAL	5,640	6,087	8,434	9,900	12,358	14,825	16,402

SOURCE: *Canadian Universities and Colleges* (published as *Universities and Colleges of Canada* beginning 1966), published biennially to 1968 – then annually (Ottawa: Canadian Universities Foundation, from 1966 Universities and Colleges of Canada, 1960-1970).

[a]In addition degrees were awarded retroactively.
[b]Including degrees awarded by associated institutions.

TABLE 4-24

Number of masters' degrees conferred by individual colleges and universities in Ontario, 1959-69

COLLEGE OR UNIVERSITY	1959-60	1960-1	1963-4	1964-5	1966-7	1967-8	1968-9
Brock							1
Carleton	2	8	17	40	92	147	106
Guelph	36	39	47	66	114	103	114
Lakehead						42	2
Laurentian							
McMaster	21	28	77	103	189	244	288
Ottawa	105	149	115	138	215	191	254
Queen's	52	70	107	115	140	165	164
Royal Military College					4	5	5
Toronto[a]	476	527	699	716	1,093	1,172	1,533
Trent							1
Waterloo	8	11	22	57	142	234	244
Waterloo Lutheran				1	6	7	27
Western	102	106	152	236	288	288	386
Windsor	5	6	38	59	81	100	95
York					28	74	146
TOTAL	807	944	1,274	1,531	2,392	2,772	3,366

SOURCE: *Canadian Universities and Colleges* (published as *Universities and Colleges of Canada* beginning 1966), published biennially to 1968 – then annually (Ottawa: Canadian Universities Foundation, from 1966 Universities and Colleges of Canada, 1960-1970).

[a]Including degrees awarded by associated institutions.

TABLE 4-25
Number of earned academic doctorates conferred by individual universities in Ontario, 1959–69

UNIVERSITY	1959–60	1960–1	1963–4	1964–5	1966–7	1967–8	1968–9
Brock							
Carleton				2	2	11	7
Guelph						5	18
Lakehead							
Laurentian							
McMaster	5	11	21	11	35	56	53
Ottawa	21	31	55	48	58	49	52
Queen's	4	10	14	22	27	39	51
Toronto[a]	74	87	94	118	141	177	192
Trent							1
Waterloo			2	3	17	45	51
Waterloo Lutheran							
Western	12	10	24	22	30	43	51
Windsor			7	3	8	12	13
York						5	6
TOTAL	116	149	217	229	318	442	495

SOURCE: *Canadian Universities and Colleges* (published as *Universities and Colleges of Canada* beginning 1966), published biennially to 1968 – then annually (Ottawa: Canadian Universities Foundation, from 1966 Universities and Colleges of Canada, 1960–70).

[a]Including degrees awarded by associated institutions.

TABLE 4-26
Projected enrolment in Ontario universities, 1970–82

YEAR	ESTIMATE A		ESTIMATE B	
	No. in 18–24 age group[a]	Total graduate and undergraduate enrolment	No. in 18–24 age group[b]	Total graduate and undergraduate enrolment
1970–1	860,930	117,100	847,000	115,200
1971–2	890,300	129,500	880,040	128,000
1972–3	908,640	140,400	908,530	140,400
1973–4	933,000	152,100	937,400	152,800
1974–5	968,690	165,600	966,300	165,200
1975–6	1,001,820	178,800	994,200	177,500
1976–7	1,037,220	192,400	1,023,750	189,900
1977–8	1,072,050	205,800	1,046,580	200,900
1978–9	1,101,020	218,000	1,068,850	211,600
1979–80	1,129,140	229,800	1,089,235	221,700
1980–1	1,150,120	239,800	1,108,200	231,100
1981–2	1,163,870	247,900	1,126,420	239,900

SOURCE: Cicely Watson and Saeed Quazi, *Ontario University and College Enrollment Projections to 1981/82 (1968 Projection)*, Enrollment Projections Series, Number 4 (Toronto: The Ontario Institute for Studies in Education, 1969).

[a]Estimated by the Department of Educational Planning, the Ontario Institute for Studies in Education.
[b]Estimated by Economic Analysis Branch, Treasury Department, Government of Ontario.

for the future. Two sets of these projections, along with the estimated numbers in the eighteen-to-twenty-four age group, are provided for the years 1970–1 to 1981–2 in Table 4-26. Estimate A is based on age-group estimates from the Department of Educational Planning of the Ontario Institute for Studies in Education, and Estimate B on estimates from the Economic Analysis Branch of the Treasury Department. Although Estimate A is somewhat higher, both tell essentially the same story of an enrolment practically doubling during the decade of the 1970s.

For Canada as a whole, the *Fourth Annual Review* of the Economic Council of Canada estimated that total post-secondary enrolment, including that at universities, teachers' colleges, and technical institutes, and that in technical courses at community colleges, would rise from 13 per cent of the eighteen-to-twenty-four age group in 1965–6 to 20 per cent in 1970–1, and to 24 per cent in 1975–6. The corresponding percentages enrolled in university alone would be 11, 16, and 20 respectively, as compared with 21, 23, and 25 in the United States. University enrolment was defined to include both full-time and part-time students at the undergraduate and graduate levels. Four part-time students were equated with one full-time student.[11]

Individual universities
The development of individual universities has become to a considerable extent a planned and controlled process involving each institution, the Department of University Affairs, the Committee on University Affairs, and the Committee of Presidents of Universities of Ontario. The role of these agencies is explored further in volume IV, chapter 2 of the present series. Table 4-27 contains a set of projections in use during 1969. Since they refer only to universities receiving provincial assistance, the totals are considerably below the estimates shown in Table 4-26, where total university enrolment is projected. They indicate large percentage increases for Brock, Guelph, Laurentian, McMaster, Trent, and York, and more moderate rates of growth for the others. Little increase is expected for the main campus at Toronto, but substantial expansion is anticipated at Erindale and Scarborough Colleges.

The projections in Table 4-27 were prepared before actual data were available for 1968–9. The total full-time enrolment for that year was estimated at 82,244, and for 1969-70, 93,462. The actual figures turned out to be 83,357 and 94,414 respectively. As far as individual universities were concerned, the projections for 1968–9 were too low for Brock, Laurentian, Toronto, Waterloo, and Western; almost exactly right for Trent and York; and too high for Carleton, Guelph, Lakehead, McMaster, Ottawa, Queen's, and Windsor. By far the largest discrepancies were the underestimates for Toronto, Waterloo, and Western, and the overestimates for Guelph and Ottawa. With respect to the figures for 1969–70, the overestimates and underestimates were in the same direction in every case.

TABLE 4-27
Projected full-time enrolment in each provincially assisted university in Ontario, 1970–5

UNIVERSITY	1970–1	1971–2	1972–3	1973–4	1974–5
Brock	2,188	2,752	3,253	3,684	4,070
Carleton	7,095	7,640	8,180	8,715	9,240
Guelph	6,546	7,186	7,885	8,730	9,655
Lakehead	2,605	2,805	2,985	3,170	3,350
Laurentian	1,739	1,968	2,270	2,467	2,686
Algoma	200	250	300	400	500
Nipissing	100	125	150	200	250
McMaster	7,801	8,720	9,831	10,662	11,440
Ottawa	7,568	7,979	8,571	9,253	9,873
Queen's	7,684	8,122	8,523	8,871	9,167
Toronto	20,120	20,370	20,680	21,090	21,460
Scarborough	2,000	2,350	2,700	3,050	3,400
Erindale	1,300	1,650	2,000	2,350	2,700
Trent	1,555	1,850	2,165	2,495	2,855
Waterloo	8,628	9,279	9,942	10,626	11,140
Western	9,960	10,630	11,320	11,820	12,155
Windsor	6,019	6,799	7,473	8,201	8,980
York	9,650	11,040	12,300	13,430	14,450
TOTAL	102,758	111,515	120,528	129,214	137,371

SOURCE: Committee on University Affairs, "Supplementary Documentation Relating to the Development of an Interim Capital Formula for Provincially-Assisted Universities in Ontario," 6 January 1969.

TABLE 4-28
Projected graduate enrolment in each provincially assisted university in Ontario, 1970–5

UNIVERSITY	1970–1	1971–2	1972–3	1973–4	1974–5
Brock	38	62	83	104	120
Carleton	845	940	1,050	1,155	1,260
Guelph	657	750	863	1,021	1,181
Lakehead	45	50	55	60	65
Laurentian	51	69	81	98	110
Algoma					
Nipissing					
McMaster	1,515	1,744	1,950	2,102	2,236
Ottawa	1,220	1,462	1,611	1,763	1,931
Queen's	1,116	1,380	1,500	1,610	1,730
Toronto	4,230	4,460	4,660	4,940	5,160
Scarborough					
Erindale					
Trent	15	25	35	45	55
Waterloo	1,286	1,391	1,523	1,647	1,755
Western	1,450	1,650	1,770	1,900	2,000
Windsor	361	415	480	553	637
York	750	840	1,000	1,130	1,250
TOTAL	13,579	15,238	16,661	18,128	19,490

SOURCE: Committee on University Affairs, "Supplementary Documentation Relating to the Development of an Interim Capital Formula for Provincially-Assisted Universities in Ontario," 6 January 1969.

Despite these differences the table gives a reasonable indication of the growth pattern anticipated during the next few years.

Projections of undergraduate enrolment are also developed and used in planning for the extension of accommodation at individual universities. These are not presented here, since they are merely complementary to the estimates of graduate enrolment given in Table 4-28. Very large percentage increases are expected at the smaller universities, particularly Trent, Brock, Laurentian, and Windsor. Large numerical increases are projected for most of the others. Toronto's rate of increase is expected to be relatively low, and, if the forecasts turn out to be accurate, that university's share of the total enrolment will be little more than one-fourth by 1974–5.

FIVE

Enrolment and certificates awarded in other post-secondary educational institutions

TEACHERS' COLLEGES

Over-all enrolment
The enrolment pattern at the teachers' colleges has been somewhat different from that of most other educational institutions. Instead of a regular yearly increase, as has come to seem customary in schools and universities, the number attending teachers' colleges has sometimes shown substantial decreases from year to year within a generally rising trend. The attraction of the colleges in any particular year depends on a number of factors. For most of the post-war period demand has been strong, and a well-qualified beginning teacher could often find a position in one of the more attractive areas of the province. The large number who preferred urban living could often choose among city schools. By the end of the 1960s, however, the seller's market had practically disappeared, and some potential candidates were not prepared to risk taking the course only to find themselves without acceptable job opportunities.

There was a tremendous surge in enrolment in 1968–9, as shown in Table 5-1, when the number of students rose from 6,853 in the previous year to 9,277, an increase of 35.4 per cent. This increase was attributed in large measure to the announcement that the minimum admission requirement the following year would be the same as that for universities. A number of candidates with a grade 13 average of less than 60 per cent apparently thought it best to avail themselves of the opportunity of attending without having to rewrite some of their papers in order to raise their standing. With this backlog out of the way, and with the higher admission requirement in force, enrolment fell in 1969–70 to 7,896. This number was still high enough to meet the province's needs quite comfortably. With elementary school enrolment reaching a level of relative stability, it was obviously an opportune time to lengthen the period of preparation and to institute stricter selection policies.

Two earlier periods of decreasing enrolment, reaching low points in 1962–3 and 1965–6, were associated with the elimination of courses which could be entered with lower academic standards. The nature of these changes is explained in volume v, chapter 1. In brief, 1962 saw the abandonment of the completing year of the program beginning with the

TABLE 5-1
Enrolment in Ontario teachers' colleges, 1945–70

TEACHERS' COLLEGE	DATE ESTABLISHED	1945–6	1950–1	1955–6	1960–1	1961–2	1962–3	1963–4	1964–5	1965–6	1966–7	1967–8	1968–9	1969–70
Hamilton	1908	87	245	423	908	889	741	881	804	626	677	780	1,015	904
Lakehead	1960				207	231	215	224	237	141	140	184	260	188
Lakeshore	1959				989	766	612	807	817	758	871	874	1,195	922
London	1900	128	236	470	1,009	910	501	571	582	546	615	554	816	697
North Bay	1909	66	141	266	412	423	382	416	405	288	322	353	546	487
Ottawa	1875	118	185	304	710	676	632	761	832	666	608	746	1,097	910
Ottawa, Univ. of	1927	147	155	228	364	358	302	235	218	230	235	316	280	278
Peterborough	1908	91	128	177	464	402	370	344	324	292	396	367	501	398
St Catharines	1965									219	333	350	458	368
Stratford	1908	113	129	273	450	377	343	363	356	354	376	396	481	372
Sudbury	1963							147	142	156	170	134	165	181
Toronto	1847	269	484	998	1,217	1,026	922	1,214	1,324	1,330	1,539	1,510	2,036	1,771
Windsor	1962						494	447	421	307	252	289	427	420
TOTAL		1,019	1,703	3,139	6,730	6,058	5,514	6,410	6,462	5,913	6,534	6,853	9,277	7,896

SOURCE: Reports of the Minister of Education of Ontario.

NOTE: Beginning with 1955–6, enrolments have been recorded as of October.

CHART 5-1
Total enrolment in Ontario teachers' colleges, 1960–70

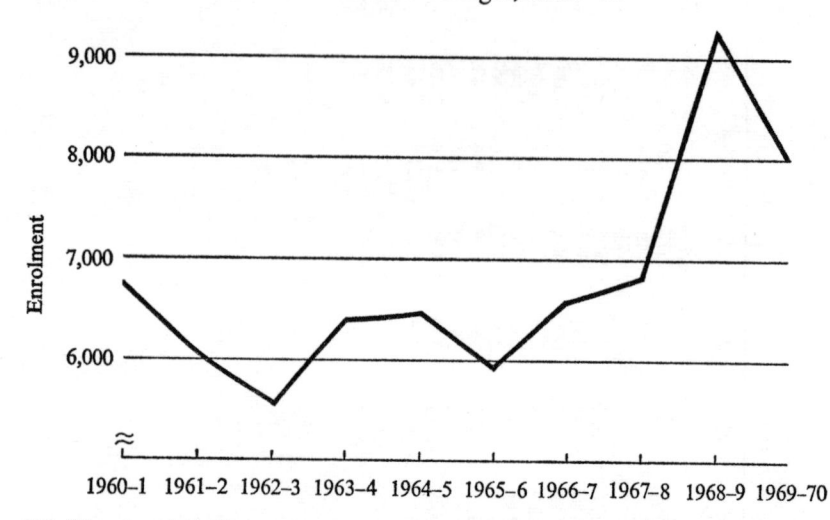

Pre-Teachers' College summer course, which could be entered from grade 12. In 1966 the second year of the two-year course, also requiring only grade 12 standing for admission, was discontinued.

There are factors other than admission requirements and employment opportunities in teaching affecting attendance at teachers' colleges, the influence of which would be difficult to assess. The creation of a system of colleges of applied arts and technology has provided a wider variety of alternatives. The increasing proportion of young people entering universities, partly because of the greater availability of financial assistance, has undoubtedly meant a reduction in the number of those willing to take a one-year course as a preparation for teaching. Salaries and status of teachers do not change quickly enough to have perceptible effects from one year to another, but presumably exert an influence over a longer period of time. The reputation of the colleges themselves is in a similar category.

Individual colleges
Comparisons of size and enrolment trends among the different colleges indicate that Toronto Teachers' College is the giant among the different colleges, and one of those that had to contend with extremely large increases in 1968–9. In a second category of size are the Hamilton, Lakeshore, London, and Ottawa Colleges, which faced a problem of similar proportions during that year. Among the smaller group, North Bay experienced the sharpest rise, while the crisis was shared in lesser proportions at the Lakehead, Peterborough, St Catharines, Stratford, and Windsor Colleges. The two colleges with the responsibility for preparing teachers for the bilingual schools, those at the University of Ottawa and Sudbury, experienced a different trend. Enrolment at the former declined, and that at the latter rose by a moderate amount, as it did also in 1969–70.

COLLEGES OF EDUCATION

General enrolment trends
In 1945–6 the Ontario College of Education, now called the College of Education, University of Toronto, had 284 students seeking academic certificates, of whom 53.9 per cent were taking the High School Assistant's course, Type B, and the other 46.1 per cent were taking both the Type A and Type B courses. Those who have taken the Type A course, leading, after successful experience, to the High School Specialist's Certificate, have always been required to take the Type B course at the same time if they have not taken it previously. At the end of the Second World War secondary school enrolment was relatively stable; the annual rate of attrition among secondary school teachers was running at a little more than 5 per cent a year; and it did not require a large number of new graduates to maintain an adequate supply.

Five years later, as shown in Table 5-2, enrolment in the academic courses had risen to 432, an increase of 52.1 per cent. The proportion of those taking both the Type A and B courses remained approximately the same. The Vocational Department, which had recently been moved to the college, had a total of forty-four students scattered among the Vocational, Industrial Arts and Crafts, and Intermediate Home Economics courses. The nature of these courses and the requirements for admission are explained in volume v, chapter 5.

The rapidly increasing shortage of teachers for secondary schools resulted in the establishment in 1955 of the special summer course, which at first involved an initial session of ten weeks, followed by a year of guided teaching and, for those who succeeded and to whom teaching proved to have sufficient appeal, a second summer session of five weeks. The second session was held for the first time in 1956. Many assumed optimistically when the course was first offered that it would appeal mainly to candidates who had completed university and gone into some other occupation, but might be enticed into teaching if they did not have to contend with the expense and loss of earning power involved in attending the regular winter session. Once this backlog had been given an opportunity to enter the profession, it was thought, the number applying for admission to the course would subside. As it happened, however, summer enrolment continued to grow, mainly for two reasons: 1 / there seemed to be a steady supply of those prepared to switch from the occupations they had entered initially, and 2 / the course had a strong appeal to those graduating from the university, since it offered them an opportunity to begin teaching a year earlier. The gain of a year meant that they had what amounted to the permanent advantage of being one rung further up on the salary scale than they would otherwise have been. Theoretically, the advantage would have ended when they reached the salary maximum, but, during a period of rapidly rising salaries, the upper limit continued to recede. A further advantage of beginning a year earlier was that it offered

228 The expansion of the educational system

TABLE 5-2
Enrolment in Ontario colleges of education by course and program, 1945–70

YEAR	COLLEGE OF EDUCATION	ACADEMIC DEPARTMENT					VOCATIONAL DEPARTMENT						TOTAL REGULAR SESSION		SPECIAL SUMMER COURSE[a]	
		Type A	Type B only	Male	Female	TOTAL	Ordinary Vocational			Industrial Arts and Crafts[b]	Intermediate Home Economics		Male	Female	First year	Second year
							Male	Female	Total							
1945-6	Univ. of Toronto	131	153			284	42	3	19	15			214	139	418	866
1950-1	Univ. of Toronto	202	230			432	76	1	45	30			348	188	1,035	895
1955-6	Univ. of Toronto	110	198	172	136	308			77	62					1,222	1,139
1960-1	Univ. of Toronto	136	323	272	187	459			281	47			566	281	1,501	1,366
1961-2	Univ. of Toronto	148	434			582	260	4	264						1,812	1,566
1962-3	Univ. of Toronto	157	426	306	277	583	242	5	247				492	227	1,952	
1963-4	Univ. of Toronto	153	319	250	222	472	235	15	250				507	309		
1964-5	Univ. of Toronto	191	375	272	294	566										
1965-6	Althouse			78	91	169	26	2	28				104	93	2,209	1,744
	Univ. of Toronto	244	482	255	302	557	164	19	183				419	321		
	Total			333	393	726	190	21	211				523	414		
1966-7	Althouse	95	144	116	123	239	40	4	44				156	127	2,281	1,962
	Univ. of Toronto	168	358	199	327	526	165	15	180				364	342		
	Total	263	502	315	450	765	205	19	224				520	469		
1967-8	Althouse	68	193	120	141	261	24	8	32				144	149	2,664	2,016
	Univ. of Toronto	215	511	305	421	726	151	24	175				456	445		
	Total	283	704	425	562	987	175	32	207				600	594		
1968-9	Althouse	103	360	251	212	463	65	5	70				316	217	3,225	2,519
	McArthur	39	155	84	110	194							84	110		
	Univ. of Toronto	264	908	487	685	1,172	172	45	217				659	730		
	Total	406	1,423	822	1,007	1,829	237	50	287				1,059	1,057		
1969-70	Althouse	225	368	264	329	593	44	8	52				308	337	812	3,041
	McArthur	105	118	84	139	223							84	139		
	Univ. of Ottawa	4	76	50	30	80							50	30		
	Univ. of Toronto	395	1,346	658	1,083	1,741	132	53	185			5	790	1,136		
	Total	729	1,908	1,056	1,581	2,637	176	61	237			10	1,232	1,642		

SOURCE: Reports of the Minister of Education of Ontario.

[a] Special summer course at Kingston and London, as well as Toronto, from 1960 on.
[b] All male.

CHART 5-2
Enrolment in regular winter and special summer courses at the Ontario colleges of education, 1960–70

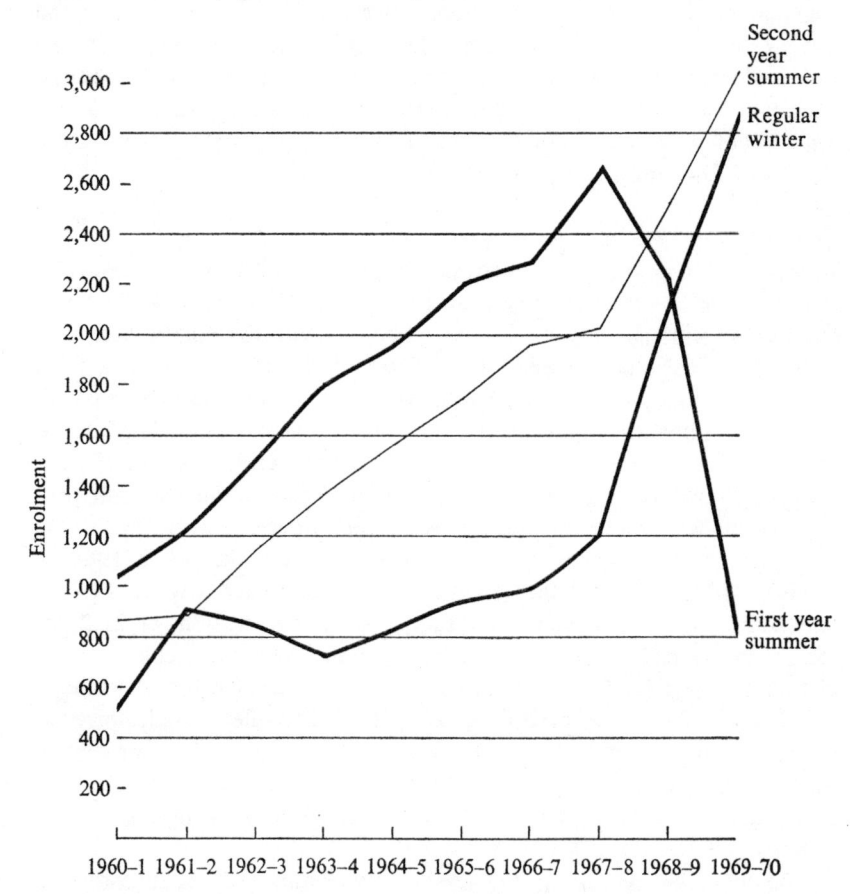

an additional year of superannuation benefits. Even at the beginning of their careers, the members of a security-minded generation are by no means unaware of the possibility that they may some day retire.

Enrolment trends in the first and second summer sessions and in the regular winter session are illustrated in Chart 5-2 for the period of the 1960s. At the beginning of the decade summer sessions were being offered not only at Toronto, but also at London and Kingston, where colleges of education were eventually established. The fact emerges clearly from the chart that these sessions were attracting the bulk of the growing number of candidates. Between 1961–2 and 1963–4 enrolment in the regular session actually declined. It was evident that only drastic action could restore this session to its pre-1955 role as the normal route to secondary school teaching. By the summer of 1967 enrolment in the first session of the special summer course reached 2,664 in the three centres, while the subsequent winter enrolment at Althouse College and the College of Education at Toronto was 1,194. In 1968–9, the last year of the first summer session in its original form, enrolment reached 3,225. At the same time enrolment in the regular course rose to 2,116. The fact that the newly established winter program at McArthur College was able to absorb 194 students could not prevent a severe strain on accommodation at the other two colleges. The problem was considerably more acute in 1969–70, when there were 2,874 students enrolled, of whom 1,926 were at the College of Education in Toronto.

Changing emphasis in academic programs
When the special summer course was first establishd, it was necessary to attend a regular winter session in order to obtain a Type A Certificate. In 1961 arrangements were made for candidates with the appropriate academic qualifications to meet the requirements by attendance at a third summer session. Most of those who chose the summer course route to certification, however, qualified for Type B Certificates only. The bulk of those seeking Type A certification attended a winter session. In 1960–1 this group constituted 29.6 per cent of the enrolment in the academic program of the winter session, and in 1966–7, 34.4 per cent. But the decline in appeal exerted by the program showed up rather sharply in 1968–9, when the phasing out of the summer course was under way. In 1968–9 only 406 of 1,829 students in the regular academic session, or 22.2 per cent, were taking Type A work. The proportions in the three colleges were comparable. In 1969–70 the corresponding percentage for all colleges together was 27.6. The percentage at each of the colleges had, however, diverged considerably, with 37.9 per cent at Althouse, 47.1 per cent at McArthur, and 22.7 per cent at Toronto. Four of the eighty students enrolled in the new University of Ottawa program were taking Type A courses.

The changing sex ratio in the academic program in the regular session is of some interest. In 1955–6 55.8 per cent of the students were men. They remained in a majority, although a decreasing one, until 1964–5. By 1966–7 they constituted only 41.2 per cent of the total, and in 1969–70, 40.0 per cent. It may be that the rising proportion of vocational teachers in the profession might be diverting a certain number of men from academic teaching. Since the background of preparation required tends to be quite different, however, it is doubtful that much of the explanation lies in that direction.

Vocational programs
By 1960–1 enrolment in the Vocational Department of the College of Education at Toronto had grown to seventy-seven seeking vocational certificates and sixty-two seeking certificates in industrial arts and crafts. The signing of an agreement in 1961 between the federal and Ontario

CHART 5-3
Enrolment in the regular session in the academic departments of the
Ontario colleges of education, 1945-70

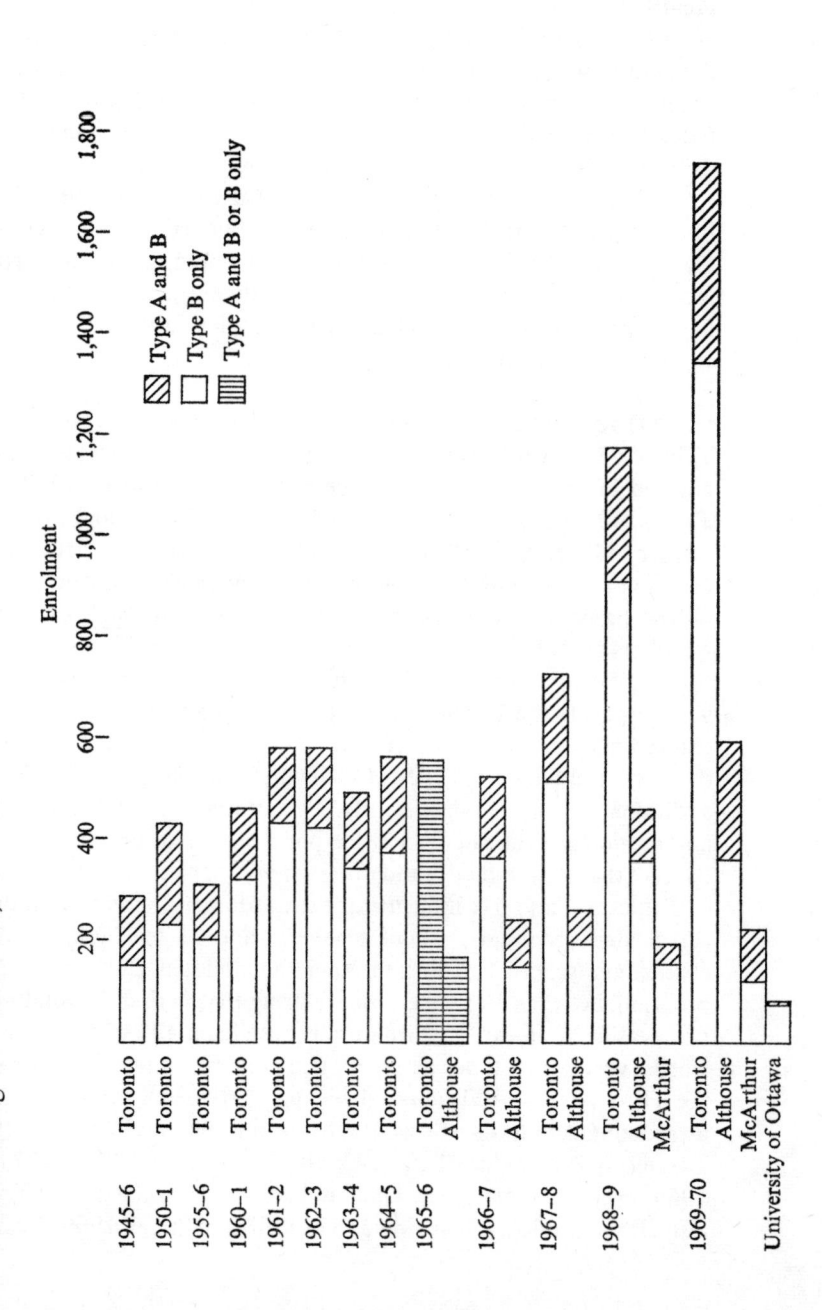

governments under the *Technical and Vocational Training Assistance Act*, which is further treated in volume II, chapter 11, had a major impact on the programs of teacher preparation in these areas. There was a great rush to take advantage of unprecedented federal grants for the construction and maintenance of new schools and additions to existing schools for technical and vocational education. Among the major results were 1 / a greatly increased need for vocational teachers, and 2 / a greatly reduced need for teachers of industrial arts and crafts, who had been chiefly in demand in schools offering only a General or academic course. The program in industrial arts and crafts was discontinued after 1961–2. The federal-provincial agreement provided for federal assistance in training the required vocational teachers under Program 7.

Enrolment in vocational programs rose to 281 in 1961–2, and, as illustrated in Chart 5-4, remained reasonably stable thereafter. Althouse College offered the program from the beginning, unlike McArthur College, which provided initially only for academic courses. The overwhelming proportion of vocational teachers are men, although the number of women has risen rapidly.

CERTIFICATES AWARDED IN COLLEGES OF EDUCATION
Tables 5-3 to 5-6 inclusive show the number of certificates of each kind granted in 1955 and in successive years from 1960 to 1969 inclusive. Tables 5-3 and 5-4 are distinguished from Tables 5-5 and 5-6 in that the former indicate the number of certificates awarded after full-time attendance at an intramural session, while the latter give the number awarded on the basis of completion of the requirements through external effort. Numbers in Tables 5-3 and 5-5 refer to "first" certificates and in Tables 5-4 and 5-6 to additional certificates. The situation is somewhat confusing with respect to the Type A Certificate. The distinction is between those who entered a Type A course after obtaining the basic Type B Certificate and those who obtained a Type B Certificate and a Type A Certificate as an additional certificate concurrently. The number of certificates awarded in any particular year does not correspond closely to enrolment because of the fact that a candidate could obtain more than one certificate.

Tables 5-3 and 5-4 indicate an extraordinary rise in the production of certificated secondary school teachers, and of teachers qualifying for elementary school teaching through the optional College of Education program, between 1955 and 1969. During that period the total number of first certificates awarded intramurally rose from 425 to 5,075 or, in other words, was twelve times as great. The greatest numerical increase was in the High School Assistant's, Type B, Certificates, of which 228 were awarded intramurally as first certificates in 1955 and 4,011 in 1969. The increase in Vocational Type B Certificates – from 48 in 1955 to 449 in 1969 – was also very great. The number of Vocational Type A Certificates also climbed quickly, reaching 216 in 1968 and 201 in 1969. Occupational

CHART 5-4
Enrolment in the regular session in the academic and vocational
departments of the Ontario colleges of education, 1950–70

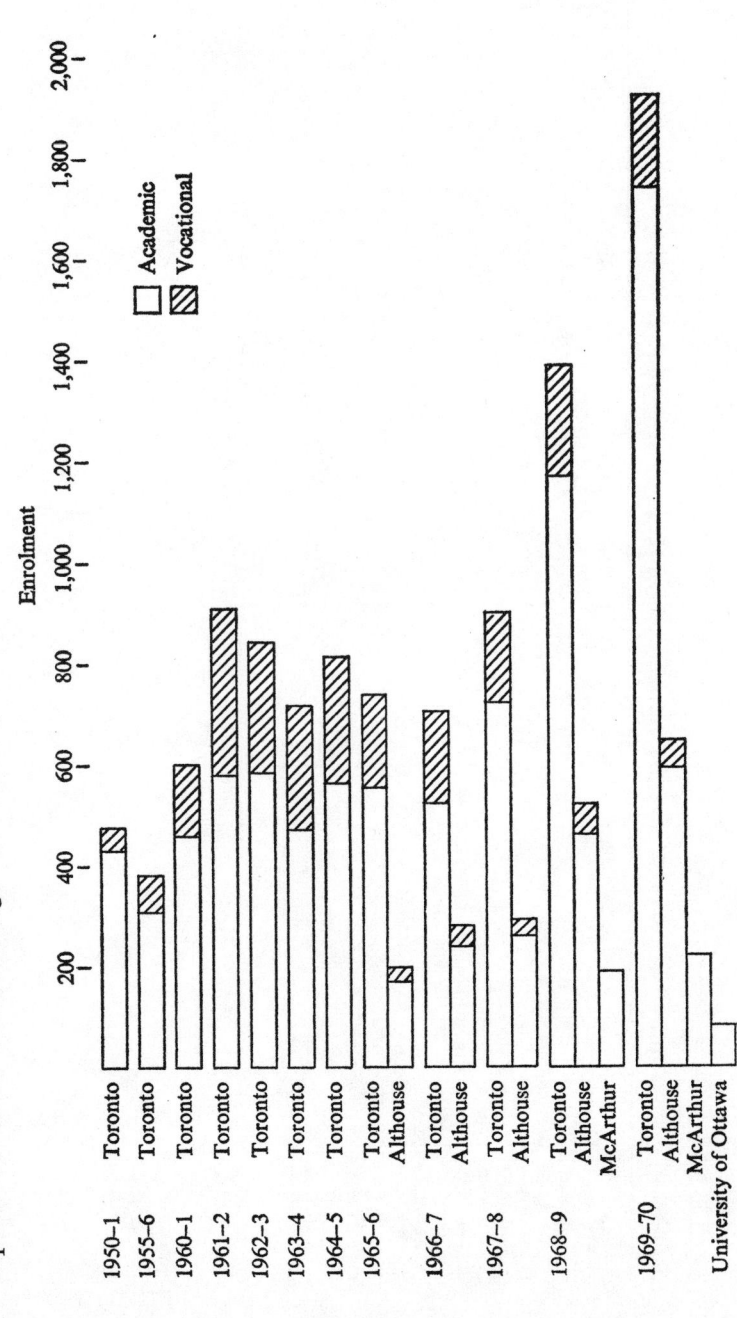

TABLE 5-3
Number of first certificates of each type awarded intramurally in the colleges of education, 1955–69

CERTIFICATE	1955	1960	1961	1962	1963	1964	1965	1966	1967	1968	1969
High School Assistant's, Type B	228	930	889	1,198	1,463	1,685	1,919	2,188	2,577	2,991	4,011
High School Assistant's, Type A	148	129	117	149	42	136	163	232	231	248	361
Vocational Type B	48	72	66	256	256	653	409	311	373	425	449
Occupational Type B, Practical Subjects					27	35	25	85	69	44	24
Occupational Type B, General Subjects											
Occupational Type A, Practical Subjects											
Occupational Type A, General Subjects											
Vocational Type A											
Intermediate Home Economics	1	1	1								
Intermediate Industrial Arts			1								
Commercial-Vocational Type B							113	127	139	184	230
TOTAL	425	1,132	1,074	1,603	1,788	2,509	2,629	2,943	3,389	3,892	5,075

SOURCE: Reports of the Minister of Education of Ontario.

TABLE 5-4
Number of additional certificates of each type awarded intramurally in the colleges of education, 1955–69

CERTIFICATE	1955	1960	1961	1962	1963	1964	1965	1966	1967	1968	1969
High School Assistant's, Type B[a]		130	148	156	174	194	190	32[b]	17[b]	16[b]	15
High School Assistant's, Type A[c]			77	213	338	457	486	615	922	945	1,177
Vocational Type B[d]				25	40		5	1	3		3
Occupational Type B, Practical Subjects[e]						26	56	24	30	4	172
Occupational Type B, General Subjects							10	10	18	22	10
Occupational Type A, Practical Subjects								13	21	12	
Occupational Type A, General Subjects									8	3	17
Vocational Type A[f]	1	59	37	60	49	50	3	2			
Intermediate Home Economics	11	50	60	53	74	73	93	172	145	216	201
Intermediate Industrial Arts	19	53	49	48	20	14	51	133	96	45	12
Elementary School Teachers' Certificate (option)	32	25	14	14	24	17	18	31	24	42	29
							36	18	27	118	311
TOTAL	63	317	385	569	719	831	948	1,051	1,311	1,423	1,947

SOURCE: Reports of the Minister of Education of Ontario.

[a]Regular 8-week summer course.
[b]Summer course for teachers with professional training.
[c]Seminar.
[d]Summer session.
[e]Summer and one-year course.
[f]Summer session.

certificates are a relatively recent phenomenon, corresponding to the provision for a wider variation of abilities and interests in the secondary school program. Most of the certificates of this type are in the category of Occupational Type B, General Subjects.

The numbers of first and additional certificates awarded extramurally, that is, the number of High School Assistant's Certificates, Type A and B, varied between 1955 and 1969 in relation to changes in regulations governing the conditions under which they might be obtained. Particularly worthy of notice in Table 5-6 is the large number of Type B Certificates awarded as additional certificates in the years between 1966 and 1969. This phenomenon reflects the easing of conditions under which a teacher with elementary certification and an appropriate degree could qualify for the Type B Certificate.

DEPARTMENT OF EDUCATION SUMMER COURSES
Summer courses offered in various centres throughout the province by the Department of Education are dealt with in volume v, chapter 9. Enrolment in these courses has increased steadily over the years, as indicated by the totals at the end of Table 5-7, as well as in Chart 5-5. The table shows the changes in the program during the post-war period. The courses that have covered the whole twenty-five year span are those in art, guidance, vocal music, physical and health education, primary methods, and special education. The highest enrolment in recent years has been in art, guidance, physical and health education, primary methods, and special education. Thus for the most part the most heavily attended courses are among the longest-established. The table provides considerable evidence of courses offered for a limited number of years to meet a passing need. Others have been offered on an experimental basis, but have not attracted a large enough enrolment to justify their continuation.

ENROLMENT IN INSTITUTIONS FOR TECHNOLOGICAL
AND TRADES TRAINING
Full-time enrolment in provincially supported institutes for technological and trades training is shown in Table 5-8 for 1962–3 to 1966–7. Figures for technology courses at Lakehead University are not included. The enrolment at all the institutes of technology increased from 3,905 to 7,638, or by 95.6 per cent, between 1962–3 and 1966–7. During that time the percentage of the total attending Ryerson shrank from 64.2 per cent to 58.8.

Among institutions for trades training, the Provincial Institute of Trades was the senior and remained much the largest. In 1966–7 its enrolment of 1,319 constituted 32.1 per cent of the total, followed by the Ontario Vocational Centre at Ottawa with 813 students, or 19.8 of the total, and the Ontario Vocational Centre at London with 697 students, or 17.0 per cent of the total. The rate of growth of these centres was fairly

TABLE 5-5
Number of first certificates of each type awarded extramurally in the colleges of education, 1955-69

CERTIFICATE	1955	1960	1961	1962	1963	1964	1965	1966	1967	1968	1969
High School Assistant's, Type B	4	133	194	247	180	138	203	464	190	309	348
High School Assistant's, Type A		2	1			5	6	9			
TOTAL	4	135	195	247	180	143	209	473	190	309	348

SOURCE: Reports of the Minister of Education of Ontario.

TABLE 5-6
Number of additional certificates of each type awarded extramurally in the colleges of education, 1955-69

CERTIFICATE	1955	1960	1961	1962	1963	1964	1965	1966	1967	1968	1969
High School Assistant's, Type B	124	22	142	127	369	437	572	909	1,008	920	1,022
High School Assistant's, Type A	29	154	156	133	44	20	15	29	29	43	35
TOTAL	153	176	298	260	413	457	587	938	1,037	963	1,057

SOURCE: Reports of the Minister of Education of Ontario.

TABLE 5-7
Enrolment in Department of Education summer courses, 1945–69

COURSE	1945	1950	1955	1960	1961	1962	1963	1964	1965	1966	1967	1968	1969
Agriculture	87	112	22	20									
Art	144	511	437	683	837	1,002	1,273	1,300	1,575	1,753	1,587	1,687	1,621
Art et Science du Langage											160	105	76
Business and Commercial Subjects											11	140	
Chassis Dynamometer													91
Compensatory Education													
Commercial Subjects	99	131	147										49
Dance													
Elementary Mathematics, Grades 1 to 6										1,765	1,353	1,029	
Elementary School Librarians (Elementary School Teacher-Librarian prior to 1968)						80	114	130	282	359	582	880	928
Elementary School Principals' Course										234	232	171	310
Elementary School Principals' Refresher Course		60	49	50									
Elementary Science											216	575	680
Elementary Social Studies												310	196
Fundamentals of Educational Television									49			54	51
Grade 13 Subjects	150	161	180	408	529	133	120	70	1,155	1,078	1,144	1,246	1,343
Guidance		116	165	259	346	565	735	915	361		354		414
Heads of Departments	80	91	91			324	404						
High School Assistant's, Type B	56	80	75	168	169	132	144	151	144	148	146		662
Home Economics	133	154	127										
Industrial Arts													
Integrated Studies				74			126	143	97	62			
Intermediate Education, Grades 7 and 8													
Intermediate Geography and History, Grades 7 and 8											128	98	105
Intermediate Mathematics, Grades 7 and 8						123	387	800	136	93	126		
Intermediate Mathematics, Grades 9 and 10						45	49						
Intermediate Science, Grades 7 and 8					96	83							

TABLE 5-7, continued

COURSE	1945	1950	1955	1960	1961	1962	1963	1964	1965	1966	1967	1968	1969
Junior Education													327
Language Arts				231	281	412	558	306	166	595	205	102	
Learning Materials Management (Audio Visual Methods Advanced prior to 1969)									96	101	120	277	10
Learning Materials Methodology (Audio Visual Methods prior to 1969)		28	66	294	395	477	614	620	776	701	844	670	608
Mathematics, Grade 11								209	202				
Mathematics, Grades 11 and 12											13		
Mathematics, Grade 13				165	206	175	175	188	240	171	269	284	221
Music, Instrumental	327	416	96	491	619	589	512	536	545	276	467	510	532
Music, Vocal			449							536			75
New Horizons for Young Children											50	50	66
New Techniques in the Teaching of Modern Languages	27												
Oral French	145	216	293	769	968	1,105	1,297	1,283	1,331	1,382	1,389	1,503	1,441
Physical and Health Education, Type B				89	80	92	148	95	98	115	113	112	104
Primary Education, Supervisors'	168	556	881	1,372	1,715	2,130	2,079	1,957	1,895	1,583	1,717	1,737	1,879
Primary Methods	28												
Refresher Latin	34												
Refresher Science	52												
Refresher History		6	24	51	58								
School Librarianship													31
Science Field Studies			90	139	83	209	212	173	264	238	324	315	344
Secondary School Principals'													
Special Education (Auxiliary Education before 1966)	127	165	255	561	715	896	986	1,111	1,293	1,212	1,377	1,661	1,629
Teaching the Deaf								88	30	62	76	48	
Teaching English as a Second Language				44	78	67	88	88	120	153	203	227	324
Teaching French to English-Speaking Pupils, Regular							134	78	151	116	88	153	194
Teaching French to English-Speaking Pupils, Special									156	97	129	198	168
Teaching French to English-Speaking Pupils, Intensive										154	114	132	106
Teaching the Trainable Retarded											125	195	222
Vocational Courses	43	275	105										
Workshop in Curriculum Building													
TOTAL	1,700	3,078	3,552	5,868	7,079	8,484	9,970	9,789	11,826	13,027	13,629	14,628	14,807

SOURCE: Reports of the Minister of Education of Ontario.

CHART 5-5
Total enrolment in Ontario Department of Education summer courses, 1960-9

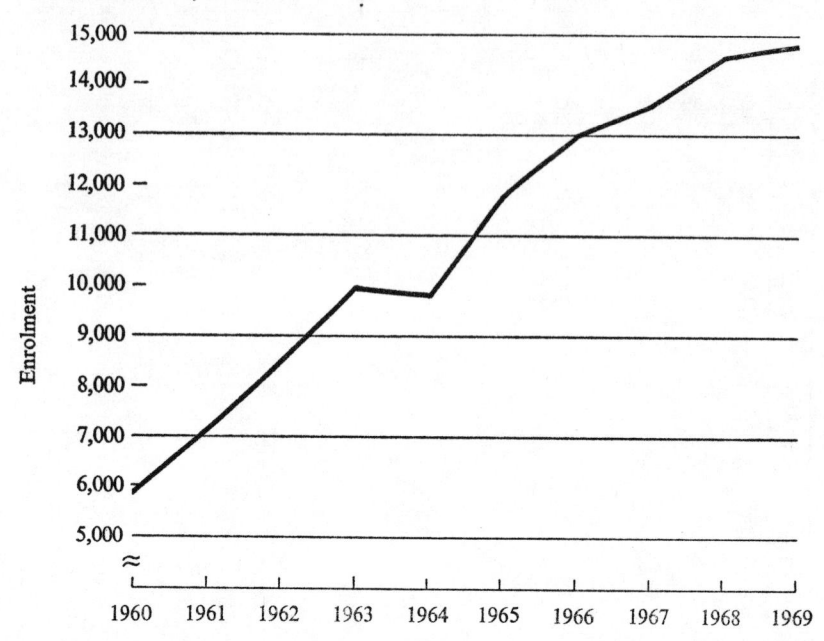

high, but the total enrolment of 4,111 in 1966-7 was not an impressive proportion of the relevant age group.

Evening class enrolment is shown in Table 5-9 for the same institutions as are listed in Table 5-8, and for the same span of years. The rate of growth was roughly comparable with that of full-time enrolment. In the institutes of technology the number increased from 5,068 in 1962-3 to 11,784 in 1966-7. In the institutes of trades and vocational centres the comparable increase was from 2,732 to 4,883.

CERTIFICATES AWARDED IN INSTITUTES OF TECHNOLOGY
Table 5-10 shows the number of certificates awarded in each major area in the provincial institutes of technology between 1960-1 and 1966-7. The total rose from 537 in the former year to 1,146 in the latter. Unfortunately the official statistics do not provide a breakdown for Ryerson for the years after 1963-4, when it assumed its present status. Thus the number of certificates by course cannot be directly compared for the periods up to and after 1964-5. It is nevertheless obvious that most certificates were in engineering technology, followed by business.

ENROLMENT IN COLLEGES OF APPLIED ARTS AND TECHNOLOGY
Total full-time and part-time enrolment in the colleges of applied arts and technology in 1967-8, the year in which most of them began operations,

TABLE 5-8

Full-time enrolment in institutions for technological and trades training supported by the Department of Education, 1962–7

INSTITUTION	1962–3	1963–4	1964–5	1965–6	1966–7
Ryerson Polytechnical Institute	2,508	2,899	3,304	3,687	4,494
Eastern Ontario Institute of Technology	522	601	709	870	1,183
Hamilton Institute of Technology	382	407	490	583	691
Northern Ontario Institute of Technology	76	118	237	386	484
Provincial Institute of Mining	87	96	126	150	184
Western Ontario Institute of Technology	330	378	455	547	602
Subtotal	3,905	4,499	5,321	6,223	7,638
Ontario Vocational Centre, London			370	430	697
Ontario Vocational Centre, Ottawa			510	619	813
Ontario Vocational Centre, Sault Ste Marie				313	549
Provincial Institute of Automotive and Allied Trades	442	456	478	380	439
Provincial Institute of Trades	871	818	987	1,080	1,319
Provincial Institute of Trades and Occupations	129	138	114	163	294
Subtotal	1,442	1,412	2,459	2,985	4,111
TOTAL	5,347	5,911	7,780	9,208	11,749

SOURCE: Reports of the Minister of Education of Ontario.

NOTE: Enrolment as of November 1.

and 1968–9 is shown in Table 5-11. Full-time enrolment only is shown for 1969–70. The number of students differs by a small amount from that reported in Tables 5-13-1 to 5-15-2 because the figures were obtained at different times during the year. It should be noted also that a uniform method of defining full-time enrolment had not been adopted by all the colleges. Some of the figures for a few of them applied to day-time enrolment. A student who attends one or more day-time classes need not be a full-time student.

Total full-time enrolment increased from 11,700 in 1967–8 to 25,173 in 1968–9, or by 115.2 per cent, and to 37,725 in 1969–70, or by 49.9 per cent. It is not altogether clear what effect the provincial austerity program will have on further expansion. Some of the colleges have been turning away considerable numbers of applicants, while others, like Northern, have had unused space. Many potential students choose not to attend at all rather than to go far from home.

TABLE 5-9

Evening class enrolment in institutions for technological and trades training supported by the Department of Education, 1962–7

INSTITUTION	1962–3	1963–4	1964–5	1965–6	1966–7
Ryerson Polytechnical Institute	4,280	4,671	6,500	7,540	9,000
Eastern Ontario Institute of Technology	345	444	890	1,088	1,518
Hamilton Institute of Technology	378	425	610	890	1,038
Northern Ontario Institute of Technology				21	39
Provincial Institute of Mining					
Western Ontario Institute of Technology	65	98	165	147	189
Subtotal	5,068	5,638	8,165	9,686	11,784
Ontario Vocational Centre, London				182	409
Ontario Vocational Centre, Ottawa				650	643
Ontario Vocational Centre, Sault Ste Marie					470
Provincial Institute of Automotive and Allied Trades	883	749	541	631	570
Provincial Institute of Trades	1,700	1,616	1,683	2,300	2,463
Provincial Institute of Trades and Occupations	149	210	159	363	328
Subtotal	2,732	2,575	2,383	4,126	4,883
TOTAL	7,800	8,213	10,548	13,812	16,667

SOURCE: Reports of the Minister of Education of Ontario.

NOTE: Enrolment as of November 1.

TABLE 5-10

Number of certificates of each type issued in provincial institutes of technology, 1960–7

COURSE	1960–1	1961–2	1962–3	1963–4	1964–5	1965–6	1966–7
All institutes							
Business	84	74	77	131	31	32	40
Engineering Technology	316	363	317	346	235	256	279
Home Economics	36	22	26	35			
Industrial Management					12	17	16
Mining	36	40	39	38			
Textiles	6	9	6	3	10	9	13
Other courses	59	106	177	189			
Ryerson[a]					680	624	798
TOTAL	537	614	642	742	968	938	1,146

SOURCE: Reports of the Minister of Education of Ontario.

[a]Figures combined with those of other institutions before 1963–4.

TABLE 5-11
Full-time and part-time enrolment in the colleges of applied arts and technology, 1967–70

COLLEGE	1967–8 Full-time	1967–8 Part-time	1968–9 Full-time	1968–9 Part-time	1969–70 Full-time
Algonquin	2,404	2,727	2,937	2,508	4,094
St Lawrence	409		883	457	1,869
Loyalist	161	124	802	562	784
Sir Sandford Fleming	380	551	478	937	1,273
Durham	201	110	428	795	705
Centennial	997	358	2,142	3,210	2,359
Humber	468	70	3,054[a]	1,025	2,636
Seneca	792	1,106	1,974	1,507	2,267
Sheridan	375	35	845	565	1,646
Mohawk	1,189	1,350	1,794	2,362	2,519
Niagara	474	110	1,409	2,700	1,812
Fanshawe	778	912	1,404	2,086	1,689
St Clair	848	273	1,210	1,275	1,543
Lambton	248	500	413	1,400	765
Conestoga			646	375	1,644
Georgian	101	25	311	223	794
Cambrian	993	399	1,556	793	2,724
Northern	644	60	632	466	718
Confederation	238	416	477	563	981
George Brown			1,778	3,957	4,903
TOTAL	11,700	9,126	25,173	27,766	37,725

SOURCE: Ontario Department of Education, Applied Arts and Technology Branch, Statistical Department.

[a] Enrolment temporarily swelled by a large Ontario Manpower retraining group.

By 1969–70 George Brown reported the largest enrolment, followed by Algonquin, which had previously been classified as the largest. The next group in terms of size were those in the larger cities, such as Centennial, Humber, and Seneca in the Metropolitan Toronto area, Mohawk in Hamilton, and Cambrian, with its three campuses in Sudbury, Sault Ste Marie, and North Bay.

Enrolment of full-time fee-paying students has been projected for some years ahead by the Applied Arts and Technology Branch. The figures shown in Table 5-12 were revised in April 1969. This group of students has constituted something in the neighbourhood of 75 per cent of total full-time enrolment, both fee-paying and non-fee-paying. Thus the anticipated increase is considerably larger than the table suggests at first glance.

The numbers of full-time students in each year of each program area in each of the colleges during 1967–8 are shown in Tables 5-13-1 and 5-13-2. The division of the table into two parts is necessitated by the complexity of the content. The colleges that made a new beginning naturally had only first-year students. Those such as Algonquin, Mohawk, St Clair, Cambrian, Northern, and George Brown, which inherited institutes of technology, institutes of trades, or vocational centres, had second-

244 The expansion of the educational system

TABLE 5-12
Projected enrolment of full-time fee-paying students in the colleges of applied arts and technology, 1970–7

YEAR	FIRST YEAR	SECOND YEAR	THIRD YEAR	TOTAL
1970–1	22,850	10,900	2,870	36,620
1971–2	29,720	14,400	3,815	47,935
1972–3	36,920	18,720	5,040	60,680
1973–4	43,650	23,260	6,550	73,460
1974–5	51,820	27,500	8,140	87,460
1975–6	58,200	32,600	9,625	100,425
1976–7	65,130	36,700	11,400	113,230

SOURCE: Ontario Department of Education, Applied Arts and Technology Branch, Statistical Department.

and third-year students, as did also Fanshawe, for which figures are not given. Centennial and Lambton, being in their second year of operations, had second-year as well as first-year students.

In all the colleges considered as a group, the following percentages of total enrolment were found in each of the program areas: three-year business, 13.3; two-year business, 10.3; one-year business, 2.3; three-year applied arts, 2.3; two-year applied arts, 7.6; one-year applied arts, 1.9; three-year technological, 19.5; two-year technical, 13.1; one-year technical, 3.6; apprenticeship, 9.0; short, 0.7; Ontario Manpower Retraining Program, 16.3. Individual colleges varied considerably in the way their students were distributed among these programs. Of the total enrolment in 1967–8, 35.2 per cent was in the three-year programs, 31.0 per cent in two-year programs, and the remainder in one-year or unclassified programs; the percentage in the third year of three-year programs was 5.4, and in the second year of two-year programs, 5.2.

Tables 5-14-1 and 5-14-2 provide similar information for 1968–9. The percentage distribution of students among program areas during that year was as follows: three-year business, 11.5; two-year business, 14.5; one-year business, 2.4; three-year applied arts, 4.4; two-year applied arts, 12.2; one-year applied arts, 1.5; three-year technological, 14.4; two-year technical, 15.6; one-year technical, 1.3; apprenticeship, 8.7; short, 0.3; and Ontario Manpower Retraining Program, 13.2. There was thus no substantial shift from one program to another. The main changes involved an increase in the proportion of second-year students in two- and three-year programs. Of the total enrolment, 30.3 per cent were now in three-year programs and 42.3 per cent in two-year programs; 4.4 per cent of the students were in the third year of three-year programs and 12.8 per cent were in the second year of two-year programs.

Tables 5-15-1 and 5-15-2 for 1969–70 are not precisely comparable to Tables 5-14-1 and 5-14-2 in that they do not show enrolment in short courses lasting less than one year; these courses had sixty-six students in 1968–9. The percentage distribution of students among program areas was as follows: three-year business, 9.1; two-year business, 11.6; one-year business, 1.9; three-year applied arts, 5.1; two-year applied arts, 13.1; one-year applied arts, 0.8; three-year technological, 10.8; two-year technical, 12.6; one-year technical, 0.4; apprenticeship, 6.6; and Ontario Manpower Retraining Program, 28.0. As compared with the previous year, there was a sharp rise in the proportion of students in the Ontario Manpower Retraining Program. This increase resulted in a proportionate decline in the business, technological, technical, and apprenticeship programs. In relation to these programs, enrolment in applied arts showed an increase. The percentage in three-year programs was 24.9, and in two-year programs, 37.4. The percentage in the third year of three-year programs was 4.7, and in the second year of two-year programs, 13.3.

COURSES OFFERED OR SPONSORED BY THE COMMUNITY
PROGRAMS (YOUTH AND RECREATION) BRANCH

The Department of Education has sponsored and assisted community groups in offering a variety of courses and programs, mostly in the adult education field. These have served educational, cultural, recreational, and social purposes. Most of them have been offered under the auspices of what was known during the major part of the post-war period as the Community Programs Branch. In 1968 this unit was combined with the Youth Branch to form the Youth and Recreation Branch. The steady increase in enrolment in the courses in which it has been involved has constituted an indication not only of its own increasingly active role, but also of a rising level of community interest and participation in the field.

The Community Programs Branch began a post-secondary diploma course in recreation in 1963, held at Guelph, from which over 120 graduates were produced during the next four years. In 1967 the course was taken over by Centennial College of Applied Arts and Technology, and six other colleges introduced similar programs in 1968. The Community Programs Branch and its successor, the Youth and Recreation Branch, have also conducted less formal short courses to train people for leadership in recreation centres and in night school and private agency programs. A Leadership Development Program has provided one residential week of training each year for three years for candidates selected for leadership potential.

Enrolment in adult leadership courses between 1960 and 1968 is shown in Table 5-16. Enrolment in all courses declined from 8,433 in 1960 to 4,500 in 1962, and then rose quickly to pass the 1960 figure by 1964. These fluctuations are not to be considered as reliable indicators of the level of activity in the branch, since they may merely reflect changes in the auspices under which various courses were offered.

For the most part because of a very large increase in enrolment in arts and craft courses and in those in drama and music, the total of recorded participants nearly doubled in 1965. Also, largely as a result of adminis-

TABLE 5-13-1
Enrolment in colleges of applied arts and technology in full-time business and applied arts programs, 1967-8

COLLEGE	BUSINESS											APPLIED ARTS								
	Three-year program				Two-year program			One-year program	TOTAL			Three-year program				Two-year program			One-year program	TOTAL
	First year	Second year	Third year	TOTAL	First year	Second year	TOTAL					First year	Second year	Third year	TOTAL	First year	Second year	TOTAL		
Algonquin	234	173	72	479	58		58	65	602							8		8	138	146
St Lawrence	27			27	29		29		56											
Loyalist	25			25	36		36	29	90											
Sir Sandford Fleming												15			15	36		36		51
Durham	49			49	33		33	10	92											
Centennial	47			47	66		66		113			128	46		174	183	158	341	4	519
Humber	78	61		139	191	57	248	11	398			44			44	48		48		92
Seneca	78			78	103		103	38	219			20			20	148		148	121	289
Sheridan	160			160	256		256		416							183		183		183
Mohawk	46			46	76		76		122							112		112		112
Niagara	164	76	42	282	112	12	124		406							74		74		74
Fanshawe	116			116	85		85	29	230											
St Clair	138	81	44	263	107	27	134		397			7		7	7	14		14	18	50
Lambton	22			22	32		32		54			18			18					18
Conestoga	28			28	36		36		64			20			20	64		64		84
Georgian	17			17	18		18		35											
Cambrian					89		89	103	192											
Northern					7		7	13	191											
Confederation	84	56	31	171	77		77	31	108			10	8	13	31	61	61			92
George Brown														13	13	19	19			32
TOTAL	1,313	447	189	1,949	1,411	96	1,507	329	3,785			262	54	26	342	870	238	1,108	281	1,731

SOURCE: Ontario Department of Education, Applied Arts and Technology Branch, Statistical Department.

TABLE 5-13-2
Enrolment in colleges of applied arts and technology in full-time technological, technical, apprenticeship, short, and Ontario Manpower Retraining programs, 1967–8

COLLEGE	TECHNOLOGICAL				TECHNICAL					APPRENTICESHIP (Average enrolment)				SHORT (LESS THAN ONE YEAR)	ONTARIO MANPOWER RETRAINING PROGRAM	TOTAL (ALL COURSES)
	Three-year				Two-year			One-year								
	First year	Second year	Third year	TOTAL	First year	Second year	TOTAL		Basic	Inter-mediate	Advanced	TOTAL				
Algonquin	241	321	186	748	86	109	195	94	152			152		116	2,053
St Lawrence	18			18	54		54									128
Loyalist	28			28	54		54									172
Sir Sandford Fleming	24			24	53		53	145						141	506
Durham	34			34	46		46									193
Centennial	52	6		58	83	20	103									1,078
Humber					69		69							1,591	1,971
Seneca	180			180	185		185									1,070
Sheridan	21			21	49		49									375
Mohawk	222	180	155	557	114		114									1,189
Niagara	94			94	52		52									450
Fanshawe																
St Clair	137	152	106	395	52		52									851
Lambton	32	33		65	34	2	36			40		40				205
Conestoga	22			22	18		18									228
Georgian	21			21	6		6	11								73
Cambrian	93			93	228	123	351	53		128		128				817
Northern	153	171	111	435	26		26									652
Confederation	23			23	58		58									281
George Brown			20	20	223	162	385	223		168	988	1,308	98	534	2,280
TOTAL	1,395	863	578	2,836	1,490	416	1,906	526	152	168	988	1,308	98	2,382	14,572

SOURCE: Ontario Department of Education, Applied Arts and Technology Branch, Statistical Department.

TABLE 5-14-1
Enrolment in colleges of applied arts and technology in full-time business and applied arts programs, 1968-9

| COLLEGE | BUSINESS ||||||||||| APPLIED ARTS |||||||||
| | Three-year program |||| Two-year program |||| One-year program | TOTAL | Three-year program |||| Two-year program |||| One-year program | TOTAL |
	First year	Second year	Third year	TOTAL	First year	Second year	TOTAL			First year	Second year	Third year	TOTAL	First year	Second year	TOTAL		
Algonquin	293	196	155	644	188	59	247	129	1,020	34			39	35	35		44	79
St Lawrence	102	56		158	142	34	176	28	362	3	5		3	52	27	79		118
Loyalist	18	11		29	61	28	89		118					34		34		37
Sir Sandford Fleming	53	44		97	61	31	92	3	192	13	12		25	41	31	72		97
Durham	47	33		80	61	54	115		195			50	50				60	110
Centennial	66	54	40	160	315	90	405	15	580	348	95	25	468	142	144	286		754
Humber	55	58		113	237	53	290	158	561	120	34		154	197	42	239	14	407
Seneca	208	81		289	283	126	409	24	722	70			70	320	120	440	184	694
Sheridan	50	40		90	95	37	132		222					358	136	494		494
Mohawk	152	105	62	319	218	113	331		650					152	72	224		224
Niagara	65	57		122	81	167	248		370					226	57	283	57	340
Fanshawe	21	11	6	38	79	41	120	105	263	28			28	312	60	372		400
St Clair	163	107	51	321	152	101	253		574	104	21		104	20	5	25		129
Lambton	21	17		38	55	42	97		135	34	21		55	29	9	38	17	110
Conestoga	77	15		92	76	23	99	6	197	24	14		38	111	50	161	10	209
Georgian	27	11		38	18	10	28	35	101					42		42		42
Cambrian	78	26		104	272	74	346	70	520					71	40	111		111
Northern	91	55	40	186	22	52	74	11	271									
Confederation					126	6	132	30	162	38	25	15	78	100	22	122		122
George Brown														17	15	32		110
TOTAL	1,587	977	354	2,918	2,542	1,141	3,683	614	7,215	816	206	90	1,112	2,259	830	3,089	386	4,587

SOURCE: Ontario Department of Education, Applied Arts and Technology Branch, Statistical Department.

TABLE 5-14-2
Enrolment in colleges of applied arts and technology in full-time technological, technical, apprenticeship, short, and Ontario Manpower Retraining programs, 1968-9

COLLEGE	TECHNOLOGICAL					TECHNICAL					APPRENTICESHIP				SHORT (LESS THAN ONE YEAR)	ONTARIO MANPOWER RETRAINING PROGRAM	TOTAL (ALL COURSES)
	First year	Second year	Third year	TOTAL	First year	Second year	One-year	TOTAL	Basic	Inter-mediate	Advanced	TOTAL			
Algonquin	427	283	220	930	310	136		446	112	54	73	239		131	2,937
St Lawrence	79	57		136	90	82		172	71	24		95			883
Loyalist	40	13		53	101	30		131	34			34		429	802
Sir Sandford Fleming	16	18		34	224	36		260	40			40			625
Durham	24	27		51	41	31		72							428
Centennial	47	24	4	75	105	35		140						101	2,142
Humber	54			54	95	44		139	206	155	93	454	16	1,783	3,069
Seneca	113	43		156	166	66	22	232	110	15		125		170	1,974
Sheridan	40	10		50	52	27		79							845
Mohawk	276	211	147	634	194	92		286							1,794
Niagara	111	57		168	105	29		134		297		297		397	1,409
Fanshawe	32	26	5	63	208	153		361					20		1,404
St Clair	159	126	118	403	65	39		104							1,210
Lambton	55	33	28	116	33	19		52							413
Conestoga	92	18		110	84	13		97	33			33			646
Georgian	51	11		62	18	4		22							311
Cambrian	68	59		127	416	188		604		166		166		68	1,556
Northern	128	106	131	365	44	20	16	64							700
Confederation	41	9		50	80	25	28	105							439
George Brown			11	11	264	202	159	466			736	736	30	267	1,779
TOTAL	1,853	1,131	664	3,648	2,695	1,271	319	3,966	606	711	902	2,219	66	3,346	25,366

SOURCE: Ontario Department of Education, Applied Arts and Technology Branch, Statistical Department.

TABLE 5-15-1
Enrolment in colleges of applied arts and technology in full-time business and applied arts programs, 1969-70

BUSINESS

COLLEGE	Three-year program				Two-year program			One-year program	TOTAL
	First year	Second year	Third year	TOTAL	First year	Second year	TOTAL		
Algonquin	323	199	180	702	176	54	230	204	1,136
St Lawrence	190	84	52	326	107	86	193	42	561
Loyalist	32	10	9	51	49	38	87	18	156
Sir Sandford Fleming	30	33	36	99	83	51	134	10	243
Durham	34	22	28	84	95	60	155		239
Centennial	96	70	72	238	198	108	306	18	562
Humber	101	40	15	156	305	184	489	55	700
Seneca	133	98	39	270	255	118	373		643
Sheridan	59	42	29	130	177	93	270		400
Mohawk	137	93	80	310	256	134	390	60	760
Niagara	37	34	43	114	166	95	261		375
Fanshawe	46	31	15	92	175	104	279	47	418
St Clair	145	154	138	437	106	99	205		642
Lambton	22	11	16	49	47	43	90		139
Conestoga	138			138	56	14	70	19	227
Georgian	26	14	11	51	54	29	83	78	212
Cambrian	17	12		29	320	222	542	86	657
Northern					18	14	32	5	186
Confederation	68	41	40	149	81	42	123	56	179
George Brown					50		50		50
TOTAL	1,634	988	803	3,425	2,774	1,588	4,362	698	8,485

APPLIED ARTS

Three-year program				Two-year program			One-year program	TOTAL
First year	Second year	Third year	TOTAL	First year	Second year	TOTAL		
76	9			179	31	210	45	255
34				67	28	95		191
				23	1	24	24	82
		11	96				90	260
			34					57
				122	48	170		
				34	23	57		
432	222	56	710	250	128	378	33	1,088
191	59	18	268	403	182	585	23	886
17			17	472	258	730	15	770
68	31	16	115	446	176	622		752
				157	105	262		262
				253	162	415		463
112	68	68	248	177	132	309	48	557
90	59		149	58	31	89		238
65	36	13	114	26	17	43		157
89	40	12	141	177	77	254		395
				56	18	74		74
				211	71	282	22	304
				17		17		17
10	6	2	10	163	99	262		272
13			21	66	29	95		116
1,197	530	196	1,923	3,357	1,616	4,973	300	7,196

SOURCE: Ontario Department of Education, Applied Arts and Technology, Statistical Department; Ontario Institute for Studies in Education, Educational Planning Department.

TABLE 5-15-2
Enrolment in colleges of applied arts and technology in full-time technological, technical, apprenticeship, and Ontario Manpower Retraining programs, 1969–70

COLLEGE	TECHNOLOGICAL[a] First year	Second year	Third year	TOTAL	TECHNICAL[a] Two-year First year	Second year	TOTAL	One-year	APPRENTICE-SHIP	ONTARIO MANPOWER RETRAINING PROGRAM	TOTAL (ALL COURSES)
Algonquin	455	95	49	599	563	357	920		270	914	4,094
St Lawrence	170	75	58	303	62	63	125		118	571	1,869
Loyalist	13	16	10	39	67	44	111		65	331	784
Sir Sandford Fleming	17	21	17	55	279	164	443	2	33	237	1,273
Durham	37			37	69	61	130			242	705
Centennial	31	32	15	78	111	42	153	22	401	77	2,359
Humber	43			43	123	42	165		164	678	2,636
Seneca	185	109	64	358	157	81	238			236	2,267
Sheridan	79	49	18	146	63	17	80	24		268	1,646
Mohawk	299	254	183	736	193	144	337		93	307	2,519
Niagara	122	44	53	219	99	56	155			600	1,812
Fanshawe	48	20	60	128	203	122	325	4	257		1,689
St Clair	199	153	79	431	81	51	132		100		1,543
Lambton	60			60	61	45	106			303	765
Conestoga	89	48	14	151	104	56	160		131	580	1,644
Georgian	38			38	74	16	90			380	794
Cambrian	162	53	64	279	282	230	512	48	148	776	2,724
Northern	103	87	71	261	57	31	88			166	718
Confederation	29	17	8	54	92	40	132			344	981
George Brown	20	15	11	46	200	165	365	45	697	3,584	4,903
TOTAL	2,199	1,088	774	4,061	2,940	1,827	4,767	145	2,477	10,594	37,725

SOURCE: Ontario Department of Education, Applied Arts and Technology, Statistical Department; Ontario Institute for Studies in Education, Educational Planning Department.

[a] All three-year courses in the technical-technological field are classified as technological and all one-year and two-year courses as technical.

252 The expansion of the educational system

CHART 5-6
Percentage of total enrolment in colleges of applied arts and technology in each program, 1967-70

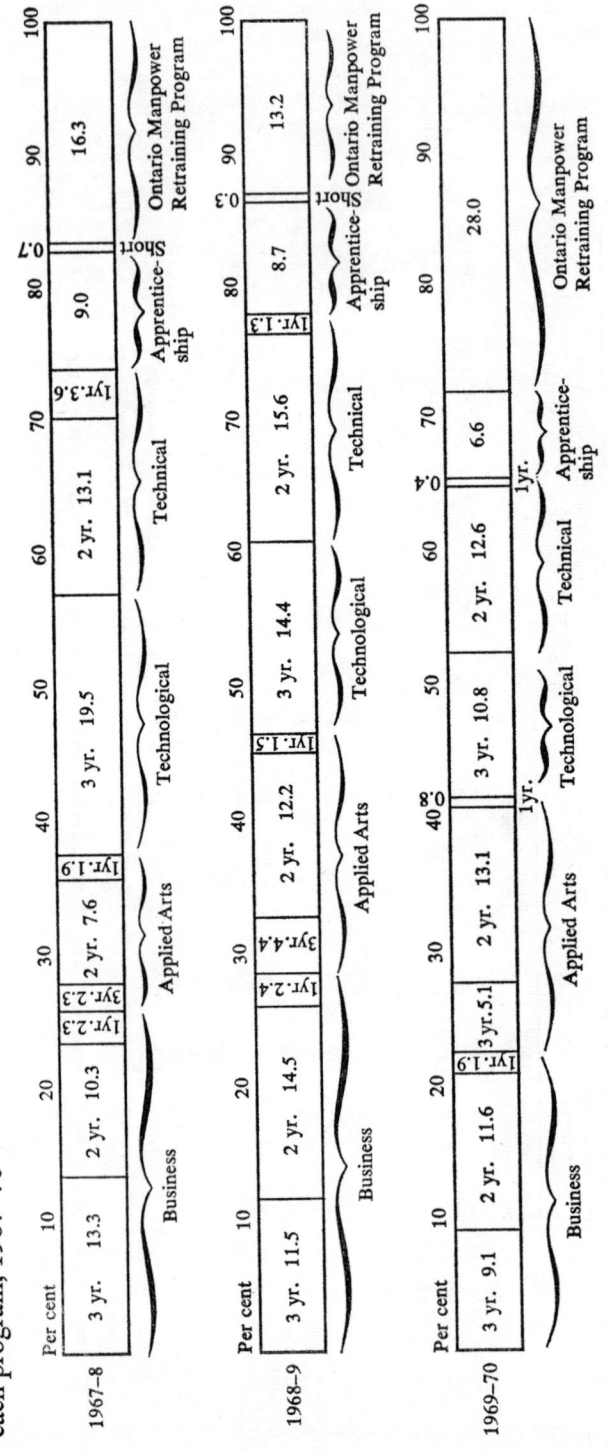

1967-8

Business	Applied Arts	Technological	Technical	Apprenticeship	Ontario Manpower Retraining Program
3 yr. 13.3 / 2 yr. 10.3	1yr. 2.3 / 3yr. 2.3 / 2 yr. 7.6 / 1yr. 1.9	3 yr. 19.5	2 yr. 13.1 / 1yr. 3.6	9.0 / 0.7	16.3

1968-9

Business	Applied Arts	Technological	Technical	Apprenticeship	Ontario Manpower Retraining Program
3 yr. 11.5 / 2 yr. 14.5	1yr. 2.4 / 3yr. 4.4 / 2 yr. 12.2 / 1yr. 1.5	3 yr. 14.4	2 yr. 15.6 / 1yr. 1.3	8.7 / 0.3	13.2

1969-70

Business	Applied Arts	Technological	Technical	Apprenticeship	Ontario Manpower Retraining Program
3 yr. 9.1 / 2 yr. 11.6	3 yr. 5.1 / 1yr. 1.9 / 2 yr. 13.1 / 1yr. 0.8	3 yr. 10.8	2 yr. 12.6 / 1yr. 0.4	6.6	28.0

TABLE 5-16
Enrolment in adult leadership courses offered by the Community Programs (Youth and Recreation) Branch, 1960-8

COURSE	1960	1961	1962	1963	1964	1965	1966	1967	1968
Facilities						246	229	260	260
General leadership						762	1,247	4,386	3,893
Group dynamics								380	1,615
Arts and crafts	1,136	879	1,043	1,775	1,941	5,004	7,622	9,875	13,815
Physical recreation	1,587	2,221	892	872	2,644	3,519	940	395	18,680
Rural leadership	775	1,177	468	1,173	1,106	677	495	245	375
Recreational directors	92	90	160	309	208	294	142	360	487
Social recreation	1,458	1,047	404	198	191	252	595	598	397
Drama and music	1,341	1,214	1,083	1,051	1,906	4,108	5,410	2,058	3,127
Senior citizens				244	525	1,983	978	191	2,445
Miscellaneous	2,044	1,603	450						
TOTAL	8,433	8,231	4,500	5,622	8,521	16,845	17,658	18,748	45,094

SOURCE: Reports of the Minister of Education of Ontario.

trative changes which led to a great increase in the number of those counted as participants in physical recreation courses, the total rose from 18,748 in 1967 to 45,094 in 1968.

Table 5-17 shows the enrolment in various courses for leaders of special groups offered by the branch during the period between 1962–3 and 1968–9. Within those six years enrolment in all such courses combined grew from 4,435 to 7,957, or by 79.4 per cent. As some of the names suggest (e.g., "seminar") these courses were generally of brief duration. Enrolment rose fairly steadily in courses for leaders of youth groups and in those for home and school or parent-teacher leaders. In others there were rapid increases and decreases from year to year corresponding to changes in policy with respect to what was to be offered. Between 1966–7 and 1967–8 the number in courses for groups from Indian communities was multiplied by nearly four, and rose by approximately another 50 per cent the following year. There was a very great increase in participation in courses for organizers of programs for older people between 1967–8 and 1968–9. The number involved in courses for playground supervisors fluctuated during the period without showing any definite trend. There was a steadily declining enrolment in rural community night school courses.

Provincial grants have been made during the post-war period to municipal governments that have passed the necessary by-law to establish a municipal recreation authority. Courses have been offered for municipal recreation directors as shown in Table 5-18, which covers 1955–6 and the period from 1960–1 to 1968–9. These courses lead to Interim A and B and Permanent A and B Certificates. The number enrolling during the period covered in the table has fluctuated considerably without showing a marked upward or downward trend. The course is characterized by a high wastage rate, with only a relatively small fraction of those enrolled ordinarily completing the course.

Beginning in 1947, when large numbers of immigrants from non-English-speaking countries were entering the province, the Department of Education provided a variety of services relating to citizenship classes. Teacher education was offered in regional seminars and in summer school courses in teaching English as a second language. Texts and resource material were made available through the federal Citizenship Branch. Certificates were issued to those who successfully completed the course in English and citizenship. The courses were offered by the Community Programs Branch until 1961, when they were turned over to the Department of the Provincial Secretary and Citizenship.

As shown in Table 5-19, the number of classes quickly increased from 126 in 1947 to 310 in 1948, and to 584 in 1949. In the same two-year interval, enrolment rose from 2,900 to 14,971. Although the number of classes continued to increase until 1954, enrolment remained fairly stable at somewhat over 20,000 between 1951 and 1954. After some decline,

TABLE 5-17

Enrolment in courses for leaders of special groups offered by the Community Programs (Youth and Recreation) Branch, 1962–9

COURSES	1962–3	1963–4	1964–5	1965–6	1966–7	1967–8	1968–9
Groups from Indian communities	203	190	253	225	275	1,060	1,551
Leaders of youth groups	96	55	398	201	266	481	772
Seminars on community recreation facilities	68	501	339	152	142	262	
Organizers of programs for older people	362	168	767	703	398	537	2,420
Provincial advanced course for community theatre directors	22	22					
Home and school or parent-teacher leaders	350	467	456	400	520	500	665
Playground supervisors	1,369	1,639	1,785	2,150	1,419	2,837	1,419
Provincial and district courses for activity leaders	356	411	820	452	428		
Rural community night school courses	1,609	1,302	1,428	1,661	1,070	514	350
Seminars and courses for recreation committee members		765	373	246	198	505	640
Leadership discussion methods			463	289	549	780	140
TOTAL	4,435	5,520	7,082	6,479	5,265	7,476	7,957

SOURCE: Reports of the Minister of Education of Ontario.

TABLE 5-18

Enrolment in training courses for municipal recreation directors offered by the Community Programs (Youth and Recreation) Branch, and number completing, 1955–69

YEAR	ENROLMENT	NO. COMPLETING	YEAR	ENROLMENT	NO. COMPLETING
1955–6	68	5	1964–5	182	31
1960–1	106	22	1965–6	212	131
1961–2	150	27	1966–7	70	31
1962–3	227	28	1967–8	189	35
1963–4	189	31	1968–9	261	32

SOURCE: Reports of the Minister of Education of Ontario.

TABLE 5-19

Enrolment in newcomer classes offered by the Community Programs Branch, 1947–61

YEAR	NO. OF CLASSES	ENROLMENT[a]	YEAR	NO. OF CLASSES	ENROLMENT[a]
1947	126	2,900	1955	835	17,549
1948	310	7,500	1956	896	16,691
1949	584	14,971	1957	919	19,361
1950	524	13,694	1958	1,096	26,117
1951	756	23,088	1959	921	20,934
1952	733	21,923	1960	655	16,184
1953	843	21,702	1961	644	15,949
1954	1,010	22,893			

SOURCE: Reports of the Minister of Education of Ontario.

[a] As of December 1 of each year.

TABLE 5-20

Number of trainees in business and industry in programs sponsored by the Applied Arts and Technology Branch of the Ontario Department of Education, 1963–8

YEAR	TYPE OF COURSE			
	Management	Supervisory	Employee-upgrading and skill	TOTAL
1963	100		30	130
1964	1,254		120	1,374
1965	2,904		3,408	6,312
1966	4,128	1,992	8,411	14,531
1967	4,370	4,752	15,618	24,740
1968	2,960	5,380	10,268	18,608

SOURCE: Ontario Department of Education, Applied Arts and Technology Branch.

TABLE 5-21

Number of trainees in Ontario under the *Technical and Vocational Training Assistance Act*, by program, 1961–7

PROGRAM NO.	1961–2[a]	1962–3	1963–4	1964–5	1965–6	1966–7
1		79,933	121,103	149,836	167,169	
2	225	3,974	4,705	5,545	6,468	7,946
3		379	1,062	5,472	7,995	14,451
4	244	104	835	2,667	8,224	17,655
5	7,344	18,511	25,211	29,699	45,310	75,394
6	829	967	1,064	1,131	1,600	2,049
7		267	228	1,414	1,229	16
8		161	226	225	254	57
9	1,015	792	793	1,151	696	700
Apprenticeship	3,435	3,440	3,735	11,342	12,455	
TOTAL	13,092	108,528	158,962	208,482	251,400	118,268

SOURCE: Annual reports of the federal Department of Labour.

[a]Each year extends from April 1 to March 31 of the following year.

TABLE 5-22

Number of trainees in Canada under the *Technical and Vocational Training Assistance Act*, by program, 1961–7

PROGRAM NO.	1961–2[a]	1962–3	1963–4	1964–5	1965–6	1966–7
1		112,081	164,420	200,327	215,413	
2	3,936	11,068	13,887	19,610	21,741	27,694
3		6,319	27,394	57,362	60,065	75,812
4	1,705	3,770	7,814	9,199	20,103	39,204
5	26,887	38,439	49,047	59,821	80,991	150,044
6	2,765	2,968	3,495	3,981	3,981	4,581
7	1,232	601	749	3,063	1,762	640
8		802	1,243	1,446	1,158	735
9	4,116	4,667	16,721	24,709	941	1,323
Apprenticeship	18,483	18,087	19,138	26,682	31,827	
TOTAL	59,124	198,802	303,908	406,200	437,982	300,033

SOURCE: Annual reports of the federal Department of Labour.

[a]Each year extends from April 1 to March 31 of the following year.

new heights were reached in 1958, just after the peak immigration year, 1957. A gradual decline in the number of classes and in enrolment occurred while the program was under the management of the branch.

ADULT TRAINING AND RETRAINING

The Technological and Trades Training Branch and its successor, the Applied Arts and Technology Branch, have sponsored short courses in business and industry since 1963, as explained in volume II, chapter 2. These courses were begun with the co-operation of the federal government under the terms of Program 4 of the Federal-Provincial Technical and Vocational Training Agreement. At first management and employee-upgrading and skill courses were offered; these were supplemented by supervisory courses in 1966. An enrolment peak was reached in 1967, when there were 24,740 participants, the majority of whom were in the employee-upgrading and skill courses. The figures are shown in Table 5-20.

The number of trainees in Ontario and in Canada as a whole in individual programs under the *Technical and Vocational Training Assistance Act* from 1961–2 to 1966–7 are shown in Tables 5-21 and 5-22 respectively. Program 1 was the vocational high school training program; Program 2 was for post-secondary school technician training; Program 3 was for trade and other occupational training; Program 4 was for training in co-operation with industry; Program 5 was for training and retraining the unemployed; Program 6 was for training and retraining the disabled; Program 7 was for the preparation of teachers, supervisors, and administrators for training and retraining programs; Program 8 was for training members of the armed services; Program 9 was for student assistance; and Program 10 (not directly involving trainees) was designed to stimulate and encourage research projects relating to technical and vocational training and manpower requirements. More detailed information on the nature of these programs is supplied in volume II, chapter 11.

Between 1962–3 and 1965–6 by far the greatest number affected by the *Technical and Vocational Training Assistance Act* in Ontario and in Canada as a whole were high school students in vocational programs, who came under Program 1. Among the other programs, Program 5 covered the bulk of the trainees. The number of these in Ontario constituted the following percentages of the total for Canada during successive years: 1961–2, 27.3; 1962–3, 48.2; 1963–4, 51.4; 1964–5, 49.6; 1965–6, 55.9; and 1966–7, 50.2. Programs 3 and 4 were showing particularly rapid growth trends in the later years in which the agreement was in force.

SIX

Status and characteristics of teachers

OVER-ALL INCREASE IN ELEMENTARY AND SECONDARY
TEACHING FORCE

The basic statistics on the growth of the teaching force during the post-war period are provided in Table 6-1. For five-year intervals up to 1960–1, and for single years to 1968–9, it shows the number of acquisitions and the number of withdrawals up to September 30 of each year, the net gain, and the total force. Figures are given separately and in combination for elementary and secondary school teachers. The totals, classified by level, were available at the time of writing for 1969–70, but not specific information about acquisitions and withdrawals. Between 1945–6 and 1969–70 the number of elementary school teachers increased from 17,970 to 57,587, a percentage increase of 220.5. The corresponding increase for secondary school teachers was from 4,751 to 32,342, or 580.7 per cent, and for the total of elementary and secondary teachers, from 22,721 to 89,929, or 295.8 per cent. Chart 6-1 illustrates these changes.

NUMBER OF ELEMENTARY SCHOOL TEACHERS

The percentage of increase in the total force of elementary school teachers by time intervals was as follows: 1945–6 to 1950–1, 18.2; 1950–1 to 1955–6, 37.9; 1955–6 to 1960–1, 24.7; 1960–1 to 1965–6, 23.1; 1965–6 to 1969–70, 28.1. The net gain was erratic in those years before 1960–1 for which information is supplied in Table 6-1. In 1950–1 it amounted to 1,203 over the previous year, at a time when 19,456 pupils were added to the enrolment. Thus at this time there was no serious problem of supply. In 1955–6, however, the net gain was only 168, while the number of pupils increased by 41,878 over the previous year. The corresponding increases in teachers and in pupil enrolment in 1960–1 were 1,546 and 44,739. Enough new teachers were thus provided to look after the enrolment increase at a pupil-teacher ratio of 28.9:1. Until 1967–8 pupil enrolment increased at somewhere between 35,000 and 45,000 per year, after which the rate of increase began to decline, while the net gain in teachers rose steadily, except for a slight decline between 1960–1 and 1961–2. Although some of the increase made it possible to reduce the pupil-teacher ratio, it is obvious that a teacher surplus was building up. It

TABLE 6-1
Numbers of acquisitions and withdrawals of teachers from elementary and secondary schools in Ontario, 1945–70

YEAR	ELEMENTARY SCHOOLS				SECONDARY SCHOOLS				TOTAL			
	Acquisitions	Withdrawals	Net gains	Total force	Acquisitions	Withdrawals	Net gains	Total force	Acquisitions	Withdrawals	Net gains	Total force
1945–6	1,869	1,584	285	17,970	635	359	276	4,751	2,504	1,943	561	22,721
1950–1	2,752	1,549	1,203	21,249	594	319	275	5,795	3,346	1,868	1,478	27,044
1955–6	3,285	3,117	168	29,301	1,044	492	552	8,036	4,329	3,609	720	37,337
1960–1	6,636	5,090	1,546	36,533	2,270	898	1,372	11,478	8,906	5,988	2,918	48,011
1961–2	6,288	5,118	1,170	38,079	3,191	1,118	2,073	12,850	9,479	6,236	3,243	50,929
1962–3	6,707	5,081	1,626	39,249	3,740	1,493	2,247	14,923	10,447	6,574	3,873	54,172
1963–4	7,224	5,349	1,875	40,875	3,679	1,644	2,035	17,170	10,903	6,993	3,910	58,045
1964–5	7,920	5,703	2,217	42,750	4,504	2,050	2,454	19,205	12,424	7,753	4,671	61,955
1965–6	9,322	6,642	2,680	44,967	5,036	2,453	2,583	21,659	14,358	9,095	5,263	66,626
1966–7	10,414	7,043	3,371	47,647	5,870	2,948	2,922	24,242	16,284	9,991	6,293	71,889
1967–8	11,045	7,476	3,569	51,018	6,140	3,101	3,039	27,164	17,185	10,577	6,608	78,182
1968–9	11,297	8,297	3,000	54,587	5,619	3,480	2,139	30,203	16,916	11,777	5,139	84,790
1969–70				57,587				32,342				89,929

SOURCE: Reports of the Minister of Education of Ontario.

CHART 6-1
Numbers in the Ontario teaching force, 1945–70

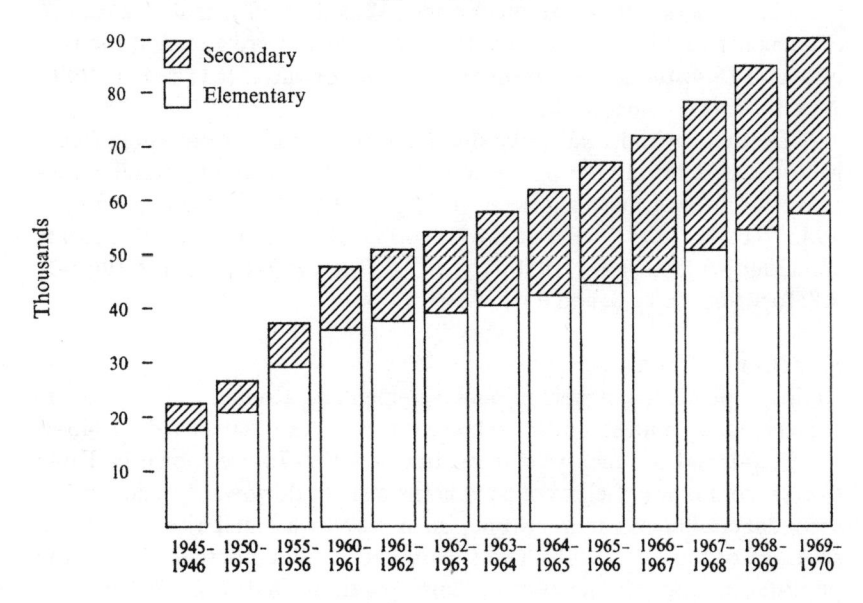

thus became practical to think of more stringent selection of candidates for teaching and a more adequate period of preparation.

The number of teachers withdrawing at the end of 1945–6 constituted 8.8 per cent of the force at the beginning of the same school year. The corresponding percentages for 1950–1, 1955–6, 1960–1, 1965–6, and 1968–9 were respectively 7.3, 10.6, 13.9, 14.8, and 15.2. This increase was attributed to the growing proportion of relatively inexperienced teachers in the force. The large percentage of annual losses in the 1960s represented a considerable training cost. The extra expense required to increase the period of training up to four years might well be compensated for, in part at least, by improved retention.

NUMBER OF SECONDARY SCHOOL TEACHERS

The number of secondary school teachers increased to a much greater degree than that of elementary school teachers, corresponding to the relatively larger rise in secondary school enrolment. Between 1945–6 and 1950–1 the percentage increase was 22.0; between 1950–1 and 1955–6, 38.7; between 1955–6 and 1960–1, 42.8; between 1960–1 and 1965–6, 88.7; and between 1965–6 and 1969–70, 49.3. An obvious consequence of this rapid growth was a relatively youthful secondary school teaching force. The recent period has provided unusually abundant opportunities for rapid promotion.

The net gain of 275 between 1949–50 and 1950–1 corresponded to an enrolment increase of 3,965. Supply and demand at that time were thus in relative equilibrium. Between 1954–5 and 1955–6 the corresponding gains in teachers and in enrolment were 552 and 14,396: that is, a gain of one teacher to 26.1 students. By 1960–1 teachers were added at the rate of one to 18.4 students; by 1965–6 at the rate of one to 9.1; and in 1969–70 at the rate of one to 14.0.

The rate of withdrawals, like that from the elementary teaching force, has increased during the post-war period, and probably for similar reasons. Withdrawals between the beginning of 1944–5 and the beginning of 1945–6 constituted 7.6 per cent of the force at the latter date. The corresponding percentage for 1950–1 was 5.5; for 1955–6, 6.1; for 1960–1, 7.8; for 1965–6, 11.3; and for 1968–9, 11.5.

PUPIL-TEACHER RATIO
Ratios of pupils to teachers in public elementary, Roman Catholic separate elementary, and secondary schools for five-year intervals from 1945–6 to 1960–1 and for each year thereafter to 1969–70 are shown in Table 6-2. In both types of elementary schools a slight downward trend, and in secondary schools a marked one, gave way to a small rise during the shortage of the late 1950s. The steady and continuous reduction of the pupil-teacher ratio in the 1960s is emphasized in Chart 6-2. The substantially less favourable position of the Roman Catholic separate school teachers was reduced to the point where they were close to equality with their public school counterparts by the end of the decade, with a ratio of 25.5:1 as compared with 25.2:1 in the public schools. The reduction in the ratio in the secondary schools from 22.2:1 in 1962–3 to 16.6:1 in 1968–9 seems remarkable. It must not, of course, be supposed that the size of the usual class was reduced to the same extent. Some teachers have expressed the view that the figures must be erroneous because they could perceive no reduction at all in the burden imposed on them. A large part of the increase in the teaching force has in fact been absorbed by a rapid growth in administrative positions and by the provision of consultants or teachers of special groups requiring unusually small classes or individual treatment. Although the very pronounced reduction in the number of small schools and the increased number of large secondary schools no doubt offers some explanation for the proliferation of administrative positions, the trend has caused misgivings in some quarters.

SEX DISTRIBUTION OF TEACHERS
Official statistics of the Department of Education have not supplied a categorization of elementary school teachers by sex since 1965–6, or of secondary school teachers since 1964–5. The situation in the period up to those dates is shown in Tables 6-3-1 and 6-3-2. There was a considerable increase in the proportion of male elementary school teachers. In 1945–6 these constituted 16.1 per cent of the total; in 1950–1, 21.6 per cent; in

TABLE 6-2

Ratio of pupils to teachers in Ontario schools, 1945–70

YEAR	ELEMENTARY SCHOOLS		SECONDARY SCHOOLS
	Public	Roman Catholic separate	
1945–6	29.9	32.2	25.2
1950–1	29.3	32.4	22.6
1955–6	29.1	31.0	21.7
1960–1	30.0	33.4	22.9
1961–2	29.8	32.9	23.3
1962–3	29.8	32.6	22.2
1963–4	29.6	31.9	21.2
1964–5	29.4	31.4	20.6
1965–6	29.0	30.4	19.3
1966–7	28.3	29.5	18.0
1967–8	27.3	28.2	17.1
1968–9	26.0	26.7	16.6
1969–70	25.2	25.5	16.4

SOURCE: Reports of the Minister of Education of Ontario.

CHART 6-2

Pupil-teacher ratios in public elementary, Roman Catholic separate, and secondary schools, 1945–70

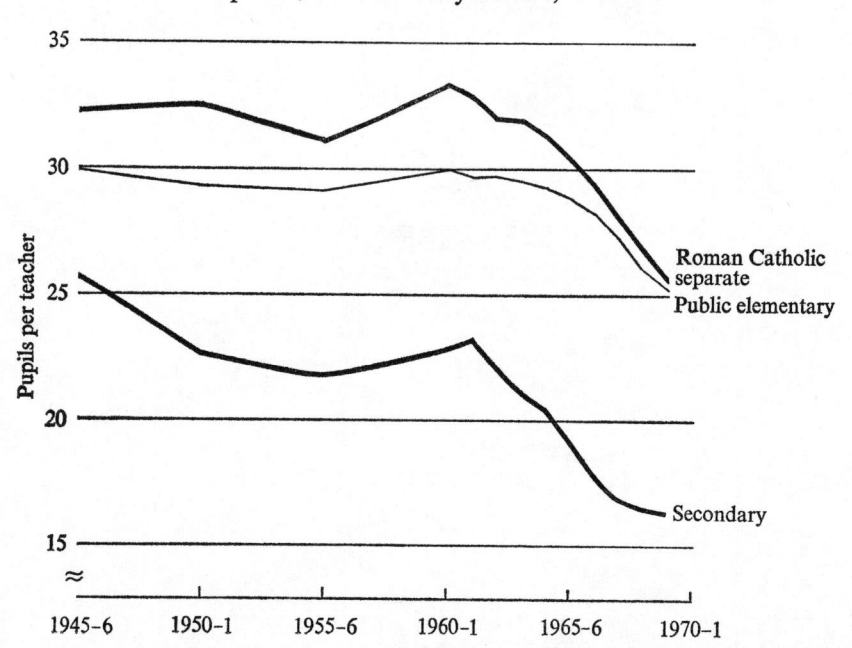

TABLE 6-3-1
Number of full-time teachers in elementary schools in Ontario by sex, 1945–70

YEAR	PUBLIC			ROMAN CATHOLIC SEPARATE			TOTAL		
	Male	Female	TOTAL	Male	Female	TOTAL	Male	Female	TOTAL
1945-6	2,521	12,089	14,610	370	2,990	3,360	2,891	15,079	17,970
1950-1	4,152	13,169	17,321	437	3,491	3,928	4,589	16,660	21,249
1955-6			23,246			6,055			29,301
1960-1	7,107	20,963	28,070	1,144	7,319	8,463	8,251	28,282	36,533
1961-2	7,753	21,177	28,930	1,332	7,817	9,149	9,085	28,994	38,079
1962-3	8,229	21,315	29,544	1,546	8,159	9,705	9,775	29,474	39,249
1963-4	8,581	21,914	30,495	1,766	8,614	10,380	10,347	30,528	40,875
1964-5	9,018	22,487	31,505	2,025	9,220	11,245	11,043	31,707	42,750
1965-6	9,479	23,304	32,783	2,338	9,846	12,184	11,817	33,150	44,967
1966-7			34,488			13,159			47,647
1967-8			36,722			14,296			51,018
1968-9			39,290			15,297			54,587
1969-70			41,373			16,214			57,587

SOURCE: Reports of the Minister of Education of Ontario.

TABLE 6-3-2
Number of full-time teachers in Ontario schools by sex, 1945–70

YEAR	ELEMENTARY			SECONDARY			TOTAL – BOTH LEVELS		
	Male	Female	TOTAL	Male	Female	TOTAL	Male	Female	TOTAL
1945-6	2,891	15,079	17,970	2,625	2,126	4,751	5,516	17,205	22,721
1950-1	4,589	16,660	21,249	3,655	2,140	5,795	8,244	18,800	27,044
1955-6			29,301			8,036			37,337
1960-1	8,251	28,282	36,533	7,626	3,852	11,478	15,877	32,134	48,011
1961-2	9,085	28,994	38,079	8,575	4,275	12,850	17,660	33,269	50,929
1962-3	9,775	29,474	39,249	10,095	4,828	14,923	19,870	34,302	54,172
1963-4	10,347	30,528	40,875	11,655	5,515	17,170	22,002	36,043	58,045
1964-5	11,043	31,707	42,750	13,009	6,196	19,205	24,052	37,903	61,955
1965-6	11,817	33,150	44,967			21,659			66,626
1966-7			47,647			24,242			71,889
1967-8			51,018			27,164			78,182
1968-9			54,587			30,203			84,790
1969-70			57,587			32,342			89,929

SOURCE: Reports of the Minister of Education of Ontario.

1960–1, 22.6 per cent; and in 1965–6, 26.3 per cent. For the public elementary schools, the percentages for these respective years were 17.3, 24.0, 25.3, and 28.9; and for the Roman Catholic separate schools, 11.0, 11.1, 13.5, and 19.2. Thus, although women have predominated to a greater extent among separate school teachers than among public elementary school teachers, the proportion of men among the former has tended to rise more rapidly.

In the secondary schools men were in an increasing majority during the twenty-year period after 1945. In 1945–6 they constituted 55.3 per cent of the total; in 1950–1, 63.1 per cent; in 1960–1, 66.4 per cent; and in 1964–5, 67.7 per cent. During the latter year 38.8 per cent of the total teaching force at both the elementary and secondary levels were men.

TEACHER ACQUISITIONS

Table 6-4 shows the number of elementary teachers acquired by Ontario schools each year between 1957–8 and 1968–9 in each of the following categories: teachers from private elementary schools, the previous year's graduates from teachers' colleges, former secondary school teachers, qualified teachers re-entering the profession, teachers with Letters of Standing, teachers on Letters of Permission, and others. Teachers' college graduates were the major source, constituting 61.4 per cent of the total in 1957–8, 69.5 per cent in 1960–1, 49.9 per cent in 1966–7, and 59.1 per cent in 1968–9. During the period under review, qualified teachers re-entering the profession, the second major source, reached a low point of 18.0 per cent in 1960–1, and a high point of 28.1 per cent in 1963–4. These trends are illustrated in Chart 6-3. There was a rapid rise in the number of Letters of Standing after 1963–4, a development that reflected, at least in part, a more liberal policy toward the recognition of equivalent qualifications obtained outside Ontario. The number of Letters of Permission fell in the early 1960s, rose to 660 in 1966–7, and then fell again. Only a small number of teachers came from private elementary schools and from secondary schools.

The numbers of teachers acquired from various sources for Ontario secondary schools between 1957 and 1969 are indicated in Table 6-5. Graduates of the Ontario colleges of education constituted 50.5 per cent of the total in 1957–8, 60.8 per cent in 1958–9, and 62.4 per cent in 1959–60. During the remainder of the 1960s, the percentage fluctuated above or below 60 per cent, without showing any definite pattern, until 1968–9, when the abandonment of the special summer course in its earlier form reduced the percentage to 43.7. The percentage of acquisitions on Letters of Permission varied from 15.4 in 1959–60 to 22.7 in 1964–5. This group, unlike the others, does not constitute cumulative additions to the teaching force. Qualified teachers re-entering the profession reached 11.6 per cent of the acquisitions in 1958–9 and 1960–1, and fell to a low point of 8.8 per cent in 1965–6. The number of Letters of

TABLE 6-4
Teacher acquisitions in Ontario elementary schools from various sources, 1957-69

SOURCE	1957-8	1958-9	1959-60	1960-1	1961-2	1962-3	1963-4	1964-5	1965-6	1966-7	1967-8	1968-9
From private elementary schools	46	72	61	64	41	49	56	54	82	58	81	75
From teachers' colleges	3,891	4,291	4,278	4,613	4,191	3,752	4,018	4,438	4,883	5,195	5,544	6,673
Former secondary school teachers	71	71	67	55	59	81	108	103	111	154	155	179
Qualified teachers re-entering profession	1,279	1,288	1,262	1,197	1,314	1,895	2,033	1,989	2,162	2,292	2,620	2,317
Letters of Standing	434	369	268	246	260	317	410	628	867	1,025	1,010	774
Letters of Permission[a]	426	528	472	281	293	390	373	484	585	660	439	312
Others	194	201	189	180	130	223	226	224	632	1,030	1,196	967
TOTAL	6,341	6,820	6,597	6,636	6,288	6,707	7,224	7,920	9,322	10,414	11,045	11,297

SOURCE: Reports of the Minister of Education of Ontario.

[a] Letters of Permission issued for following year.

268 The expansion of the educational system

CHART 6-3
Percentages of teacher acquisitions in Ontario elementary schools from major sources, 1957–69

Others
Qualified teachers re-entering the profession
Teachers' college graduates of previous year

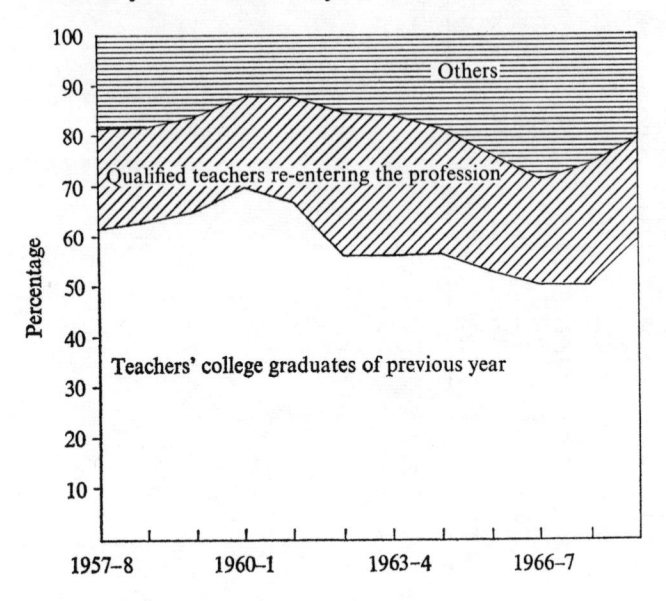

CHART 6-4
Percentages of teacher acquisitions in Ontario secondary schools from major sources, 1957–69

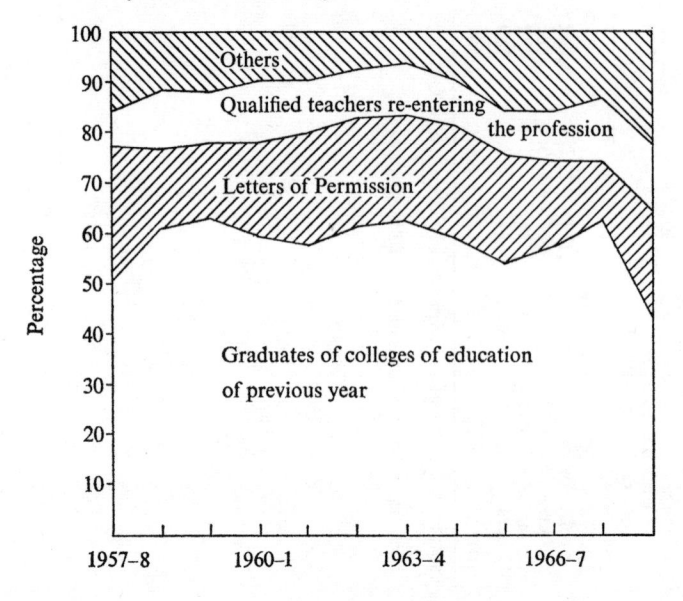

Others
Qualified teachers re-entering the profession
Letters of Permission
Graduates of colleges of education of previous year

TABLE 6-5
Teacher acquisitions in Ontario secondary schools from various sources, 1957-69

SOURCE	1957-8	1958-9	1959-60	1960-1	1961-2	1962-3	1963-4	1964-5	1965-6	1966-7	1967-8	1968-9
From private secondary schools	22	31	37	42	58	53	63	67	83	81	190	104
Ontario colleges of education[a]	779	1,020	1,152	1,342	1,826	2,273	2,288	2,638	2,696	3,351	3,833	2,455
Former elementary teachers qualified to teach in secondary schools	61	60	69	82	135	139	124	145	166	117	112	110
Qualified teachers re-entering profession	182	195	192	264	332	354	376	417	442	571	728	757
Letters of Standing	109	66	52	73	74	34	29	94	226	335	330	585
Letters of Permission[b]	340	267	284	432	705	820	788	1,022	1,089	1,013	710	1,144
Others	50	40	60	35	61	67	11	121	334	402	237	464
TOTAL	1,543	1,679	1,846	2,270	3,191	3,740	3,679	4,504	5,036	5,870	6,140	5,619

SOURCE: Reports of the Minister of Education of Ontario.
[a] Not including those who had only the first session of the special summer course.
[b] Letters of Permission issued for following year.

standing increased from 94 in 1964–5 to 226 in 1965–6 and to 585 in 1968–9, constituting 2.1 per cent, 4.5 per cent, and 10.4 per cent of the total in these respective years.

TEACHER WITHDRAWALS

The number of withdrawals from the elementary school teaching force for each year between 1957–8 and 1968–9 for each of nine categories of reasons is shown in Table 6-6. The category "marriage" has been used for many years, although the practice of regarding it as excluding teaching appears increasingly unrealistic. Marriage perhaps should be redesignated as "undertaking full-time household duties" for those for whom it means withdrawal from teaching, and combined with "resumption of household duties." The latter as a reason for withdrawal has been by far the most important, accounting for between 34.9 and 42.5 per cent of the withdrawals over the twelve-year period, as shown in Table 6-7. Increasing numbers have left to teach in institutions other than publicly supported elementary schools in Ontario, including secondary schools, private schools, teachers' colleges, elementary schools outside Ontario, and, in recent years, colleges of applied arts and technology. The second category in Tables 6-6 and 6-7 includes these, as well as teachers who gave up full-time in favour of part-time teaching. The percentage in this category increased from 11.3 in 1957–8 to 24.9 in 1965–6, and then declined slightly. The percentage withdrawing in favour of employment in other occupations fell to some extent during the period covered, as did that in the "marriage" category. The percentage of those retiring, on the other hand, rose for a number of years and more recently has remained relatively stable at about 11 per cent. Among the "others" are those who abandoned teaching in favour of supervisory or administrative positions in education. Earlier reports do not indicate the number of these separately.

Tables 6-8 and 6-9 provide information about withdrawals from the secondary school teaching force corresponding to that in Tables 6-6 and 6-7, dealing with the elementary force. In recent years the most important reason for withdrawal has been to teach in institutions other than publicly supported secondary schools. In 1967–8 141 teachers were recruited to teach in colleges of applied arts and technology alone. Resumption of household duties has generally been the second most important reason for withdrawal, accounting for between 16.9 and 23.8 per cent of the cases during the twelve-year period. As few as 10.9 and as many as 20.8 per cent of the withdrawals have gone to employment in non-teaching occupations. The percentage retiring declined fairly steadily from 17.8 per cent in 1957–8 to 8.0 in 1966–7, and then rose slightly to 8.8 in 1968–9. There has been an almost uninterrupted increase in the number seeking further full-time education in various types of institutions. In the "others" category are those who have assumed full-time supervisory or administrative positions. As was true of the elementary teaching force,

TABLE 6-6
Number of withdrawals from elementary school teaching force for various reasons, 1957-69

REASON FOR WITHDRAWAL	1957-8	1958-9	1959-60	1960-1	1961-2	1962-3	1963-4	1964-5	1965-6	1966-7	1967-8	1968-9
To enrol in teachers' colleges, universities, and other educational institutions	804	897	1,074	865	792	462	501	564	519	605	756	869
To teach in institutions other than Ontario elementary schools, or part-time in such schools	467	632	837	905	993	1,055	977	1,237	1,656	1,704	1,756	1,736
Employment in non-teaching occupations	317	323	406	365	344	392	465	351	397	389	403	409
Resumption of household duties	1,537	1,661	1,894	1,834	1,789	2,097	2,281	2,272	2,463	2,556	2,632	2,975
Marriage	349	385	381	351	382	298	283	255	270	266	237	268
Retirement	339	319	395	454	503	491	533	667	764	745	824	988
Illness	82	114	90	115	111	102	108	125	137	140	167	140
Death	46	38	35	45	46	45	36	44	55	61	81	61
Others	184	284	193	156	158	139	165	188	381	577	620[a]	851[a]
TOTAL	4,125	4,653	5,305	5,090	5,118	5,081	5,349	5,703	6,642	7,043	7,476	8,297

SOURCE: Reports of the Minister of Education of Ontario.

[a] Including withdrawals to supervisory or administrative positions in education, 333 in 1967-8 and 453 in 1968-9.

TABLE 6-7
Percentages of withdrawals from elementary school teaching force for various reasons, 1957–69

REASON FOR WITHDRAWAL	1957–8	1958–9	1959–60	1960–1	1961–2	1962–3	1963–4	1964–5	1965–6	1966–7	1967–8	1968–9
To enrol in teachers' colleges, universities, and other educational institutions	19.5	19.3	20.2	17.0	15.5	9.1	9.4	9.9	7.8	8.6	10.1	10.6
To teach in institutions other than Ontario elementary schools, or part-time in such schools	11.3	13.6	15.8	17.7	19.4	20.8	18.3	21.7	24.9	24.2	23.5	20.9
Employment in non-teaching occupations	7.7	6.9	7.7	7.2	6.7	7.7	8.7	6.2	6.0	5.5	5.4	4.9
Resumption of household duties	37.2	35.7	35.7	36.0	34.9	41.2	42.5	39.7	37.1	36.2	35.2	35.8
Marriage	8.5	8.3	7.2	6.9	7.5	5.9	5.3	4.5	4.1	3.8	3.2	3.2
Retirement	8.2	6.8	7.4	8.9	9.8	9.7	10.0	11.7	11.5	10.6	11.0	11.9
Illness	2.0	2.5	1.7	2.3	2.2	2.0	2.0	2.2	2.1	2.0	2.2	1.7
Death	1.1	0.8	0.7	0.9	0.9	0.9	0.7	0.8	0.8	0.9	1.1	0.7
Others	4.5	6.1	3.6	3.1	3.1	2.7	3.1	3.3	5.7	8.2	8.3[a]	10.3[a]
TOTAL	100.0	100.0	100.0	100.0	100.0	100.0	100.0	100.0	100.0	100.0	100.0	100.0

SOURCE: Calculated from figures contained in Reports of the Minister of Education of Ontario.

[a] Including withdrawals to supervisory or administrative positions in education, 333 in 1967–8 and 453 in 1968–9.

TABLE 6-8
Number of withdrawals from secondary school teaching force for various reasons, 1957-69

REASON FOR WITHDRAWAL	1957-8	1958-9	1959-60	1960-1	1961-2	1962-3	1963-4	1964-5	1965-6	1966-7	1967-8	1968-9
To enrol in teachers' colleges, universities, and other educational institutions	63	81	97	114	139	216	248	320	407	471	482	588
To teach in institutions other than Ontario publicly supported secondary schools	102	145	181	185	204	294	296	424	503	764	851	898
Employment in non-teaching occupations	79	129	91	129	184	234	342	256	374	353	359	454
Resumption of household duties	122	133	153	189	244	355	278	389	453	541	645	722
Marriage	46	76	61	67	71	88	199	106	82	95	103	97
Retirement	114	136	136	170	152	175	81	240	253	237	254	305
Illness	9	19	20	24	31	21	29	38	43	52	61	48
Death	24	24	27	19	19	35	23	32	37	38	36	40
Others	80	45	66	1	74	75	148	245	301	397	310	328
TOTAL	639	788	832	898	1,118	1,493	1,644	2,050	2,453	2,948	3,101	3,480

SOURCE: Reports of the Minister of Education of Ontario.

TABLE 6-9
Percentages of withdrawals from secondary school teaching force for various reasons, 1957–69

REASON FOR WITHDRAWAL	1957–8	1958–9	1959–60	1960–1	1961–2	1962–3	1963–4	1964–5	1965–6	1966–7	1967–8	1968–9
To enrol in teachers' colleges, universities, and other educational institutions	9.9	10.3	11.7	12.7	12.4	14.5	15.1	15.6	16.6	16.0	15.5	16.9
To teach in institutions other than Ontario publicly supported secondary schools	16.0	18.4	21.9	20.6	18.2	19.7	18.0	20.6	20.5	25.8	27.4	25.8
Employment in non-teaching occupations	12.4	16.4	10.9	14.4	16.5	15.7	20.8	12.5	15.2	12.0	11.6	13.0
Resumption of household duties	19.0	16.9	18.4	21.1	21.8	23.8	16.9	18.9	18.5	18.4	20.8	20.7
Marriage	7.2	9.6	7.3	7.5	6.4	5.9	12.1	5.2	3.3	3.2	3.3	2.8
Retirement	17.8	17.3	16.3	18.9	13.6	11.7	4.9	11.7	10.3	8.0	8.2	8.8
Illness	1.4	2.4	2.4	2.7	2.8	1.4	1.8	1.9	1.8	1.8	2.0	1.4
Death	3.8	3.0	3.2	2.1	1.7	2.3	1.4	1.6	1.5	1.3	1.2	1.1
Others	12.5	5.7	7.9	*	6.6	5.0	9.0	12.0	12.3	13.5	10.0	9.5
TOTAL	100.0	100.0	100.0	100.0	100.0	100.0	100.0	100.0	100.0	100.0	100.0	100.0

SOURCE: Calculated from figures contained in Reports of the Minister of Education of Ontario.

*Negligible.

these were not separately identified in the official statistics until 1967–8, when they numbered 194.

TEACHERS' SALARIES

During the immediate post-war period teachers received what appear in today's values to be extremely low salaries. When unemployment was most serious during the worst days of the depression of the 1930s, the surplus of teachers had enabled school boards to reduce salaries by substantial amounts. For those who managed to retain their jobs, however, the situation was by no means as bad as it was for many other groups. As wages and salaries began to improve during the war, despite government controls, the relative position of the teachers worsened, and pessimists saw bleak prospects for the profession. The effects of the teacher shortages of the 1950s and 1960s, combined with the developing power of the teachers' federations, proved the more optimistic forecasts correct.

Tables 6-10 to 6-14 provide information, as far as the ministers' reports supply it, on salary distributions of public and Roman Catholic separate school teachers and of secondary school teachers for certain intervals from 1950–1 to 1966–7 and for 1967–8. The values in the scales used in successive tables differ to take account of the generally rising salary levels. Table 6-15 provides assistance in interpreting the preceding tables by identifying median salaries from 1950–1 to 1967–8, in most cases for each sex as well as for the total group in the three categories. The lack of completeness of the data, and the change in the period of reporting in 1967–8, do not prohibit a tracing of the general trend. The fact that some of the figures were, according to the ministers' reports, based on samples, need not be considered a matter of serious concern.

Of the 16,717 public elementary school teachers included in the distribution in Table 6-10, 7,100, or 42.5 per cent, were getting salaries between $1,551 and $2,050, and about one in four were getting between $2,051 and $2,550 in 1950. According to Table 6-15, the median for teachers of both sexes during that year was $2,130. Fewer than 1 per cent were in the $4,551–$5,050 range, and only eleven individuals were getting between $5,051 and $5,550. Data for the Roman Catholic separate schools are not available for that period, but it is a well known fact that salaries in those schools were substantially lower. In secondary schools 23.2 per cent were getting between $2,551 and $3,050, and 20.7 per cent were in the next higher category. The median of $3,334 was $1,204 above that for public elementary school teachers.

There was a marked improvement in the salary position of public elementary school teachers by 1955–6, as shown in Table 6-11. By that time 30.9 per cent were getting between $2,251 and $2,850, and 23.0 per cent between $2,851 and $3,450. The median for teachers of both sexes was $3,130. That for female teachers was $3,010, and for male teachers,

TABLE 6-10
Salary frequency distribution for full-time teachers in Ontario schools as of September 1950

SALARY RANGE $	PUBLIC ELEMENTARY SCHOOLS[a]	SECONDARY SCHOOLS
Under 1,551	262	9
1,551–2,050	7,100	38
2,051–2,550	4,156	752
2,551–3,050	2,408	1,296
3,051–3,550	1,770	1,158
3,551–4,050	598	986
4,051–4,550	262	889
4,551–5,050	150	383
5,051–5,550	11	60
5,551–6,050		23
TOTAL	16,717	5,594

SOURCE: Report of the Minister of Education of Ontario, 1950.

[a]No data available for Roman Catholic separate schools.

$3,690, reflecting the greater experience and predominance of administrative positions among the latter. During the same year well over half the teachers in Roman Catholic separate schools were getting less than $2,251 a year. The medians, at $2,470 for males, $2,140 for females, and $2,220 for both sexes, were approximately 70 per cent of those of public school teachers.

The late 1940s and early 1950s constituted a period when the Ontario Secondary School Teachers' Federation was establishing bargaining procedures for dealing with school boards. At the time of writing S.G.B. Robinson, who served as General Secretary of the federation during that period, and for many years thereafter, was in the process of recording these developments. The publication of the results of his efforts promises to provide a permanent record of major developments such as the extension of salary schedules, with minima, maxima, and annual increments for teachers in each salary category; the devising of the "pink letter," which was used to mobilize teachers for effective action in salary campaigns; and the increasing aggressiveness of teachers in favour of special raises and improved schedules. In a preliminary version of his work, Robinson notes that Toronto accepted a maximum of $4,500 for non-specialists in 1950, and raised it to $5,400 in 1951. Trenton approved a maximum of $4,100 in 1950, and raised it to $5,200 in 1951, and other boards took similar action. The figures for specialists were ordinarily $200 higher than those for non-specialists. The $200 annual increment was widely replacing the $100 increment, a development that was to have very important implications for general salary levels.

TABLE 6-11
Salary frequency distribution for full-time teachers in
Ontario schools as of September 1955

SALARY RANGE $	ELEMENTARY SCHOOLS Public	Roman Catholic separate	SECONDARY SCHOOLS
Under 2,251	1,367	3,084	
2,251–2,850	6,811	1,538	23
2,851–3,450	5,075	736	802
3,451–4,050	2,966	131	1,213
4,051–4,650	2,116	22	1,267
4,651–5,250	1,750	2	1,060
5,251–5,850	1,057	2	918
5,851–6,450	500		1,189
6,451–7,050	161		684
7,051–7,650	122		83
Over 7,650	93		66
TOTAL	22,018	5,515	7,305[a]

SOURCE: Report of the Minister of Education of Ontario, 1955.

[a]The total number of teachers shown will not exactly agree with statistics shown elsewhere owing to a difference in time of reporting.

According to Table 6-11 salaries for secondary school teachers in 1955–6 were fairly evenly distributed over categories ranging from $3,451 to $6,450. The median of $4,820 for both sexes was 44.6 per cent higher than it had been five years earlier. The median for males, at $4,850, was $390 higher than that for females. There were eighty-three teachers or principals, constituting just over 1 per cent of the group on which the table is based, receiving between $7,051 and $7,650, and sixty-six at a still higher level.

In 1960–1, as shown in Table 6-12, the largest concentration of public elementary school teachers, 32.8 per cent, was in the range between $3,051 and $3,850, while 20.7 per cent were in the next higher bracket. Of the total of 28,070 teachers, 85.7 per cent were receiving $6,250 or less. The median salary of $4,218 per annum was $1,088 higher than it had been five years earlier, and the spread between the medians for men and women was $818. In the Roman Catholic separate school group, 42.7 per cent were getting less than $3,051, and 74.4 per cent less than $3,851. The median of $3,215 was approximately $1,000 below that for public elementary school teachers.

Only 668 of the group of 11,478 secondary school teachers, or 5.8 per cent, were getting $4,650 or less in 1960–1. The percentages in successive $800 categories above this figure were 14.7, 15.7, 13.4, 13.8, 11.0, and 12.1. There were 1,549, or 13.5 per cent of the total group, in categories above $9,450, four of whom were receiving $14,250 or more. The median for both sexes was $7,078, an increase of 46.8 per cent over the 1955–6

TABLE 6-12

Salary frequency distribution for full-time teachers in Ontario schools as of September 1960

SALARY RANGE $	ELEMENTARY SCHOOLS Public	ELEMENTARY SCHOOLS Roman Catholic separate	SECONDARY SCHOOLS
Under 3,051	1,699	3,610	
3,051–3,850	9,213	2,686	
3,851–4,650	5,823	1,438	668
4,651–5,450	3,728	640	1,690
5,451–6,250	3,589	85	1,797
6,251–7,050	1,959	4	1,536
7,051–7,850	859		1,580
7,851–8,650	461		1,266
8,651–9,450	307		1,392
9,451–10,250	158		990
10,251–11,050	155		310
11,051–11,850	112		100
11,851–12,650	7		72
12,651–13,450			45
13,451–14,250			28
Over 14,250			4
TOTAL	28,070	8,463	11,478

SOURCE: Report of the Minister of Education of Ontario, 1960.

figure. The difference between the medians for male and female teachers was now $750, indicating clearly that it takes something more than legislation against salary differentials based on sex in order to ensure equal pay. The highest administrative positions in education were of course largely restricted to men.

In 1966–7 5.3 per cent of 23,720 public elementary school teachers were getting $4,000 or less, 25.6 per cent between $4,001 and $5,000, 24.5 per cent between $5,001 and $6,000, and 44.6 per cent larger amounts. The median for men was $6,749, and for women, $5,500, representing increases of $1,847 and $1,416 respectively over 1960–1. In 1966–7 18.4 per cent of the group of Roman Catholic separate school teachers received $4,000 or less, and 49.3 per cent received $5,000 or less. Fifty-one individuals in this group were in the highest category, receiving over $13,000. The medians were $5,391 and $4,941 for men and women respectively. These figures were below the corresponding ones for public school teachers by $1,358 and $559.

In 1966–7 6.5 per cent of secondary school teachers were getting between $5,001 and $6,000; 16.0 per cent between $6,001 and $7,000; 17.8 per cent between $7,001 and $8,000; 15.0 per cent between $8,001 and $9,000; 12.9 per cent between $9,001 and $10,000; 9.4 per cent between $10,001 and $11,000; 8.9 per cent between $11,001 and $12,000; and 12.9 per cent over $12,000. The medians for men and women were $8,868 and $7,904 respectively.

TABLE 6-13
Salary frequency distribution for full-time teachers in Ontario schools as of December 1966

SALARY RANGE $	ELEMENTARY SCHOOLS Public	ELEMENTARY SCHOOLS Roman Catholic separate	SECONDARY SCHOOLS
Under 3,001	72	247	22
3,001–4,000	1,174	1,222	17
4,001–5,000	6,075	2,467	70
5,001–6,000	5,822	1,957	1,000
6,001–7,000	3,934	1,267	2,439
7,001–8,000	2,892	471	2,713
8,001–9,000	1,145	177	2,287
9,001–10,000	825	77	1,964
10,001–11,000	501	30	1,436
11,001–12,000	411	9	1,357
12,001–13,000	258	1	1,053
Over 13,000	611	51	921
TOTAL	23,720	7,976	15,279

SOURCE: Report of the Minister of Education of Ontario, 1966.

Table 6-14 shows the changes after a further one-year interval. The largest group of public elementary school teachers were in the $4,500–$5,999 salary range, with 42.5 per cent of the entire force receiving the latter amount or less. At the same time 29.7 per cent were getting between $6,000 and $7,499, and 27.8 per cent larger amounts. The medians, again not available for the entire group, had risen by $349 and $236 for males and females respectively. The difference between the medians for the two sexes was now $1,358. In 1967–8 1,851, or 12.5 per cent, of the Roman Catholic separate school teachers were getting $4,499 or less. At the same time 42.3 per cent were in the $4,500–$5,999 range, and the remaining 45.2 per cent were in higher categories. The medians of $5,794 and $5,218 for males and females respectively were $1,300 and $518 below the corresponding figures for public school teachers.

By 1967–8 24.3 per cent of 27,634 secondary school teachers were getting between $6,000 and $7,499, 25.6 per cent between $7,500 and $8,999, 18.1 between $9,000 and $10,499, 11.5 per cent between $10,500 and $11,999, and 19.1 per cent $12,000 or more. Only 1.3 per cent were getting less than $6,000. The medians were $9,157 and $7,956 for males and females respectively.

COMPARISON WITH TEACHERS' SALARIES IN THE UNITED STATES

Some salary statistics are offered in Table 6-16 to provide a basis for a rough comparison between the financial position of American teachers and that of their Ontario counterparts. It should be kept in mind that the amounts reported are in the dollars of the respective countries. When due

TABLE 6-14
Salary frequency distribution for full-time teachers in Ontario schools as of April 1968

SALARY RANGE $	ELEMENTARY SCHOOLS Public	Roman Catholic separate	SECONDARY SCHOOLS
Under 3,000	24	74	4
3,000–4,499	1,261	1,777	84
4,500–5,999	14,782	6,269	267
6,000–7,499	11,231	4,559	6,723
7,500–8,999	5,379	1,432	7,075
9,000–10,499	2,346	453	4,999
10,500–11,999	991	150	3,191
12,000–13,499	748	62	2,346
13,500–14,999	422	18	1,728
15,000–16,499	277	3	575
16,500–17,999	322	6	307
18,000–19,499	6		221
Over 19,499		1	114
TOTAL	37,789	14,804	27,634

SOURCE: Report of the Minister of Education of Ontario, 1968.

allowance has been made for this difference, it is nevertheless possible to draw some tentative conclusions. 1 / Since 1954–5 American elementary school teachers have consistently received substantially higher salaries than their Ontario counterparts. 2 / At the secondary school level the reverse has been true. Each of these generalizations merits some further consideration.

On the basis of Tables 6-15 and 6-16, median public elementary school salaries in Ontario for 1955–6, 1960–1, and 1965–6 were 86.6, 87.6, and 82.0 per cent of the American averages for the same respective years. As indicated in chapter 1, Ontario per capita income has been consistently around 80 per cent of the American average during the post-war period. Thus in these terms the relative position of the Ontario group within their own society has tended to be somewhat more favourable. Although only medians for the separate sex groups in Ontario are available for the more recent period, it appears that Ontario salaries have advanced more quickly than have those in American elementary schools.

At the secondary school level there is not the least doubt which group was in the more favourable position. In 1955–6 the median for American teachers at this level was $4,194, and for Ontario teachers, $4,820. In 1960–1 the comparable figures were $5,276 and $7,078, and in 1964–5, $6,266 and $7,220. Again, while direct comparisons cannot be made for subsequent years on the basis of the tables, it appears that Ontario teachers increased their relative advantage after 1964–5.

There are other factors that must be considered before a really adequate comparison of the economic status of teachers in the United States and

TABLE 6-15
Median salaries of teachers and principals in Ontario schools by sex, 1950–69 (in dollars)

| YEAR | ELEMENTARY ||| ||| SECONDARY |||
| | Public ||| Roman Catholic separate ||| |||
	Male	Female	Total	Male	Female	Total	Male	Female	Total
1950–1[a]			2,130						
1951–2	2,845	2,351							3,334
1952–3	3,142	2,565	2,673						3,855
1953–4	3,276	2,824	2,789				4,353	3,891	4,140
1954–5	3,422	2,820	2,935	2,392	1,995	2,030	4,650	4,058	4,350
1955–6	3,690	3,010	3,130	2,470	2,140	2,200	4,730	4,217	4,526
1956–7	3,948	3,215	3,349	2,626	2,275	2,309	4,850	4,460	4,820
1957–8	4,210	3,421	3,570	2,856	2,457	2,495	5,335	4,782	5,131
1958–9	4,509	3,695	3,826	3,053	2,688	2,728	5,912	5,287	5,687
1959–60	4,748	3,947	4,090	3,235	2,932	2,964	6,477	5,754	6,196
1960–1	4,902	4,084	4,218	3,496	3,174	3,215	7,157	6,421	6,870
1961–2	4,908	4,161	4,289	3,636	3,332	3,374	7,355	6,605	7,078
1962–3	4,958	4,229	4,382	3,728	3,494	3,539	7,339	6,506	7,041
1963–4	5,035	4,297	4,474	3,914	3,661	3,707	7,215	6,486	6,958
1964–5	5,261	4,515	4,687	4,129	3,919	3,959	7,271	6,489	7,017
1965–6	5,510	4,737	4,907	4,445	4,128	4,186	7,481	6,608	7,220
1966–7	6,749	5,500		5,391	4,941		8,868	7,904	
1967–8	7,094	5,736		5,794	5,218		9,157	7,956	
1968–9[b]	7,231	6,108		6,311	5,713		9,418	8,008	

SOURCE: Reports of the Minister of Education of Ontario.

[a]Salaries as reported in the fall of each academic year.
[b]Salaries as of April 1968.

TABLE 6-16
Salaries of elementary and secondary school teachers in the United States, 1955–69

YEAR	AVERAGE SALARY (IN $ US)			PERCENTAGE DISTRIBUTION OF TEACHERS BY SALARY			
	Elementary	Secondary	Total	Under $4,500	$4,500–$5,499	$5,500–$6,499	$6,500 and over
1955–6	3,615	4,194	3,816	77.7	22.3[a]		
1958–9	4,373	4,894	4,571	59.1	40.9		
1959–60	4,607	5,113	4,797	48.7	26.7	15.7	8.9
1960–1	4,815	5,276	4,995	42.5	28.2	17.4	11.9
1961–2	5,075	5,543	5,275	35.2	27.2	19.3	18.3
1962–3	5,340	5,776	5,515	26.6	28.9	22.6	21.9
1963–4	5,560	5,980	5,732	22.0	28.0	23.4	26.6
1964–5	5,805	6,266	5,995	16.9	28.6	24.2	30.4
1965–6	5,985	6,451	6,195	13.5	27.0	24.7	34.8
1966–7	6,279	6,761	6,485	8.8	22.7	26.8	41.7
1967–8	6,622	7,109	6,830	4.4	19.7	26.7	49.2
1968–9	7,077	7,569	7,296	2.3	13.2	24.0	60.5

SOURCE: National Education Association Research Division; Research Report, 1967 – R 19, *Estimates of School Statistics, 1967–8*. Copyright 1967 by the National Education Association. All rights reserved.

[a]Includes salaries of $5,500 and over.

Ontario can be made. The necessary data for Ontario exist, but have been beyond the reach of the present writer because of the resources it would require to tabulate and analyze them. Certain aspects of the situation are nevertheless well enough known to justify a number of observations in the light of the more exact information provided about American teachers in Tables 6-17, 6-18, and 6-19.

Only a relatively small proportion of Ontario elementary school teachers have had university degrees, or indeed any substantial academic credit beyond grade 13. In 1964 and 1967, as shown in Table 6-17, the percentages of American elementary teachers with less than a bachelor's degree, normally obtained after four years of study beyond grade 12, were respectively 15.9 and 10.3. Not only were the great majority holders of the bachelor's degree, but a substantial proportion had the master's degree as well. Thus the Ontario teachers were receiving returns on a much smaller educational investment.

As was true of elementary school teachers, it is also apparent that Ontario secondary school teachers had a generally lower level of education than their American counterparts. Although teachers of academic subjects in Ontario schools were normally required to have degrees, most vocational teachers did not. Table 6-17 indicates that in the United States only 1.5 per cent of all secondary school teachers had less than a bachelor's degree in 1967, and almost one in four had a master's degree. Even if some allowance is made for the fact that an Ontario honours degree rep-

TABLE 6-17

Percentage distribution of public elementary and secondary school classroom teachers in the United States by degrees held, 1964 and 1967

HIGHEST DEGREE HELD	1964			1967				
	Elementary school	Secondary school	TOTAL	Elementary school	Secondary school	Men	Women	TOTAL
No degree	3.8	0.4	2.3	2.4	0.8	0.8	2.1	1.6
2-year degree	12.1	0.6	6.8	7.9	0.7	1.1	6.2	4.5
Bachelor's degree	66.7	62.6	64.8	72.9	63.0	58.3	73.1	68.2
Master's degree	16.6	33.5	24.3	15.7	34.1	38.1	17.6	24.4
Professional degree, 6 years	0.7	2.4	1.5	1.1	1.3	1.5	1.0	1.2
Doctor's degree	0.1	0.4	0.3		0.1	0.2		0.1

SOURCE: National Education Association, Washington, DC; annual National Sample Survey of Classroom Teachers, unpublished data.

resented seventeen years of formal study, and thus should be classed higher than the American four-year degree, it must be recognized that a decreasing proportion of Ontario secondary school teachers had such degrees.

The median ages of American teachers are shown for the same two years in Table 6-18. While the median for elementary school teachers fell from forty-three to thirty-nine during the three-year interval, there is little question that, even in 1967, this figure was considerably higher than that for the Ontario group, which was being augmented year after year by large numbers of young people just one year away from high school. It is certainly not to be doubted that the percentage in Ontario aged twenty-four and under was much higher than the 10 and 14 per cent recorded in the United States in 1964 and 1967 respectively. It stands to reason that those with a greater stake in the profession in terms of professional preparation may be expected to give, on the average, more years of service. Some observers have warned, however, that the effect of this factor on retention is not as great as is generally supposed. It may be predicted, nevertheless, that the average age of elementary school teachers in Ontario will rise as the period of preparation lengthens and as the teaching force requires a smaller proportion of new recruits each year. Other things being equal, the average Ontario salary will rise more quickly than that in the United States.

Secondary school teachers in the United States were, on the average, seven years younger than elementary school teachers in 1964, and five years younger in 1967. It seems a safe deduction that there was a smaller difference in age between American and Ontario teachers at the secondary than at the elementary school level.

The experience factor is dealt with explicitly for American teachers in Table 6-19. Between 1964 and 1967 the median length of experience for elementary school teachers fell from twelve to ten years. In Ontario the unofficial estimate is that the comparable figure was actually under three years in the latter part of the 1960s. With the appearance of a teacher surplus, a change may be anticipated, but it is unlikely that the two situations will be comparable for some time to come. Somewhat similar observations might be made about the secondary school teaching force.

When all factors are considered, it appears that teaching in the public elementary schools in Ontario has been relatively more highly remunerated than in the elementary schools in the United States, despite somewhat lower dollar income. This conclusion does not necessarily mean that a higher value is placed on education in Ontario. A more likely explanation lies in the generally lower level of education in the Ontario population than in that of the United States. Grade 13 graduates with one year's further preparation, and grade 12 graduates with two years, have probably been scarcer in Ontario than college graduates in the United States. The relatively more rapid growth of the school population in Ontario

TABLE 6-18
Percentage distribution of public elementary and secondary school classroom teachers in the United States by age, 1964 and 1967

AGE	1964			1967					
	Elementary school	Secondary school	TOTAL	Elementary school	Secondary school	Men	Women	TOTAL
24 years or less	10.0	11.1	10.5	14.0	16.0	13.1	15.9	15.0
25–29 years	12.4	19.9	15.8	16.1	22.3	25.4	15.8	19.0
30–34 years	11.4	14.9	13.0	9.7	11.9	15.7	8.2	10.7
35–39 years	9.1	13.0	10.9	10.7	9.7	13.1	8.8	10.2
40–49 years	22.4	19.3	21.0	20.8	19.9	20.9	20.2	20.4
50–59 years	25.9	17.7	22.1	20.2	15.5	9.3	22.3	17.9
60 years or more	8.9	4.1	6.7	8.5	4.7	2.5	8.8	6.7
Median years	43	36	39	39	34	33	40	37

SOURCE: National Education Association, Washington, DC; annual National Sample Survey of Classroom Teachers, unpublished data.

TABLE 6-19
Percentage distribution of public elementary and secondary school classroom teachers in the United States by teaching experience, 1964 and 1967

EXPERIENCE	1964			1967				
	Elementary school	Secondary school	TOTAL	Elementary school	Secondary school	Men	Women	TOTAL
1 year	5.8	8.0	6.8	6.2	9.4	8.9	7.1	7.7
2-3 years	11.1	14.5	12.6	14.7	18.7	18.2	15.9	16.6
4-6 years	14.3	18.1	16.1	15.5	18.5	19.5	15.6	16.9
7-9 years	10.1	11.2	10.6	11.7	13.3	16.3	10.5	12.4
10-14 years	15.3	15.8	15.5	17.6	13.7	14.8	16.2	15.7
15-19 years	11.6	11.2	11.4	10.3	10.8	11.7	9.9	10.5
20-29 years	19.4	11.0	15.6	14.3	8.9	5.7	14.7	11.7
30 years or more	12.4	10.1	11.3	9.7	6.7	4.9	10.1	8.3
Median years	12	9	11	10	7	7	10	8

SOURCE: National Education Association, Washington, DC; annual National Sample Survey of Classroom Teachers, unpublished data.

rounds out the explanation. Ultimately supply and demand are the major determinants of the salaries of teachers, as of other groups.

These comments take into account only teachers in public elementary schools in Ontario, which correspond superficially to the group in the United States with which the comparison has been made. But, in fact, the Roman Catholic separate schools, which receive most of their financial sustenance from public funds, are more appropriately considered with the public schools than equated with American parochial schools. When all Ontario elementary school teachers are grouped together, the comparison is much more difficult to interpret in their favour, although, as noted earlier, the difference between the public and separate school teachers has been narrowing rapidly.

ACADEMIC STAFF IN UNIVERSITIES

Those who attended the National Conference on Engineering, Scientific and Technical Manpower at St Andrews-By-The-Sea in 1956 addressed themselves to the need for a tremendous increase in university teaching staff to meet the projected expansion of enrolment. Although they were on the right track, some of their expressions of concern were nevertheless based on a gross underestimate of what would be needed. What was described as the barest minimum requirement, assuming that the proportion of the age group currently enrolled in the universities would remain constant, called for 18,000 more university teachers for the whole of Canada by 1980. A more realistic estimate, which assumed a continuation of the existing rate of increase in university attendance, implied a 350 per cent increase in staff over the same period, or a total of 38,000.[1]

The prospects looked gloomy to B.S. Keirstead, Professor of Economics at the University of Toronto, who appraised the situation during the same year.

It is an economic commonplace that an increase in demand will stimulate an increase in supply by creating a higher price. There is, however, little comfort for the universities in this reflection. In the first place the higher price, or higher reward, offered by industry to Bachelors is the cause of the diminution of graduate students in our graduate schools. Graduate fellowships in the United States have jumped to would-be competitive levels, to $2,500–$3,000 for example, but without stemming the drift from graduate study. I doubt if Canadian universities will be able to offer fellowships of this order. When it comes to raising salaries, so as to be able to compete with government and business in the market for the Ph.D.'s and M.A.'s we must remember that if we can raise our bidding price, so can our competitors and they can always outbid us. After all most of our money comes from our competitors in the labour market. They can quite easily keep us on an allowance which will ensure that we cannot successfully compete with them.[2]

Keirstead did not think there were very good prospects of attracting many people from the United States. Salaries that failed to bring back half the Canadian graduates from American universities seemed hardly likely to attract native Americans. The prospects of inducing migration from the United Kingdom appeared somewhat better, but in some important fields there were serious shortages there too, and the best British scholars preferred to remain in their own universities.

Warnings at the conference in Ottawa at which Keirstead made his comments suggested that a crash program was needed to expand graduate schools. There was, however, very little immediate evidence of a positive response. The number of PhD candidates declined during the following year. Between 1956 and 1962 the number of PhDs granted by Canadian universities in all disciplines increased only from 292 to 321.

In *Post-Secondary Education in Ontario, 1962–1970*,[3] the Committee of Presidents strongly emphasized the need for a more serious effort to expand the graduate schools. The insignificant increase in the number of doctorates granted by Canadian universities during the previous five years represented a slight rise in the humanities and social sciences, practically no change in engineering, and a decrease in the physical and biological sciences. There had been an increase in masters' degrees awarded in all fields, again most noticeably in the humanities and the social sciences. The total for Ontario was estimated at somewhat over one thousand. There were no grounds for complacency in this figure as far as the university staffing problem was concerned when account was taken of the fact that many of them were advanced professional degrees in such fields as social work and business administration, and that the holders were more likely to be recruited for practice than for teaching. The committee recommended a crash program in graduate schools that would approximately double the enrolment in the next few years.

A strong case was made for more financial assistance to graduate students. The presidents declared that, unless available fellowships were very greatly increased, both in value and in number, no sizeable expansion of graduate work could take place. Under existing conditions there was only one Canada Council fellowship for every four excellent applicants, and only half enough National Research Council fellowships for those who merited them. The presidents asked not only for a great increase in fellowships, but also for a special per capita grant to the universities themselves to help cover the extra costs that would have to be met.

The response of the provincial government was to establish an Ontario Graduate Fellowship program, which was hailed as farsighted and generous. It involved the award of fellowships to graduates with a better than average standing who were prepared to enter graduate schools in Ontario with the expectation of a career in university teaching. In 1964–5 there were 5,421 graduate students in Ontario universities, of whom 1,149, or

TABLE 6-20
Number of full-time teaching staff in the provincially assisted universities of Ontario, 1964–9

UNIVERSITY	1964–5	1965–6	1966–7	1967–8	1968–9
Brock	7	25	60	79	94
Carleton	158	187	219	321	367
Guelph	290	220	314	379	455
Lakehead	31	44	89	117	146
Laurentian	49	57	86	110	133
Algoma				11	18
Nipissing				6	10
McMaster	230	293	307	421	472
Ottawa	255	319	369	448	520
Queen's	333	365	449	512	557
Toronto – Main	956	1,034	1,281	1,532	1,776
Erindale		8	4	19	34
Scarborough	14	30	36	71	83
Trent	15	30	54	76	97
Waterloo	215	297	368	448	461
Western	382	442	532	639	695
Windsor	154	165	206	250	296
York	77	124	223	312	471
TOTAL	3,166	3,640	4,597	5,751	6,685

SOURCE: Reports of the Minister of University Affairs of Ontario.

about 21 per cent, were Ontario Graduate Fellows. Of this total 513 were enrolled in PhD courses.

The minister reviewed the projections of supply in relation to future need in the Legislature in February 1965. Assuming a student-faculty ratio of 13.5 to 1, and allowing for some flexibility, he foresaw a need for a total of between 6,800 and 7,000 faculty members by 1970 or 1971.[4] The estimate of graduate enrolment for 1965–6 was 6,726, a number that was expected to double by 1970–1. Davis questioned a suggestion by A.E. Thompson, Leader of the Opposition, that as many as half these might be available for university teaching, but nevertheless felt that the supply would be adequate.[5]

In 1968 the minister referred to the results of the fellowship program with satisfaction.

... the record here speaks for itself. It is one of our most successful ventures. It is no coincidence that the inauguration of this form of graduate assistance and the upsurge and growth of our graduate schools have run parallel courses. Given this well established foundation we can expect that this growth in the graduate area will continue at a pace probably in excess of that of the undergraduate level.[6]

The number of full-time teaching staff in the provincially assisted universities of Ontario between 1964–5 and 1968–9 is shown in Table 6-20.

Over the four-year span, the number rose from 3,166 to 6,685; that is, it more than doubled. In most of the established universities the pattern was similar.

RATIO OF STUDENTS TO STAFF IN UNIVERSITIES
The ratio of students to staff for each provincially assisted university and for all universities combined from 1964–5 to 1968–9 is shown in Table 6-21. By any comparison with other provinces, states, or countries, this ratio has been regarded as very favourable. The opinion has occasionally been expressed in official quarters that the efforts of faculty members might well be stretched a little further in order to help meet the rapidly developing problem of financing higher education. University authorities have been accused of failing to take full advantage of the best methods of instruction and of modern educational media. In view of the provincial government's policy of interfering as little as possible with the autonomy of the universities, the existence of these views has had relatively little influence. From the universities' point of view, any substantial increase in the number of students per faculty member would accentuate the depersonalization of the educational process that has caused so many complaints from students in recent years. The growing proportion of graduate students in the total enrolment has made heavy demands on faculty time. In the struggle to attract outstanding scholars, furthermore, the existence of a favourable student-staff ratio, with its implication for research opportunities, has been a potent selling point. Even if all provincial universities were put in a similar position, there would still be a problem of recruiting from outside. These arguments have not been completely convincing to those who hold the purse strings and, whether desirable or otherwise, it is possible that pressure may build up to persuade the universities to raise the ratio.

A study of Table 6-21 indicates wide variations in student-staff ratio among the universities. Where the ratio has been unusually low, the reason has usually been that the institution concerned has been in an early stage of development, and has necessarily had to maintain many partially filled classes in order to provide a reasonably varied program. Were this the only factor at work, however, one might expect such universities as Brock, Lakehead, Trent, and York to show a steadily rising ratio. Such a development has by no means consistently occurred. Another factor that should generally militate against a high ratio is the existence of a large proportion of graduate students. While Ottawa's low ratio might be explained in this way, it leaves Toronto's relatively high one unaccounted for. Toronto has, of course, received some of the sharpest criticism for maintaining inordinately large classes.

FACULTY SALARIES IN UNIVERSITIES
Information on university faculty salaries has been collected rather casu-

TABLE 6-21
Ratio of students to instructors in each provincially assisted university in Ontario, 1960–9[a]

UNIVERSITY	1964–5	1965–6	1966–7	1967–8	1968–9
Brock	17.7	14.4	8.8	8.8	8.8
Carleton	17.3	16.4	17.0	16.1	16.3
Guelph	6.6	11.0	10.5	11.5	11.3
Lakehead	15.0	18.9	13.3	13.5	13.9
Laurentian	11.3	16.4	13.1	12.1	12.0
Algoma				7.2	16.0
Nipissing				8.3	5.4
McMaster	14.4	12.9	15.1	12.3	13.3
Ottawa	15.0	12.1	11.2	10.9	11.8
Queen's	12.1	12.7	11.4	11.3	12.1
Toronto – Main	15.9	16.1	11.6	12.3	11.5
Erindale				7.9	13.5
Scarborough		6.4	13.9	13.5	17.3
Trent	7.0	9.7	9.5	9.7	11.1
Waterloo	14.6	15.0	15.5	15.6	18.9
Western	13.8	13.3	14.5	13.0	14.1
Windsor	12.9	14.5	13.6	13.3	8.9
York	10.3	12.0	11.9	12.0	12.6
TOTAL	13.7	14.1	13.3	12.6	13.0

[a]Calculated from Reports of the Minister of University Affairs of Ontario.

ally during most of the period under review. Much of the available material comes from agencies such as the Canadian Association of University Teachers and the Ontario Council of University Faculty Associations, which have been interested in improving the financial position of their members.

On November 16, 1965, Stewart Fyfe wrote to the Minister of University Affairs on behalf of the Ontario Council of University Faculty Associations, enclosing certain statistics and making a case for the improvement of faculty salaries.

The demand for university teachers is increasing faster than employment opportunities in other professions because of the rapid growth in university enrolment. To improve the attractiveness of university teaching, university salaries will have to increase faster than those of other professions. Moreover, as the growth in universities is not just an Ontario problem but is a national and international phenomena, Ontario salaries must be competitive with those in other provinces, in the United States and in Great Britain, for university teachers are among the most mobile of all professions. Within Canada, Ontario universities traditionally had the highest salary scales. This is no longer the case. In several provinces, salary scales are significantly above those in Ontario, and in all other provinces with traditionally lower scales, the differential has been greatly reduced. American salary scales are currently increasing by about seven per cent per year, and it is increasingly difficult to recruit staff from British universities because of salary increases there.

A seven per cent annual increase in salary scales would appear to be the absolute minimum required to attract and retain adequate staff in these circumstances. In fact, since 1961 university salaries have been falling behind those of comparable professions.[7]

The reason for approaching the minister was not to propose any direct government intervention, but to point out that the universities' ability to increase salaries rested on the size of government grants. These were not considered large enough to meet the need as estimated by the council.

The statistical analysis that accompanied the letter to the minister reiterated the familiar theme that university academic staffs in Canadian universities had experienced a decline in income position in comparison with the place they had held in the pre-war income structure. What was identified as far more important was that a period of marked improvement had given way to one of retrogression. The technique used to demonstrate these trends was to take 1937–8 as the base year and to show how salaries would have risen subsequently had university staffs benefited to the same extent as the rest of the population from productivity gains, and had their salaries been adjusted to the same extent to compensate for inflation. The actual salary increases for corresponding years were placed next to these theoretical figures, and the difference, which was always to the disadvantage of university salaries, and consequently labeled "shortfall," was placed alongside. Two sets of figures were obtained, one comparing the growth in university salaries with an index of earned income per capita and the other with an index of average wage or salary. According to the first of these comparisons university salaries in 1963–4 were $7,241 less on the average than they would have been had the 1937–8 relative position been maintained, and by the second comparison they were $2,778 less. By these respective estimates, the shortfall was 44 and 23 per cent of actual salaries. What particularly concerned the council was that the corresponding shortfall in 1960–1 had been 42 and 22 per cent by the respective estimates.

Further statistics showed the increase in median salaries of the professorial ranks in Ontario and in all of Canada between 1960–1 and 1963–4 as compared with other occupational groups. The average annual percentage increases for professors, associate professors, assistant professors, and lecturers were respectively 3.5, 3.1, 3.5, and 3.8. The corresponding percentage for all professionals was 5.0; for lawyers and notaries, 5.0; for consulting engineers and architects, 1.8; for medical doctors and surgeons, 5.7; and for wages and salaries, 4.0.

Whether or not the 1937–8 situation represents a reasonable basis for comparison is open to question. Those on fixed salaries are always in an optimum relative position in a period of severe deflation, and tend to fall behind with increasing inflation. A critic might make a case for picking some point midway between the extremes as a base year on the grounds that it is conceivable that university faculty could be overpaid in relation to other groups at certain stages of the cycle. In the complete absence of any objective means of relating university salaries to social contributions or to any quantitative measure of social justice, the main determinant must be supply and demand. Those who organize salary campaigns have often predicted that if salaries did not increase at a specified rate, outstanding people could not be attracted. When this rate has not been achieved, however, there has been no documented evidence that the predicted consequences have materialized. It would admittedly be difficult, if not impossible, for members of a faculty to collect such evidence.

The rapid rise in salaries of secondary school teachers has often been cited as a reason why university salaries should be increased. The brief of the Ontario Council of University Faculty Associations to the Prime Minister of Ontario in 1963 pointed out what could happen.

It is hard to justify the anomalous situation in which a university teacher, usually with a Ph.D., can be receiving at age thirty-six a salary of less than $8,000, whereas a classmate with whom he attended university is receiving at least $9,600 in the Ontario secondary school system. It is also hard to justify a situation where it is possible for a professor to receive a lower salary than his wife is paid as a secondary school teacher (general degree – level 2), both having graduated from university in the same year. These are not isolated examples or exceptional cases.[8]

It is probable that this kind of comparison has been of considerable assistance in making a case for increased university salaries. The school teachers have benefited from the fact that citizenship and certification requirements have given them something approaching a closed shop, while universities have been part of the international market.

In *From the Sixties to the Seventies*,[9] the Presidents' Research Committee observed the difficulty of making a satisfactory appraisal of the salary situation in Ontario because of the incompleteness of the data. Yet it was possible to present some revealing figures. In 1965–6 only 10 per cent of Toronto's full professors, including department heads, received more than $19,000; the top 10 per cent at the same rank received over $18,000 at Queen's, over $18,000 at McMaster, over $17,500 at York, and over $16,000 at Western. For all Ontario universities, only 5 per cent of full professors had salaries over $18,000. The report concluded that the province was not in a position to compete for the very best.

The Canadian Association of University Teachers (CAUT) offered figures making possible comparisons between 1961–2 and 1965–6 for the following Ontario universities: Windsor, Carleton, McMaster, OAC-OVC/Guelph, Ottawa, Queen's, Toronto (except for the federated colleges and the Ontario College of Education), Waterloo, and Waterloo Lutheran. In these universities mean salaries for full professors in 1961–2 ranged

TABLE 6-22
Mean salaries by rank and yearly percentage increases in Ontario universities, 1966-9 (in dollars)

RANK	1966-7	1967-8	PERCENTAGE INCREASE (1966-7 TO 1967-8)	1968-9	PERCENTAGE INCREASE (1967-8 TO 1968-9)
Full professor	16,329	18,154	11.2	$19,556	7.7
Associate professor	12,070	13,350	10.6	14,235	6.6
Assistant professor	9,547	10,533	10.3	11,262	6.9
Next lower rank	7,689	8,397	9.2	9,041	7.7
ALL RANKS	11,433	12,508	9.4	13,576	8.5

SOURCE: *C.A.U.T. Bulletin*, XVII, 3, February 1969, 15-19.

from $9,500 to $13,799, and in 1965-6, from $13,566 to $16,150. For associate professors the corresponding ranges were from $8,150 to $10,121 and from $9,970 to $11,488; and for assistant professors, from $7,000 to $8,000 and from $8,500 to $9,100. The annual increase in average salaries had been in the range of 5 to 6 per cent. Between January 1962 and January 1966 the consumer price index had risen from 129.7 to 141.2.

The CAUT presented a set of fairly detailed figures in February 1969, applying to the current year and the two preceding ones.[10] Between 1966-7 and 1967-8 mean salaries for all ranks rose by 9.4 per cent; for full, associate, and assistant professors and the next lower rank, the respective percentage increases were 11.2, 10.6, 10.3, and 9.2. Between 1967-8 and 1968-9 the over-all percentage increase was 8.5, and for the four respective categories, 7.7, 6.6, 6.9, and 7.7. The fact that the over-all increase was greater than that for any individual rank might reflect promotions or the policy in hiring new staff members. For example, under the first of these two possible explanations, the effect of a large number of promotions to the next higher rank might depress the average salary at that rank and yet represent a relatively large increase for the individuals concerned.

Table 6-23 shows the average salary for all ranks combined at each Ontario university for the four years from 1966-7 to 1969-70. The figures do not take into account differences in average age and experience at various universities, and thus do not justify uncritical direct comparisons. Since some of the newer universities tend to have relatively youthful faculties, they are shown in a less favourable light than the facts warrant. This bias is probably reduced, although not eliminated, in Table 6-24, where mean salaries for each rank are shown for 1968-9.

As indicated in Table 6-24, the increases in the mean salaries for all ranks differed considerably from one university to another during the successive years between 1966-7 to 1967-8 and 1968-9 to 1969-70.

TABLE 6-23
Mean salaries and annual percentage increases for all ranks in each Ontario university, 1966-70 (rounded to the nearest hundred dollars)

UNIVERSITY	MEAN SALARIES				PERCENTAGE INCREASE		
	1966-7	1967-8	1968-9	1969-70	From 1966-7 to 1967-8	From 1967-8 to 1968-9	From 1968-9 to 1969-70
Brock	9,700	10,600	12,000	13,200	9.3	13.2	10.0
Carleton	10,700	11,400	12,700	13,800	6.5	11.4	8.7
Guelph	11,200	11,700	13,100	14,300	4.5	12.0	9.2
Lakehead	9,500	10,400	11,600	12,700	9.5	11.5	9.5
Laurentian	9,100	10,000	11,500	12,500	10.0	15.0	8.7
McMaster	11,800	13,100	14,200	15,700	11.0	8.4	10.6
Ottawa	10,500	11,700	12,500	14,400	11.4	6.8	15.2
Queen's	12,200	13,700	14,600	15,900	12.3	6.6	8.9
RMC	11,800	12,500	13,600	14,400	5.9	8.8	5.9
Toronto	12,700	13,900	14,700	15,900	9.4	5.8	8.2
Trent	10,300	11,400	12,600	14,000	10.7	10.5	11.1
Waterloo	10,700	12,000	13,600	15,500	12.1	13.3	14.0
Waterloo Lutheran	9,200	10,300	11,500	12,100[a]	12.0	11.7	10.5
Western	11,300	12,900	13,800	15,400	14.2	7.0	11.6
Windsor	11,100	12,200	13,400	14,500	9.9	9.8	8.2
York	10,300	11,400	12,500	13,500	10.7	9.6	8.0

SOURCE: *C.A.U.T. Bulletin*, XVII, 3, February 1969, 20, Table 2; *C.A.U.T. Bulletin*, XVIII, 2, Winter 1970, 57, Table 1.

[a]Excluding deans.

TABLE 6-24
Mean salaries by rank in each Ontario university, 1968-9 (in dollars)

UNIVERSITY	FULL PROFESSORS WHO ARE DEPARTMENT HEADS	OTHER FULL PROFESSORS	ALL FULL PROFESSORS	ASSOCIATE PROFESSORS	ASSISTANT PROFESSORS	RANK BELOW ASSISTANT PROFESSORS
Brock	17,629	17,000	17,488	13,420	10,663	8,780
Carleton	18,153	17,750	17,856	13,623	10,744	8,752
Guelph	20,278	18,055	18,865	14,467	11,251	8,980
Lakehead	17,289	16,800	17,138	13,718	11,149	9,056
Laurentian	17,554		17,517	13,669	10,725	8,746
McMaster	19,821	19,203	19,375	14,188	11,481	9,366
Ottawa	19,241	17,084	18,121	13,932	10,744	8,602
Queen's	21,920	18,618	19,687	14,373	11,565	9,778
RMC	21,071	17,768	18,869	13,856	11,770	9,629
Toronto	24,159	20,322	21,024	14,751	11,815	9,202
Trent	18,992	17,617	18,533	13,693	10,369	8,650
Waterloo	21,165	18,718	19,286	13,923	10,780	8,369
Waterloo Lutheran	18,500	17,128	17,750	13,498	10,558	8,438
Western	21,508	19,031	19,711	14,110	11,391	9,346
Windsor	17,795	17,383	17,548	14,368	11,684	9,713
York	19,876	18,829	19,413	13,978	11,298	9,020

SOURCE: *C.A.U.T. Bulletin*, XVII, 3, February 1969, 28-35.

Over the whole period the rates of increase tended to balance out. In 1969–70 the means were highest at the University of Toronto and Queen's. The age levels at these two institutions are relatively high.

The salaries of many university faculty members fail to indicate their real income. There are stipends for summer school teaching and research and fees for outside consulting work, and in some cases a proportion of a research grant is paid directly to the recipient, even though his involvement in the research does not reduce his regular salary. Since these extra benefits are spread very unevenly, and there is very little reliable information about them, it is impossible to get a clear and accurate impression of the financial implications of holding a faculty position.

TEACHERS' COLLEGE INSTRUCTORS

The number of instructors in each of the teachers' colleges for 1951–2, 1955–6, 1960–1, and each subsequent year up to and including 1969–70 is shown in Table 6-25. For the most part the increase has been fairly regular, and has not varied in close relationship to fluctuations in enrolment. Thus in years of very heavy enrolment increase, such as 1968–9, the instructors have had a comparatively difficult time. A temporary decline in staff in certain colleges has tended to accompany the opening of a new college in the same general area. For example, the opening of the college at St Catharines in 1965–6 was accompanied by a reduction in the staff at Hamilton from thirty-two to twenty-seven. The over-all decline between 1968–9 and 1969–70 is accounted for by the incorporation of the Lakehead Teachers' College and the University of Ottawa Teachers' College into Lakehead University and the University of Ottawa respectively.

Table 6-26 shows the ratio of students to instructors in the teachers' colleges for the same years as those given in Table 6-25. Generally speaking, the burden of teaching and supervision has been relatively great. Among the years shown, the situation was at its best in 1967–8, when the ratio was 22.2:1. The figure rose to 28.5:1 in 1968–9, although the situation was still not as bad as in 1955–6 and 1960–1. The lower enrolment produced a noticeable improvement in 1969–70. Variations among colleges were not as great at that time as they had been in some earlier years.

SALARIES OF TEACHERS' COLLEGE INSTRUCTORS

The range between minimum and maximum salaries for teachers' college masters, with the effective dates of change between 1947 and 1969, is shown in Table 6-27. The difference between minimum and maximum has never been very great, nor has it taken the individual master very long to go from one to the other. The revisions have been made at quite regular intervals. There are a number of ways of evaluating the salary situation in the teachers' colleges. Members of university faculties, contemplating the

TABLE 6-25
Number of instructors in Ontario teachers' colleges, 1951–70

TEACHERS' COLLEGE	1951–2	1955–6	1960–1	1961–2	1962–3	1963–4	1964–5	1965–6	1966–7	1967–8	1968–9	1969–70
Hamilton	10	13	30	33	32	32	32	27	31	35	35	35
Lakehead			4	6	7	9	9	10	8	7	8	
Lakeshore			29	32	32	30	30	30	32	36	38	41
London	10	13	32	32	22	22	23	25	26	31	32	29
North Bay	9	10	13	14	14	16	16	15	18	19	18	17
Ottawa	7	10	21	23	23	23	27	27	28	31	34	39
Ottawa, Univ. of	6	6	12	12	12	9	10	10	12	16	16	16
Peterborough	7	9	13	13	14	14	15	15	14	16	16	14
St Catharines								7	8	11	14	16
Stratford	8	11	14	14	14	14	14	14	14	15	16	12
Sudbury						5	5	5	7	10	13	
Toronto	18	25	41	42	40	39	48	48	54	65	69	79
Windsor					13	15	15	15	16	16	16	16
TOTAL	75	97	209	221	223	228	244	248	268	308	325	314

SOURCE: Ontario, Department of Education, *Calendars of the Teachers' Colleges.*

TABLE 6-26
Ratio of students to instructors in Ontario teachers' colleges, 1951–70[a]

TEACHERS' COLLEGE	1951–2	1955–6	1960–1	1961–2	1962–3	1963–4	1964–5	1965–6	1966–7	1967–8	1968–9	1969–70
Hamilton	24.5	32.5	30.3	26.9	23.2	27.5	25.1	23.2	21.8	22.3	29.0	25.8
Lakehead			51.8	38.5	30.7	24.9	26.3	14.1	17.5	26.3	32.5	
Lakeshore			34.1	23.9	19.1	26.9	27.2	25.3	27.2	24.3	31.4	22.5
London	23.6	36.2	31.5	28.4	22.8	26.0	25.3	21.8	23.7	17.9	25.5	24.0
North Bay	15.7	26.6	31.7	30.2	27.3	26.0	25.3	19.2	17.9	18.6	30.3	28.6
Ottawa	26.4	30.4	33.8	29.4	27.5	33.1	30.8	24.7	21.7	24.1	32.3	23.3
Ottawa, Univ. of	25.8	38.0	30.3	29.8	25.2	26.1	21.8	23.0	19.6	19.8	17.5	
Peterborough	18.3	19.7	35.7	30.9	26.4	24.6	21.6	19.5	28.3	22.9	31.3	24.9
St Catharines								31.3	41.6	31.8	32.7	26.3
Stratford	16.1	24.8	32.1	26.9	24.5	25.9	25.4	25.3	26.8	26.4	30.1	23.2
Sudbury						29.4	28.4	31.2	24.3	13.4	12.7	15.1
Toronto	26.9	39.9	29.7	24.4	23.0	31.1	27.6	27.7	28.5	23.2	29.5	22.4
Windsor					38.0	29.8	28.1	20.5	15.8	18.1	26.7	26.2
TOTAL	22.7	32.4	32.2	27.4	24.7	28.1	26.5	23.8	24.4	22.2	28.5	25.1

[a] Calculated from figures contained in the Reports of the Minister of Education of Ontario and Ontario, Department of Education, *Calendars of the Teachers' Colleges.*

TABLE 6-27
Salary scales for teachers' college masters, 1947–69

EFFECTIVE DATE OF REVISIONS	SALARY RANGE Minimum	Maximum	EFFECTIVE DATE OF REVISIONS	SALARY RANGE Minimum	Maximum
1947	3,800	4,600	Sept. 1, 1959	7,500	9,500
April 1, 1949	4,000	5,000	Oct. 1, 1959	7,800	10,000
Jan. 23, 1951	4,000	5,500	April 1, 1960	8,600	11,000
July 24, 1951	4,000	6,000	Sept. 1, 1962	9,000	11,500
Feb. 12, 1953	4,600	6,700	April 1, 1964	10,000	12,500
April 1, 1954	4,900	7,000	Oct. 1, 1965	11,000	13,500
May 5, 1955	5,500	8,000	Oct. 1, 1966	12,000	14,500
Oct. 1, 1956	5,700	8,100	Oct. 1, 1967	12,197	15,445
April 1, 1957	6,600	9,000	Oct. 1, 1968	12,562	16,071
April 1, 1959	7,200	9,500	Oct. 1, 1969	under review	

SOURCE: Ontario, Department of Civil Service – Pay and Classification Standards Section.

CHART 6-5
Numbers of full-time instructors in institutions for technological and trades training and Ryerson Polytechnical Institute, 1960–7

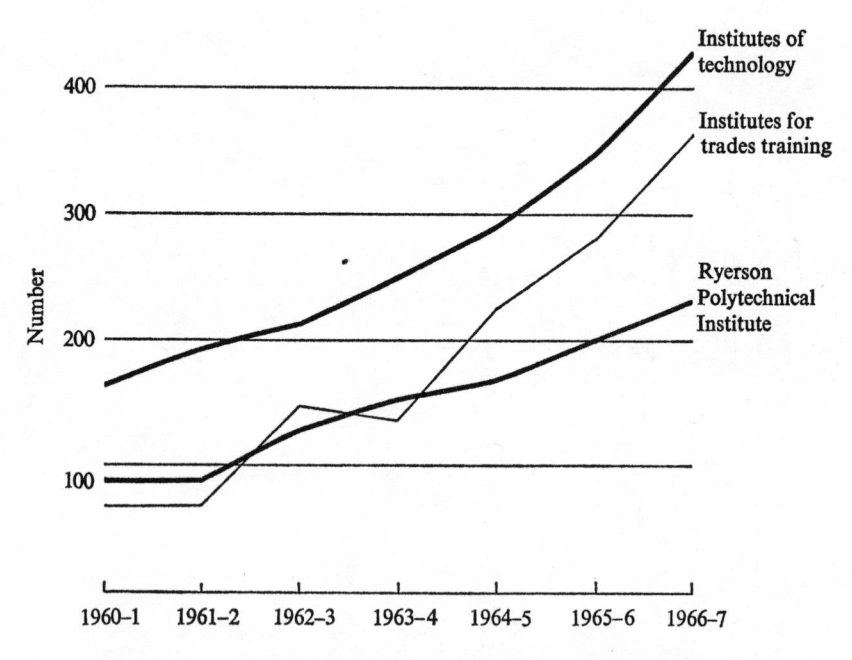

accession of the colleges, have taken the view that the masters are remunerated at a higher level than they themselves when judged by academic qualifications. Such a judgment ignores the much higher student–staff ratio, the longer academic year in all the colleges, and the unattractive facilities in a considerable number of them. Furthermore, if it is considered desirable to establish any movement of people from the

TABLE 6-28
Number of full-time faculty in institutions for technological and trades training supported by the Department of Education, 1960–7

INSTITUTION	1960–1	1961–2	1962–3	1963–4	1964–5	1965–6	1966–7
Ryerson Polytechnical Institute	90	89	130	153	167	201	232
Eastern Ontario Institute of Technology			28	32	42	51	72
Hamilton Institute of Technology			24	25	30	35	43
Northern Ontario Institute of Technology			5	10	17	23	35
Provincial Institute of Mining			7	7	8	9	12
Western Ontario Institute of Technology			18	22	24	27	35
SUBTOTAL	164	191	212	249	288	346	429
Ontario Vocational Centre, London					32	50	70
Ontario Vocational Centre, Ottawa					33	47	59
Ontario Vocational Centre, Sault Ste Marie						29	45
Provincial Institute of Automotive and Allied Trades			39	40	42	39	43
Provincial Institute of Trades	68	68	96	83	100	93	110
Provincial Institute of Trades and Occupations	68	68	12	13	17	22	36
SUBTOTAL			147	136	224	280	363
TOTAL	232	259	359	385	512	626	792

SOURCE: Reports of the Minister of Education of Ontario.

TABLE 6-29
Number of part-time faculty in institutions for technological and trades training supported by the Department of Education, 1960–7

INSTITUTION	1960–1	1961–2	1962–3	1963–4	1964–5	1965–6	1966–7
Ryerson Polytechnical Institute	8	16	29	31	48	50	80
Eastern Ontario Institute of Technology			3	3		1	1
Hamilton Institute of Technology			2	2			
Northern Ontario Institute of Technology					3	6	5
Provincial Institute of Mining					1	1	1
Western Ontario Institute of Technology			2	2	1		6
SUBTOTAL	23	32	36	38	53	58	93
Ontario Vocational Centre, London					2	3	39
Ontario Vocational Centre, Ottawa							
Ontario Vocational Centre, Sault Ste Marie						2	5
Provincial Institute of Automotive and Allied Trades							
Provincial Institute of Trades						7	17
Provincial Institute of Trades and Occupations					2	12	61
SUBTOTAL					2		
TOTAL	23	32	36	38	55	70	154

SOURCE: Reports of the Minister of Education of Ontario.

TABLE 6-30
Number of faculty in colleges of applied arts and technology, 1967–70

COLLEGE	1967–8	1968–9	1969–70 Male	Female	TOTAL
Algonquin	164	211	269	60	329
Cambrian	93	132	175	16	191
Centennial	64	146			
Conestoga		55	75	25	100
Confederation	18	25	65	9	74
Durham	14	35	48	3	51
Fanshawe	91	129	118	15	133
George Brown		185	104	10	114
Georgian	9	29	36	9	45
Humber	30	178	119	31	150
Lambton	26	49	53	6	59
Loyalist	15	44	118	23	141
Mohawk	86	118	52	8	60
Niagara	33	99	86	18	104
Northern	62	63	81	5	86
St Clair	45	61	87	13	100
St Lawrence	25	70	108	30	138
Seneca	66	136	66	20	86
Sheridan	34	75	80	18	98
Sir Sandford Fleming	23	55	71	13	84
TOTAL	898	1,895	1,811	332	2,143

SOURCE: Colleges of Applied Arts and Technology, Finance Department.

higher administrative positions in the local school systems to teaching positions in the colleges, it is obvious that salaries in the latter are not sufficiently high, or at least not sufficiently flexible, to encourage such a flow.

INSTRUCTORS IN INSTITUTIONS FOR TECHNOLOGICAL AND TRADES TRAINING

The numbers and distribution of instructors in institutions for technological and trades training, of which all but Ryerson had been absorbed in the colleges of applied arts and technology by 1968–9, are shown in Table 6-28. The total number in all these institutions increased from 232 in 1960–1 to 792 in 1966–7, that is, by 241.4 per cent. The percentage increase during that period in institutes of technology, including Ryerson, was 161.6, and in institutions for trades training, 433.8 per cent. Ryerson's percentage of the total number of instructors in institutes of technology declined from 61.3 in 1962–3 to 54.1 in 1966–7. Among the institutes for trades training, the Provincial Institute of Trades in Toronto had much the largest number, although rapid increases occurred in the Ontario Vocational Centres at London and Ottawa during the brief period of their separate existence.

The number of part-time instructors in these institutions is shown in

Table 6-29. In 1960–1 these constituted 9.9 per cent of the total of full-time instructors, and by 1966–7, 19.4 per cent. During the latter year the corresponding percentage for institutes of technology was 21.7, and for institutions for trades training, 16.8.

INSTRUCTORS IN COLLEGES OF APPLIED ARTS
AND TECHNOLOGY

Table 6-30 shows the number of instructors in colleges of applied arts and technology for 1967–8, 1968–9, and 1969–70. The sex classification was available only for the last of these three years. The numerical increase between 1967–8 and 1968–9 was 997, and the percentage increase, 110. The corresponding numerical increase for the next year was 248, and the percentage increase, 13.7. The percentage of male staff members in 1969–70 was 84.5.

SEVEN

The financing of education

ONTARIO'S ECONOMIC GROWTH

Ontario's ability to finance education, as well as other benefits, is closely related to the gross provincial product. Table 7-1 shows the figures for 1945 to 1969 in current dollars, and for 1945 to 1968 in constant dollar values on a 1949 base. Annual changes in dollar amounts were positive throughout the period except between 1945 and 1946. The percentage increase in current dollar values was 487.5 between 1945 and 1968, and in constant dollar values, 172.6 between the same years. For five-year intervals the percentages of increase in current dollar values were as follows: 1945–50, 47.9; 1950–5, 57.7; 1955–60, 35.7; 1960–5, 42.8. The comparable increase between 1965 and 1968 was 30.0 per cent, and between 1965 and 1969, 34.6 per cent.

Ontario's rate of growth can be compared with that of Canada as a whole by referring to the figures in Table 7-2, which gives the amount and rate of change in the Canadian gross national product for successive years from 1945 on. The approximate percentage increase in the rate of change between 1945 and 1968 was 505.1, and, in terms of constant dollars, 175.6. For five-year intervals the percentage increases in current dollar values were as follows: 1945–50, 52.5; 1950–5, 55.0; 1955–60, 35.5; 1960–5, 45.2. The comparable percentage for 1965–8 was 30.1. The percentage increases in constant dollar values were as follows: 1945–50, 12.8; 1950–5, 30.7; 1955–60, 22.2; 1960–5, 32.0; 1965–8, 15.9.

PROVINCIAL REVENUE

The amount of funds available to the provincial government during the post-war period has increased dramatically. The Ontario Committee on Taxation pointed out that, despite constitutional provisions limiting the government to direct taxation within the province, "flexible interpretations and official ingenuity have managed to devise a variety of taxes designed to generate revenues sufficient to meet expenditure programs." While considerable allowance must be made for inflationary reductions in the value of the dollar, there has been a very evident trend toward increasing public disposal of personal income. Only such a trend could have made possible the extraordinary recent expansion of educational facilities.

Taking the estimates made by the Treasurer of Ontario in his Budget

TABLE 7-1
Ontario gross provincial product, 1945–69[a]

YEAR	CURRENT DOLLARS IN BILLIONS	ANNUAL CHANGE (PER CENT)	CONSTANT DOLLARS IN BILLIONS 1949 = 100	ANNUAL CHANGE (PER CENT)
1945	4.8		6.2	
1946	4.6	−3.8	5.8	−6.6
1947	5.1	12.2	6.0	2.3
1948	5.8	13.1	6.1	1.7
1949	6.3	8.9	6.3	4.1
1950	7.1	11.8	6.9	9.8
1951	8.1	14.6	7.1	2.6
1952	9.3	15.0	7.9	10.4
1953	10.0	6.7	8.4	6.7
1954	10.1	1.9	8.4	0.2
1955	11.2	10.3	9.2	9.6
1956	12.4	10.5	9.8	6.8
1957	13.2	7.2	10.4	5.6
1958	13.8	4.0	10.6	1.9
1959	14.7	6.9	11.1	4.6
1960	15.2	3.1	11.3	1.9
1961	15.7	3.7	11.6	3.1
1962	16.8	6.5	12.2	5.0
1963	18.1	7.9	13.0	5.8
1964	19.9	10.0	13.9	7.5
1965	21.7	8.9	14.7	5.2
1966	24.2	11.6	15.6	6.7
1967	26.0	7.6	16.3	4.0
1968	28.2	8.0	16.9	4.0
1969	29.2	7.8		

[a]Calculated from System of National Accounts, *National Income and Expenditure Account, 1926–1968*, August 1969, DBS, National Income and Expenditure Division; *Ontario Statistical Review, 1968*, Economic Analysis Branch, Economic and Statistical Services Division, Department of Treasury and Economics, June 1969; Ontario, Department of Treasury and Economics. Percentages calculated on exact amounts.

Address of 1970, net general revenue in 1970–1 was nearly twenty-six times as great as in 1945–6. Although there was continuous growth throughout the period, most of the increase in absolute terms was in the 1960s. Net general revenue in 1970–1 was over five times that in 1960–1. It is evident that the province found the means of financing a substantial increase in services.

Provincial net general revenue for five-year intervals from the end of the Second World War to 1960–1 and for individual years thereafter is shown in Table 7-3. Net general revenue is derived directly from the provincial revenue system, and is obtained by combining net ordinary revenue and net capital receipts from physical assets. It includes funds from such taxation sources as the Income Tax Collection Agreement with the federal government, the retail sales tax, corporation taxes, the gasoline tax, the succession duty, a share of the federal estate tax, the motor vehicle fuel tax, the tobacco tax, the race tracks tax, the tax on mines profits,

TABLE 7-2

Canadian gross national product, 1945–68[a]

YEAR	CURRENT DOLLARS IN BILLIONS	ANNUAL CHANGE (PER CENT)	CONSTANT DOLLARS IN BILLIONS 1949 = 100	ANNUAL CHANGE (PER CENT)
1945	11.8		15.6	
1946	11.9	0.2	15.2	−2.7
1947	13.2	10.8	15.4	1.8
1948	15.1	14.9	15.8	2.5
1949	16.3	7.8	16.3	3.0
1950	18.0	10.2	17.6	8.1
1951	21.1	17.3	18.5	5.0
1952	24.0	14.2	20.3	9.6
1953	25.3	5.3	21.4	5.3
1954	25.2	−0.4	20.9	−2.0
1955	27.9	10.5	23.0	9.9
1956	31.4	12.5	25.0	8.7
1957	32.9	4.9	25.7	2.8
1958	34.1	3.6	26.2	2.2
1959	36.3	6.4	27.3	4.1
1960	37.8	4.2	28.1	2.9
1961	39.1	3.4	28.9	2.8
1962	42.4	8.4	30.9	6.9
1963	45.5	7.3	32.6	5.3
1964	49.8	9.5	34.8	6.9
1965	54.9	10.3	37.1	6.6
1966	61.4	11.9	39.7	7.0
1967	65.6	6.8	41.0	3.3
1968	71.4	8.9	43.0	4.8

[a]Calculated from System of National Accounts, *National Income and Expenditure Account, 1926–1968*, August 1969, DBS, National Income and Expenditure Division; *Ontario Statistical Review, 1968*, Economic Analysis Branch, Economic and Statistical Services Division, Department of Treasury and Economics, June 1969; Ontario, Department of Treasury and Economics. Percentages calculated on exact amounts.

acreage, and gas, the land transfer tax, the hospitals tax, the security transfers tax, the logging tax, and others. The first four in the list have been by far the most lucrative in recent years. The nature of some of the major revenue sources and the advantages and disadvantages of raising funds from them are discussed in volume II, chapter 9. In addition to taxation, revenues are obtained from other sources such as the Liquor Control Board of Ontario, post-secondary education adjustment payments from the federal government, and income from various departments of the provincial government. It was estimated in the Treasurer's Budget Address of 1969 that income from these non-tax sources would constitute slightly over 20 per cent of total net general revenue.

The chief sources of provincial revenues are given individually in Table 7-4 for the years 1962–3 to 1970–1. At the beginning of that period corporation taxes were the chief revenue producer, followed in succession by the retail sales tax, the gasoline tax, and income tax. By 1965–6 income tax was at the head of the list, followed by corporation taxes, the gasoline

CHART 7-1
Gross provincial product in Ontario and gross national product in Canada in current and constant dollars, 1945–69

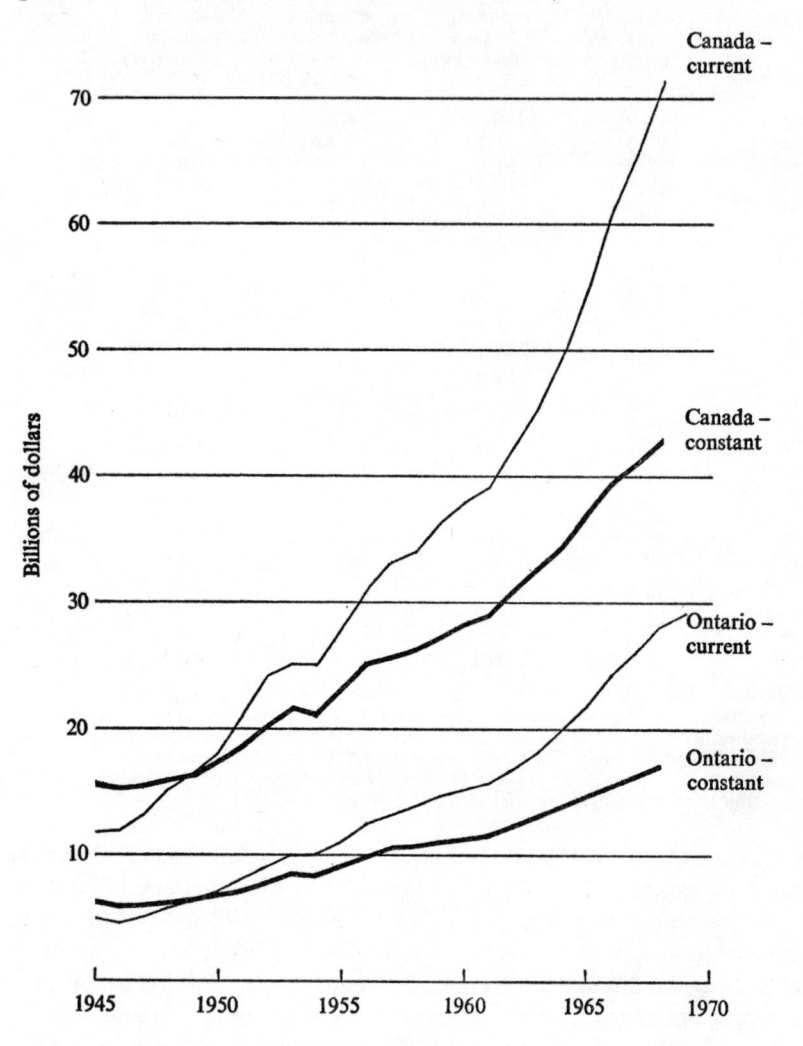

tax, and the retail sales tax. According to the estimates for 1970–1, the retail sales tax was in second place. Revenue from the Liquor Control Board of Ontario was consistently in fifth place. Federal payments for post-secondary education made a rapidly increasing contribution beginning in 1967–8.

Table 7-6 shows the payments made by the federal government to the Ontario government under various educational assistance programs from 1960 to 1966. The conditions under which these were made are dealt with in volume II, chapter 11. The very large increase from approximately

TABLE 7-3

Net general revenue of government of Ontario, 1945–71

YEAR	NET GENERAL REVENUE (IN $ MILLIONS)	YEAR	NET GENERAL REVENUE (IN $ MILLIONS)
1945–6	128	1964–5	1,239
1950–1	265	1965–6	1,444
1955–6	428	1966–7	1,811
1960–1	742	1967–8	2,158
1961–2	827	1968–9	2,604
1962–3	993	1969–70[a]	3,292
1963–4	1,079	1970–1[b]	3,739

SOURCE: Public Accounts of the Province of Ontario for the Fiscal Year Ended 31st March (Toronto: Queen's Printer); Budget Statements of the Treasurer of Ontario, 1970.

[a]Interim, as reported in the Treasurer's Budget Address, 1970.
[b]Estimate.

$12.5 million in 1962 to over $127 million in 1963 resulted from the coming into effect of the federal-provincial agreement under the *Technical and Vocational Training Assistance Act*, passed in 1960. Subsequent payments affecting schools declined after the great rush of technical and vocational construction subsided, but payments for the maintenance of various other programs continued for the most part to rise. The agreement expired in 1967, and the federal government assumed responsibility for making direct payments to individuals and educational agencies under the *Adult Occupational Training Act*. In the same year the federal government abandoned direct subsidies to the universities and began to make post-secondary education adjustment payments to the provinces. Under this arrangement Ontario received about $19.5 million in 1967–8. In the Treasurer's Budget Address in 1969, receipts for 1968–9 were estimated on the basis of interim reports at $83 million, but actually reached $117.3 million. The estimate for 1969–70 was $147 million, which was to include $30 million relating to 1967–8 spending. The Budget Address for 1970–1 indicated actual payments of only $104 million for 1969–70; the estimate for 1970–1 at that time was $150 million.

The financial contributions of the federal government to Ontario and to Canada as a whole for individual programs under the *Technical and Vocational Training Assistance Act* from 1961–2 to 1966–7 are shown in Tables 7-7 and 7-8 respectively. The purposes of these programs are stated briefly in chapter 5 of the present volume and explained more fully in volume II, chapter 11.

Throughout the period Program 5 absorbed the largest share of the funds as far as Ontario was concerned. It constituted the following percentages of the total granted during the successive years between 1961–2

TABLE 7-4
Ontario government net general revenue by major sources, 1962–71 (in thousands of dollars)

SOURCE	1962-3	1963-4	1964-5	1965-6	1966-7	1967-8	1968-9	1969-70[a]	1970-1[b]
Taxation									
Income tax collection agreement	151,844	164,370	195,842	292,404	393,837	551,004	620,476	762,000	948,000
Retail sales tax	175,715	186,535	195,299	220,998	385,575	435,666	485,588	636,900	679,000
Corporation taxes	185,718	209,672	232,543	252,376	274,500	302,273	332,964	480,000	457,000
Gasoline tax	173,136	183,649	221,189	236,829	266,391	283,221	337,284	358,000	376,000
Succession duty	44,149	44,121	48,682	56,968	57,913	59,638	68,472	72,000	72,500
Share of federal estate tax			15,116	16,838	19,743	20,628	21,677	26,800	26,000
Motor vehicle fuel tax	8,204	9,390	12,007	14,678	18,196	21,527	26,298	29,700	33,000
Tobacco tax				2,002	18,553	18,983	54,220	70,600	72,000
Other taxation	39,837	38,304	45,974	52,519	52,826	64,076	80,402	82,200	93,800
Total taxation	778,603	836,041	966,652	1,145,612	1,487,534	1,757,016	2,027,381	2,518,200	2,757,300
Other revenue									
LCBO	87,500	97,100	113,000	125,200	133,700	149,142	192,577	182,000	192,400
Other	127,509	145,995	159,329	173,434	190,035	251,794	384,428	591,800	789,600
Total other revenue	215,009	243,095	272,329	298,634	323,735	400,936	577,005	773,800	982,000
Total net general revenue	993,612	1,079,136	1,238,981	1,444,246	1,811,269	2,157,952	2,604,386	3,292,000	3,739,300
Post-secondary education adjustment payment						19,479	117,296	104,000	150,000

SOURCE: Ontario Budgets, 1968 and 1970.

[a] Interim.
[b] Estimate.

TABLE 7-5

Major sources of Ontario government net general revenue as percentages of total, 1962-71

SOURCE	1962-3	1963-4	1964-5	1965-6	1966-7	1967-8	1968-9	1969-70[a]	1970-1[b]
Taxation									
Income tax collection agreement	15.3	15.2	15.8	20.3	21.7	25.5	23.8	23.1	25.4
Retail sales tax	17.7	17.3	15.8	15.3	21.3	20.2	18.6	19.3	18.2
Corporation taxes	18.7	19.5	18.7	17.6	15.2	14.0	12.8	14.6	12.2
Gasoline tax	17.5	17.0	17.9	16.4	14.7	13.2	13.0	10.9	10.0
Succession duty	4.4	4.1	3.9	3.9	3.2	2.7	2.6	2.2	1.9
Share of federal estate tax			1.2	1.2	1.1	1.0	0.8	0.8	0.7
Motor vehicle fuel tax	0.8	0.9	1.0	1.0*	1.0	1.0	1.0	0.9	0.9
Tobacco tax						0.9	2.1	2.2	1.9
Other taxation	4.0	3.5	3.7	3.6	2.9	3.0	3.1	2.5	2.5
Total taxation	78.4	77.5	78.0	79.3	82.1	81.5	77.8	76.5	73.7
Other revenue									
LCBO	8.8	9.0	9.1	8.7	7.4	6.9	7.4	5.5	5.1
Other	12.8	13.5	12.9	12.0	10.5	11.6	14.8	18.0	21.2
Total other revenue	21.6	22.5	22.0	20.7	17.9	18.5	22.2	23.5	26.3
Total net general revenue	100.0	100.0	100.0	100.0	100.0	100.0	100.0	100.0	100.0

SOURCE: Ontario Budgets, 1968 and 1970.

*Negligible.

[a]Interim.
[b]Estimate.

TABLE 7-6
Payments made by the federal government to Ontario for education, 1960–6 (in thousands of dollars)

TYPE OF EDUCATION	1960	1961	1962	1963	1964	1965	1966
Technical and vocational training – total	3,062	3,292	11,930	126,631	69,188	27,732	54,638
Capital assistance to trade schools, etc.				119,357	59,350	16,140	31,398
Vocational high school training				841	841	538	1,144
Technician training				948	857	1,142	1,283
Occupational training				544	940	1,374	3,819
Apprenticeship training				626	734	200	273
Assistance to students				100	100	100	100
Training of unemployed workers				3,928	6,118	7,954	16,021
Training of disabled persons				215	220	249	373
Other				72	28	35	227
Citizenship and language instruction for immigrants	198	184	193	180	187	190	230
Other training					46	43	
Schools operated by municipal authorities	112	234	423	355	217	457	501
TOTAL	3,372	3,710	12,546	127,166	69,638	28,422	55,369

SOURCE: *Canada Year Book: Official Statistical Annual of the Resources, History, Institutions, and Social and Economic Conditions of Canada* (Dominion Bureau of Statistics, Canada Year Book Division).

TABLE 7-7

Federal financial contributions to training in Ontario under the *Technical and Vocational Training Assistance Act*, by program, 1961–7 (in dollars)

PROGRAM NO.	1961-2[a]	1962-3	1963-4	1964-5	1965-6	1966-7
1	823,800	841,000	841,000	537,952	1,144,048	684,634
2	258,232	947,974	856,565	1,142,307	1,283,754	1,520,345
3	292,512	544,157	940,586	1,373,492	3,819,058	4,116,410
4	2,458	162	6,226	1,260	148,038	271,120
5	936,390	3,927,656	6,117,780	7,953,196	16,005,145	31,493,379
6	192,954	214,989	220,340	248,660	373,138	304,314
7	129,795	62,435	13,400	33,943	36,763	525,920
8	4,159	4,810	8,549		43,537	6,209
9	100,000	100,000	100,000	100,000	100,000	100,000
10						91,155
Apprenticeship	565,005	626,273	733,679	200,152	272,945	544,711
TOTAL	3,305,305	7,269,456	9,838,125	11,590,962	23,226,426	39,658,197

SOURCE: Annual reports of the federal Department of Labour.

[a]Each year extends from April 1 to March 31 of the following year.

TABLE 7-8
Federal financial contributions to training in Canada under the *Technical and Vocational Training Assistance Act*, by program, 1961–7 (in dollars)

PROGRAM NO.	1961–2[a]	1962–3	1963–4	1964–5	1965–6	1966–7
1	1,964,730	1,930,000	2,765,435	3,575,000	2,278,257	1,626,106
2	3,351,896	6,794,211	7,064,083	10,238,560	3,934,113	4,128,901
3[b]	5,429,502	8,172,691	10,288,190	14,028,189	15,383,600	18,731,282
4	31,177	56,478	88,017	329,074	629,380	1,194,025
5	3,941,585	7,751,223	10,492,333	13,600,000	23,979,351	54,232,229
6	368,186	748,602	604,996	655,000	799,895	818,703
7	212,641	232,943	380,503	614,609	429,243	1,081,921
8	26,833	69,246	58,827	61,922	73,452	114,474
9	332,254	319,055	315,653	290,750	194,961	204,239
10						114,071
Apprenticeship	2,160,854	2,172,146	2,334,891	694,879	920,106	1,174,175
TOTAL	17,819,658	28,246,595	34,392,928	44,087,983	48,622,358	83,420,126

SOURCE: Annual reports of the federal Department of Labour.

[a] Each year extends from April 1 to March 31 of the following year.
[b] From 1964–5 on, contributions for classroom training of apprentices was included under Program 3.

and 1966–7: 28.3, 54.0, 62.2, 68.6, 68.9, and 79.4. Program I accounted for a relatively high proportion of the total only during the first three years. During the later years Program 3 took the second highest proportion of the funds; the percentages for the six years were 8.8, 7.5, 9.6, 11.8, 16.4, and 10.4 respectively. For Canada as a whole it was not until 1965–6 that Program 5 forged ahead of the others in terms of costs. Its percentages of the whole for the respective six years were 22.1, 27.4, 30.5, 30.8, 49.3, and 65.0. During the same period the percentages of the total devoted to Program 3 were 30.5, 28.9, 29.9, 31.8, 31.6, and 22.5. For all programs considered together, Ontario's share rose from 18.5 per cent in 1961–2 to 47.5 per cent in 1966–7.

DEBT

Provincial
Throughout the post-war period the provincial government has maintained relatively cautious fiscal policies. Premier Frost, who acted as Provincial Treasurer from 1944 to 1955, and again in 1958, took pride in announcing that his last budget was intended to produce the sixteenth consecutive surplus on ordinary account. The capital construction program for 1957–8 was expected to amount to $215.7 million, but over half of it was being paid for out of current revenues. While net debt had risen, Frost pointed out that production, personal income, and revenues had increased much more quickly. In 1944 net debt constituted 14.4 per cent of the total personal income of the population, as compared with 9.4 per cent in 1958.

As shown in Table 7-9, total net debt rose quite slowly from 1960–1 on. There was no substantial increase in per capita net debt between 1961–2 and 1967–8, even in dollar values. Despite an increase to $214.34 in 1968–9, the percentage of average personal income was well below 9 per cent. An actual decline to $206.05 was projected for 1970–1 in the bud-

TABLE 7-9

Total and per capita net provincial debt, 1944–70

YEAR	TOTAL NET DEBT (IN $ MILLIONS)	PER CAPITA NET DEBT (IN $)	YEAR	TOTAL NET DEBT (IN $ MILLIONS)	PER CAPITA NET DEBT (IN $)
1944–5	482.7	120.85	1964–5	1,365.3	202.00
1949–50	510.0	114.46	1965–6	1,380.5	199.09
1954–5	660.7	126.07	1966–7	1,360.5	191.22
1960–1	1,092.6	175.83	1967–8	1,450.5	199.16
1961–2	1,209.1	191.01	1968–9	1,591.5	214.34
1962–3	1,284.1	198.65	1969–70[a]	1,566.0	206.05
1963–4	1,344.7	203.53			

SOURCE: Ontario Budget, 1969, Table c11.

[a]Estimate.

TABLE 7-10
Net public debt of the government of Canada, 1946–69

YEAR	NET DEBT (IN $ MILLIONS)	NET DEBT AS PERCENTAGE OF GNP[a]	YEAR	NET DEBT (IN $ MILLIONS)	NET DEBT AS PERCENTAGE OF GNP[a]
1946	13,421	113.4	1964	15,070	34.7
1950	11,645	71.3	1965	15,504	32.7
1956	11,280	41.6	1966	15,543	29.8
1960	12,089	34.6	1967	15,965	27.4
1961	12,437	34.3	1968	16,760	27.0
1962	13,228	35.3	1969[b]	17,326	25.7
1963	13,920	34.3			

SOURCE: *The National Finances, an Analysis of the Revenues and Expenditures of the Government of Canada, 1969–70*, Canadian Tax Foundation (Toronto, 1969).

[a]Based on gross national product for the calendar year ended in the fiscal year.
[b]Preliminary.

get for that year. The Treasurer, Charles MacNaughton, announced in 1969 that the government would continue to avoid borrowing as a major means of meeting its financial obligations. In his subsequent Budget Address in March 1970 he repeated the same resolution in very similar words.

Federal
In the late 1940s and in the 1950s the Canadian government kept the absolute debt level fairly constant, as shown in Table 7-10. The fact that Ontario was unable to avoid substantial increases, although they were well within the province's capacity to handle, was often cited to show that the federal government was in a substantially better position to meet its obligations. Despite the gradual increase in federal debt in the 1960s, the amount constituted a steadily declining percentage of the gross national product.

PROVINCIAL EXPENDITURE FOR EDUCATION
There was a very marked increase not only in the total amount of provincial expenditure on education, but also, up to the 1970s, in the proportion of the provincial budget devoted to that purpose. In 1950–1 net ordinary expenditure by the Department of Education amounted to $51.8 million out of a total of $249.8 million, or a little more than one-fifth of the total. In 1955–6 the corresponding amounts were $91.1 million and $424.5 million, and in 1960–1, $209.1 million and $739.0 million. Table 7-11 shows net general expenditure of the various departments and units of the provincial government for 1964–71. Although the figures are not strictly comparable with those given for the earlier years, the same general trend can be followed. In 1964–5 the Departments of Education and University Affairs spent 32.9 per cent of the total for all departments and

TABLE 7-11
Net general expenditure by ministerial responsibility in Ontario government, 1964–71 (in thousands of dollars)

DEPARTMENT	1964–5	1965–6	1966–7	1967–8	1968–9	1969–70[a]	1970–1[b]
Education	416,853	437,124	554,839	691,814	806,928	974,845	1,102,437
Highways	299,036	336,147	390,568	423,026	438,641	453,679	490,854
Health	154,601	164,045	226,544	329,588	387,418	567,715	677,872
University Affairs	233	75,980	107,422	216,858	284,897	358,884	424,307
Municipal Affairs	41,547	46,817	50,197	69,654	186,154	206,653	243,174
Social and Family Services	69,170	84,843	82,121	93,247	112,707	116,333	133,781
Public Debt – interest	62,441	63,175	62,022	64,163	72,293	71,581	74,799
Public Works	50,775	49,568	63,062	68,856	82,116	83,854	98,823
Justice	34,166	39,424	46,830	64,091	86,576	99,678	105,130
Lands and Forests	30,230	33,377	43,589	51,879	60,176	63,511	67,729
Treasury and Economics	19,978	24,514	28,342	34,905	39,401	48,561	66,867
Agriculture and Food	20,482	24,699	30,815	36,401	42,795	49,737	53,135
Correctional Services	16,884	19,499	25,400	31,541	42,745	48,154	48,029
Energy and Resources Management	11,470	11,078	16,415	19,478	24,029	26,265	30,404
Trade and Development	9,857	7,258	14,023	12,415	13,628	21,397	27,453
Labour	5,087	6,885	9,752	9,811	12,280	14,043	15,777
Transport	7,208	8,005	9,135	10,623	12,013	13,093	14,054
Tourism and Information	5,003	6,138	9,017	11,532	11,447	13,719	12,850
Provincial Secretary and Citizenship	5,180	5,696	5,420	5,894	6,168	7,993	8,506
Mines	3,545	3,944	3,312	3,810	5,105	6,892	9,865
Financial and Commercial Affairs			1,969	3,355	3,908	4,281	4,700
Civil Service	1,013	1,189	1,443	1,692	2,196	2,631	2,820
Provincial Auditor	534	548	657	755	850	812	979
Prime Minister	215	236	256	300	357	398	384
Lieutenant Governor	26	47	32	33	35	39	40
Treasury Board			486	747	1,003	1,536	2,010
Revenue		5,962	7,461	8,232	9,504	10,225	11,239
Total	1,265,534	1,456,198	1,791,129	2,264,700	2,745,370	3,266,509	3,728,018

SOURCE: Ontario Budgets, 1968 and 1970.

[a]Interim.
[b]Estimate.

318 The expansion of the educational system

CHART 7-2
Net general expenditure by ministerial responsibility in selected departments of the Ontario government, 1964–71

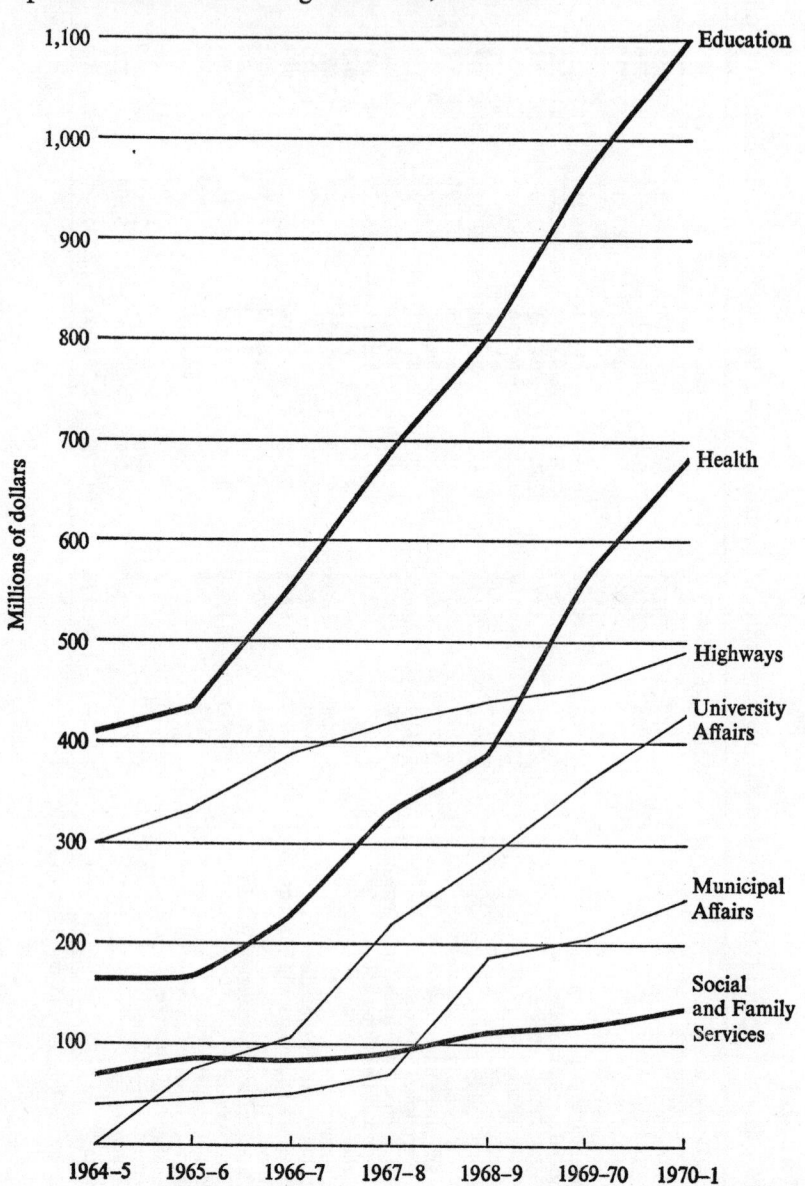

TABLE 7-12
Percentage of total net general expenditure spent by the
Departments of Education and University Affairs, 1964–71

YEAR	DEPARTMENT OF EDUCATION	DEPARTMENT OF UNIVERSITY AFFAIRS	BOTH DEPARTMENTS
1964–5	32.9	*	32.9
1965–6	30.0	5.2	35.2
1966–7	31.0	6.0	37.0
1967–8	30.5	9.6	40.1
1968–9	29.4	10.4	39.8
1969–70[a]	29.8	11.0	40.8
1970–1[b]	29.6	11.4	41.0

SOURCE: Ontario Budget, 1970.
*Negligible.
[a]Interim.
[b]Estimate.

units, a figure which includes provision for the sinking fund. The corresponding percentages for the six subsequent years were 35.2, 37.0 40.1, 39.8, 40.8, and 41.0. Chart 7-2 shows the relative rate of increase in six of the departments that spend comparatively large amounts. The sharp upward trend in Education and University Affairs stands out from that in Highways and Social and Family Services, and to a lesser extent from that in Health and Municipal Affairs.

Table 7-12 is designed simply to emphasize the rising proportion of total net general expenditure handled by the Departments of Education and University Affairs. Percentages are given separately and in combination for the two departments for 1964–5 to 1970–1.

Net general expenditure by the Department of Education in major categories for the years 1965–6 to 1970–1 is shown in Table 7-13. The figures given for 1969–70 are based on interim calculations made for the 1970 Budget Address, and those for 1970–1 are estimates. The amount of assistance to school boards for each year differs from the total general legislative grant given in Table 7-17, since it applies to the budget year while the general legislative grant applies to the calendar year. For the six years referred to in the table, the percentages of funds spent on assistance to school boards amounted respectively to 77.1, 71.1, 71.1, 70.2, 73.1, and 73.9. The item that showed the fastest relative growth in the six-year period was expenditure for technical and technological institutions, where the respective percentages of the total were 1.9, 4.6, 5.5, 6.7, 7.0, and 8.1. The assumption of financial responsibility for the new network of colleges of applied arts and technology accounts for this increase. Under "other" are included the costs of operating the Department of Education itself, and of providing for the services discussed in volume II, chapter 2. This category accounted for 7.1 per cent of the cost in 1965–6, and, according to estimates, for 8.2 per cent in 1970–1.

TABLE 7-13
Net general expenditure by the Ontario Department of Education on various items, 1965–71 (in thousands of dollars)

ITEM OF EXPENDITURE	1965–6	1966–7	1967–8	1968–9	1969–70[a]	1970–1[b]
Assistance to school boards	336,962	394,267	491,041	566,330	712,168	814,800
Construction and equipment of additional vocational units for school boards, etc.	21,243	43,857	57,600	66,727	49,703	40,000
Teachers' Superannuation Fund	39,472	42,939	47,752	54,952	64,520	67,032
Technical and technological institutions	8,268	25,603	37,763	53,663	68,315	89,721
Other	31,179	48,173	57,658	65,256	80,139	90,884
TOTAL	437,124	554,839	691,814	806,928	974,845	1,102,437

SOURCE: Ontario Budget, 1969, 1970.

[a]Interim.
[b]Estimate.

TABLE 7-14

Expenditure by the Department of Education on
summer courses for teachers, 1950–69
(in thousands of dollars)

YEAR	EXPENDITURE	YEAR	EXPENDITURE
1950–1	127	1964–5	534
1954–5	147	1965–6	684
1959–60	292	1966–7	927
1960–1	308	1967–8	1,119
1962–3	411	1968–9	1,325

SOURCE: *Public Accounts of the Province of Ontario for the Fiscal Year Ended 31st March* (Toronto: Queen's Printer).

TABLE 7-15

Net general expenditure by the Ontario Department of
University Affairs on various items, 1965–71 (in thousands of dollars)

ITEM OF EXPENDITURE	1965–6	1966–7	1967–8	1968–9	1969–70[a]	1970–1[b]
Grants to universities and colleges	69,087	96,562	193,844	252,282	314,885	374,665
Student awards	6,518	9,926	21,986	28,403	37,967	43,040
Other	375	934	1,028	4,212	6,032	6,602
TOTAL	75,980	107,422	216,858	284,897	358,884	424,307

SOURCE: Ontario Budget, 1970.

[a] Interim.
[b] Estimate.

The amounts expended on one particular service item, summer courses for teachers, are shown in Table 7-14 for intervals of approximately five years from 1950–1 to 1960–1, for 1962–3, and for single years from 1964–5 on. These amounts increased steadily to somewhat less than ten times as much in 1968–9 as in 1950–1. These costs accompanied the large increase in enrolment already observed.

Information is supplied in Table 7-15 for the Department of University Affairs corresponding to that for the Department of Education in Table 7-13. During the six successive years grants to universities and colleges rose from $69.1 million to $374.7 million. The percentages of the total accounted for by this item amounted respectively to 90.9, 89.9, 89.4, 88.6, 87.7, and 88.3. During the six-year period the total amount of the grants was multiplied by nearly five times.

The Department of Education spends a relatively small proportion of its annual budget in making grants to assist voluntary non-profit associations in the conduct of their activities. They pursue a wide variety of educational, cultural, and recreational objectives. They are asked each year for a statement about the nature of their activities in order to justify a renewal of the grant or an increase in the amount. Because of the impos-

TABLE 7-16
Miscellaneous grants by the Department of Education for 1969–70

ORGANIZATION	AMOUNT (IN DOLLARS)
Air Cadet League of Canada	3,000
Association canadienne-française d'éducation d'Ontario	2,500
Boy Scouts' Association	15,000
Boys' Clubs of Canada	5,000
Canadian Association for Adult Education	10,000
Canadian Education Association	52,000
Canadian Library Association	2,000
Canadian National Institute for the Blind	125,000
Champlain Society	5,000
Consumers' Association of Canada	2,000
English Catholic Education Association of Ontario	2,500
Federation of Catholic Parent-Teacher Associations	1,000
Frontier College	7,500
Institut canadien-français d'Ottawa	500
Institute of Public Administration of Canada	10,000
L'Association canadienne des éducateurs de langue française	1,500
L'Association des commissions des écoles bilingues d'Ontario	300
Navy League of Canada	3,000
Northern Ontario Public and Secondary School Trustees' Association	300
Ontario Educational Association	10,000
Ontario Federation of Home and School Associations	8,000
Ontario Federation of School Athletic Associations	15,000
Ontario Girl Guides Association	15,000
Ontario Institute of Painters	1,000
Ontario Library Association	1,000
Ontario Public School Trustees' Association	10,000
Ontario School Trustees' Council	11,300
Ontario Separate School Trustees' Association	300
Ontario Society for Crippled Children	6,000
Ontario Temperance Federation	3,500
Royal Life Saving Society of Canada	2,000
United Nations Association in Canada	3,500
Workers' Educational Association	6,000
Miscellaneous (to be paid as may be directed by the Minister)	499,300
TOTAL	840,000

SOURCE: *Public Accounts of the Province of Ontario for the Fiscal Year Ended 31st March 1969*, the Legislative Assembly of Ontario (Toronto: Queen's Printer, 1969), pp. 4–36.

sibility of placing any exact value on their individual contributions, the process of determining how much each will receive is inevitably arbitrary. The contents of the list of organizations varies somewhat each year as additions and deletions are made. Table 7.16 indicates the recipients for 1969–70, along with the amounts awarded. The grants varied from $300 for certain trustees' associations to $125,000 given to the Canadian National Institute for the Blind.

General legislative grants for the calendar years 1945 to 1969 for different classifications of elementary and secondary school pupils are shown in Table 7-17. These amounts do not include payments by the provincial government to school boards for services rendered, such as for the education of pupils from certain unorganized areas and for the use of schools for practice teaching. The legislative grants in the second last column have been paid for purposes that have differed over the years. Earlier special grants were incorporated in the general legislative grants beginning in

TABLE 7-17
General legislative grants to school boards, 1945–69

| CALENDAR YEAR | GENERAL LEGISLATIVE GRANTS ||| Secondary |||| TOTAL GENERAL | LEGISLATIVE GRANTS[a] | GRAND TOTAL |
| | Elementary ||| | | | | | | |
	Public	Roman Catholic separate	Total elementary	Academic	Vocational[b]	Total secondary				
1945	15,054,682	2,366,091	17,420,773	5,556,523	3,023,124	8,579,647	26,000,420	599,783	26,600,203
1946	16,505,851	2,558,009	19,063,860	6,406,703	3,181,837	9,588,540	28,652,400	583,635	29,236,035
1947	16,492,262	2,621,999	19,114,261	7,156,174	3,366,903	10,523,077	29,637,338	496,998	30,134,336
1948	18,823,524	3,178,073	22,001,597	8,675,900	3,811,220	12,487,120	34,488,717	464,812	34,953,529
1949	20,255,898	3,569,361	23,825,259	8,860,180	4,275,541	13,135,721	36,960,980	517,916	37,478,896
1950	22,855,028	4,654,442	27,509,470	10,578,979	3,544,331	14,123,310	41,632,780	906,806	42,539,586
1951	25,234,450	5,488,935	30,723,385	12,366,762	3,233,614	15,600,376	46,323,761	552,237	46,875,998
1952	29,174,724	6,836,124	36,010,848	14,071,863	3,983,986	18,055,849	54,066,697	688,130	54,754,827
1953	31,175,745	7,460,444	38,636,189	15,527,536	3,492,872	19,020,408	57,656,597	15,380	57,671,977
1954	34,359,603	8,789,361	43,148,964	16,599,237	3,153,979	19,753,216	62,902,180	2,194	62,904,374
1955	36,883,215	9,932,076	46,815,291	18,427,187	3,262,244	21,689,431	68,504,722	3,408,481	71,913,203
1956	38,930,822	11,251,019	50,181,841	19,969,082	3,465,398	23,434,480	73,616,321	5,445,672	79,061,993
1957	45,739,285	13,090,046	58,829,331	20,941,900	3,654,702	24,596,602	83,425,933	13,060,015	96,485,948
1958	66,602,160	21,199,669	87,801,829	34,111,152	6,233,869	40,345,021	128,146,850	21,107	128,167,957
1959	74,265,417	26,000,466	100,265,883	39,470,622	8,449,781	47,920,403	148,186,286		148,186,286
1960	78,390,624	29,251,485	107,642,109	45,631,466	5,467,359	51,098,825	158,740,934		158,740,934
1961	83,519,798	33,604,283	117,124,081	46,693,831	11,425,637	58,119,468	175,243,549	6,034,684	181,278,233
1962	86,313,357	37,238,770	123,552,127	51,477,034	9,465,618	60,942,652	184,494,779	16,651,908	201,146,687
1963	90,046,121	42,364,728	132,410,849	50,435,484	15,873,562	66,309,046	198,719,895	29,959,558	228,679,453
1964	120,342,850	66,806,654	187,149,504	62,735,967	35,322,096	98,058,063	285,207,567	289,429	285,496,996
1965	131,301,678	75,626,684	206,928,362	69,811,379	51,787,971	121,599,350	328,527,712		328,527,712
1966	147,836,815	88,009,650	235,846,465	75,223,596	61,986,827	137,210,423	373,056,888		373,056,888
1967	179,133,936	121,757,214	300,891,150	87,838,055	83,310,347	171,148,402	472,039,552		472,039,552
1968	216,186,123	147,589,673	363,775,796	95,245,086	93,819,320	189,064,406	552,840,202		552,840,202
1969	241,128,018	165,696,408	406,824,426			227,609,119	634,433,545		634,433,545

SOURCE: Reports of the Minister of Education of Ontario.

[a] Commencing with 1963 the former special grants were incorporated into the general legislative grant.
[b] For 1962–8 additional payments in the amounts of $116,880,945, $108,645,957, $24,209,090, $25,578,365, $72,496,797, $92,024,748, and $48,179,321 respectively were made for the construction and equipment of vocational accommodation under the terms of agreements between the government of Canada and the government of the province of Ontario. Other payments totalling $1,846,968 and $18,726,971 respectively were made by the province in the 1967 and 1968 calendar years to compensate for the phasing out of participation by the government of Canada in this area.

CHART 7-3
Provincial grants for elementary and secondary schools in Ontario, 1945–69

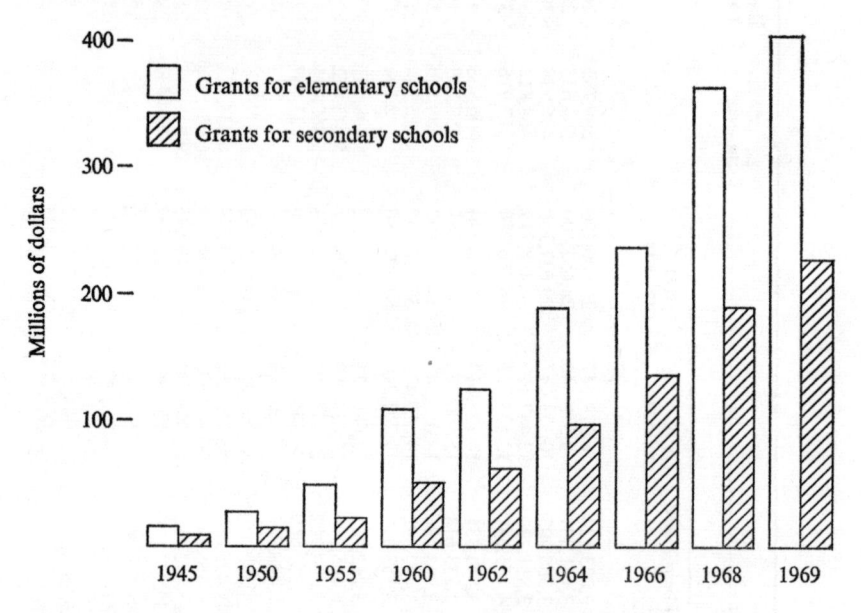

1953. The large amounts paid under this heading in 1955–7 were special per pupil grants, which again were incorporated in the general legislative grants in 1958. From 1961 to 1964 the legislative grant was the Residential and Farm School Tax Assistance Grant. The conditions under which these grants were paid are explained in volume II, chapter 8. The tables do not take account of additional payments made for the construction and equipment of vocational schools and additions to schools under the terms of the federal-provincial agreement of 1961. For the years 1962 to 1968 inclusive, the respective amounts were $116.9 million, $108.6 million, $24.2 million, $25.6 million, $72.5 million, $92.0 million, and $48.2 million. In 1967 and 1968 additional payments of $1.8 million and $18.7 million respectively were made to compensate for the phasing out of participation in this area by the federal government.

The grants rose by very large amounts during the twenty-five-year period. The total for 1969 was nearly twenty-four times as high as that for 1945. In 1945 elementary school grants represented 67.0 per cent of the total general legislative grants; in 1950, 66.1; in 1955, 68.3; in 1960, 67.8; in 1965, 63.0; in 1968, 65.8; and in 1969, 64.1. The proportion thus varied little throughout the period. The remaining proportion, the percentage of the total awarded for secondary schools, thus also remained relatively stable. The absolute and relative increases in elementary and secondary school awards are shown in Chart 7-3.

There was a steady change in the proportion of elementary school grants

CHART 7-4
Provincial grants for public elementary and Roman Catholic separate schools in Ontario, 1945-69

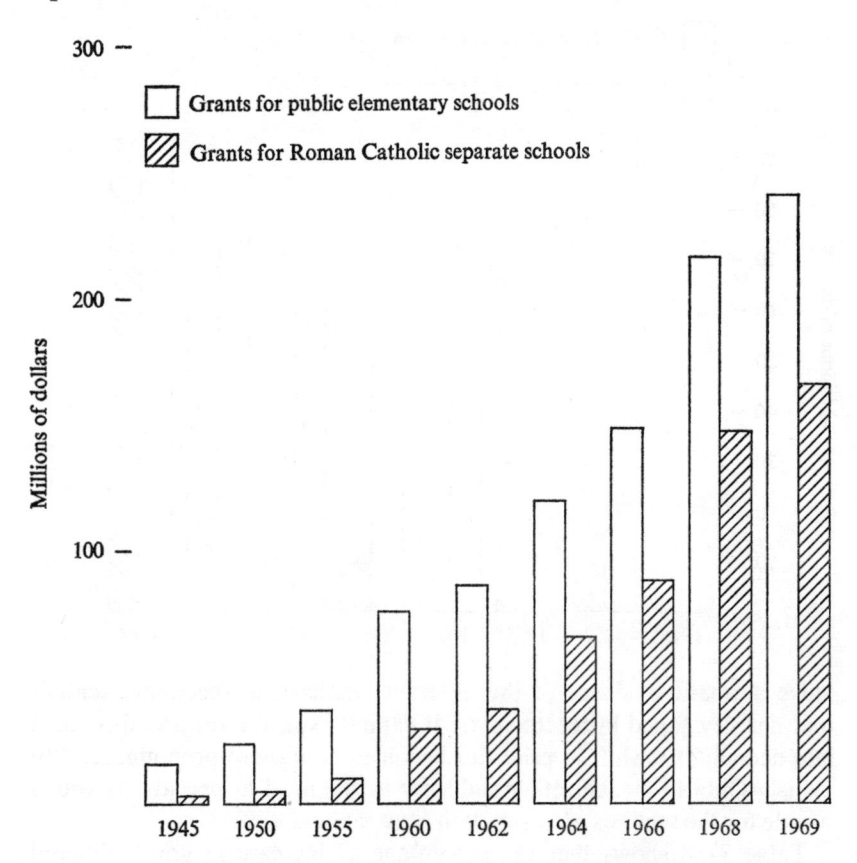

[Bar chart: Millions of dollars vs years 1945, 1950, 1955, 1960, 1962, 1964, 1966, 1968, 1969. Legend: Grants for public elementary schools; Grants for Roman Catholic separate schools.]

in favour of the Roman Catholic separate schools. In 1945 public school grants accounted for 86.4 per cent of elementary grants; in 1950, 83.1 per cent; in 1955, 78.8 per cent; in 1960, 72.8 per cent; in 1965, 63.5 per cent; in 1968, 59.4 per cent; and in 1969, 59.3 per cent. The reasons for this change were 1 / the relative increase in the number of children attending Roman Catholic separate schools, and 2 / more favourable conditions under which grants were awarded for these schools. An account of these changes may be found in volume II, chapter 8.

Grants for academic secondary schools increased in relation to those for vocational schools before the 1960s, after which there was a sharp reversal of the trend. In 1945 academic grants constituted 64.8 per cent of total secondary grants; in 1950, 74.9 per cent; in 1955, 85.0 per cent; in 1960, 89.3 per cent; in 1961, 80.3 per cent; in 1962, 84.5 per cent; in 1963, 76.1 per cent; in 1965, 57.4 per cent; and in 1968, 50.4 per cent. The two types of grants are not differentiated for 1969. This pattern pro-

CHART 7-5
Provincial grants for academic and vocational programs in Ontario secondary schools, 1945–68

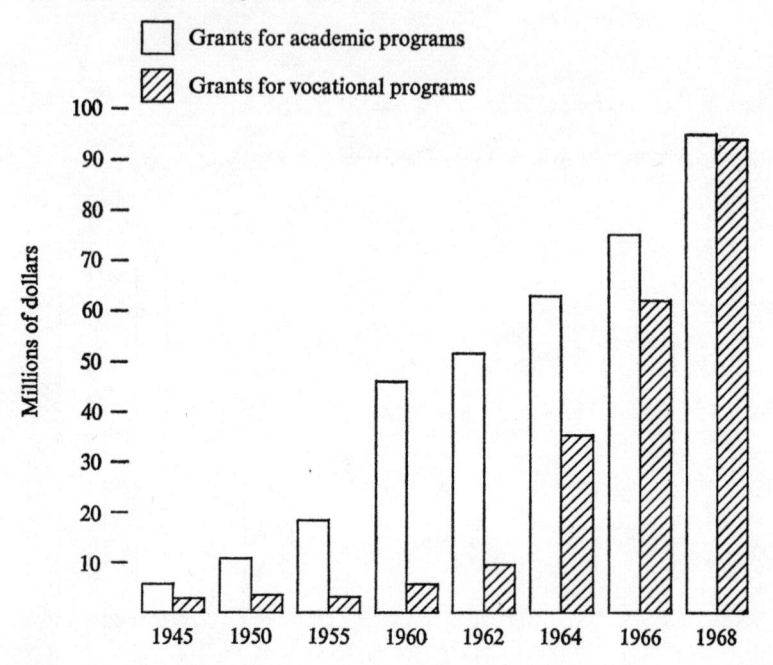

vides dramatic evidence of the different emphasis in secondary schools that has developed in recent years. If capital expenditures are also taken into account, the shift in priorities becomes even more pronounced. Obviously Ontario awoke rather suddenly to the need to prepare its young people for the realities of the modern occupational world.

Table 7-18 shows that the percentage of increase in grants differed considerably year by year. There were relatively small increases in 1946, 1947, 1949, 1953, 1954, 1956, and 1960. In 1958, when a new grant scheme was introduced, there were major increases both for elementary and secondary schools. The over-all percentage increase was considerably less, however, because the special per pupil grant was incorporated into the general legislative grant. Something of a similar nature happened in 1964.

REVENUES OF SCHOOL BOARDS
Table 7-19 gives a summary of the main sources of school board revenues for 1950, 1955, 1960, and individual years to 1968.* The total of receipts

*Unlike certain tables in the minister's reports, Table 7-19 counts grants made to the Metropolitan Toronto School Board as regular grants. This readjustment does not affect the total revenue of the boards, but redistributes it in terms of source.

TABLE 7-18

Percentage increase of provincial grants to school boards, 1945–69[a]

YEAR	PERCENTAGE OF INCREASE OVER PREVIOUS YEAR'S GRANTS			YEAR	PERCENTAGE OF INCREASE OVER PREVIOUS YEAR'S GRANTS		
	Elementary	Secondary	TOTAL[b]		Elementary	Secondary	TOTAL[b]
1945	100.0	100.0	100.0	1958	49.2	64.0	32.8
1946	9.4	11.7	9.9	1959	14.2	18.8	15.6
1947	0.3	9.8	3.1	1960	7.4	6.6	7.1
1948	15.1	18.7	16.0	1961	8.8	13.7	14.2
1949	8.3	5.2	7.2	1962	5.5	4.8	11.0
1950	15.5	7.5	13.5	1963	7.2	8.8	13.7
1951	11.7	10.4	10.2	1964	41.3	47.9	24.8
1952	17.2	15.7	16.8	1965	10.6	24.0	15.1
1953	7.3	5.3	5.3	1966	14.0	12.8	13.6
1954	11.7	3.8	9.1	1967	27.6	24.7	26.5
1955	8.5	9.8	14.3	1968	20.9	10.5	17.1
1956	7.2	8.0	9.9	1969	11.8	20.4	14.8
1957	17.2	5.0	22.0				

[a]Calculated from figures in Reports of the Minister of Education of Ontario.
[b]The totals include special grants payments made under the Residential and Farm School Assistance Grants.

from the provincial government is larger than the grant totals given in Table 7-17 because of the inclusion of payments for the education of non-resident pupils from the territorial districts and Ontario government establishments, those for the transportation of non-resident elementary school pupils, and those for the use of schools for practice teaching. Local revenues do not include fees paid by one board to another, since these do not constitute a net gain for the entire system. Other revenues consist of items such as proceeds from the sale of school sites, buildings, and equipment; payments by the federal government; and fees paid by individuals.

Table 7-19 shows total revenue increasing from about $62.1 million in 1945 to $1,243.9 million in 1968, or by about twenty times. The amount of the increase from 1945 to 1950 was approximately $56 million, and the percentage increase was 89.7; from 1950 to 1955 the corresponding figures were $103.0 million and 87.5 per cent; from 1955 to 1960, $206.2 million and 93.4 per cent; from 1960 to 1965, $323.5 million and 75.8 per cent; and from 1965 to 1968, $493.4 million and 65.7 per cent. Receipts from the provincial government were down to 37.5 per cent of the total in 1955, but rose steadily in the 1960s. The local taxpayer contributed $34.3 million in 1945 and $633.0 million in 1968. There were obviously considerable grounds for comment about the rising burden of local taxation.

The Ontario Committee on Taxation examined the basis for complaints about the high level of municipal taxation. While the data used were somewhat stale, even when the committee's report was made in 1967, the conclusions still have some relevance. It was observed that municipal tax levies took approximately 3 per cent of personal income in 1945, and by

TABLE 7-19
Revenues of Ontario school boards from major sources, 1945–68[a]

YEAR	PROVINCIAL GRANTS (IN $ THOUSANDS)	GRANTS AS PERCENTAGE OF TOTAL REVENUE	LOCAL TAXATION (IN $ THOUSANDS)	LOCAL TAXATION AS PERCENTAGE OF TOTAL REVENUE	OTHER REVENUES[b] (IN $ THOUSANDS)	OTHER REVENUES AS PERCENTAGE OF TOTAL REVENUE	TOTAL REVENUE (IN $ THOUSANDS)
1945	26,607	42.9	34,345	55.3	1,116	1.8	62,068
1950	46,742	39.7	68,282	58.0	2,716	2.3	117,740
1955	82,898	37.5	127,001	57.5	10,908	4.9	220,807
1960	160,791	37.6	253,900	59.5	12,294	2.9	426,985
1961	183,888	38.5	280,598	58.8	12,588	2.6	477,074
1962	204,415	38.4	300,327	56.5	27,034	5.1	531,776
1963	234,786	40.4	327,020	56.3	18,963	3.3	580,769
1964	298,316	43.6	368,747	53.9	16,892	2.5	683,955
1965	332,034	44.2	395,985	52.8	22,455	3.0	750,474
1966	386,351	44.2	458,256	52.4	29,837	3.4	874,444
1967	469,555	44.6	550,362	52.2	33,691	3.2	1,053,608
1968	571,099	45.9	632,971	50.9	39,807	3.2	1,243,877

[a]Calculated from Reports of the Minister of Education of Ontario.
[b]Including proceeds from the sale of school sites, buildings, and equipment; payments by the federal government; and fees paid by individuals.

CHART 7-6
Total school board revenues and receipts from local taxation, 1945–68

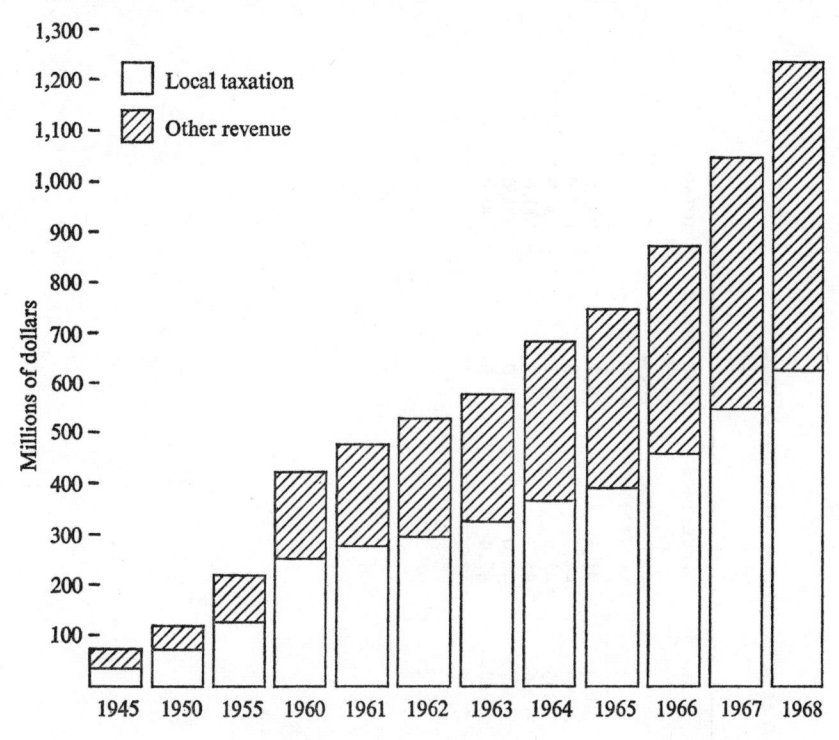

☐ Local taxation
▨ Other revenue

1963, 5.8 per cent. While this percentage was presumed to have increased after the latter year, it was still far below the distress level of 10.4 per cent reached in the depression year of 1933. While the committee expressed its concern with the height of the existing level of property taxes, it thought it desirable to see the matter in perspective.[1]

There were changes in the balance of revenues from local taxation, the provincial government, and other sources from 1945 to 1968. After rising substantially between 1945 and 1950, and falling again by 1955, the percentage obtained from local taxation remained fairly steady until 1963. From the latter year on, the percentage contributed by the provincial government gradually increased. Table 7-20 brings out the relationship between these two revenue sources. Provincial contributions as a percentage of the sum of the two rose from 39.1 in 1955 to 47.4 per cent in 1968.

A more detailed breakdown of revenue sources is provided in Table 7-21 for the period from 1950 to 1968. Provincial government grants include grants made to the Metropolitan Toronto School Board. Income from the federal government is shown only for the later years. Tuition fees are shown as a single entry before 1965, and as "transfers from other boards" and "individuals" thereafter. While fees paid by individuals rep-

TABLE 7-20
Receipts from the provincial government and local taxation as percentages of the sum of receipts from both sources, 1945–68

YEAR	PERCENTAGE FROM PROVINCIAL GOVERNMENT	PERCENTAGE FROM LOCAL TAXATION	TOTAL	YEAR	PERCENTAGE FROM PROVINCIAL GOVERNMENT	PERCENTAGE FROM LOCAL TAXATION	TOTAL
1945	49.6	50.4	100.0	1963	41.3	58.7	100.0
1950	40.6	59.4	100.0	1964	44.7	55.3	100.0
1955	39.1	60.9	100.0	1965	45.6	54.4	100.0
1960	38.5	61.5	100.0	1966	45.7	54.3	100.0
1961	39.3	60.7	100.0	1967	46.0	54.0	100.0
1962	40.0	60.0	100.0	1968	47.4	52.6	100.0

SOURCE: Reports of the Minister of Education of Ontario.

TABLE 7-21
Revenues of Ontario school boards from various sources, 1950–68 (in thousands of dollars)

SOURCE	1950	1955	1960	1961	1962	1963	1964	1965	1966	1967	1968
Local taxation	68,282	127,001	253,901	280,598	300,325	327,021	368,747	395,985	458,256	550,362	632,971
Provincial government – grants	46,742	81,610	158,962	181,546	200,455	230,044	285,741	325,961	378,686	460,600	557,407
other		1,289	1,828	2,342	3,961	4,741	12,575	6,073	7,665	8,955	13,692
Federal government								6,418	5,706	8,497	9,385
Sales of property and insurance proceeds			482	654	907	1,236		1,652	2,276	2,574	5,637
Sales of buildings and equipment	2,716		50	66	265	126					
Other		10,908	11,762	11,868	25,862	17,601	16,892	12,004	19,549	20,124	21,494
Subtotal	117,740	220,808	426,985	477,074	531,775	580,769	683,955	748,093	872,138	1,051,112	1,240,586
Fees from other boards[a]		6,890	14,161	15,791	16,373	20,463	24,324	22,647	22,946	24,878	29,993
from individuals								2,381	2,306	2,496	3,291
TOTAL	117,740	227,698	441,146	492,865	548,148	601,232	708,279	773,121	897,390	1,078,486	1,273,870

SOURCE: Reports of the Minister of Education of Ontario.

[a] Figures for the years before 1965 show fees from other boards and from individuals combined.

resent a net gain for the system, transfers from other boards do not. When the two figures are combined, one is forced, in trying to obtain a clear idea of the revenue situation, either to count both or omit both. The table is set up so that either can be done.

Tables 7-22 to 7-25 present the same type of breakdown of revenue by sources for each type of board. In those cases where grants to the Metropolitan Toronto School Board are applicable, they have been treated as provincial government grants and not as local taxation. As in Table 7-21, each table shows a division of fees after 1964 into those representing transfers from one board to another and those received from individuals.

For elementary school boards the percentage of the revenue subtotal contributed by local taxation in 1950, as shown in Table 7-22, was 58.4, and receipts from the provincial government constituted 39.0 per cent. Local taxation contributed 60.7 per cent in 1955, 58.9 per cent in 1960, 51.8 per cent in 1965, 50.3 per cent in 1967, and 47.3 per cent in 1968. For the same selected years the percentages contributed by the provincial government were 39.0, 35.3, 37.8, 45.7, 47.1, and 50.0. Tuition fees from other boards and from individuals amounted to 0.9 per cent of all revenues in 1955 and 0.7 in 1968.

The pattern of revenues for public elementary schools was much like that for all elementary schools in 1950, as indicated in Table 7-23, when 59.3 per cent of revenues came from local taxation and 38.7 per cent from the provincial government. After that year, reflecting the increasing weight of provincial support given to Roman Catholic separate school boards, the percentage for public elementary schools raised by local taxation was considerably higher than that for the total of all elementary school boards. The percentages for 1955, 1960, 1965, 1967, and 1968 were respectively 63.0, 63.3, 59.8, 59.6, and 56.6. The percentages contributed by the provincial government for the same years were respectively 33.3, 33.6, 37.8, 37.6, and 40.7. Tuition fees constituted a declining percentage of total revenue during the 1960s, and even decreased in absolute amount between 1966 and 1967.

Table 7-24 shows the distribution of revenue sources for Roman Catholic separate school boards. In 1950 these boards raised 53.5 per cent of their revenues from local taxation. For 1955, 1960, 1965, 1967, and 1968, the corresponding percentages were 47.5, 39.0, 26.5, 23.9, and 21.6. In other words, since 1950 the provincial government has assumed most of the financial burden of supporting the Roman Catholic separate schools. The grants are, of course, paid partly to compensate for corporation taxes which it is a practical impossibility for supporters of the schools to claim. While no one can make any adequate estimate of how much this amount might be, it could hardly constitute the major part of the school grant. The schools are to a large extent financed out of revenue levied from all taxpayers. The relative positions of the two types of school boards are shown in Chart 7-7.

TABLE 7-22
Revenues of Ontario elementary school boards from various sources, 1950-68 (in thousands of dollars)

SOURCE	1950	1955	1960	1961	1962	1963	1964	1965	1966	1967	1968
Local taxation	48,069	93,389	168,152	181,638	187,614	196,801	216,159	234,119	268,412	313,055	350,138
Provincial government – grants	32,044	53,834	107,703	121,576	138,591	154,006	185,402	206,050	238,596	292,937	368,818
other		497	327	504	233	338	4,321	410	1,024	725	995
Federal government								3,566	3,477	5,273	5,708
Sales of property and insurance proceeds			470	628	854	1,190		1,537	1,939	2,272	4,714
Sales of buildings and equipment	2,127	6,128	34	37	45	71	9,306	6,039	11,449	8,579	9,527
Other			8,997	8,758	9,534	9,418					
Subtotal	82,240	153,848	285,683	313,141	336,871	361,824	415,188	451,721	524,897	622,841	739,900
Fees from other boards[a]		1,416	2,653	3,018	2,871	4,166	4,932	4,250	4,594	4,291	4,918
from individuals								359	446	492	535
TOTAL	82,240	155,264	288,336	316,159	339,742	365,990	420,120	456,330	529,937	627,624	745,353

SOURCE: Reports of the Minister of Education of Ontario.

[a] Figures for the years before 1965 show fees from other boards and from individuals combined.

TABLE 7-23
Revenues of Ontario public elementary school boards from various sources, 1950-68 (in thousands of dollars)

SOURCE	1950	1955	1960	1961	1962	1963	1964	1965	1966	1967	1968
Local taxation	41,438	82,445	147,816	158,895	163,136	170,839	189,213	205,402	234,968	274,349	307,873
Provincial government – grants	27,020	43,317	78,306	87,136	97,390	105,953	119,514	129,521	148,552	172,688	220,684
other		311	278	269	192	271	3,031	338	822	564	695
Federal government								3,159	2,907	4,417	4,582
Sales of property and insurance proceeds			435	592	751	912		1,371	1,532	1,990	3,505
Sales of buildings and equipment			23	35	40	58					
Other	1,393	4,753	6,706	6,755	6,868	6,838	7,527	3,647	7,225	6,598	6,530
Subtotal	69,851	130,826	233,564	253,682	268,377	284,871	319,285	343,438	396,006	460,606	543,869
Fees from other boards		1,222	2,173	2,523	2,287	2,567	2,967	2,425	2,726	2,403	2,879
from individuals								245	283	225	316
TOTAL	69,851	132,048	235,737	256,205	270,664	287,438	322,252	346,108	399,015	463,234	547,064

SOURCE: Reports of the Minister of Education of Ontario.

TABLE 7-24
Revenues of Ontario Roman Catholic separate school boards from various sources, 1950–68 (in thousands of dollars)

SOURCE	1950	1955	1960	1961	1962	1963	1964	1965	1966	1967	1968
Local taxation	6,631	10,944	20,336	22,743	24,478	25,962	26,946	28,717	33,444	38,706	42,265
Provincial government – grants	5,024	10,517	29,397	34,440	41,201	48,053	65,888	76,529	90,044	120,249	148,134
other		186	49	235	41	67	1,290	72	202	161	300
Federal government								407	570	856	1,126
Sales of property and insurance proceeds			35	36	103	278		166	407	282	1,209
Sales of buildings and equipment			11	2	5	13					
Other	734	1,375	2,291	2,003	2,666	2,580	1,779	2,392	4,224	1,981	2,997
Subtotal	12,389	23,022	52,119	59,459	68,494	76,953	95,903	108,283	128,891	162,235	196,031
Fees from other boards[a]		194	480	495	584	1,599	1,965	1,825	1,868	1,888	2,039
from individuals								114	163	267	219
TOTAL	12,389	23,216	52,599	59,954	69,078	78,552	97,868	110,222	130,922	164,390	198,289

SOURCE: Reports of the Minister of Education of Ontario.

[a] Figures for the years before 1965 show fees from other boards and from individuals combined.

The financing of education 335

CHART 7-7
Local taxes, receipts from the provincial government, and other revenues as percentages of the total revenue for public elementary and Roman Catholic separate school boards, 1950–68

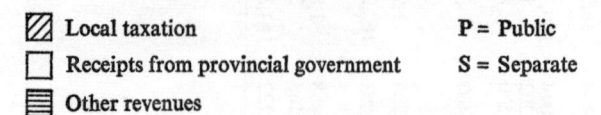

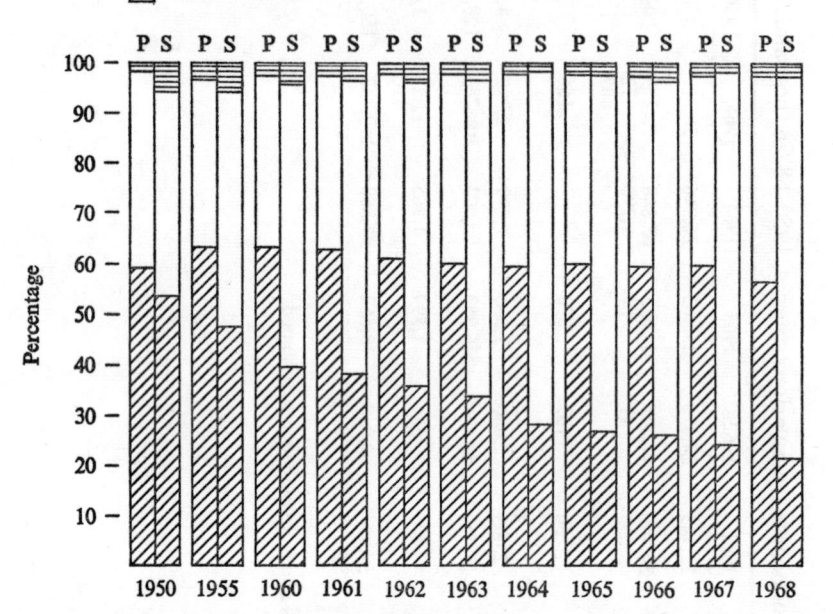

- ▨ Local taxation
- ☐ Receipts from provincial government
- ☰ Other revenues

P = Public
S = Separate

Revenue sources for all secondary school boards are shown in Table 7-25. Between 1950 and 1968 total revenue, including fees, increased from $35.5 million to $528.5 million, or by about fifteen times. In 1950, 1955, 1960, 1965, 1967, and 1968 the percentages of this total represented by local taxation were respectively 56.9, 50.2, 60.7, 54.6, 55.4, and 56.5. For the same years the respective percentages represented by receipts from the provincial government were 41.4, 42.7, 37.3, 42.4, 41.1, and 40.2. Tuition fees, paid both by other boards and by individuals, were a considerably larger item than they were in the accounts of elementary school boards. In 1955, 1960, 1965, 1967, and 1968 they constituted 7.6, 7.5, 6.4, 5.0, and 5.3 per cent of total income including fees.

There have been continual complaints from elected municipal officials throughout the post-war period that levies by school boards have been growing at an unreasonable rate. Part of the cause of their dissatisfaction has of course been that they believe they have been blamed by an undiscriminating public because their obligation to operate the tax-collecting machinery has made them appear responsible for increases over which they have had no control. They have also tended to feel that school boards

TABLE 7-25
Revenues of Ontario secondary school boards from various sources, 1950–68 (in thousands of dollars)

SOURCE	1950	1955	1960	1961	1962	1963	1964	1965	1966	1967	1968
Local taxation	20,213	33,612	85,748	98,960	112,712	130,219	152,588	161,866	189,844	237,307	282,833
Provincial government – grants	14,698	27,776	51,260	59,970	61,863	76,039	100,339	119,911	140,090	167,663	188,589
other		792	1,501	1,838	3,728	4,403	8,254	5,663	6,641	8,230	12,697
Federal government								2,852	2,229	3,224	3,677
Sales of property and insurance proceeds			12	26	53	46		115	337	302	923
Sales of buildings and equipment			16	29	220	55					
Other	589	4,780	2,765	3,110	16,328	8,183	7,586	5,965	8,100	11,545	11,967
Subtotal	35,500	66,960	141,302	163,933	194,904	218,945	268,767	296,372	347,241	428,271	500,686
Fees from other boards[a]		5,474	11,508	12,773	13,502	16,297	19,392	18,397	18,352	20,587	25,075
from individuals								2,022	1,860	2,004	2,756
TOTAL	35,500	72,434	152,810	176,706	208,406	235,242	288,159	316,791	367,453	450,862	528,517

SOURCE: Reports of the Minister of Education of Ontario.

[a] Figures for the years before 1965 show fees from other boards and from individuals combined.

TABLE 7-26
Education levies as a percentage of total municipal taxation in Ontario, 1945–68

YEAR	PER CENT	YEAR	PER CENT
1945	32.2	1957	43.1
1946	32.0	1958	42.5
1947	33.4	1959	44.2
1948	34.3	1960	44.4
1949	35.2	1961	44.9
1950	35.7	1962	45.1
1951	37.7	1963	45.3
1952	38.5	1964	45.3
1953	40.1	1965	44.5
1954	39.8	1966	45.7
1955	41.6	1967	48.2
1956	42.9	1968	49.2

SOURCE: *1967 Annual Report of Municipal Statistics*, Department of Municipal Affairs (Toronto: Queen's Printer, 1968).

have been appropriating tax room that should be shared more equitably with them. While there is no easy way to determine the ideal method of apportioning funds between education on the one hand and municipal services such as welfare, water works, sidewalks, police and fire protection, and other such items on the other, it is of some interest to observe the actual shift toward the former. As indicated in Table 7-26, education got a little more than 32 cents of the local tax dollar in 1945 and close to 50 cents by 1968. While a complete assessment of the situation depends on taking into account all sources of revenue, particularly provincial grants, it is easy to observe the factual basis for the complaints of municipal councils.

SCHOOL BOARD EXPENDITURE

Operating expenditure by Ontario school boards of different types is shown in Tables 7-27 to 7-33 inclusive. The reporting procedure was changed in 1965 so that instructional supplies and administration costs were given separately instead of being combined with plant operation and maintenance. Also, beginning in 1967 educational services and pupil welfare services were removed from the general category of other operating expenditure.

Between 1950 and 1968 total expenditure by all school boards increased from approximately $112 million to $1,248 million, or by about eleven times, as shown in Table 7-27. The amount roughly doubled every five years during the 1950s, and nearly tripled between 1960 and 1968. Salaries for instructors constituted 57.7 per cent of the total in 1950 and 56.4 per cent in 1968, with only small variations during the intervening years. Plant operation and maintenance, including administration and instructional supplies, took 26.6 per cent of the total in 1950, 21.8 per cent

TABLE 7-27

Expenditure by Ontario school boards on various items, 1950–68 (in thousands of dollars)

ITEM	1950	1955	1960	1961	1962	1963	1964	1965	1966	1967	1968
Administration								32,444	38,992	46,432	56,245
Instruction											
Salaries	64,590	126,794	247,006	271,136	297,251	328,626	362,842	413,983	480,324	564,948	704,739
Supplies								38,789	46,073	48,015	61,186
Educational services										19,101	19,055
Pupil welfare services										6,348	7,264
Plant operation and maintenance[a]	29,845	52,523	93,916	103,130	112,189	127,516	151,667	92,337	105,954	124,153	150,619
Transportation	3,782	7,782	13,268	15,014	16,970	19,118	21,617	25,526	30,401	35,853	41,840
Capital expenditure from revenue	4,357	8,378	19,425	19,999	23,502	25,342	35,754	37,613	50,279	58,412	58,993
Debt charges	9,479	21,834	48,105	56,081	60,446	67,573	86,484	93,172	100,518	118,070	134,771
Other operating expenditure		4,858	8,262	9,496	21,859	14,985	15,289	18,691	20,474	14,539	13,605
TOTAL	112,053	222,169	429,982	474,856	532,217	583,160	673,653	752,555	873,015	1,035,871	1,248,317

SOURCE: Reports of the Minister of Education of Ontario.

[a] Including instructional supplies and administration before 1965.

in 1960, and 21.5 per cent in 1968. The cost of administration was 4.3 per cent of the total in 1965 and virtually the same at 4.5 per cent in 1968. Other expenditure items in general also tended to keep much the same relative position.

Expenditure by elementary school boards of both types is shown in Table 7-28. The increase in the total by about nine and one-half times between 1950 and 1968 was substantially less than that for elementary and secondary school boards combined. In 1950 instructional salaries took 60.0 per cent of the total, as compared with 57.8 per cent in 1960, 54.0 per cent in 1965, and 55.0 per cent in 1968. Plant operation and maintenance, including administration and instructional supplies, fell from 26.4 per cent in 1950 to 21.6 per cent in 1968. Large relative increases occurred in transportation costs and debt charges.

Expenditure by public elementary school boards, according to Table 7-29, was multiplied by a little over eight times from 1950 to 1968. Instructional salaries took 61.3 per cent of the total in 1950, 59.1 per cent in 1960, and 55.5 per cent in 1968. Plant operation and maintenance showed the same pattern of decline as in both types of elementary schools combined. Debt charges were multiplied by about fifteen times between 1950 and 1968.

Expenditures by Roman Catholic separate school boards were over seventeen times as great in 1968 as in 1950, rising from $11.2 million to $195.1 million, as shown in Table 7-30. The cost of instructional salaries was generally relatively lower than for the public elementary school boards during the earlier years, amounting to 52.8 per cent of the total in 1950. By 1968 there had been a slight rise to 53.7 per cent. During the eighteen-year period transportation costs increased from $139,000 to $7,413,000, or by over fifty times, representing a great increase in pupil service. Debt charges multiplied in the same interval by more than twenty times.

Expenditure by secondary school boards, according to Table 7-31, increased from $34.4 million in 1950 to $503.2 million in 1968, or by about fifteen times. Instructional salaries took 52.3 per cent of the total in 1950, 56.5 per cent in 1965, and 58.6 per cent in 1968. Thus the general trend for this item was the opposite to that in the elementary school systems. The percentage of expenditure on plant operation and maintenance, including administration and instructional supplies, declined from 27.2 in 1950 to 21.3 in 1968. Transportation costs rose more slowly than expenditures in general, while capital expenditure from revenue and debt charges increased at a rate that was fairly consistent with the total expenditure trend.

Expenditure for academic secondary schools increased by between eight and nine times between 1950 and 1967, according to Table 7-32. Instructional salaries took 53.9 per cent of the total in 1950 and 56.6 per cent in 1967. Other items showed much the same trend as for secondary schools as a whole. As shown in Table 7-33, the increase in the cost of

TABLE 7-28
Expenditure by Ontario elementary school boards on various items, 1950–68 (in thousands of dollars)

ITEM	1950	1955	1960	1961	1962	1963	1964	1965	1966	1967	1968
Administration								18,760	22,980	27,384	33,598
Instruction	46,590	90,098	165,643	178,707	191,500	204,247	220,788				
Salaries								246,021	281,707	328,141	409,910
Supplies								20,208	25,955	26,266	33,858
Educational services										10,056	12,157
Pupil welfare services										2,105	2,331
Plant operation and maintenance[a]	20,468	36,966	64,089	68,739	73,709	80,229	89,946	59,032	67,332	77,252	93,478
Transportation	1,801	3,724	6,758	7,825	8,994	10,499	12,143	14,808	18,786	23,175	27,787
Capital expenditure from revenue	3,283	5,879	13,083	13,055	15,304	15,953	21,047	23,953	32,816	36,875	36,158
Debt charges	5,474	14,457	31,382	36,685	39,561	44,139	57,971	63,715	68,081	77,793	88,986
Other operating expenditure		2,793	5,651	5,960	6,445	6,125	6,839	9,182	9,291	5,861	6,810
TOTAL	77,616	153,917	286,606	310,971	335,513	361,192	408,734	455,679	526,948	614,908	745,073

SOURCE: Reports of the Minister of Education of Ontario.

[a] Including instructional supplies and administration before 1965.

TABLE 7-29
Expenditure by Ontario public elementary school boards on various items, 1950–68 (in thousands of dollars)

ITEM	1950	1955	1960	1961	1962	1963	1964	1965	1966	1967	1968
Administration								14,769	17,871	20,863	25,197
Instruction											
Salaries	40,668	78,311	138,289	147,340	155,377	163,710	174,303	190,692	215,554	245,191	305,178
Supplies								15,311	19,282	18,987	24,308
Educational services										7,395	8,564
Pupil welfare services										1,795	1,986
Plant operation and maintenance[a]	17,196	31,811	53,866	57,487	61,088	66,018	72,190	48,087	53,180	59,589	71,740
Transportation	1,662	3,132	5,200	5,951	6,669	7,659	8,793	10,644	13,750	17,072	20,374
Capital expenditure from revenue	2,628	4,789	10,936	11,120	10,942	11,886	11,690	13,922	20,951	23,657	23,826
Debt charges	4,237	10,570	22,103	25,791	28,438	30,370	42,643	45,929	48,521	55,465	63,373
Other operating expenditure		2,314	3,485	3,903	4,633	4,509	4,666	7,614	7,760	5,026	5,394
TOTAL	66,391	130,927	233,879	251,592	267,147	284,152	314,285	346,968	396,869	455,040	549,940

SOURCE: Reports of the Minister of Education of Ontario.

[a] Including instructional supplies and administration before 1965.

TABLE 7-30
Expenditure by Ontario Roman Catholic separate school boards on various items, 1950-68 (in thousands of dollars)

ITEM	1950	1955	1960	1961	1962	1963	1964	1965	1966	1967	1968
Administration								3,991	5,109	6,521	8,401
Instruction											
Salaries	5,922	11,787	27,354	31,367	36,123	40,537	46,485	55,329	66,153	82,950	104,732
Supplies								4,897	6,673	7,279	9,550
Educational services										2,661	3,593
Pupil welfare services										310	345
Plant operation and maintenance[a]	3,272	5,155	10,223	11,252	12,621	14,211	17,756	10,945	14,152	17,663	21,738
Transportation	139	592	1,558	1,874	2,325	2,840	3,350	4,164	5,036	6,103	7,413
Capital expenditure from revenue	655	1,090	2,147	1,935	4,362	4,067	9,357	10,031	11,865	13,218	12,332
Debt charges	1,238	3,887	9,279	10,894	11,123	13,769	15,328	17,786	19,560	22,328	25,613
Other operating expenditure		479	2,166	2,057	1,812	1,616	2,173	1,568	1,531	835	1,416
TOTAL	11,226	22,990	52,727	59,379	68,366	77,040	94,449	108,711	130,079	159,868	195,133

SOURCE: Reports of the Minister of Education of Ontario.

[a] Including instructional supplies and administration before 1965.

TABLE 7-31
Expenditure by Ontario secondary school boards on various items, 1950–68 (in thousands of dollars)

ITEM	1950	1955	1960	1961	1962	1963	1964	1965	1966	1967	1968
Administration								13,684	16,012	19,048	22,647
Instruction											
Salaries	18,000	36,696	81,363	92,429	105,751	124,379	142,054	167,962	198,617	236,807	294,829
Supplies								18,581	20,118	21,749	27,328
Educational services										9,045	6,898
Pupil welfare services										4,243	4,933
Plant operation and maintenance[a]	9,377	15,557	29,827	34,391	38,480	47,287	61,721	33,305	38,622	46,901	57,141
Transportation	1,981	4,058	6,510	7,189	7,976	8,619	9,474	10,718	11,615	12,678	14,053
Capital expenditure from revenue	1,074	2,499	6,342	6,944	8,198	9,389	14,707	13,660	17,463	21,537	22,835
Debt charges	4,005	7,377	16,723	19,396	20,885	23,434	28,513	29,457	32,437	40,277	45,785
Other operating expenditure		2,065	2,611	3,536	15,414	8,860	8,450	9,509	11,183	8,678	6,795
TOTAL	34,437	68,252	143,376	163,885	196,704	221,968	264,919	296,876	346,067	420,963	503,244

SOURCE: Reports of the Minister of Education of Ontario.

[a]Including instructional supplies and administration before 1965.

TABLE 7-32

Expenditure by Ontario secondary school boards on various items, academic schools, 1950-67 (in thousands of dollars)

ITEM	1950	1955	1960	1961	1962	1963	1964	1965	1966	1967
Administration	13,307	26,083	61,135	70,148	79,376	78,806	84,413	7,383	8,354	9,701
Instruction										
Salaries								95,647	107,319	122,661
Supplies								9,741	9,804	10,043
Educational services										4,962
Pupil welfare services										2,051
Plant operation and maintenance[a]	5,440	10,763	20,912	24,265	26,431	27,178	32,575	17,471	19,322	22,386
Transportation	1,981	4,057	6,391	7,024	7,642	6,283	6,031	6,371	6,626	6,792
Capital expenditure from revenue	666	1,726	5,005	4,949	5,300	5,566	7,991	8,013	10,213	11,108
Debt charges	3,294	6,330	13,963	16,010	16,779	16,942	19,089	18,873	20,257	23,434
Other operating expenditure		1,570	2,046	2,530	3,475	6,928	6,511	4,986	5,603	3,581
TOTAL	24,688	50,529	109,452	124,926	139,003	141,703	156,610	168,485	187,498	216,719

SOURCE: Reports of the Minister of Education of Ontario.

[a] Including instructional supplies and administration before 1965.

TABLE 7-33

Expenditure by Ontario secondary school boards on various items, vocational schools, 1950–67 (in thousands of dollars)

ITEM	1950	1955	1960	1961	1962	1963	1964	1965	1966	1967
Administration								6,301	7,658	9,347
Instruction										
Salaries	4,693	10,613	20,228	22,281	26,375	45,573	57,641	72,315	91,298	114,146
Supplies								8,840	10,314	11,706
Educational services										4,083
Pupil welfare services										2,192
Plant operation and maintenance[a]	3,937	4,794	8,915	10,126	12,049	20,109	29,146	15,834	19,300	24,515
Transportation			119	165	334	2,336	3,443	4,347	4,989	5,886
Capital expenditure from revenue	408	773	1,337	1,995	2,898	3,823	6,716	5,647	7,250	10,429
Debt charges	709	1,048	2,760	3,386	4,106	6,492	9,424	10,584	12,180	16,843
Other operating expenditure	495	565	1,006	11,939	1,932	1,939	4,523	5,580	5,097	
TOTAL	9,747	17,723	33,924	38,959	57,701	80,265	108,309	128,391	158,569	204,244

SOURCE: Reports of the Minister of Education of Ontario.

[a] Including instructional supplies and administration before 1965.

TABLE 7-34

Expenditure on instruction as a percentage of total Ontario school board expenditure, 1950–68[a]

YEAR	ELEMENTARY			SECONDARY			TOTAL
	Public	Roman Catholic separate	TOTAL	Academic	Vocational	TOTAL	
1950	36.3	5.3	41.6	11.9	4.2	16.1	57.7
1955	35.2	5.3	40.5	11.7	4.8	16.5	57.0
1960	32.2	6.4	38.6	14.2	4.7	18.9	57.5
1961	31.0	6.6	37.6	14.8	4.7	19.5	57.1
1962	29.2	6.8	36.0	14.9	5.0	19.9	55.9
1963	28.1	7.0	35.1	13.5	7.8	21.3	56.4
1964	25.9	6.9	32.8	12.5	8.6	21.1	53.9
1965	25.3	7.4	32.7	12.7	9.6	22.3	55.0
1966	24.7	7.6	32.3	12.3	10.4	22.7	55.0
1967	23.7	8.0	31.7	11.8	11.0	22.8	54.5
1968	24.4	8.4	32.8			23.6	56.4

[a]Calculated from Reports of the Minister of Education of Ontario.

vocational schools from $9.7 million to $204.2 million represented more than a twenty-fold increase. The distribution of expenditure over various items was not much different from that for academic schools.

Table 7-34 indicates how total instructional costs of all boards were distributed between the two publicly supported elementary school systems, between academic and vocational secondary schools or departments, and between the elementary and secondary levels. The final column gives the percentage of total school board expenditure that went for instruction. This percentage remained fairly constant in the 1950s, but declined somewhat after 1962, hovering around 55 per cent for several years. A comparison of the public elementary and Roman Catholic separate school expenditures shows that the two followed opposite trends. The percentage of the total for instruction in the former declined from 36.3 in 1950 to 24.4 in 1968, while that in the latter rose from 5.3 to 8.4 in the same period. For the two systems combined, the total fell from 41.6 to 32.8 per cent. That is, 41.6¢ of every dollar of expenditure on public education went for elementary school teachers' salaries in 1950, and 32.8¢ in 1968. The percentage of total expenditure for academic secondary school instruction increased from 11.9 in 1950 to 14.9 in 1962, and then declined to 11.8 in 1967. On the other hand, the percentage for vocational instruction rose steadily from 4.2 in 1950 to 11.0 in 1967. The total for both forms of secondary school instruction increased regularly from 16.1 per cent in 1950 to 23.6 per cent in 1968.

The annual per pupil cost based on average daily attendance for day school education for five-year intervals up to 1960–1 and for single years thereafter up to 1966–7 is shown in Table 7-35. Account should be taken of the shift to calculations based on average daily enrolment in 1967–8

TABLE 7-35

Annual per pupil cost of average daily attendance for day school education in Ontario, 1945-69 (in dollars)

YEAR	ELEMENTARY		SECONDARY	
	Public	Roman Catholic separate	Academic	Vocational
1945-6	94.45	59.37	167.49	266.15
1950-1	151.34	96.36	286.35	353.71
1955-6	221.63	133.55	428.84	506.37
1960-1			594.54	734.07
1961-2	321.05	214.52	592.84	743.79
1962-3	336.08	234.59	596.38	765.56
1963-4[a]	365.08	254.76	636.04	754.03
1964-5	380.02	294.32	683.19	814.32
1965-6	409.15	328.73	760.38	855.31
1966-7[b]	456.00	377.00	841.00	949.00
1967-8[c]	484.00	427.00	845.00	1,037.00
1968-9[c]	574.00	506.00		1,077.00[d]

SOURCE: Reports of the Minister of Education of Ontario.

NOTE: Cost covers current operations, capital charges, capital outlays from current funds, and transportation; from 1963 other or miscellaneous is also included.

[a] Figures for 1963 have been adjusted to include Metropolitan Toronto expenditures where applicable.
[b] Per pupil cost of average daily enrolment was elementary: public, $434.00; Roman Catholic separate, $360.00; secondary: academic, $802.00; vocational, $887.00.
[c] Per pupil cost of average daily enrolment.
[d] Total secondary.

and 1968-9. If this change is ignored, which it may be without doing serious violence to the general conclusions, it may be said that the average cost per public elementary school pupil increased by more than six times between 1945-6 and 1968-9. The corresponding cost for Roman Catholic separate school pupils increased by about eight and one-half times. Up to 1967-8, the per student cost in academic secondary schools increased by about five times and that for vocational secondary schools by about four times. The figure of $1,077 for 1968-9 applies to both groups combined.

SCHOOL BOARD DEBT

The debt position of Ontario municipalities and school boards for selected years up to 1960, and for every year from 1960 to 1967, is shown in Table 7-36. An index is included, with 1939 taken as the base year. The situation improved for both types of agencies during the war. Between 1945 and 1967 school board debt grew from approximately $43 million to nearly $958 million, or by more than twenty-two times. The comparable figures for municipalities were $124 million and $1,165 million,

TABLE 7-36
Municipal and school board debt, 1945–67

YEAR	AMOUNT (IN $ THOUSANDS)			INDEX (1939 = 100)		
	Gross debt			Gross debt		
	Municipal	*School board*	*Total*	*Municipal*	*School board*	*Total*
1945	123,954	43,042	166,996	57.6	72.4	60.8
1951	197,141	120,916	318,057	91.5	203.2	115.7
1955	291,513	238,284	529,797	135.4	400.5	192.7
1960	611,896	514,249	1,126,145	284.1	864.3	409.7
1961	670,539	555,990	1,226,529	311.4	934.5	446.2
1962	751,595	586,761	1,338,356	349.0	986.2	486.9
1963	828,320	629,493	1,457,813	384.6	1,058.0	530.4
1964	951,802	671,192	1,622,994	442.0	1,128.1	590.5
1965	1,018,876	697,495	1,716,371	473.1	1,172.3	
1966	1,074,888	824,641	1,899,529	499.1	1,386.0	
1967	1,165,166	957,712	2,122,878	541.0	1,609.6	

SOURCE: The Ontario Committee on Taxation, Ontario Department of Municipal Affairs, Annual Report of Municipal Statistics.

a little more than a nine-fold increase. In terms of the 1939 index, the figure reached by the school boards was 1,609.6, and by the municipalities, 541.0. Debt increase at this level was much greater than at either of the provincial or federal levels. Although municipal governments and school boards have the financial backing of the province, the situation is not to be regarded as desirable.

The Ontario Committee on Taxation reported that "in recent years" school board gross debt as a percentage of provincial domestic product had become stabilized at approximately 4 per cent. This figure was significantly higher than the 1939 level of 3 per cent, and much above the war-time low level of 1 per cent. The committee found the existing trend quite unsatisfactory.[2]

UNIVERSITY INCOME

The percentage of income of the provincially assisted universities from the major sources for 1965–6 to 1968–9 is shown in Table 7-37. During the 1950s students' fees typically constituted between one-fourth and one-third of total operating costs. The percentage declined gradually until it reached an over-all level of 24.8 in 1965–6, after which it declined very sharply, reaching 18.9 in 1967–8 and 17.0 in 1968–9. During the same period gifts for operating purposes, never a very robust item since private donors usually prefer to contribute to scholarship funds or individually identifiable building projects, declined from 0.6 per cent in 1965–6 to 0.4 in 1968–9. There are not many citizens or private organizations that are prepared to enter into a partnership with government to share in the maintenance of what have come to be regarded as public institutions.

Endowment income during the period in question was reduced sharply in relative terms, although not in actual amount. The minute percentage of income from this source emphasizes the public status of the provincially assisted universities. The cessation of direct federal grants in 1967 in favour of transfer payments to the provincial government did not interrupt the trend toward increasing dependence of the universities on public financing. By 1968–9 the government's contribution had reached 79.0 per cent and promised to go higher. Other income referred to in Table 7-37 covers municipal grants and research funds contributed by various agencies.

The relative degree of reliance on the two major sources of income – fees and federal and provincial grants – is shown in Table 7-38 for individual universities during the same recent four-year period. Some of the established universities, such as McMaster, Queen's, Toronto, and Western, had a relatively large proportion of their income accounted for by other sources of funds, such as research grants and endowment. The newer universities, on the other hand, were almost entirely dependent on fees and provincial grants, unless they were sponsored by local government in their own areas. Algoma and Nipissing Colleges, affiliates of Laurentian University, began their existence in the latter category. The status of Brock and Trent as "emerging" institutions goes far to explain the small percentage of maintenance costs they have recovered in fees. Carleton has been conspicuous in the high percentage of costs raised by fees. It is hardly surprising that that university particularly welcomed the introduction in 1967 of the formula system for awarding provincial grants. This scheme is discussed in volume II, chapter 12.

Provincial assistance during the early 1950s was on a scale that seems small by current standards. In his Budget Address in 1957 the Honourable Dana Porter stated that, during the previous decade, operating grants had increased from $3.8 million to $8.7 million. During the previous five-year period total capital grants had amounted to $17.6 million. Current and capital grants for the subsequent year alone would total more than half this amount.[3]

The amount of provincial government grants to the provincially assisted universities between 1957–8 and 1969–70 is shown in Table 7-39. At the beginning of the period, Brock, Trent, and York did not exist, nor did Scarborough and Erindale Colleges. The nucleus of the University of Guelph, consisting of the Ontario Agricultural College, Macdonald Institute, and the Ontario Veterinary College, received financial support from the Department of Agriculture. Laurentian's parent institution, as a denominational college, received no financial support from the province. The University of Ottawa received assistance only for its medical school. Essex College, affiliated with Assumption, was eligible for provincial grants before the creation of the University of Windsor, although Assump-

TABLE 7-37
Percentages of total income of provincially assisted
universities of Ontario by source, 1965-9

SOURCE OF INCOME	1965-6	1966-7	1967-8	1968-9
Student fees	24.8	21.2	18.9	17.0
Gifts for operating purposes	0.6	0.4	0.4	0.4
Endowment income	1.5	1.1	0.8	0.4
Other income	5.8	4.8	3.8	3.2
Subtotal	32.7	27.5	23.9	21.0
Federal grant	10.8	19.2		
Provincial grant	56.5	53.3		
Subtotal	67.3	72.5	76.1	79.0
TOTAL	100.0	100.0	100.0	100.0

SOURCE: Reports of the Minister of University Affairs of Ontario.

TABLE 7-38
Student fees and grants from provincial and federal governments as
percentages of total income of provincially assisted universities of
Ontario, 1965-9

UNIVERSITY	1965-6 Fees	1965-6 Grants	1966-7 Fees	1966-7 Grants	1967-8 Fees	1967-8 Grants	1968-9 Fees	1968-9 Grants
Brock	21.0	72.0	15.8	80.7	15.4	81.5	17.0	81.2
Carleton	36.2	61.6	31.7	66.6	26.7	72.0	24.0	74.4
Guelph	25.6	64.9	16.9	77.0	17.4	79.1	15.6	82.1
Lakehead	38.8	57.2	24.4	72.8	22.7	76.1	20.3	78.8
Laurentian	29.0	63.8	24.6	69.3	21.6	70.9	21.5	74.1
Algoma					27.2	54.6	34.0	57.0
Nipissing				55.6	22.0	46.5	35.0	52.0
McMaster	20.3	64.1	22.0	70.4	20.9	76.0	16.0	78.3
Ottawa	28.0	70.2	27.9	70.5	18.6	76.8	14.8	80.0
Queen's	26.6	58.5	22.3	65.5	22.5	74.6	19.4	77.7
Toronto–Main	19.1	72.4	16.2	76.2	13.9	79.2	12.5	82.5
Erindale		99.3		100.0	10.6	89.3	16.8	83.1
Scarborough	10.9	89.0	16.8	82.7	19.1	80.4	20.6	79.3
Trent	16.1	81.6	13.4	86.6	13.9	86.1	16.0	84.0
Waterloo	30.9	66.0	23.5	72.3	19.8	76.2	17.4	80.5
Western	30.9	60.1	22.7	69.1	19.3	72.5	17.0	75.6
Windsor	34.2	63.2	29.8	67.3	25.6	72.6	24.0	75.8
York	29.1	68.1	26.2	71.1	24.1	68.5	23.7	73.2

SOURCE: Reports of the Minister of University Affairs of Ontario.

tion was not. Waterloo College Associate Faculties was in a similar position in relation to Waterloo College.

Total provincial operating grants amounted to $8.9 million in 1957–8, an amount which more than doubled in the next four years, and approximately doubled again in the next three, that is, by 1964–5, and again in the next two, or by 1966–7. Another doubling in the next year included the absorption of the direct payments formerly made by the federal

352 The expansion of the educational system

TABLE 7-39
Provincial operating grants to provincially assisted universities of Ontario, 1957–70 (in thousands of dollars)

UNIVERSITY	1957–8	1958–9	1959–60	1960–1	1961–2	1962–3	1963–4	1964–5	1965–6	1966–7	1967–8	1968–9	1969–70[a]
Brock													
Carleton	225	325	400	485	600	915	130	355	612	1,498	2,309	3,304	4,698
Guelph							1,350	1,852	2,775	3,640	8,213	11,133	13,962
Lakehead							80	600	2,375	5,698	9,921	13,344	16,225
Laurentian	50	100	105	135	150	185	210	325	518	1,503	3,063	4,453	5,474
Algoma				125	250	350	425	712	982	1,526	2,576	3,430	4,237
Nipissing											165		432
McMaster										90	125		196
Ottawa	400	650	780	975	1,325	1,545	2,225	3,368	4,588	6,043	12,523	17,325	19,987
Queen's	400	450	475	550	600	915	1,225	1,292	4,083	5,016	13,474	17,755	20,194
Toronto – Main	825	925	1,075	1,300	1,475	1,680	2,365	3,823	4,930	6,027	12,769	16,206	19,741
Erindale	5,907	6,632	8,482	10,332	11,575	12,935	16,029	19,104	24,168	28,441	48,044	57,030	63,623
Scarborough							80	200	300	335	832	1,304	2,449
Trent							80	300	1,010	1,412	2,220	2,934	3,403
Waterloo							205	430	638	1,488	2,327	3,115	3,729
Western	100	150	250	375	600	865	1,575	2,544	4,078	5,938	13,650	18,965	23,956
Windsor	825	925	1,035	1,175	1,475	1,680	2,675	4,094	5,860	7,947	15,659	20,434	26,783
York	150	275	300	400	550	665	1,450	1,638	2,242	2,738	5,879	8,485	11,056
			25	250	400	700	900	1,330	2,306	3,842	7,622	12,032	16,403
TOTAL	8,882	10,432	12,927	16,102	19,000	22,435	31,004	41,967	61,465	83,242	161,371	211,249	256,548

SOURCE: Reports of the Minister of University Affairs of Ontario.

[a]Estimate.

government. By 1969-70 the estimated total had reached $256.5 million. At the beginning of the period covered by the table the University of Toronto received 66.5 per cent of the total; by 1965-6 this percentage had fallen to 41.5, and by 1969-70 to 27.1. For the same three years Western received 9.3, 9.5, and 10.4 per cent; Queen's received 9.3, 8.0, and 7.7 per cent; and McMaster received 4.5, 7.5, and 7.8 per cent of the total respectively. These changes, of course, reflected varying rates of growth at the different institutions.

Federal grants showed a much different pattern of growth. Since they were based on fixed amounts per capita, which remained the same from one year to another until they were deliberately changed, they increased only in relation to the growth of the population. While they were a factor of major importance in 1957-8 when they constituted nearly half the provincial grant, they were only 34.2 per cent of the provincial grant in 1963-4 and, despite a raising of the rate, only 13.8 per cent by 1966-7. That is, they completely failed to keep up with the universities' need for assistance. The subsequent arrangement, whatever the real or fancied diminution of the universities' independence with the loss of direct payments from an additional source, was much more generous. Federal operating grants to each provincially assisted university between 1957-8 and 1966-7 are shown in Table 7-40, and combined federal and provincial grants for the same years in Table 7-41.

Table 7-42 shows the increasing amount of capital grants made to the provincially assisted universities between 1957-8 and 1969-70. The procedures by which the funds were made available are dealt with in volume II, chapter 12. There was no great increase in the annual amount between 1957-8 and 1959-60, but after the latter year it practically doubled every two years until 1966-7. During the next three years the total rose from $93.1 million to $119.0 million, that is, by about 27.8 per cent. A study of the amounts given to individual universities suggests that grants were awarded rather arbitrarily. There was no objective basis in earlier years for determining need, and almost any procedure employed was bound to result in accusations of political influence and favouritism. Thus the development of a formula for capital grants was anticipated with enthusiasm in certain quarters at the end of the decade.

For recent years the amounts mentioned in Table 7-42 refer to assistance provided through the Ontario Universities Capital Aid Corporation. Grants for health science facilities, replacements and renovations, land acquisition, and general services and site development were provided under special funds. All forms of capital assistance constituted much larger sums than those shown. For example, the grand total for 1965-6 was approximately $163.3 million,[4] that for 1967-8, more than $180 million,[5] and that for 1969-70, more than $170 million.

The Department of University Affairs issued notes in 1968 on the costs of higher education in Ontario which help to lend meaning to some of the

TABLE 7-40
Federal operating grants to provincially assisted universities of Ontario, 1957–67 (in thousands of dollars)

UNIVERSITY	1957–8	1958–9	1959–60	1960–1	1961–2	1962–3	1963–4	1964–5	1965–6	1966–7
Brock								35	87	198
Carleton	140	230	256	318	399	629	655	685	681	1,562
Guelph								456	501	1,250
Lakehead	19	30	24	30	32	36	44	76	103	346
Laurentian	20	40	48	58	74	95	116	156	131	385
Algoma										
Nipissing										
McMaster	281	444	463	514	549	779	852	937	925	2,568
Ottawa	444	708	742	764	785	1,053	1,044	989	837	2,476
Queen's	637	1,010	976	964	975	1,216	1,185	1,127	1,145	2,694
Toronto – Main	2,245	3,380	3,346	3,283	3,098	3,970	3,925	3,918	3,619	8,959
Erindale										
Scarborough									121	185
Trent								30	69	2,294
Waterloo	618	956	956	1,039	1,086	1,456	1,514	1,481	1,472	3,589
Western	162	274	292	326	358	500	506	499	532	1,261
Windsor				23	63	109	163	223	364	1,261
York								753	931	
TOTAL	4,566	7,072	7,243	7,521	7,672	10,354	10,610	11,365	11,518	29,028

SOURCE: Reports of the Minister of University Affairs of Ontario.

TABLE 7-41
Combined provincial and federal operating grants to provincially assisted universities of Ontario, 1957–67 (in thousands of dollars)

UNIVERSITY	1957-8	1958-9	1959-60	1960-1	1961-2	1962-3	1963-4	1964-5	1965-6	1966-7
Brock								390	699	1,696
Carleton	365	554	656	803	999	1,544	2,005	2,537	3,456	5,202
Guelph							130	1,056	2,876	6,948
Lakehead	69	130	129	165	182	221	254	401	621	1,849
Laurentian	20	41	48	183	324	445	541	868	1,113	1,910
Algoma										90
Nipissing										60
McMaster	681	1,094	1,243	1,489	1,874	2,324	3,077	4,305	5,513	8,611
Ottawa	844	1,158	1,217	1,314	1,385	1,968	2,269	2,281	4,920	7,492
Queen's	1,462	1,935	2,051	2,264	2,450	2,896	3,550	4,950	6,075	8,721
Toronto – Main	8,952	11,087	11,828	13,615	14,674	16,905	19,954	23,021	27,787	37,400
Erindale							80	200	300	335
Scarborough							80	300	1,131	1,412
Trent							205	460	708	1,673
Waterloo	100	150	390	577	853	1,376	2,181	3,298	5,009	8,232
Western	1,443	1,880	1,991	2,214	2,561	3,136	4,198	5,574	7,332	11,536
Windsor	312	549	592	726	908	1,165	1,956	2,137	2,774	3,999
York			25	273	463	809	1,063	1,553	2,670	5,103
TOTAL	14,248	18,578	20,170	23,623	26,673	32,789	41,623	53,331	72,984	112,269

SOURCE: Reports of the Minister of University Affairs of Ontario.

TABLE 7-42
Regular provincial capital grants to provincially assisted universities of Ontario, 1957–70 (in thousands of dollars)

UNIVERSITY	1957–8	1958–9	1959–60	1960–1	1961–2	1962–3	1963–4	1964–5	1965–6	1966–7	1967–8	1968–9	1969–70[a]
Brock							293	300	1,595	4,425	2,950	4,250	2,620
Carleton	1,000	1,000	1,000	800	1,000	2,000	3,000	4,450	5,450	7,400	8,090	8,575	5,880
Guelph								250	1,600	6,825	17,700	14,430	6,525
Lakehead			125	125	713	250	300	500	1,230	1,520	5,625	9,235	6,015
Laurentian					250	125	1,750	2,000	1,949	510	2,500	5,705	2,060
Algoma													
Nipissing													
McMaster	2,000	1,000	1,500	1,250	1,200	2,000	3,500	3,000	6,150	7,875	6,467	11,945	20,525
Ottawa	1,000	1,000	1,000	800	800	1,250	1,300	600	8,445	8,800	763	3,014	7,860
Queen's	1,000	1,000	1,250	1,250	1,200	2,000	3,500	4,250	4,875	2,075	3,100	8,535	7,540
Toronto – Main	2,000	2,000	3,000	3,925	6,025	6,025	2,925	6,000	8,250	10,400	13,400	13,930	16,485
Erindale							300			850	2,400	2,275	6,905
Scarborough							700			3,900	1,625	350	550
Trent							300	3,500	10,450	2,750	5,975	8,085	990
Waterloo	500	1,000	1,000	1,500	1,500	1,800	3,000	300	2,295	13,500	11,750	12,820	6,530
Western	1,000	1,000	1,000	1,000	1,200	2,000	3,500	5,000	10,100	6,675	2,700	8,665	5,125
Windsor	1,000	1,000	750	1,500	1,500	1,750	3,700	3,250	7,050	2,600	2,225	5,440	5,575
York				550	1,150	2,000	6,400	5,200	5,800	13,000	12,725	14,720	17,815
								7,000	14,000				
TOTAL	9,500	9,000	10,625	12,700	16,538	21,200	34,468	45,600	89,239	93,105	99,995	131,974	119,000

SOURCE: Reports of the Minister of University Affairs of Ontario.

[a]Estimate.

TABLE 7-43

Operating and capital funds provided to colleges of applied arts and technology by Ontario government, 1966-70 (in thousands of dollars)

COLLEGE	1966-7 Operating	1966-7 Capital	1967-8 Operating	1967-8 Capital	1968-9 Operating	1968-9 Capital	1969-70[a] Operating	1969-70[a] Capital
Algonquin	170		2,038		5,049	4,523	5,797	4,000
Cambrian	355		1,970	579	3,435	421	3,936	2,500
Centennial	3,328		1,494	302	3,447	945	3,256	
Conestoga			670	549	1,496	4,814	1,806	3,000
Confederation	50		650	173	1,291	1,012	1,983	2,500
Durham	675		714		984	737	1,296	1,000
Fanshawe	150		1,183	68	2,615	2,622	2,603	800
George Brown			280		4,560	280	2,616	
Georgian	50		253		1,012	783	1,059	1,500
Humber	50		980		2,194	3,251	2,810	3,500
Lambton	362		848	50	1,424	1,000	1,449	1,500
Loyalist				139	833	1,379	1,127	1,500
Mohawk	666		699		2,975		3,485	
Niagara	812		825	370	1,789	3,215	2,438	2,600
Northern	634		1,200	417	1,554	3,711	2,016	3,000
St Clair	880		948	600	1,937	3,975	2,564	3,700
St Lawrence	50		750		2,059	1,705	2,304	3,500
Seneca	575		1,381	1,985	2,789	2,422	3,879	3,000
Sheridan	52		1,298	925	2,296	380	2,630	2,000
Sir Sandford Fleming	248		1,300	157	1,261	325	1,866	1,500
TOTAL	9,107		19,481	6,314	45,000	37,500	50,920	41,100

SOURCE: Figures supplied by Applied Arts and Technology Branch, Finance Department.

[a] Estimate.

statistics. Total investment in post-secondary education during the previous year constituted about 2 per cent of the gross provincial product. The investment in capital and operating grants for each resident of Ontario averaged about $80 a year, and that for each student attending a university or community college, about $3,500 a year.[6]

According to figures reported by the Economic Planning Branch of the Department of Treasury and Economics in October 1968, the average cost per student in Ontario universities in 1968–9 was $3,300. Projected figures for the next seven years were as follows: 1969–70, $3,564; 1970–1, $3,849; 1971–2, $4,157; 1972–3, $4,490; 1973–4, $4,849; 1974–5, $5,237; 1975–6, $5,656. On the basis of an estimated total enrolment of 169,000, the cost for 1974–5 would be $885 million.

INCOME OF THE COLLEGES OF APPLIED ARTS
AND TECHNOLOGY

The extent of provincial financial support for the colleges of applied arts and technology between 1966–7 and 1969–70 is shown in Table 7-43. Operating grants more than doubled each year between 1966–7 (when few of the colleges were in operation) and 1967–8, as they did again between 1967–8 and 1968–9. The next year's increase was comparatively small. The estimates for 1970–1 indicated that the grants to all the colleges together would rise to $69.5 million, and that total provincial expenditure for operations relating to the colleges, including support for the Ontario Council of Regents, principal instalments and interest on debentures for capital purposes, and payments on the unfunded liability of the pension plan, would amount to $77.5 million. Capital costs were at a fairly uniform level in 1968–9 and 1969–70.

The average cost per student at the colleges of applied arts and technology was $1,810 in 1968–9. According to the estimate of the Economic Planning Branch of the Department of Treasury and Economics already referred to, this figure was expected to rise as follows between 1970–1 and 1975–6: 1970–1, $2,053; 1971–2, $2,186; 1972–3, $2,328; 1973–4, $2,479; 1974–5, $2,640; and 1975–6, $2,812. That is, a rise of nearly 75 per cent in the per-student cost was anticipated for the six-year period. Two sets of estimates of the total operating costs of the colleges were prepared at the same time. On the basis of a minimum increase in enrolment amounting to 68,000, the total operating costs of the colleges would amount to $192.9 million in 1975–6. Allowing for a maximum enrolment of 114,300, the operating costs would be $321.4 million.

EXPENDITURE FOR PUBLIC LIBRARIES

The total amounts spent on public libraries, as well as the amount contributed by provincial grants and the percentage that these grants constituted of the total, are shown in Table 7-44 for the years 1960–8. The estimated amount of grants for 1969 and 1970 is also shown, although

TABLE 7-44

Expenditure for public libraries in Ontario, 1960–8 (in thousands of dollars)

YEAR	PROVINCIAL GRANTS	TOTAL EXPENDITURE	PROVINCIAL GRANTS AS PERCENTAGE OF TOTAL EXPENDITURE
1960	1,500	10,553	14.2
1961	2,000	11,899	16.8
1962	2,193	12,994	16.9
1963	2,283	14,250	16.0
1964	2,720	15,853	17.2
1965	3,316	18,030	18.4
1966	4,756	21,028	22.6
1967	5,919	25,302	23.4
1968	6,600	28,938	22.8

SOURCE: Reports of the Minister of Education of Ontario; Ontario Department of Education, Public Library Statistics; Expenditure Estimates for Ontario.

figures for the total expenditure for these two years were not available at the time of writing. Between 1960 and 1968 the percentage accounted for by provincial grants rose gradually from 14.2 to 22.8. The remainder was raised by municipal councils.

Notes

INTRODUCTION

1 "The More You Learn, the More You Earn," *School Administration*, III, 2, February 1966, 28.
2 Edward F. Denison, *The Sources of Economic Growth in the United States and the Alternatives Before Us*, Supplementary Paper No. 13 (New York: Committee for Economic Development, 1962).
3 Theodore W. Schultz, *The Economic Value of Education* (New York: Columbia University Press, 1963), p. 45.
4 Economic Council of Canada, *Second Annual Review, Towards Sustained and Balanced Economic Growth*, December 1965, pp. 92–3.
5 *Ibid.*, p. 78.
6 John R. Nicholson, "The Three-Pronged Attack: Education – Re-training – Immigration," *Human Resource Development in the Province of Ontario* (Toronto: Report of the Ontario Economic Council, 1965), p. 8.
7 Paul Goodman, *Compulsory Mis-Education and The Community of Scholars* (New York: Random House, Vintage Books, 1962, 1964), pp. 52–3. *Compulsory Mis-Education* is also available in a cloth edition from Horizon Press. *The Community of Scholars* is available in a cloth edition from Random House.
8 David A. Dodge, "Education: Cause or Effect of Economic Growth," speech delivered during the Secondary School Principals' Course, Queen's University, Kingston, 21 July 1969, p. 10. Mimeographed.
9 *Ibid.*, p. 7.
10 "Education Cutbacks Are 'Self-Defeating,'" *School Progress*, XXXIX, 3, March 1968, 3.
11 Ontario, Legislative Assembly, *Debates*, 28th leg., 2nd sess., 2 December 1969, p. 9221.
12 "Research Notes. Show Generation Gap Not So Wide as Social Strata Gap," *Phi Delta Kappan*, L, 7, March 1969, 417.
13 Edgar Z. Friedenberg, *Coming of Age in America: Growth and Acquiescence* (New York: Random House, 1963, 1965), p. 3.
14 *Ibid.*, pp. 4–5.
15 *Ibid.*, p. 4.
16 Goodman, *Compulsory Mis-Education and The Community of Scholars*, pp. 273–4.
17 *Ibid.*, p. 274.
18 Seymour L. Halleck, "Why

They'd Rather Do Their Own Thing," *Think*, XXXIV, 5, September-October 1968, 3.
19 *Ibid.*, p. 4.
20 Arnold Toynbee, "Education in the Perspective of History," *The Teacher and The Taught*, ed. Ronald Gross (New York: Dell Publishing Co. Inc., 1963), pp. 134–5.
21 J.J. Deutsch, "The Future of Technical Manpower in Canada," *Headmaster*, Spring 1968, pp. 39–40.
22 Margaret Mead, "The Changing American Family," *Children*, September-October 1963, p. 174.
23 "Research Notes. NIMH Study: Tutoring Ups Infant I.Q.'s Dramatically," *Phi Delta Kappan*, L, 7, March 1969, 415.
24 Goodman, *Compulsory Mis-Education and The Community of Scholars*, pp. 200–1.
25 *Ibid.*, pp. 16–17.
26 Pierre Teilhard de Chardin, *The Future of Man* (New York: Harper & Row, 1964), p. 52.
27 Elizabeth L. Simpson, "The Individual in the Group," *Phi Delta Kappan*, L, 6, February 1969, 322–3.
28 *Ibid.*, p. 324.
29 National Conference on Engineering, Scientific and Technical Manpower, brief to the Conference, St Andrews-By-The-Sea, New Brunswick, 9–11 September 1956, p. ii.
30 Lewis S. Beattie and Edward F. Sheffield, *The Development of Student Potential*, Conference Study 3 (Ottawa: Canadian Conference on Education, 1962), p. 7.
31 Frank E. Jones, "The Social Bases of Education," report prepared for the Second Canadian Conference on Children at Quebec City, October 1965, pp. 13–17. Mimeographed.
32 T.E. Reid, "Priorities in Educational Expenditure: The Essential Basis," *Dalhousie Review*, XLVIII, 3, Autumn 1968, 387.
33 John Porter, *The Vertical Mosaic* (Toronto: University of Toronto Press, 1965), p. 90.
34 A.B. Hodgetts, *What Culture? What Heritage?: A Study of Civic Education in Canada* (Toronto: Ontario Institute for Studies in Education, 1968), p. 13.
35 *Ibid.*, p. 14.

CHAPTER 1
1 Information in this and subsequent paragraphs on immigration was obtained from the Ontario Department of Treasury and Economics, Manpower Analysis Section, Economic Analysis Branch, Office of the Chief Economist, "Population Projections 1967–1975," July 1967.
2 John R. Nicholson, "The Three-Pronged Attack: Education – Re-training – Immigration," *Human Resource Development in the Province of Ontario* (Toronto: Report of the Ontario Economic Council, 1965), p. 8.

CHAPTER 2
1 Charles E. Phillips, *The Development of Education in*

Canada (Toronto: W.J. Gage, 1957), p. 135.
2 *Report of the Royal Commission on Education in Ontario, 1950*, J.A. Hope, chairman (Toronto: King's Printer, 1950), p. 13.
3 *Ibid.*, p. 17.
4 Phillips, *Development of Education in Canada*, p. 225.
5 J.M. McCutcheon, *Public Education in Ontario* (Toronto: T.H. Best, 1941), p. 65.
6 *Report of the Royal Commission on Education in Ontario, 1950*, p. 19.
7 Phillips, *Development of Education in Canada*, p. 184.
8 Economic Council of Canada, *Fourth Annual Review, The Canadian Economy from the 1960's to the 1970's* (Ottawa: Queen's Printer, 1967), p. 65.
9 Ontario, Legislative Assembly, *Debates*, 27th leg., 2nd sess., 28 April 1964, p. 2541.

CHAPTER 3
1 David M. Cameron, "The Politics of Education in Ontario, with Special Reference to the Financial Structure" (PhD thesis, University of Toronto, 1969), p. 346.
2 Ontario, Legislative Assembly, *Debates*, 27th leg., 3rd sess., 3 June 1965, p. 3616.
3 *Ibid.*, 5th sess., 29 May 1967, p. 3949.
4 Francis R. St John Library Consultants Inc., *A Survey of Libraries in the Province of Ontario 1965* (Toronto: Ontario Library Association through the co-operation of the Ontario Department of Education, 1965), p. 41. Mimeographed.

CHAPTER 4
1 Committee of Presidents of Provincially Assisted Universities and Colleges of Ontario, *The Structure of Post-Secondary Education in Ontario*, Supplementary Report No. 1 (Toronto, 1963), p. 10.
2 Claude T. Bissell, ed., *Canada's Crisis in Higher Education: Proceedings of a Conference held by the National Conference of Canadian Universities*, Ottawa, 12–14 November 1956, p. 4.
3 Ontario, Legislative Assembly, *Debates*, 25th leg., 1st sess., 1 February 1956, p. 23.
4 University of Toronto, *President's Report for the Year Ended 1959* (Toronto: University of Toronto Press, 1959), p. 1.
5 Ontario, Legislative Assembly, *Debates*, 26th leg., 1st sess., 28 March 1960, p. 1812.
6 R.W.B. Jackson, *The Problem of Numbers in University Enrolment*, Bulletin No. 18 (Toronto: Canadian Education Association, and Department of Educational Research, Ontario College of Education, University of Toronto, 1963).
7 Committee of Presidents of Universities of Ontario, Presidents' Research Committee, *From the Sixties to the Seventies: An Appraisal of Higher Education in Ontario* (Toronto,

June 1966), p. 62.
8 Edward F. Sheffield, *Enrolment to 1976–77 in Canadian Universities and Colleges (1963 projection)* (Ottawa: Canadian Universities Foundation, 1964).
9 Commission to Study the Development of Graduate Programmes in Ontario Universities, *Report to the Committee on University Affairs and the Committee of Presidents of Provincially-Assisted Universities*, J.W.T. Spinks, chairman (Toronto, November 1966), pp. 24–5.
10 Gail C.A. Cook and David A.A. Stager, *Student Financial Assistance Programs: A Report to the Ontario Committee on Student Awards* (Toronto: Institute for the Quantitative Analysis of Social and Economic Policy, University of Toronto, November 1969), p. 7, Table 1-2.
11 Economic Council of Canada, *Fourth Annual Review, The Canadian Economy from the 1960's to the 1970's* (Ottawa: Queen's Printer, 1967), p. 70.

CHAPTER 6
1 National Conference on Engineering, Scientific and Technical Manpower, brief to the Conference, St Andrews-By-The-Sea, New Brunswick, 9–11 September 1956, p. 6.
2 Claude T. Bissell, ed., *Canada's Crisis in Higher Education: Proceedings of a Conference held by the National Conference of Canadian Universities*, Ottawa, 12–14 November 1956,

p. 160.
3 *Post-Secondary Education in Ontario, 1962–1970*, Report of the Presidents of the Universities of Ontario to the Advisory Committee on University Affairs, May 1962, revised January 1963 (Toronto, 1963), p. 20.
4 Ontario, Legislative Assembly, *Debates*, 27th leg., 3rd sess., 22 February 1965, p. 660.
5 *Ibid.*, 24 February 1965, pp. 748–9.
6 *Ibid.*, 28th leg., 1st sess., 10 June 1968, p. 4166.
7 Stewart Fyfe to William G. Davis, 16 November 1965.
8 "University Education in Ontario," brief prepared for presentation to the Prime Minister of Ontario by the Ontario Council of University Faculty Associations, 19 December 1963, p. 26. Mimeographed.
9 Committee of Presidents of Universities of Ontario, Presidents' Research Committee, *From the Sixties to the Seventies: An Appraisal of Higher Education in Ontario* (Toronto, June 1966), pp. 21–2.
10 "Traitements de L'Exercise 1968–1969," *C.A.U.T. Bulletin*, XVII, 3, February 1969, 10–35.

CHAPTER 7
1 Ontario, Committee on Taxation, *Report of the Ontario Committee on Taxation*, II: *The Local Revenue System* (Toronto: Queen's Printer, 1967), pp. 82–3.

2 *Ibid.*, I: *Approach, Background and Conclusions*, p. 119.
3 Ontario, Legislative Assembly, *Debates*, 25th leg., 3rd sess., 21 February 1957, pp. 527–8.
4 *Ibid.*, 27th leg., 3rd sess., 10 February 1965, pp. 417–18.
5 *Ibid.*, 5th sess., 5 June 1967, p. 4262.
6 Ontario, Department of University Affairs, "Notes on the Costs of Higher Education in Ontario," 20 March 1969.

Contents of volumes in
ONTARIO'S EDUCATIVE SOCIETY

I / THE EXPANSION OF THE EDUCATIONAL SYSTEM
Introduction: Current issues in education
1 Characteristics of the Ontario population
2 Enrolment in schools and in courses sponsored by the Department of Education
3 Educational institutions
4 University enrolment and degrees awarded
5 Enrolment and certificates awarded in other post-secondary educational institutions
6 Status and characteristics of teachers
7 The financing of education

II / THE ADMINISTRATIVE STRUCTURE
1 The evolution of the structure of the Department of Education
2 The role and functions of the department after 1965
3 Principles of local organization and administration
4 The development of local administrative units for public elementary and secondary schools before 1968
5 The consolidation of local administrative units in 1969
6 The development of the separate school system
7 The development of an educational system for Metropolitan Toronto
8 Provincial financial assistance to schools
9 Provincial and local revenues
10 Budgetary practices
11 Federal financial assistance for provincial non-university programs
12 University finance
13 Educational activities of provincial government departments other than Education and University Affairs
14 Interprovincial co-operation
15 Educational concerns of the federal government

III / SCHOOLS, PUPILS, AND TEACHERS
1 Aims of education
2 The development of different types of schools
3 School organization and administration
4 The organization of the school program
5 The evolution of curriculum
6 Significant development in certain curricular areas
7 The role of measurement and evaluation
8 Educational media
9 Education for special groups

10 Special education
11 School buildings, facilities, and equipment
12 The role and status of teachers
13 Teacher welfare
14 The Provincial Committee on Aims and Objectives of Education in the Schools of Ontario

IV / POST-SECONDARY AND ADULT EDUCATION
1 The role of the university
2 Developing relationships between the universities and the provincial government and inter-university co-ordination
3 Highlights in the development of each Ontario university
4 University government
5 Observations on certain university programs
6 University teaching
7 Evaluation of student success
8 University research
9 Miscellaneous university functions and services
10 Student activities and attitudes
11 Student assistance
12 University faculty affairs
13 Institutes of technology
14 Other institutions for technological and trades training
15 Origin, nature, and purposes of the colleges of applied arts and technology
16 Organization and functioning of the colleges of applied arts and technology
17 The process of education in the colleges of applied arts and technology
18 The Ontario College of Art
19 Nursing education
20 Government programs for adult training and retraining
21 Training within business and industry

V / SUPPORTING INSTITUTIONS AND SERVICES
1 The development of facilities and certification requirements for the preparation of elementary school teachers
2 The development of the educational process in institutions for the preparation of elementary school teachers
3 Issues in teacher education with particular application to the elementary school level
4 The report of the Minister's Committee on the Training of Elementary School Teachers
5 The development of the colleges of education
6 Requirements for admission to colleges of education and courses and certificates offered
7 The response of the colleges of education to the shortage of secondary school teachers
8 Ideas about the preparation of secondary school teachers
9 In-service teacher education
10 Research and development: definitions and issues
11 Structures for educational research and development before 1965
12 Contributions of various agencies to educational research in Ontario before 1965
13 The creation and development of the Ontario Institute for Studies in Education
14 Activities in research, development, and graduate studies at the Ontario Institute for Studies in Education

15 The Ontario grade 13 departmental examination system
16 Departmental essay-type examinations in grade 12
17 Departmental objective testing in grade 12
18 Objective testing for university admission
19 Radio and television
20 The provincial library system
21 Miscellaneous educative institutions

VI / SIGNIFICANT DEVELOPMENTS IN LOCAL SCHOOL SYSTEMS
1 Approaches to teaching
2 Curricular experimentation, research, and innovation
3 Buildings and facilities
4 Distinctive schools
5 Extended use of school facilities
6 Administration and operation of school systems and schools
7 Special services, classes, and schools
8 Education for employment
9 Research
10 In-service teacher education
11 Centennial celebrations

VII / EDUCATIONAL CONTRIBUTIONS OF ASSOCIATIONS
1 Broadly based education associations
2 Federations of elementary and secondary school teachers
3 Other associations of educators for professional and fraternal purposes
4 Associations providing general support for education
5 Associations for the promotion of specific causes relating to formal education
6 Associations for the promotion of special education
7 Organizations of school trustees
8 Associations of school administrators
9 Associations of administrators of miscellaneous agencies
10 Associations of university officials
11 Associations of university teachers and students
12 Associations concerned with scholarship
13 Professional associations
14 Adult education
15 Community cultural and recreational associations
16 Youth groups
17 Religious organizations
18 Service clubs and associations
19 Social welfare organizations
20 Associations concerned with health
21 Associations for the welfare of special groups
22 Associations for the promotion of social, economic, and cultural causes
23 Charitable foundations
24 Associations concerned with international causes